C
FOR
ENGINEERS

Brian Bramer B.Tech., Ph.D., C.Eng., M.I.E.E., M.I.E.E.E
Principal Lecturer in Computing Science,
Department of Computing Science,
De Montfort University,
Leicester.

Susan Bramer B.A.
Lecturer in Computing Science,
Department of Computing Science,
De Montfort University,
Leicester.

Edward Arnold
A division of Hodder & Stoughton
LONDON MELBOURNE AUCKLAND

© 1993 Brian Bramer and Susan Bramer

First published in Great Britain 1993

British Library Cataloguing in Publication Data

Bramer, Brian
  C for Engineers
  I. Title   II. Bramer, Susan
  005.362

  ISBN 0-340-57014-8

Printed and bound in Great Britain for Edward Arnold,
a division of Hodder and Stoughton Limited, Mill Road,
Dunton Green, Sevenoaks, Kent TN13 2YA by
St Edmundsbury Press Limited, Bury St Edmunds, Suffolk
and Hartnolls Ltd, Bodmin, Cornwall.

Preface

This book is intended as a learning text for students of Computer Science, Electronic Engineering, Information Technology and other courses, in a module which introduces programming in the ANSI C language. In addition, the book may also be used for self-instruction by experienced programmers who wish to program in ANSI C.

This learning text would normally accompany a course of practical/tutorial sessions which may be backed by lectures. Each chapter is a self-contained unit that can be read by the student and many include exercises to be attempted during tutorial/practical sessions (answers to the exercises are given in Appendix B). To complete each chapter is a problem that should be attempted and may be used by instructors as a means of assessment.

Good programming practice is encouraged throughout the book by the use of modular and structured programming techniques. To illustrate and support concepts introduced within the text a large number of sample programs are presented (associated with each program is a discussion which dissects the program code line by line). Except for a few programs which contain machine or compiler specific code the programs should run under any ANSI compatible compiler (the programs have been tested on IBM PC compatible microcomputers using Turbo C and Microsoft C and on Apollo Domain DN4500 and Hewlett Packard 720 UNIX based workstations).

This book is a self contained text and makes no assumptions about previous programming experience. In a formal course other modules could provide support in the area of Software Engineering (to reinforce the modular and structured programming techniques outlined in this book) and assembly language programming (to support the chapters on pointers and the latter chapters on accessing low-level system dependent facilities).

Although this book is suitable for a wide range of courses, particular support is given to students on mathematical, engineering or physical science based courses. For example, the text introduces mathematical library functions at an early stage (Chapter 5), contains a chapter devoted to the problems associated with evaluating mathematical series (Chapter 16) and describes techniques to access low-level system dependent facilities (Chapters 30 to 32). The majority of programs, however, deal with the general problems of storing and manipulating different types of data and are applicable to a range of subject areas.

Outline of the book

Chapter 1 provides a general introduction to computer systems, information representation, and computer hardware and software fundamentals. Chapter 2 contains a general discussion the of problems faced when implementing large complex software systems and presents an overview of program design, coding and testing.

Chapter 3 introduces C functions, discussing their place in modular programming, and describes the role of the editor, preprocessor, compiler, linker and run time system. Chapter 4 describes, by means of a simple program, the outline structure of a C program and the role of constants, variables, expressions, statements, etc. Input/output and mathematical functions are introduced in Chapter 5 together with sample programs which read data, perform a calculation and print results. Chapter 6 discusses program layout and the detection of compile, link and run time errors (program listings are presented which contain typical errors).

Chapters 7 and 8 discuss integral and real data types and describe functions to perform input/output operations. Chapters 9 and 10 introduce the *operators* which are used to build up expressions and the concept of operator *precedence* and *associativity*.

Conditional statements and program loop control statements, which are important tools in the implementation of well structured programs, are described in Chapters 11 to 14. Functions, which are critical to the implementation of modular programs, are described in Chapter 15. The techniques are then used in Chapter 16 in the implementation of algorithms to evaluate mathematical functions such as sine(x), sqrt(x), etc.

Chapter 17 discusses *data hiding* and describes how it may be achieved in C programs (this topic is continued in Chapter 21 when multi-file programs are discussed).

Chapters 18, 19 and 20 introduce arrays (Chapter 19 dealing specifically with strings and Chapter 20 with multi-dimensional arrays) and Chapter 22 introduces structures.

Although C programs may be implemented with minimal use of pointers it is wise to have an understanding of pointers and where they may be used to advantage. Chapter 23 introduces basic pointer operations and Chapters 24 and 25 discuss advanced pointer operations.

Chapter 26 describes the preprocessor directives and the construction and use of header files (which are very important in modular programming in C).

Chapter 27 describes basic file input/output facilities, providing more details of the functions which have been used in earlier chapters.

Chapters 28 describes dynamic memory management techniques and Chapter 29 the advanced use of functions; both of which are required in the implementation of sophisticated programs. Chapters 30, 31, 32 and 33 describe techniques to access low-level system dependent facilities. Finally Chapter 34 gives an **overview** of the C + + language.

Recommendations to tutors

It is recommended that the sample programs and exercises are entered and tested (the sample programs and answers to exercises may be obtained from the authors, see below). This should given an indication of any differences between the target environment and the ANSI C environments used to test the programs. Students can then be provided with information to enable them to overcome any problems.

To obtain copies of the sample programs and exercises call email bb@dmu.ac.uk

or send a floppy disk to: Dr Brian Bramer
Department of Computing Science,
De Montfort University,
The Gateway,
Leicester LE1 9BH,
U.K.

Acknowledgements and dedications

We wish to acknowledge the assistance of colleagues who helped with the preparation of this book. This book is dedicated to our lovely daughters Elinor and Isobel who assisted as much with its production as they did with the previous one !

Brian Bramer, Susan Bramer, 1993

Contents

1

Computer systems: an overview

1.1 The ANSI C standard

C was designed in the 1970s by Denis Ritchie (Kernighan & Ritchie, 1978) as a *system implementation* language for the UNIX operating system (a *system implementation* language has 'high-level' program and data constructs plus 'low-level' facilities such as bit-manipulation and the ability to access memory directly). Prior to that time operating systems and other low-level programs had been implemented in assembly language which, although efficient when written by a **good** programmer, is very difficult to write and is processor dependent. Using C to implement UNIX enabled it to be portable across a wide variety of computer systems based on different processors. Assembly languages, however, are still used to implement hardware dependent operations which cannot be done in C or functions where speed is critical (Chapter 31 will discuss linking assembly language functions to C).

In 1989 ANSI (American National Standards Institute) approved an updated C standard (Kernighan & Ritchie 1988) which remedied many of the deficiencies in the original C. In particular ANSI C provides *function prototypes* which enables the compiler to cross check the definition of a function with its use (i.e. the number and type of arguments) and specifies a standard library with an extensive set of functions for input/output, string manipulation, etc. In addition, features which were either loosely specified or not specified at all in the original C were specified precisely. The programs in this book will adhere to the ANSI C standard which is supported by the majority of modern C compilers (updates from the original C will be noted where appropriate).

The C language was designed to be used by professional programmers who, it is assumed, know what they are doing and as such lacks many of the restrictions and checks of more modern languages such as Pascal and Modula 2, e.g. lack of rigorous type checking, array bound checking, etc. C is, however, a very powerful and flexible language allowing fast program development and is used extensively in industry and commerce to implement programs to solve problems in a wide range of application areas.

To understand many of the low level facilities of C an appreciation of computer hardware and information storage is useful. The remainder of this chapter introduces these topics and may be skipped by readers who already have this knowledge.

1.1.1 The C++ language

The C++ programming language is a superset of the original C language with enhancements to support object orientated programming techniques. In traditional programming languages the data and associated functions are distinct, in that the data is declared and then the functions are implemented. Objected orientated programming languages contain facilities which support the encapsulation of a set of data types and associated functions into integrated entities called objects. Chapter 34 contains an brief introduction to C++.

1.2 Computer hardware

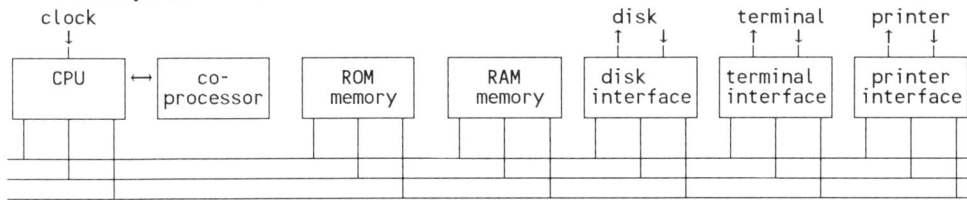

Fig. 1.1 Typical microcomputer configuration using a common bus system

Fig 1.1 is a simplified representation of the hardware (physical components) of a simple single processor computer system comprising:

1   CPU (Central Processing Unit), e.g. microprocessor integrated circuit chip.
2   Co-processor (if fitted), e.g. for real number calculations or graphics.
3   Main or primary memory:
   (a) ROM (Read Only Memory) which contains permanent programs, e.g. power-up test programs and the 'bootstrap loader' which loads the operating system off disk;
   (b) RAM (Random Access read/write Memory) which is used to hold programs being executed and data being processed.
4   Disk interface which controls a floppy disk and/or hard disk as secondary memory for saving programs and data as files.
5   Terminal interface which controls the display screen and the keyboard.
6   Input/output interface devices for connecting external devices such as printers, modems, data acquisition subsystems, etc.

In Fig. 1.1 an *information highway or bus system* connects the components of the system:

Address Bus which carries the address of the memory location or I/O device being accessed.

Data Bus which carries the data signals.

Control Bus which carries the control signals between the CPU and the other components of the system, e.g. signals to indicate when a valid address is on the address bus and if data is to be read or written.

A program consists of a sequence of instructions and associated data stored in main memory. In outline the CPU consists of two major components:

The control unit which *fetches* instructions from the main memory, decodes them to determine the operation required and then sets up instruction *execution*, e.g. to add two numbers together.

The Arithmetic/logic unit (ALU) which, under the direction of the control unit, performs operations upon numeric and other data.

Each instruction that the computer hardware can execute has a particular binary pattern, with sequences of such binary patterns in the memory of the computer forming a program. Programs in this form are in a language called *machine code*, i.e. the language that the hardware of the computer understands. Before a program written in the C language can be executed it must be converted into machine code using a program called a compiler.

During program execution main memory is used to store the machine code and data. The majority of modern computer systems use a memory store built up of bytes of storage with each byte having an assigned location address. Fig. 1.2 shows such a memory organisation with the first byte of memory having address 0, the next 1, the next 2, etc.

```
address          memory bytes          comments
   0          ┌─────────────────┐      first byte in memory
   1          ├─────────────────┤      second byte in memory
   2          ├─────────────────┤      third byte in memory
   3          ├─────────────────┤           etc.
   4          ├─────────────────┤
   5          ├─────────────────┤
              └─────────────────┘

maximum-2     ┌─────────────────┐
maximum-1     ├─────────────────┤
maximum       ├─────────────────┤      last byte in memory
              └─────────────────┘
```

Fig. 1.2 The organisation of computer primary memory

In C there are a range of *data types* used to represent different types of data, e.g. characters, integer numbers, real numbers, etc. A program starts with *declarations* which specify the names and *data types* of *variables* which will be used to store data, e.g. a variable called x may be used to hold an integer numeric value. Knowing the *data type* of each variable enables the compiler to allocate memory to store the variable and to convert between different data types in calculations. For example, character data requires one byte of storage, an integer number two or four bytes and a real number four or eight bytes. The place in memory where the variable is stored is called its *address* which is used by the program to reference the variable in operations (generally the C programmer need not be concerned with the actual values of addresses but it helps to know what an address is and what it is used for).

Information, such as program text, is held on disk (secondary memory) in a file structure which is organised and controlled by the operating system (see next section). Facilities are provided which enable the user to enter a program from the keyboard, correct any errors and save the result as a named file. The file can then be compiled, linked and executed.

1.3 Computer software

Before a computer can process information (i.e. carry out calculations or read a character from a keyboard) it requires a program. A program is a series of instructions stored in the main memory that are executed sequentially by the processor. The programs of a computer system are called its software and include:

System software includes the operating system which manages the overall operation of the computer system and software to support program execution, user interaction, etc.

Application programs for solving end-user problems, e.g. word processors, spreadsheets, accounting programs, CAD design tools, etc.

When a computer is switched on the operating system is read from disk into main memory (by a *bootstrap loader* in ROM). The *bootstrap loader* then passes control to the operating system which, after initialisation, prompts the user for command input. The facilities provided by the operating system and support software include:

1   Control of the disk file system, e.g. opening/closing/reading/writing, etc.
2   Editors for the creation and modification of programs and data.
3   An assembler which translates programs in assembly language (see section 1.5.1) into object code (object code contains machine code instructions plus information for the linker).
4   Compilers which translates programs in high-level languages (see section 1.5.2) into object code.
5   A linker which links various object code program modules into a complete executable machine code program.
6   Execution and debugging of systems, application and user programs.

A native compiler (or assembler) produces code suitable for execution on the host computer or systems with a compatible processor. A cross compiler (or assembler) executing on one computer (the host) generates code suitable for another computer (the target) usually with a different processor. The resultant output object code is then linked (on the host) with libraries to provide I/O facilities, etc. (Bramer 1990).

1.4 Instruction and data storage

Within the computer hardware **memory** is used to store the instructions of the program being executed and the data to be processed. The data is the information to be processed by the computer system which may be simple numbers for mathematical calculations, text such as names and addresses or more complex structures such as pictures or drawings.

1.4.1 Representation of integer numbers

Within modern computer systems the basic element of storage is the *binary digit (or bit)* which can represent a 0 or a 1. The reason for this is that it is very easy to build electronic switches where an off/on condition is used to represent a 0/1 binary value. Although a single bit can only have two states, 0 or 1, a sequence of bits can be used to represent a larger range of values. Such a sequence is called a word of storage and is usually 8, 16, 32, 64 or 128 bits in length. An 8-bit word, for example, can represent an unsigned positive number in the range 0 to 11111111 binary (0 to 255 decimal) thus:

bit	7	6	5	4	3	2	1	0
bit value	2^7	2^6	2^5	2^4	2^3	2^2	2^1	2^0

In the diagram above the least significant or rightmost bit, bit 0, represents 2^0 or 1 and the most significant or leftmost bit, bit 7, represents 2^7 or 128 decimal (the convention for identifying the bits within a word is that the rightmost or least significant bit is numbered 0). The combinations of 1s and 0s of the 8-bit word thus represent an unsigned value in the range 0 to 11111111 binary (0 to 255 decimal). The general term given to an 8-bit storage word is a **byte** which is used by the majority of modern computer systems as their fundamental unit of storage. To represent values that are too large to store in 8-bits a number of bytes may be used. For example, a 16-bit number (made up from two bytes) can represent an unsigned value in the range 0 to 65535 decimal.

Many commercial and scientific calculations require the use of signed numbers and the majority of modern computer systems use *twos complement binary arithmetic* in which the most significant bit is used to store the sign (1 for a negative number and 0 for a positive number). Using twos complement binary arithmetic an 8-bit number can represent values in the range -128 to +127 and a 16-bit number values in the range -32768 to +32767. In the C the *data types* used to represent integer numbers are short int, int and long int which may be *signed* or *unsigned* (the programmer would use the most appropriate for the application). In practice short int and int are at least 16-bit and long int is at least 32-bit (Table 1.1 shows the numeric values which can be represented).

In practice it would be both difficult and error prone to enter data directly in binary form, so hexadecimal (base 16) or decimal are more commonly used.

data size	unsigned range	signed range
8-bit	0 to 255	-128 to +127
16-bit	0 to 65535	-32768 to +32767
32-bit	0 to 4294967295	-2147483648 to 2147483647

Table 1.1 Numeric range of 8-, 16- and 32-bit unsigned and signed numbers

1.4.2 Representation of real numbers

Integer numbers are suitable for whole number calculations (i.e. no fractional component) and where a limited number range is acceptable. The majority of scientific and engineering applications use numbers with fractional components and which can vary in size from very small to very large values, e.g. from the size of atomic particles to intergalactic distances. C provides float, double and long double real number *data types* which are represented internally in floating point format.

In the floating point number system the real value is represented by a signed fractional component called the mantissa and a signed exponent. For example, decimal floating point numbers (using base 10) can be represented:

$$\text{mantissa} * 10^{\text{exponent}} \text{ where } 0.1 >= \text{mantissa} < 1.0$$

To maintain accuracy the absolute value of the mantissa is maintained within the range shown (this process is called normalisation), e.g. 6520000.0 would be $0.652*10^7$ and -0.00000000652 would be $-0.652*10^{-8}$. In practice many printers cannot print superscripts so the above examples would be printed as 0.652E7 and -0.652E-8 where the E indicates an exponent of 10.

Within computer systems the fractional component is held as a binary fraction and the exponent is a power of 2 (or possibly 16). Typically the number would be stored in 32 bits with 24 bits to hold the signed mantissa and 8 bits for the signed exponent. In this case the accuracy of the mantissa is 23 binary bits (which is equivalent to 6 or 7 decimal figures of accuracy), and the range of the exponent would be -128 to +127. Greater accuracy can be obtained by using 64-bit storage in which 53 bits may be used to store the signed mantissa (giving 15 to 17 decimal figures of accuracy) and 11 bits for the exponent.

1.4.3 Character data

Character data is used within a computer to represent text (such as names and addresses) and consists of the usual printable characters, e.g. the alphabet A-Z and a-z, digits 0-9 and other characters such as +, -, *, /, !, $, %, and &.

Each character is stored in a byte of memory and represented by a particular binary pattern or character code. To enable different computers, terminals and printers to be connected together there are a number of standard character codes. The most commonly used character code is ASCII (American Standard Code for Information Interchange), which is listed in Appendix A. The character A, for example, is represented by the binary pattern 01000001 (41 hexadecimal), and B by 01000010 (42 hexadecimal). The majority of computer users do not need to know or even be aware of these codes as the keyboard and display equipment converts between the characters and the internal codes, i.e. if the user hits the key A on the keyboard the binary value 01000001 is sent to the computer.

In C characters are represented by a *data type* called char which is stored in a *byte*. A point to note is that C makes no guarantee about the character set used to store the char data type or even the way the characters are ordered, i.e. in ASCII the alphabet is consecutively ordered with A represented by decimal 65, B by 66, C by 67, up to Z which is 90 (but a particular machine may use some other character code, e.g. EBCDIC).

1.4.4 Instruction representation

A computer program is made up of a sequence of instructions which are represented by binary patterns. For example, the binary pattern 0100 0010 0100 0011 (4243 hexadecimal), when executed by the Motorola MC68000 microprocessor, would set the lower 16 bits of the data register D3 to 0. Each instruction that the computer hardware can execute has a particular binary pattern, with sequences of such binary patterns in the memory of the computer forming a program. Programs in this form are in a language called *machine code*, i.e. the language the hardware of the computer understands. It is clear that if humans had to write programs in machine code, programming would be a very error prone and time consuming task.

1.5 Low and high-level languages

1.5.1 Assembly languages

In assembly languages each machine instruction is represented by a meaningful mnemonic (ADD, SUB, DIV) and data specified in binary, hexadecimal, decimal and character form. For example, the MC68000 instruction which clears the lower 16 bits of data register D3 (0100001001000011 in machine code) would be written in 68000 assembly language:

```
CLR.W     D3
```

where CLR.W is the instruction or operation-code mnemonic and D3 is the position of the data being operated upon (called the operand). The computer hardware can *only* *understand* machine code, so before it can be executed an assembly language program has to be converted into machine code. This is done by a program called an assembler which takes each assembly language statement and converts it on a one-to-one basis into the equivalent machine code instruction which can then be executed.

Assembly language programming is difficult because it is only one level above machine code and hence orientated to a particular computer (each type or model of central processing unit has its own machine code language). For example, a program which had been implemented in assembly language on an MC68000 microcomputer would have to be totally rewritten if transferred to an Intel 8086 based system. Even with the above disadvantages assembly language programming is still required in many industrial applications, e.g. time critical functions in a real-time control system.

Machine code and assembly languages are described as low-level languages in that they are orientated towards the computer hardware. High-level languages on the other hand are problem orientated and computer independent.

1.5.2 High-level problem solving languages

High-level languages are written in an English or mathematical notation which is orientated towards solving practical problems (Hunt 1982). Some examples of high-level languages are:

FORTRAN FORmula TRANslation: a language widely used for mathematical, scientific and engineering applications;

PASCAL a general purpose problem solving language;

C a systems implementation language;

Modula 2 a modern general purpose and systems implementation language;

Ada a modern systems implementation language designed for real-time applications.

After the program source code has been entered into the computer it has to be converted into machine code by a program called a compiler. Each statement in a high-level language can be converted into a number of machine code instructions. For example, consider the following statement in C (where x is a *variable*):

```
x = 7 + 2 * (267 - 23);
```

The equivalent in 68000 assembly language is (the variable is in data register D0):

```
MOVE.L      #267,D0
SUB.W       #23,D0
ADD.W       D0,D0
ADD.W       #7,D0
```

and in 68000 machine code (hexadecimal byte values) is:

```
20 3C 00 00 01 0B 04 40 00 17 D0 40 06 40 00 07
```

In general the compilation process is not 100% efficient so a program written in a high-level language will take more memory and run more slowly than an equivalent assembly language program written by a **good** programmer. However, the advantages of working in a language which is orientated towards solving problems rather than the computer hardware means the majority of application programs are written in high-level languages.

An additional advantage of using high-level languages is that such languages are less computer dependent than assembly languages (depending upon the quality of the international standard of the language and the particular implementation being used).

2

Program design, coding and testing

2.1 General requirements for software systems

As end-user requirements become more exacting system software grows in complexity and size. Systems consisting of 200,000 to 500,000 lines of code, once beyond imagination, are now commonly found in a single product. In general, software systems have a number of overall requirements:

Correctness and reliability, which outweigh all the other requirements. Faults in programs can range in effect from being costly, for example, incorrectly ordered stock for a supermarket, to disastrous, for example, a fault that could lead to an explosion in a computer controlled chemical process.

Flexibility and reusability. To be commercially viable, components of software systems must be capable of being used across a range of products and computer systems (Bramer 1988). This flexibility is more often provided by the use of high level languages than assembly language, but all programs are more easily adapted to changing requirements (and they will change), if written in a modular manner and well documented.

Efficiency. As a software system grows in size and complexity it also tends to run slower. Slow response time may be annoying to an engineer using a CAD system but it could prove disastrous in a jet aircraft travelling at Mach 2. Efficiency is the usual reason for coding in assembly language, but it must never be pursued at the expense of correctness and only in extreme cases at the expense of flexibility. Today it is generally simpler and cheaper to purchase faster hardware than to spend time gaining marginal improvements in software efficiency.

Maintainability. This deals with the problem of updating and improving software regardless of complexity. Modifying systems consisting of hundreds of thousands of lines of code written by software engineers who have since moved on is a daunting task. Will new staff be able to understand the code as originally written ? If not, product maintenance will be very costly, time consuming and prone to error.

In an era of increasing system size and complexity an important issue is productivity. A software system consisting of 500,000 lines of code may take 150 man-years to implement. Without use of modern techniques and tools such systems may never become operational. CASE (Computer Aided Software Engineering) tools aid with software specification, design, debugging, integration, performance analysis, verification, and maintenance (Chikofsky and Rubenstein 1988, Wallace & Fujii 1989, Oman 1990). The functionality offered by software development tools depends to a large extent on the complexity and size of the project and hence the funds available to purchase tools and support software and hardware. In practice this can range from a simple editor, compiler and run-time system on a PC to a CASE system running on a high powered professional workstation (Oman 1990).

2.2 Documentation

Documentation is vitally important if a program is to be understood, not only by others, but by the original programmer at a later stage. A major aim when writing a program (apart from making it work) is to make it readable. The program code should be documented, as it is written, by inserting comments at appropriate places.

2.3 System analysis

The object of the analysis phase is to find out exactly what the end-user wants the final program to do (the programmer himself may be the end-user). A problem is that often users do not know what they want because they do not know the capabilities of modern computer systems. It is the job of full time professional analysts to discover the real requirements and analyse complex problems. From the analysis phase, a requirements specification is drawn up, which specifies exactly what the program will do. When complete, the finished program can be checked against this document.

All the exercises and problems presented in this book are in effect specifications of programs to be written. It may appear from these specifications that the end product is obvious, and no analysis was required. Even simple problems, however, do require some analysis if only to find out what type of data is to be processed and how much there will be, e.g. will a file contain 100 items or 1000000000 (which will not fit onto a floppy disk).

2.4 Program design - stepwise refinement

It is recognised that human beings can only carry between five and ten separate operations in their heads at a time. If a program is more than 10 or 20 lines of code (depending upon experience and complexity of problem), any attempt to design and code the entire program in one go will lead to a badly conceived and incorrect program. One design technique is stepwise refinement, whereby a task is visualised initially at a very simple level and subsequently refined in more and more detail. Initially the design is carried out using *pseudo code* or *structured English*.

2.4.1 Design exercise - a simple calculator

Design a calculator where numeric values may be entered as decimal or hexadecimal numbers, simple arithmetic performed and the result displayed in decimal. The initial specification of the calculator program is:

1   16-bit integer arithmetic (maximum numeric range is -32768 to 32767).
2   Entry of numeric data may be in decimal and hexadecimal.
3   Operations: add, subtract, multiply and divide using straight left to right evaluation.
4   Display the results as a signed decimal number on entry of an = character.

The approach to be taken is to design (and code and test) small parts of the problem at a time. This is a very useful method, particularly when controlling new equipment or experiments, where it is sometimes a major problem to control just one solenoid or valve or motor, never mind large parts of a complex process control system. It is often difficult to get general purpose input/output interfaces to do exactly what is required (even if the requirements are quite simple) and 'talking' to external equipment complicates things further. Once the problems of controlling the elementary components of a system have been overcome the software produced can then be used to form modules of the complete system. In the case of the calculator program nothing can be done until numeric values can be written to the screen and read from the keyboard and these are the first problems to be tackled. Once input/output functions have been implemented the real working parts of the calculator program can be designed, implemented and tested.

It is assumed that the following input/output subroutines are available (if not available one would have to start programming I/O devices to read and write characters):

```
write_character(character_out)    write character to the screen
read_character(character_in)      read a character from the keyboard
newline                           writes a newline to the screen
```

Calculator stage 1 refinement

Implement and test a subroutine to write a 16-bit decimal number to the display screen.

```
main program (* to test write_decimal *)
write_decimal(0)
newline
write_decimal(-10)
newline
write_decimal(10)
newline
write_decimal(30000)
newline
write_decimal(-30000)
stop

(* write number as a signed 16-bit decimal integer, suppress leading 0's *)
SUBROUTINE write_decimal(number)
IF number=0
    write_character('0')
ELSE
    IF number<0
        write_character('-')
        number = -number
    END IF
    print_0 = FALSE        (* used to suppress leading zeros *)
    divisor = 10000
    LOOP                              (* print next digit *)
        quotient=number/divisor
        IF quotient<>0 OR (quotient=0 AND print_0)
            print_0 = TRUE
            character = quotient + ASCII '0'
            write_character(character)
        END IF
        number= REMAINDER OF number/divisor
        divisor = divisor / 10
    UNTIL divisor = 0
END IF
RETURN
```

Only minimal testing of write_decimal is performed. When read_decimal is implemented (next stage) more extensive testing of both routines can be carried out.

Calculator stage 2 refinement

Implement and test a subroutine to read a signed decimal number from the keyboard. Call routine when a digit is read from the keyboard and terminate on a non digit character.

```
main program
number = 0
REPEAT
    read_character(character)
    IF character IN ['0' - '9'] THEN
        read_decimal(number, character)
    newline
    write_decimal(number)
    newline
FOREVER

(* read a decimal number from the keyboard (exit on non digit)
    on entry : character contains first digit character
    on exit  : number    contains the decimal value read
               character last character read              *)
read_decimal(number, character)
number = 0
REPEAT
    write_character(character)
    number = number * 10 + (character - ord ('0'))
    read_character(character)
UNTIL character < > IN ['0' - '9']
RETURN
```

The specification called for hexadecimal input in addition to decimal. It would be reasonable to implement and test this while the problem of implementing read_decimal was fresh in one's mind.

Calculator stage 3 refinement

Implement and test a subroutine to read a hexadecimal number from the keyboard. Call routine when a '$' is read from the keyboard and terminate on a non hex-digit character. Allow hex digits preceded by $ character

```
main program
number = 0
REPEAT
    read_character(character)
    IF character IN ['0' - '9'] THEN
        read_decimal(number, character)
    ELSE
        IF character = '$' THEN
            read_hexadecimal(number, character)
    newline
    write_decimal(number)
    newline
FOREVER
```

```
(* read a hexadecimal number (exit on non hex character)
    on exit  : number    contains the hexadecimal value read
               character last character read                *)
read_hexadecimal(number, character)
number = 0
read_character(character)
WHILE character IN [0' - '9', 'A' -  'F'] DO
    write_character(character)
    IF character in ['0' - '9'] THEN
        tempnum = character - ord ('0')
    ELSE
        tempnum = character - ord ('A') + 10
    number = number * 16 + tempnum
    read_character(character)
RETURN
```

At this point basic numeric input/output is complete (extensions can be added later) and it is time to start implementing the operations of the calculator.

Calculator stage 4 refinement

Implement and test a subroutine to allow entry of '+'   '-'   '*'   '/' operators, do calculations and print result when '=' is entered:

```
main program
REPEAT
    result = 0                        (* result of overall calculation *)
    number = 0                        (* current number being typed *)
    operator_character = '+'              (* initial operator *)
    REPEAT
       read_character(character)
       IF character IN ['0' - '9'] THEN
           read_decimal(number, character)
           calculate(result, number, operator_character)
       ELSE
           IF character = '$' THEN
               read_hexadecimal(number, character)
               calculate(result,number)
           ELSE
               IF character IN  ['+' '-' '*' '/'] THEN
                   operator_character = character
                   write_character(character)
    UNTIL character = '='
    write_character(character)
    write_decimal(result)
    newline
FOREVER
```

```
(* perform the operation - result = result operator number *)
SUBROUTINE calculate(result, number, operator character)
CASE operator_character OF
    '+' THEN result  = result + number
    '-' THEN result  = result - number
    '*' THEN result  = result * number
    '/' THEN result  = result / number
number = 0
operator_character = '+'
RETURN
```

Calculator stage 5 refinement

Examine program and tidy up. A larger program would require this at several stages

2.4.2 Design exercise - discussion

The refinement of each stage can stop when the design is of sufficient detail that it can be translated directly into program instruction statements, or calls to existing modules. The design process is generally iterative and modifications to existing stages may be needed. This can occur when a new situation arises that requires a backtrack in the design process. If possible, modifications should be carried out at the design stage; once a program has been coded, modification becomes much more expensive (see Fig. 2.2).

Possible extensions to the calculator program are:

1   To add a write_hexadecimal subroutine to display the result in hexadecimal as well as decimal.
2   To abort the calculation when the ESC key is pressed.
3   To check for overflow on operations such as + and * and display an error message.
4   Extend the calculation part of the program to take account of operator precedence (* and / usually have a higher priority than + and -) and to make use of () to change the order of evaluation. Ensure that multiple operators may not be entered (5 +* 8) or an operator missed entirely.
5   Allow the entry of the DEL or backspace key to delete the last character entered.
6   Extend the read_decimal and write_decimal subroutines to accept real numbers with fractional components (hexadecimal I/O can still be integer only reading and printing the whole number part of the real).

In practice, critical situations may occur where there is no means of recovering from an error condition, and the program would terminate with a **fatal error** or **unrecoverable error** message to the user. Such critical situations should be discovered during the specification and design phases, and some means to recover from them found.

The approach taken above was one of incremental design and implementation in which a few modules at a time are designed, implemented and tested. Another approach is to design the whole system to the point where it can be coded and then implement and test. Problems can occur during implementation when it is realised that critical issues have been overlooked at the analysis stage. Although the use of prototyping tools can help overcome some of these problems there is no easy answer and reference should be made to Software Engineering texts for detailed discussion (Steward 1987).

2.4.3 Implementation of the calculator program in C

The implementation of the calculator program in C entails the mapping of the structures of the program into the C equivalent, i.e.

IF structures map directly into the C **if** statement (Chapter 11)

WHILE structures map directly into the C **while** statement (Chapter 12)

REPEAT .. UNTIL structures will map into the C **do .. while** statement by inverting the terminating condition (Chapter 12)

CASE structure will map into the C **switch** statement (Chapter 14)

The input/output subroutines can be provided by the C functions:

`write_character(character)` by `putchar(character)`

`read_character(character)` by `character = getchar()`

    (getchar usually echoes the character; however, most systems have a variation which does not echo)

`newline` by `putchar('\n')`

2.5 Testing

Although methods of thorough testing are beyond the scope of this book, the subject is introduced in the following section. Unless a program has been formally proved, confidence in it can only be determined by thorough testing. Two approaches are:

Black Box Testing. All reasonable combinations of input to a module are tried out, the results are predicted **in advance** and compared with the actual results. Such test data should, if possible, be devised at the program specification and design stage before any coding is carried out.

White Box Testing. Test data is devised to follow every possible path through the module. Again, results must be predicted in advance; it is easy to convince oneself that incorrect results are correct once a program has produced them.

In practice, a combination of these methods is often used. For example, white box testing (together with the display of internal variables) is often used when homing in on a fault. When testing any particular input value, it is important to test:

    (a) normal values;

    (b) ends of ranges;

    (c) other special values (e.g. 0 often causes trouble);

and (d) possible invalid values.

Suppose, for example, valid numerical data input to a module should be -7 to +7 inclusive. A suitable set of test data could be -7, -1, 0, +1, +7, -8 and +8 where the latter two values should be rejected as invalid input.

    It is often useful to arrange for someone else to test one's programs. The situation that is not considered when testing will often have been left out during the design and implementation stages as well.

3

Outline structure of a C program

This chapter will describe, in outline, the structure of a C program and then go on to discuss the C programming environment in terms of program creation, compilation, linking and execution.

3.1 Program modules and C functions

A large software system can consist of many individual programs, each of which may contain 200,000 lines or more of program statements. Attempting to design, code and test a large program as a single entity is virtually impossible, so it is broken down into logical components called modules, which, in C, are implemented as *functions*.

During the program specification and design stages logical tasks or sequences of tasks, which will become modules, are identified and specified. Once a specification of the logical steps performed by each module has been drawn up (modules can contain other modules and call other modules as required) the individual modules, which become *functions*, can then be designed, coded and tested.

3.1.1 Function *identifiers*

A large C program many contain hundreds of functions each of which has its own **unique** name or *identifier*. The function *identifiers* are constructed from upper and lower case alphabetic letters, digits and the _ (underscore) character, with the proviso that the first letter must be alphabetic, e.g.:

```
test   Test   TEST   read_voltage   print_results   set_temperature   test_set_4
```

Note that C is case sensitive, i.e. in the above examples the names test, Test and TEST are different identifiers.

The programmer selects names that have some meaning within the overall context of the program, e.g. the function read_voltage may read a voltage from an experiment via an analogue to digital converter. To support program development there are a large number of functions available in *standard libraries* (see section 3.1.3).

3.1.2 Function call and return

A function *calls* (transfers control to) another function by naming it in a *program statement* (discussed in the next chapter) and passes any information required in the form of *parameters* (also called *arguments*). When the task is complete the function returns control to calling function together with any results. Functions may call other functions or even themselves (recursion).

3.1.3 Standard library functions

Facilities such as input/output (file open, close, read, write) and string processing are provided by *standard libraries* which contain functions which must be explicitly called by the C program, see Table 3.1. Associated with each of the *standard libraries* is a *standard header file* which contains information about the library functions. A C program starts with *preprocessor* directives to include the contents of specified *header files* which are used by the compiler to check functions calls (details later).

function name	header file	operation performed by function
printf	stdio.h	general output function to print to the display screen
scanf	stdio.h	general input function to read from the keyboard
fopen	stdio.h	file open
strcpy	string.h	copy a string
strcmp	string.h	compare strings
sqrt	math.h	evaluates the square root of a real number
sin	math.h	evaluates the sine of an angle in radians

Table 3.1 Examples of standard library functions with associated header file name

3.1.4 The function *main*

When a C program is executed the operating system *calls* (transfers control to) a function called main which can then call other functions to read data (e.g. scanf), process information (mathematical functions such as sin and cos), write results (e.g. printf), etc. Every C program must therefore have one (and only one) function called main. When execution is complete main returns control to the operating system.

```
preprocessor directives
int main(void)
{
    declarations
    statements
}
```

Fig. 3.1 Outline structure of a C program consisting of the function main

Fig. 3.1 shows the outline structure of a simple C program which consists of the function main (more details in the next chapter):

> *preprocessor directives*, e.g. to define a macro or include a header file (details later)
>
> **int main(void)** indicates that the function main follows
>
> **{** indicates the start of the function main
>
>> *declarations* list functions and *variables* used within main
>>
>> *statements*   specify the computing operations to be carried out
>
> **}** matches the { and indicates the end of the function main

The operations specified in the statements act on *variables* which are used to store data (characters, integer and real numbers, etc). Before a variable can be used its name or *identifier* and *data type* must be declared in a *declaration* (discussed in the next chapter).

3.2 Program creation, compilation and execution

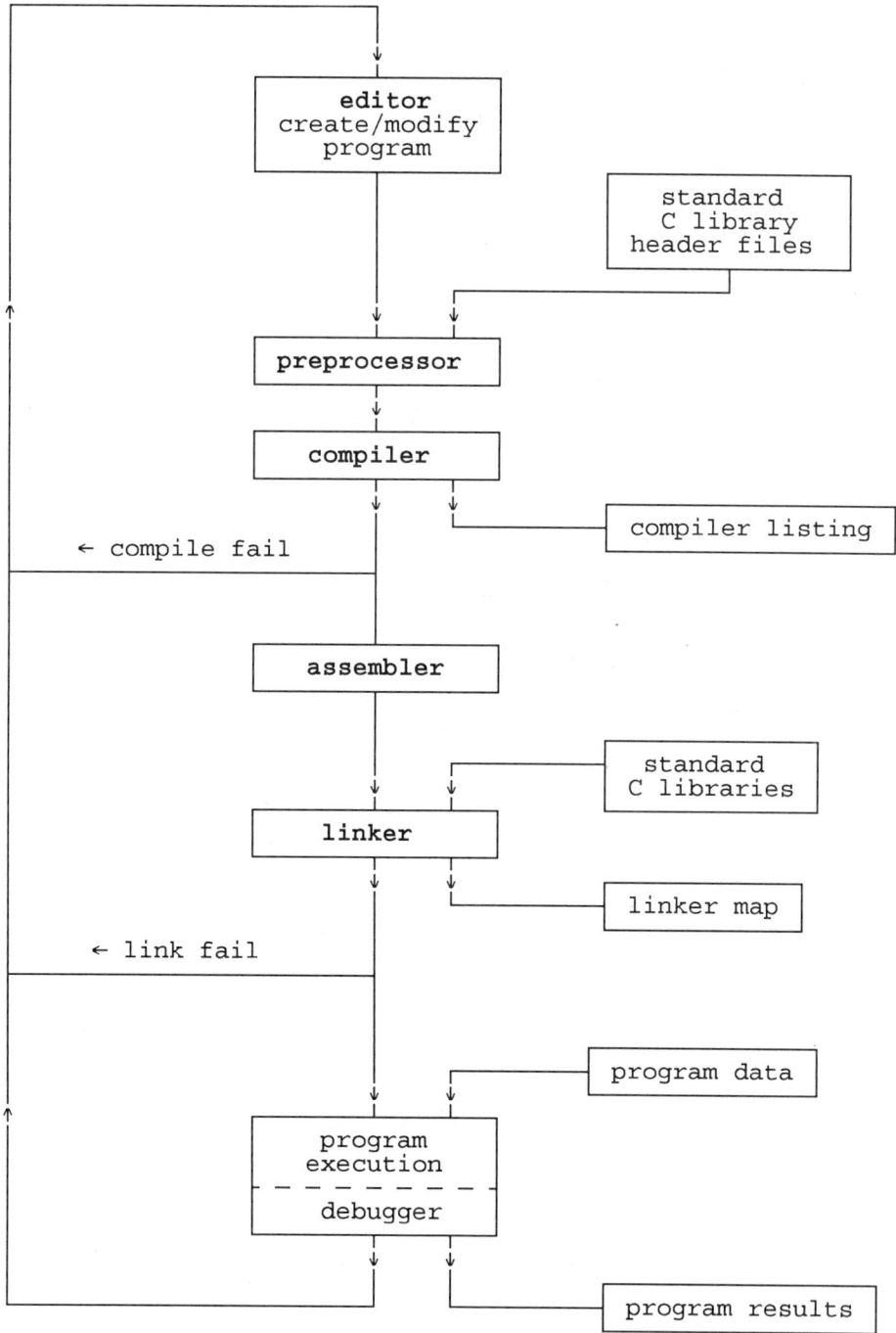

Fig. 3.2 Program creation, compilation, linking and execution

Fig. 3.2 shows the sequence of events from the creation of a C program to its execution:

Editor. The editor is used to create the program text or modify existing programs.

Preprocessor. The program starts with preprocessor directives which enable macro substitution, conditional compilation and the inclusion of other text files into the program, e.g. *header files* which supply details about library functions. The preprocessor reads the program source file, expands any macros, includes any header files and writes the result to an intermediate text file which is read by the compiler.

Compiler. The compiler converts the file from the preprocessor either into assembly language or directly into object code which contains executable machine code instructions plus information for the linker, e.g. details of standard functions required.

Assembler. Converts the assembly language program file generated by the compiler into object code (some systems can generate a combined compiler assembler listing which shows the original C code and the generated assembly language statements).

Linker. Except for very specialist programs (e.g. an embedded controller) the majority of programs require standard library functions. The linker adds object code files, either standard libraries or other files supplied by the user, to form the executable program file (in a machine code to be executed under the control of the operating system).

Program execution. The user issues commands to the operating system to run the program. During program execution data may be entered, either from the keyboard or files, and results output, either to the display screen or files.

Debugger. Some C environments contain an optional debugger which assists in error detection, e.g. at run time program execution can be traced, breakpoints inserted (to halt the program at a particular point), variables examined, etc. When the program works correctly the debugger is removed and the program runs by itself.

The editor, compiler, assembler, linker and debugger may be separate programs (to be invoked separately . by the user) or components of an integrated environment, e.g. Microsoft's C Programmer's Workbench or Borland's Turbo C IDE. An integrated environment contains an editor enabling the user to type in the program and, by hitting a keyboard key or mouse button, invoke the compilation/link process. If compilation or link fails control returns to the editor with error messages to enable the user to (hopefully) identify the cause. If the compilation/link completes without errors the user can progress to program execution where the program can be run under the control of the debugger.

Few programs work correctly first time and an iterative error correction process is required. For example, errors may be reported at various points during the above process:

During compilation: a *syntax* error indicates that the program does not conform to the rules of the language, e.g. the structure of a statement is incorrect.

During linking: multiple definitions of a reference (two functions of the same name) or undefined reference (a function called in the program was not found).

At execution time: the program crashes with a *run time* error (e.g. division by 0) or the program does not do what the specification required (the results are incorrect).

If errors occur the program text has to be modified (using the editor) and the compilation, link and execute cycle invoked again. This iterative process continues until the program runs correctly (error correction is discussed further in Chapter 6).

3.3 Editing, compiling and executing the program

The sequence of commands required to edit, compile and run a program depends upon the operating system, editor, compiler and linker being used. The following examples assume a source file called *prog.c*, with user input shown in **bold**.

Using the MS-DOS operating system with the WordStar word processor (as the editor) and the Microsoft C compiler the command sequence would be:

```
c:> ws prog.c/n          edit source file prog.c in non-document mode
                          type in C source program
c:> cl /W4 prog.c        compile the C program (warning level 4)
                          the compiler will display any errors or warnings
c:> prog                 if OK execute the program in file prog.exe
```

or using the Microsoft C Programmers Workbench integrated environment:

```
c:> pwb                  invoke the Programmers Workbench
```

To compile with Turbo C the compilation stage would be:

```
c:> tcc -w prog.c        compile the C program (all warnings on)
```

When using the UNIX operating system the command sequence could be:

```
$ vi prog.c              use vi editor or similar to type in C source program
$ cc prog.c              compile the C program into file a.out (default)
$ a.out                  execute the program in file a.out
```

When a program is executed the printf function (discussed in Chapter 5) writes to the standard output stream **stdout** which is usually directed to the display screen (if nothing appears on the screen check that **stdout** has not been redirected to a disk file). Under UNIX and MS-DOS **stdout** can be redirected at execution time:

```
$ a.out > result         execute and print to the file result
```

The corresponding input function scanf (discussed in Chapter 5) reads from the standard input stream **stdin** which is usually directed to the keyboard.

It is sometimes necessary to interrupt program execution (e.g. it is looping). How this is achieved is system dependent (e.g. UNIX uses the CTRL/C or CTRL/Q key) and may require a reboot of the operating system (e.g. with MS-DOS).

Problem for Chapter 3

From manuals determine what C program development environment you are using.
Does it conform to the ANSI C standard ?
It is an integrated environment or is the editor a separate program ?

On the next page is Program 4.1 which calculates the area of a circle $= \pi * radius^2$:

   (a) Using the editor type in the program (exactly as it is).
   (b) Compile and link the program.
   (c) If errors occur use the editor to modify the program to remove the cause.

Repeat the process until the program compiles and links without error. Execute the program. Do the following results appear on the screen ?

```
radius = 2.000000, area = 12.566370
```

4

Starting to program in ANSI C

Chapter 3 introduced the outline structure of a C program. This chapter presents a simple C program and then discusses *constants, variables, statements, expressions*, etc. which contribute towards the complete program. At this stage much of the description will be at an introductory level and later chapters will provide detail.

4.1 Program to calculate the area of a circle

```
/* Program 4.1 - from circle radius calculate area  */

#include <stdio.h>                                   /* preprocessor directive */

int main(void)                                       /* start of function main */
{
    float radius,                               /* declare radius of circle */
          area;                                 /* declare area of circle */

    radius = 2.0f;                                   /* initialise radius */
    area = 3.1415926f * radius * radius;             /* calculate area */
    printf("radius = %f, area = %f \n", radius, area);    /* print result */
    return 0;                                        /* terminate program */
}
```

Program 4.1 To calculate the area of a circle

Fig. 3.1 introduced the structure of a C program consisting of the function main. Program 4.1 is a C program which, given the radius of a circle, calculates its area and prints the result to the display screen. The area of the circle is calculated thus:

$$area = \pi * radius^2$$

Note that text within /* ...... */ is *program comment* which is effectively ignored by the C compiler. Program comment enables the human reader to gain a better understanding of the purpose and structure of the program than is available from the C program code alone. Program 4.1 begins with a comment which briefly describes the objective of the program and further comments expand on the role of particular lines of code.

4.2 Constants

Constants are fixed values within a program, e.g. in the Program 4.1:

1   2.0f and 3.1415926f are real number constants of *data type* float
2   "radius = %f, area = %f \n" is a constant of *data type* string
3   0 is an integer number constant of *data type* int

Data types are discussed in the next section.

4.3 Variables, data types and declarations

Variables are used within a program to store data being processed, e.g. characters (names and addresses) or numbers (data read from an experiment). So that a particular variable can be referenced in the program (to store a value in it) each variable is given a name or *identifier* (construction rules as for functions, see section 3.1.1), e.g.:

```
radius   area   Area   circle_area   Voltage   output_current   Minimum_temperature
```

Remember C is case sensitive, i.e. Area and area are different identifiers. In Program 4.1 radius and area are variables, the contents of which are accessed via the variable names in *program statements* (see next section).

Each variable in the program is of a particular *data type* which determines what type of information may be stored within it. Examples of C data types are:

data type	information stored
char	a character stored in a byte
int	a signed integer number, minimum size is 16-bits
long int	a signed integer number, minimum size is 32-bits
float	single precision real number, minimum precision 6 decimal digits
double	double precision real number, minimum precision 10 decimal digits

Before a variable can be used its name or *identifier* and *data type* must be declared in a *declaration*. This enables the compiler:

(a) to reserve storage in memory, e.g. a byte for a character or two or four bytes for an integer,

and (b) to convert between different data types, e.g. a mathematical expression may contain a mixture of integer and single and double precision real values.

In Program 4.1 variables radius and area are declared to be type float, i.e. in lines:

```
float radius,                          /* declare radius of circle */
      area;                            /* declare area of circle */
```

In a declaration the *data type* is specified followed by a list of variable names separated by commas with a ; terminating the declaration. Although, for reasons of clarity, the declarations are on separate lines the above could have been written:

```
float radius, area;                    /* declare variables */
```

When a variable is declared it may be given an *initial value*, otherwise its value is either zero or *undefined* depending on context (details in Chapters 17 and 21). For example:

```
char char_a = 'a';
int temperature, min_temperature = 50, max_temperature;
float radius = 2.0f, circle_area, sphere_area, sphere_volume;
```

In the above declarations the following variables are given initial values:

char_a	initial value 'a'	data type char	(character)
min_temperature	initial value 50	data type int	(integer number)
radius	initial value 2.0f	data type float	(single precision real number)

A variable declared with an initial value may be given a new value in an *assignment statement* (see next section). In ANSI C terminology a named area of storage used to represent a value (such as variables char_a, radius, etc.) is called an *object*.

4.4 Statements and expressions

Program *statements* specify the computing operations to be carried out, e.g. print the value of a variable or to add two variables and assign the result to another. In Program 4.1 there are four statements (each terminated by a ;), i.e.:

```
radius = 2.0f;                                        /* initialise radius */
area = 3.1415926f * radius * radius;                  /* calculate area */
printf("radius = %f, area = %f \n", radius, area);    /* print result */
return 0;                                             /* terminate program */
```

The first and second are *assignment statements* which assign a value to a variable, the third calls the function `printf` to print results on the screen and the `return` terminates the function `main` and returns control to the operating system. The assignment statements contain *expressions* which are built up from:

  (a) *operators*   + add, - subtract, * multiply, / divide (details in Chapter 9),
and (b) *operands*   data objects to be operated upon such as variables and constants.

In an assignment statement the value of the expression to the right of the = is evaluated and assigned to the variable on the left (= is the *assignment operator*), i.e.:

```
radius = 2.0f;
```

the expression to the right of the = is a constant, the value of which is assigned to the variable `radius` (which now has the value 2.0 whereas before it was *undefined*). Consider:

```
area = 3.1415926f * radius * radius;
```

The value of the expression `3.1415926f * radius * radius` is evaluated and the result assigned to variable `area`. Remember that when a variable name is used in a statement the memory location assigned to the variable is accessed either to read the current contents (e.g. `radius`) or to write a new one (e.g. `area`).

It is worth noting that the expression to the left of an = is called an *lvalue* (left value) in C terminology. Compilers use the term in error reports (see Listing 6.1 in Chapter 6).

One problem, particularly when learning to program, is that assignment statements resemble mathematical equations (where = means *equals*), however, they are distinct and should not be confused, e.g.:

```
radius = radius + 1;
```

is a meaningless mathematical equation but an acceptable assignment statement, i.e. the constant 1 is added to the value of `radius` and the result assigned to `radius`. More modern languages such as Pascal and Modula 2 attempt to get around this problem by using := for assignment.

4.5 Function calling and parameters

A function calls (transfers control) to another function to carry out a specific task by naming it in a *program statement*. For example, `printf` is the standard library function which is called to print information onto the display screen:

```
printf("Hello John Doe how are you ?");
```

Would print on the display screen:

```
Hello John Doe how are you ?
```

When a function is called the parameters, enclosed in (), pass information to the function. In the above call there is a single parameter "Hello John Doe how are you ?" which is called the *control string* (in C a string is enclosed in " characters which are not part of the string but are the string *delimiters*). Now consider the call to printf in Program 4.1:

```
printf("radius = %f, area = %f \n", radius, area);
```

This call has three parameters separated by commas; the *control string* and the variables radius and area (the values of which are to be printed, the use of printf will be described in Chapter 5). When executed Program 4.1 prints on the screen:

```
radius = 2.000000, area = 12.566370
```

followed by a *newline* (\n is the C notation for the *newline* character).

Fig. 4.1 shows the flow of instruction execution of Program 4.1 on the call to printf. Program instruction execution is sequential until an instruction transfers control elsewhere, i.e.:

(a) the call to printf in Fig. 4.1 transfers control to start of the code of printf,

(b) the code of printf is executed to print the specified information,

and (c) the final instruction of printf returns control to the instruction following the original call (in the case of Fig. 4.1 to the statement return 0;).

A simplified view of the flow of instruction execution in Program 4.1 would be:

1   the operating system sets up the program environment and calls the function main

2   storage is allocated in main memory for the variables radius and area

3   execute assignment radius = 2.0f;

4   execute assignment area = 3.1415926f * radius * radius;

5   execute function call printf(....)

      execute function printf to print information on the screen

      return to calling function (main in this case)

6   execute statement return 0;

7   deallocate variable storage and return to the operating system

```
          main (void)
          {                              start of function main
              radius = 2.0f;
              area = .....;
              printf(....); →  ──────┐
              return 0;              ↓    call function printf
  ┌──→   →  }
  │
  │    ┌────────────────────────┘
  │    │  printf(....)
  │    └→ {                              start of function printf
  │       .....
  │       .....
  ↑       }                              return to calling function
  │       ↓
  └───────┘
```

Fig. 4.1 Execution flow of Program 4.1 on the call to function printf

4.6 The *function result* of a function

Although some functions are 'stand alone', in that no data is passed in or out, the majority:

(a) require data from the calling function in the form of parameters,

and (b) return a *function result*, e.g. the square root of a number (passed as a parameter).

When a function is implemented the first line specifies the function name, the *data type* of the *function result* and any parameters. For example, in Program 4.1 the function main starts with:

```
int main(void)
```

Indicating that:

(a) the function returns a *function result* of data type int (integer),

(b) the function name is main,

and (c) it has no parameters; any parameters are enclosed in () and the keyword void indicates that there are no parameters.

The *function result* is returned via the function name (as the contents of a variable are accessed via the variable name). For example, the mathematical function sqrt evaluates the square root of a double precision real number and returns the solution as a *function result* of type double precision real:

```
x = sqrt(4.0);
```

Assuming x is a double precision real variable the sequence of events is:

1   the function sqrt is called with the parameter 4.0
2   the square root of 4.0 is evaluated, i.e. the solution is 2.0
3   sqrt exits and returns the solution as a function result (in effect the identifier sqrt now has the value 2.0)
4   the value returned via the name sqrt is assigned to the variable x (the value 2.0)

Because the result of a particular function is returned via its name an expression may contain a number of function calls in addition to variable names, constants, etc. For example, the **mathematical equation** for sin 2Θ is:

$$\sin 2\Theta = 2 \sin \Theta \cos \Theta$$

The **program statements** to evaluate sin 2Θ of a double precision real variable angle are:

```
angle = 3.14159 * 25.0 /180.0;          /* angle 25° in radians */
x = 2.0 * sin(angle) * cos(angle);      /* calculate sin 2Θ */
```

The functions sin and cos are called (in which order the standard does **not** specify) returning the *function results* sin = 0.422618 and cos = 0.906308 (both of type double). Then the complete expression is evaluated and the result assigned to variable x, i.e. the angle is 25° hence the value of sin 2Θ would be 0.766044 (more details in Program 5.2).

The function sqrt has a parameter and returns a value but this is not always the case. For example, function getchar waits for a keyboard hit and returns a character:

```
ch = getchar();
```

Although there is no parameter the () are still required to tell C that this a function call, otherwise it would take getchar as a variable name. Even if a function returns a result it does not have to be used. For example, the function printf returns an int which reports the number of characters printed (which was ignored in Program 4.1).

4.7 The *function result* of the function *main*

When a program is executed the operating system sets up the program environment and then calls the function main. When main terminates it returns a *function result* of type int which the operating system can use as a test of successful program completion (0 indicates success and non zero some error condition). The test for successful program completion would be used if a sequence of programs are to be executed where the later programs depend upon the success of those preceding. The return statement is used to terminate a function and return the function result, e.g. in Program 4.1 to indicate success:

```
return 0;                                    /* terminate program */
```

4.8 Review of Program 4.1

In summary the sequence of statements in Program 4.1 is:

1   #include <stdio.h> is a *preprocessor directive* to include a copy of the standard header file stdio.h at this point in the program (stdio.h provides the compiler with information about the standard library function printf)

2   int main(void) indicates that the code of the function main follows

3   { indicates the start of the function main

4   Declare the variables radius and area to be of data type float (single precision real).

5   radius = 2.0f; is an *assignment statement* which assigns the value 2.0 to the variable radius

6   area = 3.1415926f * radius * radius; is an *assignment statement* which evaluates 3.1415926f * radius * radius and assigns the result to the variable area

7   printf("radius = %f, area = %f \n", radius, area); is a *statement* which calls function printf to print the results of the program (printf is described in Chapter 5)

8   return 0; terminates the function main and returns a function result of 0 (success) to the operating system

9   } indicates the end of the function main

The blank lines are inserted to improve the overall layout of the program.

Problem for Chapter 4

If not complete finish off the Problem for Chapter 3, i.e. get Program 4.1 working.

One at time put errors in the program, compile/link and execute (if possible) and comment on the result (Chapter 6 discusses error detection), e.g.:

    (a) miss area, from the declaration
    (b) miss the = from an assignment statement
    (c) miss the ; from the end of a statement
    (d) miss an * from the calculation of area
    (e) miss a " in the call to function printf
    (f) mistype the name of function printf
    (g) miss out the line radius = 2.0f; completely
and (h) miss out the line return 0; completely

5

Using standard library functions

Higher-level facilities such as input/output (file open, close, read, write) and mathematical functions (sin, cos, sqrt, etc.) are provided by *standard libraries* which contain functions which must be explicitly called by the C program. This chapter introduces the basic keyboard input (scanf) and screen output (printf) functions and the mathematical functions sqrt, sin and cos. This is at an introductory level and further details are provided later.

5.1 Introduction to the *printf* function

The standard library function printf is used to print information to the standard output stream **stdout** (usually the display screen), e.g.:

```
printf("Hello John Doe how are you ?\n");
```

will print the string enclosed in " delimiters, i.e.:

```
Hello John Doe how are you ?
```

followed by a *newline*. In this case there is a single parameter to printf, called the *control string*, which contains the characters to print and the character sequence \n which is the C notation for the *newline character* (which moves the cursor to the start of the next line on the screen). Now consider the call to printf in Program 4.1:

```
printf("radius = %f, area = %f \n", radius, area);
```

This call to printf has three parameters (separated by commas - ignore the comma inside the string which is part of the text to be printed) which are used to pass information into the function:

1 The *control string* "radius = %f, area = %f \n" which controls the printing of information onto the screen.
2 The variable radius, the numeric value of which is to be printed on the screen.
3 The variable area, the numeric value of which is to be printed on the screen.

In addition to the characters to be printed the control string contains the *conversion specification* %f (also called a *format control*). The effect of the %f conversion specifications is to print the value of the following parameters (variables radius and area) as signed decimal real numbers, i.e. %f **converts** the value of the parameter into a sequence of characters to be printed on the screen. The effect of the call to printf in Program 4.1 is:

1 to print the text string "radius = "
2 the first %f prints the value of the second parameter (variable radius, i.e. 2.0)
3 to print the text string " area = "
4 the second %f prints the value of the third parameter (variable area)
5 " \n" to print a space followed by a newline character

There are corresponding conversion specifications for integers (%d), characters (%c), etc.

5.2 Introduction to mathematical functions (sqrt, sin & cos)

```
 1 /* Program 5.1 - from circle radius calculate area and recalculate radius */
 2
 3 #include <stdio.h>                              /* standard I/O library */
 4 #include <math.h>                               /* standard maths library */
 5
 6 int main(void)
 7 {
 8     float radius = 2.0f,           /* radius of circle, initial value 2.0 */
 9           area,                              /* area of circle */
10           radius_check;                      /* check of radius */
11
12     area = 3.1415926f * radius * radius;        /* calculate area */
13     printf("radius = %f, area = %f", radius, area);
14     radius_check = sqrt(area / 3.1415926f);      /* recalculate radius */
15     printf(", radius check = %f \n", radius_check);
16     return 0;
17 }
```

Program 5.1 Calculate circle area then recalculate radius

Program 5.1 is an extension of Program 4.1 in that after the area has been calculated (using the circle radius) the radius is recalculated, i.e.:

$$\text{radius} = (\text{area} / \pi)^{1/2}$$

The line numbers down the left hand side of Program 5.1 are **not** part of the program but are there to enable identification of particular lines when discussing the programs within the text of this book. For example, the sequence of statements in Program 5.1 is:

line

3   `#include <stdio.h>` includes the standard header file `<stdio.h>`

4   `#include <math.h>` includes the header file `<math.h>` which provides information about the `sqrt` function used in line 14 (without this the program would not work, discussed in the next section)

8   declares variable `radius` and initialises its value to 2.0f

9   declares variable `area`

10 declares variable `radius_check`

12 `area = 3.1415926f * radius * radius;` calculates the circle area and assigns the result to variable `area`

13 `printf("radius = %f, area = %f", radius, area);` print the values of `radius` and `area`

14 `radius_check = sqrt(area / 3.1415926f);` uses the `sqrt` function to calculate the radius from the area and assigns the result to the variable `radius_check` (sqrt is discussed in the next section)

15 `printf(", radius check = %f \n", radius_check);` prints the value of `radius_check`

C library functions which print to the screen or disk files append new information directly on to the end of any existing information. When executed Program 5.1 prints:

`radius = 2.000000, area = 12.566370, radius check = 2.000000`

followed by a *newline* (at the end of the second `printf` call).

5.2.1 Using the mathematical function *sqrt* (square root)

In C facilities such as I/O and mathematical functions are provided by standard libraries. An implication of this is that C knows nothing about the library functions in terms of their names, number and type of parameters (data to be passed to and from the function) and function result returned (if any). The compiler, however, requires this information before it can check that a function call in the program is correct. Associated with each of the *standard libraries* is a *standard header file* which contains *function prototypes* and other information which gives details about the library functions (*function prototypes* will be discussed in Chapter 15.3). A C program starts with *preprocessor* directives to include specified header files which can then be used by the compiler to check functions calls.

The preprocessor directive #include <math.h> in Program 5.1 reads the header file <math.h> which contains the *function prototypes* of all the mathematical functions. This informs the compiler that sqrt has one parameter of type double (double precision real) and returns a function result of type double. The operations performed by the function call:

```
radius_check = sqrt(area / 3.1415926f);
```

are:

1 the *expression* area / 3.1415926f is evaluated as a float (i.e. both operands are float)
2 the result is converted to a double to be passed as a parameter to sqrt
3 sqrt is called with the double parameter
4 sqrt evaluates the square root of the parameter
5 sqrt terminates and returns control to main with the function result which is a double
6 the double function result is converted to a float and assigned to radius_check

Unlike more modern languages such as Pascal and Modula 2 C does not have to know about a function before the function is called (to maintain compatibility with the original C which did not have function prototypes). How a particular parameter is passed on a function call when C has not got a *function prototype* depends upon its data type (parameter passing will be covered in detail in Chapter 15). In the case of a parameter of type float it is converted to a double. This happens to be suitable for the sqrt function but would cause problems if the function expected some other type such as an int. In addition, if a function prototype is missing C assumes that any function result is of data type int.

Thus if, in Program 5.1, the #include <math.h> had been missed sqrt would have been called correctly with a parameter of type double but the function result returned from sqrt would have been assumed to be of type int (to be converted to float before assigning to radius_check). This would result in unpredictable behaviour which can range from rubbish returned from the function call to a crash of the program, e.g. a segmentation fault on an Apollo DN4500. Missing #include directives is a fairly common error and a modern compiler will issue a warning message if a function prototype is not available when a function is called (see example in Chapter 6).

Exercise 5.1 (*see Appendix B for sample answer*)

1 Enter Program 5.1 compile, link and execute it.

2 Repeat with the preprocessor directive #include <math.h> removed, what happens ?

3 Replace line 15 with the following (see sample answer for further discussion):

```
printf(" converted %d \n", printf(", radius check = %f \n", radius_check));
```

5.2.2 Using the mathematical functions *sin* (sine) and *cos* (cosine)

```
 1 /* Program 5.2 - calculate sin(2A) = 2 * sin(A) * cos(A)             *
 2  *                         cos(2A) = cos(A)*cos(A)-sin(A)*sin(A)     */
 3
 4 #include <stdio.h>
 5 #include <math.h>
 6
 7 int main(void)
 8 {
 9     float angle = 25.0f, sin_2a, cos_2a;
10
11     angle = 3.14159f * angle /180.0f;                       /* angle in radians */
12     sin_2a = 2.0f * sin(angle) * cos(angle);                      /* sin 2A */
13     cos_2a = cos(angle) * cos(angle) - sin(angle) * sin(angle);   /* cos 2A */
14     printf("angle A = %f, sin(A) = %f, cos(A) = %f \n",
15             angle, sin(angle), cos(angle));
16     printf("sin(2A) = %f and %f ", sin_2a, sin(2.0f * angle));
17     printf("and cos(2A) = %f and %f \n", cos_2a, cos(2.0f * angle));
18     return 0;
19 }
```

Program 5.2 To evaluate sin 2Θ and cos 2Θ

The **mathematical equations** for sin 2Θ (see Chapter 4.5) and cos 2Θ are:

$$\sin 2\Theta = 2 \sin \Theta \cos \Theta$$
$$\cos 2\Theta = \cos^2\Theta - \sin^2\Theta$$

Program 5.2 evaluates sin 2Θ and cos 2Θ using the `sin` and `cos` functions from the mathematical library `<math.h>`. Both functions take a `double` precision parameter, the angle in radians, and return a function result of type `double`. The program evaluates the values of sin 2Θ and cos 2Θ using the above equations, and then prints the values together with function results from `sin` and `cos` called with the angle 2Θ. The program sequence is:

9   declare variables and initialise the `angle` to 25°
11   convert the `angle` in degrees to radians (for `sin` and `cos`)
12-13 calculate sin 2Θ (variable `sin_2a`) and cos 2Θ (variable `cos_2a`) using above equations (Chapter 4.6 explained how an expression may contain a number of function calls in addition to variable names, constants, etc.)
14-15 print the value of `angle`, `sin(angle)` and `cos(angle)`
16   print `sin_2a` calculated in line 12 and the value returned by `sin(2Θ)`
17   print `cos_2a` calculated in line 13 and the value returned by `cos(2Θ)`

In the calls to `printf` some of the parameters are variables and some are expressions, e.g. in the call to `printf` in line 16 the second parameter `sin_2a` is a variable and the third parameter `sin(2.0f * angle)` is an expression. This is an example of the general rule of C that anywhere where it is permissible to use the value of a variable (of some type) an expression (of the same type) may be used.

A run of the program on an **IBM PC** compatible under Microsoft C version 6.00 was:

```
angle A = 0.436332, sin(A) = 0.422618, cos(A) = 0.906308
sin(2A) = 0.766044 and 0.766044 and cos(2A) = 0.642788 and 0.642788
```

5.3 Numeric keyboard input using the *scanf* function

```
 1 /* Program 5.3 - read radius of circle from the keyboard      *
 2  *              calculate circle area and recalculate radius   */
 3
 4 #include <stdio.h>
 5 #include <math.h>
 6
 7 int main(void)
 8 {
 9     const float pi = 3.1415926f;                    /* constant pi */
10     float radius = 2.0f,                          /* radius of circle */
11           area,                                   /* area of circle */
12           radius_check;                           /* check of radius */
13
14     printf("Enter radius of circle (real number) ? ");
15     scanf("%f", &radius);                           /* read radius */
16     area = pi * radius * radius;                  /* calculate area */
17     printf("radius = %f, area = %f", radius, area);
18     radius_check = sqrt(area / pi);              /* calculate radius */
19     printf(", radius check = %f \n", radius_check);
20     return 0;
21 }
```

Program 5.3 Using *scanf* to read a real number from the keyboard

A problem with Program 5.1 is that if the area of another circle is required the program has to be modified, recompiled and linked. Program 5.3 is similar to Program 5.1 except that the circle radius is read from the keyboard. The lines which contain updated code are:

9   const float pi = 3.1415926f; declares pi with the value 3.1415926f (discussed below)
14 prompts the user to enter the radius of the circle on the keyboard
15 scanf("%f", &radius); reads a real number from the keyboard and returns the value in the variable radius (discussed in the next section)

The standard library function scanf reads information from the keyboard (see next section). The "%f" conversion specification in line 15 instructs scanf to read a real signed decimal number from the keyboard and return the value in the second parameter, &radius.

In Program 5.1 the value of π was specified twice, in lines 12 and 14, as the float constant 3.1415926f. A good optimising compiler may realise that this is the same value and generate one copy of it, otherwise, two copies will be generated wasting memory. In Program 5.1 this is not a problem but many mathematical, engineering and scientific programs make extensive use of constants and generating a separate copy at each point in the program would be very inefficient as well as a source of errors due to mistyping.

In line 9 of Program 5.3 π is declared as the non-modifiable variable pi (also called a *named constant*) which is then used in lines 16 and 18. The *type qualifier* const (new to ANSI C) tells the compiler that the following objects are to be treated as constants and may not be altered. If the compiler knows something is a constant it can optimise the code more efficiently and generate warnings if the programmer attempts to alter its value (see example in Chapter 6). It is recommended that const qualified objects are declared first so that the declarations stand out in the program.

5.3.1 The *scanf* control string

The function scanf, which reads characters from the standard input stream **stdin** (usually the keyboard), is called with the following parameters:

(a) the *control string* which controls the reading of characters from the keyboard and their conversion into values to be assigned to variables of various data types,

and (b) other parameters; in the main a list of addresses of (or *pointers* to) variables.

The control string may contain:

1   **Spaces** which cause the input stream to be read up to the next non **white space** character (**white space** is the C term for spaces, tabs and newlines).
2   **Conversion specifications** beginning with % which specify how characters in the input stream are matched and converted (%d for decimal int and %f for float, more details in Chapters 7 and 8). If converted successfully the value is returned in the variable **whose address** is given by the corresponding parameter.
3   Characters other than **white space** and conversion specifications; the next character in the input stream must match this character.

Apart from character input **white space** in the input text stream is skipped, scanf reads across spaces, tabs, newlines, etc. to find its input, e.g. in line 15 of Program 5.3 any spaces or newlines typed before the number will be ignored.

It is important to note that text streams normally operate on a line by line basis with each line consisting of zero or more characters terminated by the newline character. As characters are typed on the keyboard they are automatically echoed to the screen and the line is formed in an input buffer and only when newline (or *end of file*) is entered is it passed to scanf. The scanf function then processes the line carrying out conversions as specified by the control string. If all the conversions specified cannot be satisfied by the current line of text scanf will request another line, e.g. if a control string "%f%f" specifies two numbers are to be entered and the user only enters one.

5.3.2 Parameters to the *scanf* function

Parameters in C are passed into a function using *call by value*, i.e. copies of the *actual parameters* are made in temporary variables and these are passed. Consider:

```
sin_a = sin(angle);
radius_check = sqrt(area / 3.1415926f);
```

In the first statement a **copy** of the value of the variable angle is passed to sin. In the second statement the value of the expression area / 3.1415926f is evaluated and this is passed to sqrt.

Call by value prevents code within the function inadvertently accessing the *actual parameters* and corrupting them. Now consider line 15 of Program 5.3:

```
scanf("%f", &radius);
```

To be able to return the number read from the keyboard scanf needs to be able to access the original memory area allocated to the variable radius. An & before a variable name tells the compiler that the *memory address* of the variable (called a *pointer* in C) is to be passed to the function at execution time. In line 15 scanf uses the address passed by the second parameter to access the memory area allocated to radius. This method of passing parameters is known as *call by reference* (more discussion in Chapter 15).

5.3.3 The function result of *scanf*

In addition to returning values read from the keyboard (into the parameters) function scanf also returns as an int function result the number of successful conversions which should be checked by the program (using an **IF statement**, see Chapter 11 Program 11.2):

1   If no conversions occurred 0 is returned.
2   If a matching failure occurs (e.g. a non-numeric character in a decimal number) conversion stops and the number of successful conversions returned (the faulty character is left in the input stream where the program can read it and take action, see Program 13.2).
3   If *end of file* occurs before any conversions the value EOF (defined in <stdio.h>) is returned (discussed in Chapter 7.3). How *end of file* is entered is system dependent, e.g. under:

> MS-DOS is CTRL/Z or newline followed by CTRL/Z
> UNIX is newline followed by CTRL/D

Thus it is possible for all input to be verified and action taken in case of error, e.g. an error message printed and the user prompted for more input (see Chapter 13 Program 13.2).

Exercise 5.2 (*see Appendix B for sample answer*)

Type in Program 5.3, compile and link and then execute with various data (in particular enter invalid characters). Extend the program to evaluate sphere surface area $= 4\pi *$ radius^2 and volume $= \frac{4}{3}\pi *$ radius^3 and then recalculate the radius from the sphere volume (note that the mathematical function pow(x,y) evaluates x^y).

Remove the & from before variable name radius in the call to scanf in line 15 of Program 5.3. Compile, link and execute the program. What happens ?

Problem for Chapter 5

Type in Program 5.2, compile, link and execute (a run of the program is given at the end of section 5.2.2). Modify the program to read the angle from the keyboard using the scanf function.

The program calls the functions sin and cos several times with the same parameter (variable angle). Modify the program to evaluate the sin and cos of angle only once and then extend it to evaluate tan 2Θ, i.e.:

$$\tan 2\Theta = 2 \tan \Theta / (1 - \tan^2\Theta)$$

The value of tan Θ may be evaluated using the standard maths function tan(Θ).

6

Program layout, documentation and debugging

6.1 The C character set

```
a b c d e f g h i j k l m n o p q r s t u v w x y z
A B C D E F G H I J K L M N O P Q R S T U V W X Y Z
0 1 2 3 4 5 6 7 8 9
! " # % & ' ( ) * + , - . / : ; < = > ? [ \ ] ^ _ { | } ~
space, horizontal and vertical tab, form feed, newline
```

Table 6.1 The C character set

The ANSI C standard talks about two character sets:

   (a) the character set that the program will be written in,

and (b) the character set used at execution time.

When the program is being compiled and executed on the same machine these two character sets are the same. They **may** differ when using a cross compiler where the program is compiled and linked on a host machine and executed on a target machine (which may use a different character set). In such cases the compiler and system documentation will discuss any problems.

The ANSI standard requires an alphabet of 96 characters, as shown in Table 6.1, which are available on the majority of computer systems and terminals. Note:

1   If some of the character set is missing (e.g. # [\ ] ^ { | } ~ are not available on some terminals) this can be overcome by the use of **trigraphs**, see compiler manual.

2   The C language is character *case sensitive*, hence the names printf, PRINTF and Printf will be treated by the compiler as different identifiers (if the linker prints the error messages *undefined reference* or *unresolved reference* check that the names of functions are spelt correctly and in the correct combination of upper and lower case).

3   C is a free format language and the compiler (not preprocessor) does not worry about the layout of the program. In particular the characters **space**, **tab** and **newline** are called **white space** and have no special effect on the program (discussed below).

6.2 Programming style: documentation and layout

Good program layout and documentation is important for various reasons, including:

   (a) it simplifies error detection and correction by the original programmer,

and (b) it improves the maintainability of the program in that other programmers can understand the objectives of the program and how it works.

6.2.1 Documentation and comments

One aim when writing a program (apart from making it work) is to make it readable. The program code should be documented, as it is written, by inserting comments at appropriate places. General guidelines on comments are:

1   The source file should begin with a general description describing its overall function and how it is used, e.g. it contains a program, or a library of functions, or a header file, etc. Additional details such as which specialist support libraries it needs and who implemented it, when were modifications made, etc. are useful particularly when a large team is working on a program consisting of many source files.

2   Every function should begin with a general description followed by details of how it is used, e.g. global variables accessed, parameters passed in and out, function result returned (if any), etc. Implementation and modification details should be included.

3   If the use of a variable is not clear from its name add a comment to the line (so far the programs have been so simple that often the variable name alone is sufficient),

4   Place comments before or within any section of program code which is complex or may be difficult to follow.

In C a comment starts with /* (no space between the characters) and is terminated by */. When compiled the comment is **replaced by a space** and so becomes **white space** (see below). Comments may not appear within strings and comments may not appear within comments, i.e. in /* --- /* --- */ --- */ the first */ will terminate the comment.

6.2.2 Program layout

Within certain limits C does not care how a program looks. For example consider the following version of Program 5.3 (which will compile, link and execute correctly):

```
/* Program 5.3a */
#include <stdio.h>
#include <math.h>
int main(void){const float pi=3.1415926f;float radius,area,radius_check;
printf("Enter radius of circle (real number) ? ");scanf("%f",&radius);area
=pi*radius*radius;printf("radius = %f, area = %f",radius,area);radius_check=
sqrt(area/pi);printf(", radius check = %f \n",radius_check);return 0;}
```

Not only do the comments fail to indicate what the program does but the code layout is a mess with several statements or parts of statements per line. With certain exceptions, C ignores spaces, tabs and newlines treating them as **white space**. Exceptions include:

(a) *preprocessor directives* must be on separate lines (newline is the terminator **not** ;),
(b) **white space** separates keywords, identifiers, etc., i.e. between float and radius,
and (c) **white space** must not occur in the middle of *keywords*, *identifiers*, *strings* and *character constants*.

Space characters within a string are part of the string (not **white space**) and a string cannot contain a newline character. For example, the following statement would generate the error message *unterminated string* or similar.

```
    printf("Enter radius of
circle (real number) ? ");
```

If a very long string is required use can be made of the string joining feature (new in ANSI C) by which adjacent strings (separated by **white space**) are concatenated:

```
printf("Enter radius of "
       "circle (real number) ? ");
```

The two strings are joined to form `"Enter radius of circle (real number) ? "`.

If a line becomes too long it is generally possible to replace a space character by a newline. For example, line 9 of Program 5.2 could be written:

```
float angle = 25.0f,
      sin_2a,
      cos_2a;
```

There are occasions where inserting a newline is not possible. For example, preprocessor directives must be on one line and terminated by a newline, yet macro definitions can be very long (described in Chapter 26). To overcome this problem the sequence **backslash newline** (no spaces following the \) becomes *invisible* to the C system, e.g. the preprocessor will accept:

```
#include \
     <stdio.h>
```

General guidelines on program layout or style are:

1   Place at least one blank line following preprocessor directives, between functions and between declarations and statements within a function.
2   Write one statement per line.
3   Use spaces to make declarations and statements readable, e.g. around operators in assignment statements, following commas in declarations and function calls, etc.
4   Variable and function names should be chosen to indicate their use in the program.
5   If making the program slightly longer improves its readability do it ! Some programmers have an unfortunate tendency (encouraged by many books) to write terse, cryptic and unreadable code (thinking that this is a sign of a good programmer).
6   Use indentation to show the logical structure of the code. For example, in the programs so far the declarations and statements within `main` have been indented four spaces to highlight the beginning and the end of the function. More examples of indentation will be shown when control structures are introduced in Chapter 11.
7   Use some pattern to separate functions making a new one immediately visible, e.g. a comment consisting of a complete line of `/*****************************************/`.

Companies tend to have their own *house style* of program layout to ensure consistency across the organisation. The precise form of the style is not critical but once a style has been chosen it should be used consistently.

6.3 Detection of compile, link and run time errors

At the simplest level errors in programs tend to be either syntactic or semantic:

syntactic: the program constructs or statements do not conform to the syntax (rules) of the programming language being used;

semantic: the program does not do what the specification states, i.e. the program gives run time errors or prints incorrect results.

```
Line#  Source Line                              Microsoft C Compiler Version 6.00

    1 /* Program 5.3b - read radius of circle from the keyboard    *
    2 *                   calculate circle area and check radius      */
    3
    4 #include <stdio.h>
    5
    6 int main(void)
    7 {
    8     const float pi = 3.1415926f;
    9     float radius, area, radius_check;
   10
   11     pi = 10.0f;
***** P5_3B.C(11) : error C2166: lvalue specifies const object
   12     printf("Enter radius of circle (real number) ? ")
   13     scanf("%f", radius);
***** P5_3B.C(13) : error C2146: syntax error : missing ';' before identifier 'scanf'
   14     area = pi * radius   radius;
***** P5_3B.C(14) : error C2146: syntax error : missing ';' before identifier 'radius'
   15     printf("radius = %d, area = %f", radius, area);
   16     radius_check = sqrt(areax / pi);
***** P5_3B.C(16) : warning C4016: 'sqrt' : no function return type, using int
***** P5_3B.C(16) : warning C4071: 'sqrt' : no function prototype given
***** P5_3B.C(16) : error C2065: 'areax' : undefined
   17     print(", radius check = %f \n, radius_check);
***** P5_3B.C(17) : warning C4016: 'print' : no function return type, using int
***** P5_3B.C(17) : warning C4071: 'print' : no function prototype given
***** P5_3B.C(17) : error C2001: newline in constant
   18     return 0
***** P5_3B.C(18) : error C2143: syntax error : missing ')' before 'return'
   19 }

6 errors detected
```

Listing 6.1 Compiler listing of a C program with errors (Microsoft C)

Listing 6.1 shows a Microsoft C compiler Version 6.00 listing of a modified version of
Program 5.3 with various syntax errors reported. The error messages indicate syntax
errors in lines:

11 pi = 10.0f; attempting to alter a *const qualified* object. In C terminology an *object* is
    a named region of storage and an lvalue is an expression (on the left side of an =)
    referring to an *object*. In this case the *lvalue* refers to a const qualified *object*.

14 area = pi * radius   radius; the * operator has been missed

16 radius_check = sqrt(areax / pi); the name areax is mistyped

17 printf(", radius check = %f \n, radius_check); missing " string delimiter

Errors are also reported in lines 13 and 18 which are correct. The messages are due to:

line

13 the missing ; on the end of line 12

18 the missing " in line 17

In addition to error messages the compiler may generate warnings indicating that although the syntax of the code is correct, and the program can be linked and executed, it suspects that something may be wrong. C was designed for professional programmers who may use unorthodox techniques deliberately and the compiler will generate warnings in case the use was unintentional. For example, in Listing 6.1 there are warnings referring to lines:

16 The #include <math.h> preprocessor directive is missing and hence there is no *function prototype* for the function sqrt. The compiler is unable to check the number and type of parameters and the result returned. In will be assumed that an int is returned and hence a run time error will occur (faulty results or a program crash).

17 The function name printf has been mistyped as print and the compiler has no *function prototype*. In addition the linker will print an *undefined reference* or *unresolved reference* error message (assuming there is no function of that name).

It is worth noting that are two other errors in Listing 6.1 which the compiler has not found:

In line 13 the & is missing before the variable radius (this type of error is very difficult for the compiler to find). Section 5.3, on scanf, described how an & before a variable name tells the compiler that the *memory address* of the variable is to be passed as a parameter. In this case, because the & is missing, the **value** of radius (which could be anything as it has not been initialised) is passed to scanf which would use it as an address. What precisely happens is implementation dependent and can range from a run time error message, incorrect program results or a crash of the program.

In line 15 the %d integer number conversion has been specified and the corresponding parameter is of type float. Rubbish will probably be printed on the screen (see Chapter 8.3 for an example of incorrect conversion specifications).

The format and content of the error messages varies from compiler to compiler. Listing 6.2 is the same program used in Listing 6.1 but shows the error reports from the Whitesmiths C compiler (the line number where the error was found follows the :).

```
#error pp p5_3b.c:17 unbalanced double quotation marks
#error p1 p5_3b.c:11    const modified
#error p1 p5_3b.c:13    missing ;
#error p1 p5_3b.c:14    missing ;
#error p1 p5_3b.c:14    useless expression
#error p1 p5_3b.c:16    undeclared areax
```

Listing 6.2 Compiler error report of a C program with errors (Whitesmiths C)

6.3.1 Debugging compile time errors and warnings

The actual format of compile time error messages varies from compiler to compiler and can often be very obscure. An error may generate an error message further on in the code or even several error messages. In particular, a missing ; or } in a function can generate all sorts of spurious error messages, often in functions further down the code, and be very difficult to track down. One approach is to fix the obvious errors and recompile. This may remove some spurious error messages enabling one to narrow down the cause of any remaining errors. In a large program it may be necessary to separate the functions into different files to be compiled independently. This not only tends to narrow down the cause of errors but is good programming practice (Chapter 21 will cover multi file programs).

The level of warnings generated can generally be selected at compile time, i.e. non at all or to warning about anything in the least bit questionable. Unless one is an experienced programmer it is wise to have the level set as high as possible, the warnings can always be ignored. For example, if Program 5.3 is compiled with the Microsoft C compiler version 6.00 with warning level 4 (/W4 option) it will generate the following warning:

```
    18    radius_check = sqrt(area / pi);                    /* calculate radius */
***** P5_2.C(18) : warning C4136: conversion between different floating types
```

The function result of sqrt is of type double which is converted to a float before being assigned to radius_check. The warning indicates that the conversion between different floating types may result in a loss of precision, i.e. double has a precision of 15 decimal digits and float a precision of 7 decimal digits (more discussion in Chapter 8). In the case of Program 5.3 the warning can be ignored as the precision of float is sufficient. However, one may inadvertently use a float variable in a sequence of calculations which should be carried out in double precision and the warning will alert one to this.

6.3.2 Debugging execution time errors

The compiler can only detect errors in the syntax of the language and is limited in its generation of warnings. The linker will detect undefined references (missing functions) or multiple definitions of a reference (more than one copy of a function). Even if the program compiles and links it may still contain run-time errors which cause it to fail or give faulty results when executed.

When coding a program the programmer works from a program design which was derived from a specification. It is possible that the resultant program code does not do what the design states it should (it is assumed that the specification and design were correct). For example, consider the statement in line 12 of Program 5.1 which calculates the area of a circle:

```
area = 3.1415926f * radius * radius;
```

The programmer, when typing in the statement hits the 2 key instead of the 3, i.e.:

```
area = 2.1415926f * radius * radius;
```

To the compiler the statement is valid and would compile without errors or warnings. At execution time, however, the value of area would be incorrect and the results of any succeeding calculations which used the value would also be incorrect. In a short program this error is fairly easy to find but in a large program could be very difficult. If the cause of a run-time error is not obvious the program has to be debugged at run-time, e.g. printing intermediate results of calculations or using run-time debugging tools. The thing to remember is that proficiency in program implementation and testing is achieved by experience and there is no short-cut or magic formula.

Exercise 6.1 (*see Appendix B for sample answer*)

Program 4.1 uses the return 0; statement to return a success indicator to the operating system. Write an operating system batch file to execute the program and report success or failure. Test it with Program 4.1 and a modified version which reports failure, e.g. use return 1;.

Problem for Chapter 6

The program below, when given the radius r and height h of a cylinder, evaluates the volume = $\pi r^2 h$, curved surface area = $2\pi r h$ and total surface area = $2\pi r(r + h)$. It contains a number of errors, both in the syntax of individual statements (the rules of the C language are not observed) and the overall semantics (the program does not do what is required). Correct the errors and check the results of a run of the program, e.g.:

```
Enter radius of cylinder (real number) ? 3↲
Enter height of cylinder (real number) ? 4↲
volume = 113.097328, radius check = 3.000000
curved area = 75.398224, radius check = 3.000000
total area = 131.946884, height check = 4.000000
```

```
 1 /* Problem 6 - Calculate surface areas and volume of a cylinder */
 2
 3 #include <stdio.h>
 4 #include <math.h>
 5
 6 int main(void)
 7 {
 8     const float pi = 3.1415926f,                        /* constant pi */
 9                 two_pi = pi * 2.5f;                      /* constant 2pi */
10     float radius = 2.0f,                           /* radius of cylinder */
11           height = 5.0f,                           /* height of cylinder */
12           curved_area,                            /* curved surface area */
13           total_aea,                               /* total surface area */
14           volume,                                       /* and volume */
15           radius_check,                                /* check radius */
16           height_check;                                /* check height */
17
18     printf("Enter radius of cylinder (real number) ? ");
19     scanf("%f", &radius);                               /* read radius */
20     printf("Enter height of cylinder (real number) ? );
21     scanf("%f", height);                                /* read height */
22
23     /* calculate volume and then check radius */
24     volume = pi * radius * height;
25     radius_check = sqt(volume / (two_pi  height));
26     printf("\nvolume = %f, radius check = %f", volume, radius_check);
27
28     /* calculate curved area and then check radius * /
29     curved_area = two_pi * radius * height;
30     radius_check = curved_area * radius / (two_pi * height);
31     printf("\ncurved area = %f, radius check = %f, curved_area radius_check);
32
33     /* calculate total area and then check height */
34     total_area = pi * height * (radius + height);
35     height_check = (total_area / two_pi - radius;
36     printf("\ntotal area = %f, height check = ", total_area, height_check);
37 }
```

Problem for Chapter 6   A program with a number of semantic and syntax errors

7

Integral data types

In many languages integer numeric, character and logical (or boolean) data is represented using separate data types with their own rules. In C these are not separate data types but are all represented using integral types (boolean data will be introduced in Chapter 11).

7.1 Integral numeric data types

The integer data types may be *signed* (take positive or negative values) or *unsigned* (only positive values). The following table shows the integer data types (including characters) together with their minimum numeric ranges as specified by the ANSI standard:

data type	numeric range
char	integer character code range 0 to + 127
signed char	signed integer range -128 to +127
unsigned char	unsigned integer range 0 to 255
short int	signed integer minimum range -32768 to 32767
unsigned short int	unsigned integer minimum range 0 to 65535
int	signed integer minimum range -32768 to 32767
unsigned int	unsigned integer minimum range 0 to 65535
long int	signed integer minimum range -2147483648 to 2147483647
unsigned long int	unsigned integer minimum range 0 to 4294967295

The number of bits used to represent short int, int and long int is implementation dependent so long as the minimum range is maintained and the longer types provide at least as much storage as the shorter. The intention is that int is implemented as the most convenient size for the target processor (in terms of instruction set, execution speed, etc.) with short int and long int provided to meet any special requirements. It is therefore possible for the three types to be different sizes (e.g. 16, 32 and 64-bit) or all the same size (e.g. 32-bit) depending upon the processor (typically short int and int are 16-bit and long int is 32-bit). The standard header file <limits.h> (see Appendix C.5) provides details on the integral types enabling programs to determine if the specific implementation can support the application (see Chapter 9 Program 9.2).

In a declaration short int, int, and long int may be prefixed with the type specifier signed which is redundant for these types, i.e. signed int is the same as int (the type specifier signed is mainly used to force the char type to be signed, see section 7.2).

When implementing programs int is the basic 'working' integer data type where the size would not exceed the maximum for a 16-bit signed number (e.g. a counter in a short loop) otherwise the long int data type should be used. Care should be taken when signed and unsigned types are used in expression as the conversion between the types is implementation dependent (see Chapter 9.1). In practice try to avoid mixing the types, i.e. select a type for a particular set of operations and keep to it. For example, use signed types for 'normal' arithmetic work and unsigned types for operations that are naturally unsigned, e.g. memory mapped I/O register addresses (see Chapter 33).

7.1.1 Integer number constants

The C rules for integer constants are:

1   Decimal value: an integer constant which consist of a sequence of digits and which does **not** start with a 0 (zero, see octal below).
2   Octal value: an integer constant which consist of a sequence of digits and which starts with a **0 (zero)**. It may not contain the digits 8 or 9. **Be careful**, it is easy to type in a value 0356 meaning it to be decimal and forgetting that the preceding 0 makes it octal.
3   Hexadecimal value: an integer constant which starts with **0x or 0X** and which consists of digits and the letters a to f (or A to F) which represent the values 10 to 15.

An integer constant may be suffixed with the letter:

u or U   specifying that the value is unsigned
l or L   specifying that the value is long (recommend using L so not to confuse with 1)

Below are three groups of numbers each consisting of a decimal, octal and a hexadecimal constant which are equal in value (i.e. 10 decimal equals 012 octal equals 0xa hexadecimal):

```
10 = 012 = 0xa        1024 = 02000 = 0x400        30010 = 074472 = 0X753A
```

When an integer constant is specified the data type it becomes is determined as follows:

1   A plain decimal will be the first of int, long int or unsigned long int which can represent the value.
2   A plain octal or hexadecimal will be the first of int, unsigned int, long int or unsigned long int which can represent the value.
3   A constant suffixed by u or U will be the first of unsigned int or unsigned long int which can represent the value.
4   A constant suffixed by l or L will be the first of long int or unsigned long int which can represent the value.
5   A constant suffixed by u or U **and** l or L will be unsigned long int.

In order to know what type a constant may become it is necessary to know something about the way integers are represented on the target system. Some compilers will issue a warning if a constant is promoted to long without the l or L suffix.

7.2 The character data type *char*

Chapter 1 described how characters are represented within a computer system using a character code such as ASCII, e.g. character 'a' is 97 decimal, 'A' is 65, '0' is 48, etc. Many modern languages (e.g. Pascal) treat characters as a separate data type with their own special rules. This is not the case in C where any integral type can be used to represent characters with the data type char being, in effect, a byte size int. The ANSI C standard specifies the following minimum requirements for the data type char:

(a) it has a minimum size of 8 bits,
(b) its maximum value is at least +127,
and (c) its minimum value is 0 or lower.

The following points should be noted:

1 The guaranteed range for char variables is 0 to +127 (i.e. sufficient to hold English language character sets such as ASCII or EBCDIC).

2 Whether char variables are signed or unsigned is implementation dependent (the most efficient for the particular environment is selected, see section 7.2.2).

3 The character code is not specified so long as it can represent the C character set (see Chapter 6.1).

4 The character codes for the alphabet a to z and A to Z may not be contiguous (as in ASCII). To overcome this problem the library <ctype.h> (see Appendix C.2) contains functions to test characters including upper (isupper) and lower (islower) case letters and digits (isdigit) (see Chapter 11 Program 11.4 and Exercise 11.2).

7.2.1 Character constants

Character constants are enclosed in ' marks, e.g.:

```
'a'  'A'  'b'  'B'  'z'  'Z'  '1'  '2'  '9'  '@'  '#'  ')'  '\n'  '\a'
```

Note that these are constants of type int. C converts the character into the equivalent integer numeric value in the target processors character code, e.g. in ASCII 'a' becomes 97, 'A' becomes 65, '0' becomes 48, etc. There are no constants of type char.

Because character variables and constants are treated as integers they may be used directly in arithmetic expressions (unlike languages such as Pascal where integers and characters are distinct data types). For example, the following fragment of code converts a digit character (range '0' to '9') to its equivalent numeric value (range 0 to 9):

```
char ch = '5';              /* declare char variable initial value '5' */
int ch_int;                             /* declare int variable */
ch_int = ch - '0';          /* convert char to equivalent numeric value */
```

In the ASCII character code ch has the value 53 therefore the statement ch_int = ch - '0'; assigns the value 5 to ch_int, i.e. the character constant '0' has the value 48.

If a character constant (within ' marks) is prefixed with a \ it is an *escape sequence* which is used to represent special characters, see Table 7.1. For example, the character constant '\x1b' would represent the ASCII control character ESC (value 1b hexadecimal).

escape sequence	character represented		action taken
\n	NL	newline	moves to the start of the next line on page
\t	HT	horizontal tab	move horizontally one tabulate position
\v	VT	vertical tab	move vertically one tabulate position
\b	BS	backspace	move back one character position
\r	CR	carriage return	move to start of current line
\f	FF	form feed	typically new page or clear screen
\a	BEL	audible alert	ring terminal bell or sound buzzer
\\	\	backslash	display a \ character
\?	?	question mark	display a ? character
\'	'	single quote	display a ' character
\"	"	double quote	display a " character
\ooo	ooo	octal number	specify the numeric value of the character
\xhh	hh	hexadecimal number	specify the numeric value of the character

Table 7.1 Character escape codes

7.2.2 *Signed* and *unsigned* characters

Unless otherwise specified int types are signed. The char data type, however, may be signed or unsigned depending upon the implementation. So long as the restrictions imposed upon char variables are observed this is no problem, i.e. the guaranteed range of 0 to 127 can be represented in either. In many applications it is often useful to store other data than character codes in byte sized char variables and the sign of the data could well be important. In such cases the signed or unsigned type specifiers should be used:

data type	numeric range
signed char unsigned char	signed integer range -128 to +127 unsigned integer range 0 to 255

In practice one can treat these types as *signed byte* and *unsigned byte* data types. For example, one may be sampling data from an 8-bit A to D (analogue to digital) converter. It would be very wasteful of memory to store a large amount of such data in int or even short int variables (both of which may be 32-bit in a particular implementation).

7.3 Printing and reading integral types

7.3.1 Printing and reading characters

```
1  /* Program 7.1 - read a character and print its character code */
2
3  #include <stdio.h>
4
5  int main(void)
6  {
7      int ch;
8
9      printf("Please enter a character ? ");
10     ch = getchar();
11     putchar(ch);
12     printf(" Character %c, character code %d, %#o, %#x \n", ch, ch, ch, ch);
13     return 0;
14 }
```

Program 7.1 Character input and output

Program 7.1 shows the use of the function getchar to read a character from the keyboard and function putchar to write a character to the display screen (the next section will discuss the program in detail and the use of printf for printing characters and integers).

The function getchar reads a character from the standard input stream **stdin** and returns it as an int function result. It does **not** return a char because it can return, in addition to characters, an *end of file* indicator, the value of which is outside the 0 to +127 range which the ANSI C standard guarantees can be represented by a char. This *end of file* indicator is defined in <stdio.h> as the symbolic constant EOF which can be used in IF statements to test for end of input (see Chapter 11 Program 11.1).

In practice a program would read a character into an int variable, as in Program 7.1, test for EOF and if *end of file* was not found assign the int to a char variable. If *end of file* was found the program would stop reading (see Chapter 12 Program 12.1).

Text streams operate on a line by line basis (see Chapter 5.3.1) with characters entered being placed in an input buffer until newline (or *end of file*) is entered. The next character can then be read by getchar and passed to the program. Thus successive calls to getchar can read characters until the input buffer is exhausted (terminated by \n) and the next line is read from the keyboard (see Chapter 12 Program 12.1). Some C systems have functions which will read individual characters directly from the keyboard, e.g. MicroSoft C and Turbo C++ have functions getche (echo character) and getch (no echo) in <conio.h>.

The function putchar prints characters to the standard output stream **stdout**. It returns an int function result which is either the character written, if successful, otherwise EOF to indicate that an error occurred. Functions scanf and printf can also be used for character I/O, e.g. when characters are part of a formatted stream containing other data types.

7.3.2 Printing and reading integral types

conversion specification	parameter type	converted to
%c	int	single character (printed as a character)
%d or %i	int, short, char	signed decimal notation
%u	int, short, char	unsigned decimal notation
%o	int, short, char	unsigned octal notation
%x or %X	int, short, char	unsigned hexadecimal notation
%ld %lu %lx %lo	long int	as above but for long int
%		printed as a %

Table 7.2 *printf* conversion specifications for integral data types

Table 7.2 lists the printf conversion specifications for integral data types (Chapter 5.1 introduced the printf function). Note that %d, %i, %o and %x are used for int, short int and char (when printing the character in integer form). If a # follows the % when using the octal (%o) and hexadecimal (%x) conversion specifications a leading 0 or 0x will be printed (by default they are not printed).

When information is printed on the screen its position is called the *field* and the number of characters printed the *field width*. When using conversion specifications printf prints sufficient characters to display the value unless a minimum field width is specified following the %. Unless otherwise specified (see Appendix C.12.6) the value is printed right justified and padded with sufficient spaces on the left to fill the *field width*, e.g.:

%d   print an integer using a field width sufficient to print the value, e.g. two characters for 15 and three for 150

%3c   print a character with a minimum field width of 3

%7d   print an integer with a minimum field width of 7 (if the value is too large to fit into seven characters the field width is increased as required)

In Program 7.1 the functions getchar, putchar and printf are used in lines:

10   ch = getchar(); read a character from the keyboard and assign it to variable ch

11   putchar(ch); prints the character in variable ch on the display screen

12   printf(" Character %c, character code %d, %#o, %#x \n", ch, ch, ch, ch);
prints ch as a character (%c conversion) followed by the character code in decimal (%d), octal with leading 0 (%#o) and hexadecimal with leading 0x (%#x).

A run of the program on an IBM PC compatible under MicroSoft C gave:

```
Please enter a character ? a
a  Character a, character code 97, 0141, 0x61
```

The function scanf is called with the following parameters (see Chapter 5.3):

(a) the *control string* which controls the reading of characters from the keyboard and their conversion into values to be assigned to variables of various data types,

and (b) other parameters; in the main a list of addresses of (or *pointers* to) variables.

The control string may contain **conversion specifications** which specify how characters in the input stream are matched and converted. If converted successfully the value is returned in the variable **whose address** is given by the corresponding parameter. Table 7.3 presents the scanf conversion specifications for integral data types. It should be noted that short int, int and long int use **different** conversion specifications. If a numeric value is to be stored in a char variable it should be read into an int and then assigned to the char.

conversion specification	parameter type	converted to
%c	char *	single character (as a character)
%d	int *	optionally signed decimal integer
%i	int *	optionally signed decimal, octal (with leading 0) or hexadecimal (leading 0x or 0X) integer
%u	int *	unsigned decimal integer
%o	int *	optionally signed octal int (optional leading 0)
%x or %X	int *	optionally signed hexadecimal int (optional 0x)
%hd %hu %ho %hx	short int *	as above, but for data type short int
%ld %lu %lo %lx	long int *	as above, but for data type long int

Table 7.3 *scanf* character conversions for integral data types
the * following the parameter type indicates that a *pointer* is required,
i.e. an & before the variable name to pass an address

7.4 The enumerative type

Consider an application where the value of a variable represents a particular component, e.g. bolt = 0, washer = 1, nut = 2, etc.:

```
int component_1, component_2;
scanf("%d", &component_1);
if (component_1 == 1) printf("\n component %d is a washer ", component_1);
```

A problem is that one has to remember that 0 represents bolts, 1 washers. etc. It would be preferable to be able to use names such as Bolt and Nut directly in the program. The enumeration type provides a compact way of doing this and improves program readability.

```
enum component_t {Bolt, Washer, Nut, Lock_nut, Nylon_nut};
```

A new integral type enum component_t is defined together with the set of mnemonic identifiers, called enumerators, {Bolts, Washers, Nuts, Lock_nuts, Nylon_nut} which it may take. The identifier component_t is called the enumeration *tag* or name.

```
enum component_t component_1, component_2;
```

declares variables component_1 and component_2 of type enum component_t.

The fragment of code processing components such as bolts, washers, nuts, etc. can now be written:

```
enum component_t {Bolt, Washer, Nut, Lock_nut, Nylon_nut};
enum component_t component_1, component_2;

scanf("%d", &component_1);
if (component_1 == Washer) printf("\n component %d is a washer", component_1);
component_2 = Lock_nut;
```

Note that a new type has not been created, just another representation of int. The enumerators are constants of type int with, by default, the first having the value 0 and each succeeding one the next integer value, i.e. in the above example Bolt = 0, Washer = 1, Nut = 2, Lock_nut = 3 and Nylon_nut = 4. The enumerators can be initialised, e.g.:

```
enum component_t {Bolt = 10, Washer = 20, Nut = 30, Lock_nut, Nylon_nut};
```

to initialise Bolt = 10, Washer = 20, Nut = 30, Lock_nut = 31 and Nylon_nut = 32. The enumerative type is really an int with I/O being performed using the normal int conversion specifications and the values 10, 20, 30, 31 and 32 in a data file may represent the components Bolts, Washers, Nuts, Lock_nuts and Nylon_nuts respectively. The identifiers used in enumerations must be unique from each other and variable names but different enumerators may have the same value.

All operations performed on enumerative types are int and C provides no range checking, e.g. the semantically meaningless operation may be performed:

```
component_2 = component_1 * Lock_nut + 250;
```

The enumerators may be used in any expression where an int constant may be used, not just those involving variables of the particular enumeration type. In addition it is possible to use enum to specify general purpose int constants, e.g.:

```
enum {Bell = '\a', Newline = '\n', Array_size = 100};

putchar(Bell);
```

In this case, because the identifier or *tag* of the enumeration is not specified (component_t above), it is not possible to declare variables of this type. The identifiers Bell, Newline, and Array_size may be used as general purpose int constants to improve program readability.

Problem for Chapter 7

Type in Program 7.1 compile and link and then execute with various data. What is the character code of the machine ?

8

Real number data types

Real number data types are required in many mathematical, scientific and engineering applications to hold numeric values that may not be represented in integer (whole number) form. For example, numeric values that:

(a) have fractional components: π has the value 3.141592653589793238462643, $e = 2.718281828459045235360287$ (the base of natural logarithms),

(b) are less than one: the permittivity of free space $\epsilon_o = 8.854 * 10^{-12}$ and the permeability of free space $\mu_o = 4\pi * 10^{-7}$,

or (c) are very large: the resistivity of mica is of the order of $5.0 * 10^{11}$ ohm meters.

The C notation for numbers such as $8.854 * 10^{-12}$ or $5.0 * 10^{11}$ is 8.854e-12 and 5.0e11 respectively (called exponential notation where e represents the power of 10).

Within the computer hardware real numbers are implemented in floating point format which has two important attributes:

Precision specifies the maximum number of decimal places that the floating value carries, e.g. the value of π above is accurate to 25 decimal digits.

Range specifies the minimum and maximum floating values that can be represented, e.g. 32-bit floating point could have a range of 1.17e-38 to 3.4e+38 (see below).

C has three real number data types:

float: single precision floating point (minimum precision of 6 decimal digits)
used for fast real calculations where accuracy is of secondary importance

double: double precision floating point with a minimum precision of 10 decimal digits
used where accuracy is important and speed less so

long double: extended precision floating point (implementation dependent)
takes advantage of very high precision floating point hardware (if available)

The number of bits used to represent real data types is implementation dependent so long as the minimum precision is maintained and each type must give at least the same range and precision as the previous type. It is therefore possible for the real types to be three distinct sizes or all the same length (float is typically 32-bit, double 64-bit and many compilers implement long double as double). The standard header file <float.h> (see Appendix C.4) provides details on the range and precision of real numbers enabling programs to determine if the specific implementation can support the application. For example, Microsoft C on an IBM PC compatible specifies the following:

data type	size bits	precision digits	range minimum	maximum
float	32	7 decimal	1.175494351e-38F	3.402823466e+38F
double	64	15 decimal	2.22507385850720e-308	1.79769313486231e+308
long double	80	19 decimal	3.36210314311209e-4932	1.18973149535723e+4932

What data type to use is application dependent, i.e. on the precision and range of the data to be processed. For example, there is no point sampling experimental data accurate to 3 decimal digits (e.g. measurements made using a good analogue meter) and then processing it using `double` variables and printing the results to 10 or 12 digits. In fact results so presented would be totally misleading (Chapter 16 discusses numeric errors).

8.1 Real number constants

If a constant contains a decimal point or an exponent it is a real number of type `double`. To specify `float` or `long double` real constants an f (or F) or l (or L) suffix is appended, e.g.:

`float`	`1.0f`	`5e11f`	`3.141592653589793238462643F`	`8.854e-12f`
`double`	`1.0`	`5e11`	`3.141592653589793238462643`	`8.854e-12`
`long double`	`1.0l`	`5e11l`	`3.141592653589793238462643L`	`8.854e-12l`

A constant may be specified to greater precision than the data type can hold, if so the value is rounded or truncated (dependent on the implementation).

8.2 Conversion between real types

Unlike Pascal or Modula 2 C is not a 'strongly typed' language allowing mixtures of data types (reals, integers, etc.) in expressions. When a mixture of data types are used in an expression a set of rules known as the **usual arithmetic conversions** is used to determine what type the overall result will be (details in Chapter 9). In the case of real data types the rule is:

**when two different real types are used in an expression the
lower precision value is implicitly converted to the higher precision type
and the arithmetic performed at that precision**

If a lower precision real is assigned the value of a higher precision real the value of the longer real is converted to shorter by truncation or rounding (implementation dependent). For example, a `double` with 15 digits of precision may be assigned to a `float` with 7 digits of precision and significant amount of information lost (more details in Chapter 10.2). A modern compiler may issue a warning message in such cases, e.g. Microsoft C:

```
***** P6_1.C(16) : warning C4136: conversion between different floating types
```

In addition, if a lower precision real is assigned the value of a higher precision real the value may be outside the range that can be held, i.e. under Microsoft C on an IBM PC compatible `float` has the range $3.4*10^{-38}$ to $3.4*10^{38}$ and `double` the range $2.2*10^{-308}$ to $1.7*10^{308}$. If the value cannot be held the behaviour is *undefined* (the program may give a run-time error or carry on with rubbish stored in the variable).

8.3 Printing and reading real numbers

Table 8.1 (next page) presents the `printf` conversion specifications for real number data types. Note that %f, %e and %g are used for **both** `float` and `double`. In addition to being able to specify the *field width* the precision (the number of digits following the decimal point) may also be specified (for clarity ▲ indicates a printed space):

%f   print a float or double; precision is 6 using a sufficient field width to print the value, e.g. 3.141592

%12f   print a float or double; precision is 6 with a field width of 12, e.g. ▲▲▲▲3.141592

%12.2f print a float or double; precision is 2 (two digits following decimal point) with a field width of 12, e.g. ▲▲▲▲▲▲▲▲3.14

%.2Lf   print a long double; precision 2 using sufficient field width to print the value, e.g. 3.14

%12.2e print a float or double in e format; precision is 2, e.g. ▲▲▲3.56e+005

Do not confuse the precision used with the conversion specifications with the precision of the real number when stored in floating point format.

conversion specification	parameter type	converted to
%f	float, double	signed decimal real number in form [-]mmm.ddd number of d's specified by precision (default 6) a precision of 0 suppresses the decimal point
%e	float, double	signed decimal real number in form [-]m.dddddе±xx the number of d's is specified by the precision (default 6) 0 precision suppresses decimal point
%g	float, double	%e is used if the exponent is less than -4 or greater than the precision otherwise %f is used
%Lf %Le %Lg	long double	as above but for long double real

Table 8.1 *printf* conversion specifications for real data types

Table 8.2 presents the scanf conversion specifications for real number data types. It should be noted that float, double and long double use **different** conversion specifications. A very common error is to use %f, %e or %g with a double variable (as with printf). This will work if, in the particular implementation, float and double are actually the same size (the code is then non-portable) otherwise rubbish is returned or the program crashes.

The reason why %f works for both float and double in the case of printf is that the parameters are passed using *call by value* where float parameters are converted to double before being passed (long double are passed as long double). The function scanf uses *call by reference* where the original parameter is accessed via its address and thus the type and size of the parameter (float, double or long double) must be specified.

conversion specification	parameter type	converted to
%f %e %g	float *	signed decimal real number type float
%lf %le %lg	double *	signed decimal real number type double
%Lf %Le %Lg	long double *	signed decimal real number type long double

Table 8.2 *scanf* character conversions for real data types
    the * following the parameter type indicates that a *pointer* is required,
    i.e. an & before the variable name to pass an address

```
 1 /* Program 8.1 - example of the use of printf */
 2
 3 #include <stdio.h>
 4
 5 int main(void)
 6 {
 7     float r_value = 3.563f, e_value = 3.563e5f;
 8     int i_value = 12, field = 3;
 9     char ch = 'A';
10
11     printf("character %3c, integer %4d, reals %6.2f, %10.2e",
12             ch, i_value, r_value, e_value);
13     printf(", integer %*d \n", field, i_value);
14     return 0;
15 }
```

Program 8.1 Using the function *printf*

Program 8.1 uses printf to display a character, integer and two reals. The sequence of events in Program 8.1 is (skipping lines discussed previously):

7-9	declare and initialise two real, two integer and a character variable
11-12	call printf to print the values of the variables
13	call printf; if an * follows the % the next parameter is used as the field width (followed by the parameter to be printed)

When executed, Program 8.1 would print (spaces are shown as ▲):

character▲▲▲A,▲integer▲▲▲12,▲reals▲▲▲3.56,▲▲3.56e+005,▲integer▲▲12

When using printf (or scanf) it is **very** important that the parameters following the control string correspond, one to one, with the conversion specifications within the control string. The programmer must ensure that the conversion specification specifies the correct type for its corresponding parameter otherwise printing (or reading) will be incorrect, e.g.: if lines 11 and 12 of Program 8.1 were replaced with:

```
    printf("character %d, integer %f, reals %c, %d",
            ch, i_value, r_value, e_value);
```

This would compile and link correctly but print rubbish at run time. For example, the result printed with the Microsoft C compiler version 6.00 on an IBM PC compatible was:

character 65, integer -0.000000, reals ♀, 0, integer   12

The real and integer variables have been printed incorrectly and the character has been printed as its equivalent integer value, i.e. the ASCII character code of the character A.

Problem for Chapter 8

Enter Program 8.1, compile, link and execute. Modify the conversion specifications within the control string and compile, link and execute. What happens ?

9

Expressions and operators

Chapter 4 introduced *program statements* which specify the computing operations to be carried out, e.g. to print the value of a variable or to add two variables and assign the result to another. For example, in an *assignment statement* the value of the *expression* to the right of the = is evaluated and the result assigned to the variable on the left:

```
r_check = sqrt(area / 3.1415926f);                    /* calculate radius */
sin_2a = 2.0f * sin(angle) * cos(angle);              /* sin 2A */
```

A general rule of C is that anywhere where it is permissible to use the value of a variable (of some type) an expression (of the same type) may be used. For example, the expression `sin(2.0f * angle)` is used as a parameter in the following call to `printf`:

```
printf(" sin(2A) = %f and %f \n", sin_2a, sin(2.0f * angle));
```

The **expressions** which are used to form statements are built up from:

    (a) *operators*   + add, - subtract, * multiply, / divide (details in section 9.3),
and (b) *operands*   data to be operated upon such as variables and constants.

For example, a simple expression would consist of two operands and an operator (called a *binary* operator because it has two operands), e.g.:

```
i + j
```

The evaluation of the expression produces a result of the same data type as the data type of the highest precision operand after any integral promotions (discussed in the next section). This result may now be:

    (a) assigned to a variable, e.g. `k = i + j`,
    (b) used as part of another expression, e.g. `m * (i + j)`,
or (c) passed as a parameter to a function, e.g. `printf("%d", i + j)`.

When terminated by ; an expression becomes a statement:

```
k = i + j;                              /* an assignment statement */
m * (i + j);            /* does nothing useful but is a valid statement */
```

9.1 Type conversion in expressions

Because expressions can contain a mixture of data types there are a number of rules which cover the *conversion* between data types. In arithmetic expressions involving integer and real data types the conversions are:

1   The *integral promotions*.
2   Conversion between integer data types.
3   Conversion between floating point data types (described in Chapter 8.2).
4   Conversion between integral and floating point data types.

The conversion process is given various names including *automatic conversion*, *implicit conversion*, *promotion*, *coercion* and *widening*.

9.1.1 The integral promotions

In C integer arithmetic is carried out at a minimum precision of int. If an expression contains a char, short int, an *enumeration type* (see Chapter 7.4) or a *bitfield* (see Chapter 22.8) the following *integral promotion* is applied:

(a) if int can hold all the values of the original type it is converted to an int ,
else (b) it is converted to an unsigned int.

The following fragment of code, from Chapter 7.2, converts a digit character (range '0' to '9') to its equivalent numeric value (range 0 to 9):

```
char ch = '5';                  /* declare char variable initial value '5' */
int ch_int;                          /* declare int variable */
ch_int = ch - '0';           /* convert char to equivalent numeric value */
```

When the expression ch - '0' is evaluated ch is promoted to an int, the int constant '0' subtracted from it and the int result assigned to the variable ch_int (remember '0' is a constant of type int, there are no constants of type char, see Chapter 7.2).

9.1.2 The *usual arithmetic* conversions

If the operands of an expression have different data types a conversion will be carried out under the following rules:

```
IF either operand is long double
     the other is converted to long double
otherwise
     IF either operand is double
          the other is converted to double
     otherwise
          IF either operand is float
               the other is converted to float
          otherwise
               the integral promotions are applied to both operands then
               IF either operand is unsigned long int
                    the other is converted to unsigned long int
               otherwise
                    IF either operand is long int
                         the other is converted to long int
                    otherwise
                         IF either operand is unsigned int
                              the other is converted to unsigned int
                         otherwise
                              both operands of a type int
```

In general, so long as there are no unsigned operands, the lower precision operand is converted or promoted to the higher, the operation performed and the result of the expression is of the higher type.

Mixing signed and unsigned types is little trouble so long as the values are positive numbers. The problem occurs when the signed value is negative and the conversion from a signed to an unsigned type is performed. The standard says that to convert a negative number to an unsigned type the largest possible number that can be held in the unsigned type plus one is added to the negative number and that is the result. Assuming a two's complement ALU this has the effect of copying the bit pattern of the signed number to the unsigned number. In practice try to avoid mixing signed and unsigned types and in particular don't try to convert a negative number to an unsigned type, i.e. select a type for a particular set of operations and keep to it. In general use signed types unless the operations are naturally unsigned, e.g. memory mapped I/O register addresses.

In addition to conversion when using operators such as +, -, *, etc., there is conversion across assignment operators (covered in Chapter 10.2).

9.2 Operator *precedence* and *associativity*

Operators are used in expressions where they operate upon *operands* (data to be operated upon such as variables and constants). To determine exactly how an expression is evaluated *operators* have rules of *precedence* and *associativity*.

Precedence determines the priority of the operators, e.g. is the expression:

i + j * k   evaluated as   (i + j) * k or i + (j * k)

The * has a higher precedence than + (see Table 9.1, next page) so the latter is the correct result. Note the () can be used to alter the order of evaluation, e.g. x = (i + j) * k.

Associativity determines how operators of the same precedence are grouped. For example, is the expression i * j / k (where * and / have the same precedence) evaluated as (i * j) / k or i * (j / k) . In C the majority of operators (but not all, see Table 9.1) associate left to right, i.e. in the above case the operations are performed from left to right, (i * j) / k.

Expressions inside **parentheses ()** are evaluated first. Hence, parentheses may be used to change the order in which operations are performed by overriding the normal rules of precedence and associativity. Even if the rules are not being overridden the use of parentheses can make a complex expression more readable by making the order of evaluation 'obvious' to the reader.

Program 9.1 shows some tests of precedence and associativity using the above expressions.

```
1  /* Program 9.1, test precedence and associativity of operators */
2
3  #include <stdio.h>
4
5  int main(void)
6  {
7      int i = 10, j = 2, k = 5;
8
9      printf(" i + j * k;   = %d \n", i + j * k);
10     printf(" (i + j) * k; = %d \n", (i + j) * k);
11     printf(" i + (j * k); = %d \n", i + (j * k));
12     printf(" i * j / k;   = %d \n", i * j / k);
13     printf(" (i * j) / k; = %d \n", (i * j) / k);
14     printf(" i * (j / k); = %d \n", i * (j / k));
15     return 0;
16 }
```

Program 9.1 Test precedence and associativity of operators

Table 9.1 shows the precedence and associativity of all the operators of C (Appendix E contains a copy of this table). As the operators are covered in the following chapters this table will be referred to.

precedence		operators	associativity
highest		. () [] ->	left to right
↑	unary	! ~ + - ++ -- * & (cast) sizeof	right to left
	multiplicative	* / %	left to right
	additive	+ -	left to right
	bitwise shifts	<< (left) >> (right)	left to right
	relational	< <= > >=	left to right
	equality	== !=	left to right
	bitwise AND	&	left to right
	bitwise OR	^	left to right
	bitwise XOR	|	left to right
	logical AND	&&	left to right
	logical OR	||	left to right
	conditional	?:	right to left
	assignment	= += -= *= /= %= &= ^= |= <<= >>=	right to left
lowest	sequence	,	left to right

Table 9.1 Precedence and associativity of operators

Exercise 9.1 (*see Appendix B for sample answer*)

Type in Program 9.1, compile, link and execute. Are the results as expected ?

9.3 Arithmetic operators

Arithmetic operators are either **unary operators** which have one operand (e.g. z = -x;) or **Binary operators** which have two operands, e.g. z = x * y; (don't confuse this term with the binary number system used to store data within the computer).

The **binary arithmetic** operators are addition +, subtraction -, multiplication *, division / and modulus or remainder % (which may not be used with real operands). For example, consider (x and y are int variables having the values 11 and 3 respectively):

expression	operation	result	comment
x + y	11 + 3	14	
x - y	11 - 3	8	
x * y	11 * 3	33	
x / y	11 / 3	3	result truncated
x % y	11 % 3	2	the remainder of 11 / 3

The following is system dependent:

1 The action taken on **overflow** and **underflow**.
2 The direction of truncation for / with negative operands.
3 The sign of the result of % with negative operands.

The **unary arithmetic** operators are - and + where:

- returns the negative value of the operand, e.g. z = -x; or z = y * -x;
+ has almost no effect except that an integral operand undergoes integral promotion (it was added for symmetry with unary -).

The precedence and associativity of all the C operators is shown in Table 9.1. Table 9.2 summarises the precedence and associativity of arithmetic operators and () with examples in Table 9.3.

precedence	operators					associativity
highest			()			left to right
↑	unary		+	-		right to left
↓	multiplicative	*	/	%		left to right
lower	additive		+	-		left to right

Table 9.2 Precedence and associativity of arithmetic operators and ()

example expression	order of evaluation
x + y - j + k	(((x + y) - j) + k)
y * (i + -x)	y * (i + (-x))
x + y * 2 - k	(x + (y * 2)) - k
x * y + -i / 9 * k - 8	((x * y) + (((-i) / 9) * k)) - 8
x + i / k	x + (i / k)

Table 9.3 Examples of the precedence and associativity of arithmetic operators

Take care when mixing types. Consider x + i / k where x is a float and i and k are int. Although x is a float the sub expression (i / k) would be evaluated as an int (losing any fractional component) then converted to a float to be added to x.

Note that the standard does not specify the order in which the operands of an operator are evaluated, e.g.:

```
x = sin(angle) * cos(angle);
```

The sin function may be called before cos or vice versa (selected to be the most efficient for the architecture of the computer concerned). In this case it does not matter but a situation may arise where two functions are accessing and modifying a common data set and the order of evaluation is critical, i.e. a program which works on one machine fails when transported to another. In such circumstances the algorithm should be broken down into to several statements the order of which ensures the correct order of evaluation of the algorithm as a whole (this may also serve to make the code more readable).

Exercise 9.2

Implement and test a program which calculates the average of up to six real numbers. If less than six numbers are entered terminate with an invalid character, e.g.:

```
10.0 20.0 30.0 $
```

Remember that scanf returns the number of successful conversions as an int function result (see Chapter 5.3.3).

9.4 The *bitwise* operators

C can be used as a replacement for assembly language in many applications, and therefore has a number of bit level operators. The following truth table shows the logical operations AND, OR (inclusive or) and EOR (exclusive or) on two bits A and B:

A	B	AND	OR	EOR
0	0	0	0	0
0	1	0	1	1
1	0	0	1	1
1	1	1	1	0

The C bitwise logical operators & (and), | (or) and ^ (exclusive or) have two integral operands and perform the specified operation upon the corresponding bits in each operand.

```
k = i & j;                      /* logical AND, i & j, assign result to k */
k = i | j;                      /* logical inclusive OR, i | j, assign result to k */
k = i ^ j;                      /* logical exclusive OR, i ^ j, assign result to k */
```

For example, assuming that i and j are byte sized variables having the values 00001010 and 01001100 respectively, the following table shows the result of &, | and ^ operations.

operation	C operator	example operation	result
AND	i & j	00001010 & 01001100	00001000
inclusive OR	i | j	00001010 | 01001100	01001110
exclusive OR	i ^ j	00001010 ^ 01001100	01000110

The operators << left shift and >> right shift have two operands; the value of the bit pattern in the left hand operand is shifted by the number of bits specified by the second operand:

```
k = i >> 3                 /* k assigned the value of i shifted right 3 bits */
k = i << j                 /* k assigned i shifted left by number of bits specified by j */
```

If in the first example i was 01001100, k would be assigned the value 00001001. Notes:

<< the bit pattern is shifted left, 0's being shifted in from the right
>> the bit pattern shifted right, the value shifted in from the left may be 0's (logical shift) or a copy of the sign bit (arithmetic shift); it is implementation dependent.

Bits shifted out are lost. Note that shifting by more bits than there are in the data word gives an implementation dependent result.

The final bitwise operator is unary ~ (logical not or one's complement) which inverts the value of every bit in the operand, i.e. 0 becomes 1 and 1 becomes 0:

```
i = ~i                              /* form one's complement of i */
```

If the value of i was 00001010 the one's complement would be 11110101. Consider:

```
k = k & 0xf                 /* clears all except the lower 4 bits of k to 0 */
k = k & ~0xf                /* clears the lower 4 bits of k to 0 */
```

Chapter 22.8 discusses the use of *bitwise* operators to store bit fields within a variable.

9.5 Casts

When evaluating an expression or part of an expression it often turns out not to have the required type. For example, consider the following where x is a float and i and k are int:

    x + i / k

Although x is a float the sub expression (i / k) would be evaluated as an int (losing any fractional component) then converted to a float to be added to x.

   A **cast**, which forces the result of an expression to have a particular type, associates from **right to left** and prefixes the expression thus:

    (type) expression

Thus the above example would be written:

    x + (float) i / k

Being of the highest priority (see Table 9.1) the cast forces the value of i to be converted to a float. When the expression (float) i / k is evaluated the value of (float) i is a float thus k is converted to a float and the expression i / k evaluated as a float to be added to x. The above expression could also be written in either of the following ways:

    ·x + i / (float) k
    x + (float) i / (float) k

Note that the following would not work:

    x + (float) (i / k)

the expression (i / k) is evaluated as an int and the result forced to a float by the cast.

   A float variable may be used in an int expression (assuming that the value will fit) discarding any fractional component, e.g. x is a float and i and k are int :

    i + (int) x / k

Casts can also be used to remove compiler warning messages such as the following from Program 5.3 when compiled using Microsoft C:

       18   radius_check = sqrt(area / pi);   /* calculate radius */
    ***** P5_3.C(18) : warning C4136: conversion between different floating types

Warning that the double function result of sqrt is converted to a float before being assigned to radius_check. Explicitly casting the result of sqrt to float removes the warning, i.e.:

    radius_check = (float) sqrt(area / pi);   /* calculate radius */

The cast indicates to the compiler that a float result is required and no warning is issued.

9.6 The *sizeof* operator

It is sometimes necessary to determine the amount of memory required to store a data structure. For example, when meeting a C system for the first time a useful exercise is to determine the number of bits used to represent types such as int, long int, float, double, etc. C provides the unary operator sizeof which returns (as an integer) the number of bytes required to store an object in memory:

    sizeof (object)

where the object may be a type such as int or float, an expression or an array (see

Chapter 18) or a structure (see Chapter 22). For example:

```
sizeof (long int)    number of bytes required to hold a long int
sizeof (x)           number of bytes required to hold the variable x
sizeof (x + y)       number of bytes required to hold the result of an expression
```

Although `sizeof` has been written as though it is a function call it is an operator. In addition, if object is a *pointer type*, `sizeof` returns the size of the *pointer type* **not** the size of the object pointed to (see Chapter 23.7).

The value returned by the `sizeof` operator is of type `size_t` (defined in `<stdlib.h>`) which is typically an `unsigned int`. The result can be cast as required, see Program 9.2.

```
 1 /* Program 9.2, display integral sizes and ranges */
 2
 3 #include <stdio.h>
 4 #include <limits.h>
 5
 6 int main(void)
 7 {
 8     printf("\nchar             size %2d bytes, range %11d to %11d ",
 9              (int) sizeof(char), CHAR_MIN, CHAR_MAX);
10     printf("\nsigned char      size %2d bytes, range %11d to %11d ",
11              (int) sizeof(signed char), SCHAR_MIN, SCHAR_MAX);
12     printf("\nunsigned char    size %2d bytes, range %11d to %11d ",
13              (int) sizeof(unsigned char), 0, UCHAR_MAX);
14     printf("\nshort int        size %2d bytes, range %11d to %11d ",
15              (int) sizeof(short int), SHRT_MIN, SHRT_MAX);
16     printf("\nunsigned short int size %2d bytes, range %11u to %11u ",
17              (int) sizeof(unsigned short int), 0, USHRT_MAX);
18     printf("\nint              size %2d bytes, range %11d to %11d ",
19              (int) sizeof(int), INT_MIN, INT_MAX);
20     printf("\nunsigned int     size %2d bytes, range %11u to %11u ",
21              (int) sizeof(unsigned int), 0, UINT_MAX);
22     printf("\nlong int         size %2d bytes, range %11ld to %11ld ",
23              (int) sizeof(long int), LONG_MIN, LONG_MAX);
24     printf("\nunsigned long int  size %2d bytes, range %11lu to %11lu ",
25              (int) sizeof(unsigned long int), 0L, ULONG_MAX);
26     return 0;
27 }
```

Program 9.2 Displays the size (in bytes) and numeric range of the integral data types

Program 9.2 displays the size (in bytes) and numeric range of the integral data types. For example, lines 22 and 23 prints the number of bytes required to store a `long int` followed by the numeric range which it can represent (defined in `<limits.h>`):

```
printf("\nlong int         size %2d bytes, range %11ld to %11ld ",
         (int) sizeof(long int), LONG_MIN, LONG_MAX);
```

The expression `(int) sizeof(long int)` evaluates the number of bytes required to store a `long int` and casts the result to an `int` (to ensure that the parameter type to `printf` corresponds to the %2d conversion specification in the control string). When run on an IBM PC compatible using Turbo C Version 1.01 the program printed:

```
char                 size  1 bytes, range         -128 to          127
signed char          size  1 bytes, range         -128 to          127
unsigned char        size  1 bytes, range            0 to          255
short int            size  2 bytes, range        -32768 to        32767
unsigned short int   size  2 bytes, range            0 to        65535
int                  size  2 bytes, range        -32768 to        32767
unsigned int         size  2 bytes, range            0 to        65535
long int             size  4 bytes, range  -2147483648 to   2147483647
unsigned long int    size  4 bytes, range            0 to   4294967295
```

When run on a Motorola MC68000 based microprocessor using Whitesmiths C (Whitesmiths 1986, Whitesmiths 1987) the program printed:

```
char                 size  1 bytes, range            0 to          255
signed char          size  1 bytes, range         -127 to          127
unsigned char        size  1 bytes, range            0 to          255
short int            size  2 bytes, range        -32768 to        32767
unsigned short int   size  2 bytes, range            0 to        65535
int                  size  4 bytes, range  -2147483648 to   2147483647
unsigned int         size  4 bytes, range            0 to   4294967295
long int             size  4 bytes, range  -2147483648 to   2147483647
unsigned long int    size  4 bytes, range            0 to   4294967295
```

The type char was signed on the IBM PC and unsigned on the Motorola MC68000. The size of an int and unsigned int was two bytes (16-bits) on the IBM PC and 4 bytes (32-bits) on the MC68000 (short int and long int were similar on the two machines).

Problems for Chapter 9

1   Implement and test a program which prints the number of bytes used to store real types together with their precision and range (the header <float.h> contains the precision and range information, see Appendix C.4).

2   Implement a program to find the roots of the quadratic equation:

$$ax^2 + bx + c = 0$$

Where the roots are determined as follows:

$$x = \frac{-b \pm \sqrt{(b^2 - 4ac)}}{2a}$$

Check the values of the roots by evaluating the quadratic equation, i.e. it should give 0.0. Test the program with various data including:

```
a = 1.0    b = -2.0    c = 1.0    roots = 1.0 and 1.0
a = 2.0    b = -6.0    c = 4.0    roots = 2.0 and 1.0
a = 2.0    b = 6.0     c = 2.0    roots = -0.381966 and -2.618034
a = 61.0   b = 159.0   c = 87.0   roots = -.781449 and -1.825108
```

The problem for Chapter 11 will discuss what happens when $(b^2 - 4ac)$ is negative and the roots are complex numbers with a real and an imaginary component.

10

Assignment operators

10.1 The = assignment operator

Chapter 9 discussed the arithmetic operators and how they are used to build up expressions, e.g.:

```
i + j * k
```

The above expression produces a result of the same data type as the data type of the highest precision operand after any integral promotions. This result may now be:

(a) assigned to a variable, e.g. x = i + j * k,
(b) used as part of another expression, e.g. (i + j * k) / x,
or (c) passed as a parameter to a function, e.g. printf("%d", i + j * k).

In C the assignment operator = is a binary operator in which the result of the expression on the right is assigned to the **variable** on the left, e.g.:

```
i = j * k
```

This is an **expression** which:

(a) evaluates j * k and assigns the result to i (after any conversion - see next section),
and (b) has an overall result the value of which is the **value** assigned to i and is of the **type** of i.

For example, if j and k are variables of type int having values of 5 and 10 respectively the expression j * k would be evaluated having a result of 50 and a data type int, then:

1   If i is an int the value 50 would be assigned to i and the result of the expression would be 50 and have the type int.
2   If i is a float the result of j * k would be converted to a float and the value 50.0 assigned to i. The result of the expression would be 50.0 and have the type float.

The result of an expression involving assignment may be used in a similar way to the result of any other expression, e.g. the result assigned to another variable:

```
x = i = j * k
```

Assignment associates from **right to left** thus the grouping of the above expression is:

```
x = (i = (j * k))
```

Such an expression is made into an *assignment statement* by a ; terminator:

```
x = i = j * k;
```

In addition, C has increment and decrement operators (discussed in Section 10.3) and *compound assignment* operators (discussed in section 10.4), e.g.:

```
i++                                         /* increment i by 1 */
i--                                         /* decrement i by 1 */
i *= 10                                      /* multiply i by 10 */
```

10.2 Data type conversion across assignment

Consider the expression:

```
i = j
```

If i and j are of different types, the value of the right hand side (which may be the result of an expression) is converted to the type of the left, which is the type of the result. If the conversion is from a lower precision type to a higher the *usual arithmetic* conversions apply, see Chapter 9.1. Problems can occur when there is a conversion from a higher precision to a lower, e.g. assigning a float to an int. In such cases the following applies:

(a) longer integers are converted to shorter by **discarding** the high-order bits;
(b) real to integer conversion causes truncation of any fractional components;
(c) longer reals are converted to shorter by truncation or rounding (implementation dependent), e.g. double to float.

Thus if the value of the higher precision cannot be stored in the lower information is lost (a modern compiler may issue a warning under such circumstances). If, in (b) and (c) above, the value is outside the range that can be held the behaviour is *undefined* (the program may give a run-time error or carry on with rubbish stored in the variable).

Note that assignments will not perform integral promotions if the operands are of the same type, e.g. in the following examples char_1 and char_2 are of data type char:

```
char_2 = char_1;
```

The value of char_1 will be assigned to char_2 (without being promoted and then the high-order bits being dropped). But integral promotion will take place in a statement such as:

```
char_2 = char_1 + 1;
```

The value of char_1 will be promoted to int, char_1 + 1 evaluated and the high-order bits of the int result dropped to convert to a char to be assigned to char_2.

Program 10.1 (next page) shows some examples of expressions using mixtures of types, consider lines:

5-10	declare variables, before main, making them external (discussed in Chapter 17.3)
14-15	prompt for entry of a char, int and long int and read in the values
16-17	prompt for entry of a float, double and long double and read the values
19	char_2 = char_1; assign char_1 to char_2 without integral promotions
20	char_3 = char_1 + 1; promote the value of char_1 to int, add 1 and then drop the high-order bits of the int result to form a char to assign to char_3
21	int_i = long_i + int_i; convert the value of int_i to long_int, add long_i and then drop the high-order bits of the long int result to assign to int_i
22	float_value = float_value + int_i; convert the value of int_i to float, add to float_value and assign the float result to float_value
23	double_value = double_value - float_value; convert the value of float_value to double, subtract from double_value and assign the result to double_value
24	ldouble_value = ldouble_value + float_value; convert the value of float_value to long double, add to ldouble_value and assign the result to ldouble_value
25	float_value = ldouble_value + float_value; convert the value of float_value to long double, add to ldouble_value and round or truncate the long double result to float to assign to float_value

```
 1 /* Program 10.1 - conversions between types   */
 2
 3 #include <stdio.h>
 4
 5 char char_1, char_2, char_3;
 6 int int_i;
 7 long int long_i;
 8 float float_value;
 9 double double_value;
10 long double ldouble_value;
11
12 int main(void)
13 {
14     printf("\nEnter a char, int and long int ? ");
15     scanf("%c %d %ld", &char_1, &int_i, &long_i);
16     printf("\nEnter a float, double and long double ? ");
17     scanf(" %g %lg %Lg", &float_value, &double_value, &ldouble_value);
18
19     char_2 = char_1;
20     char_3 = char_1 + 1;
21     int_i = long_i + int_i;
22     float_value = float_value + int_i;
23     double_value = double_value - float_value;
24     ldouble_value = ldouble_value + float_value;
25     float_value = ldouble_value + float_value;
26     printf("\nfloat %f, double %f, long double %Lf \n",
27             float_value, double_value, ldouble_value);
28     float_value = double_value * 3.0e+38F;
29     printf("float %e \n", float_value);
30     return 0;
31 }
```

Program 10.1 Conversion between types

In line 25 the expression evaluated as a long double is rounded or truncated (depending upon the implementation) to a float to be assigned to float_value. In such a case there is a loss of precision, e.g. a value with 15 decimal digits of precision may be converted to a value with 6 decimal digits of precision and a significant amount of information lost. Similarly in line 21 the high order bits of the expression evaluated as a long int are dropped to form an int to be assigned to int_i. When compiled with the Microsoft C compiler version 6 the following warnings are issued:

```
p10_1.c(20) : warning C4135: conversion between different integral types
p10_1.c(21) : warning C4135: conversion between different integral types
p10_1.c(25) : warning C4136: conversion between different floating types
p10_1.c(28) : warning C4136: conversion between different floating types
```

Warning that the conversions between the different integral and floating types results in a loss of precision (which may be critical or not depending upon the application).

When an expression is being evaluated it is possible that the destination may be unable to hold the value at all. For example, consider line 28:

```
float_value = double_value * 3.0e+38F;
```

The constant 3.0e+38F is a large value, near to the maximum that can be stored in a typical 32-bit float. If double_value is of any size the expression double_value * 3.0e+38F evaluated as a double may cause overflow when converted to float before being assigned to float_value. The following is a run of the program under Microsoft C version 6.00 (user input in **bold** with newline shown as ↴):

Enter a char, int and long int ? **x 5 10** ↴
Enter a float, double and long double ? **3.0 10.0 20.0** ↴
float 56.000000, double -8.000000, long double 38.000000

run-time error M6104: MATH
floating-point error: overflow

The program terminates with a run-time error indicating that a floating-point overflow has occurred, i.e. the result of double_value * 3.0e+38F was too large to assign to a float (maximum value 3.402823466e+38F).   Although, in the above run, the program terminated with a run-time error this is not always the case as the ANSI standard states that in such circumstances **undefined behaviour** occurs. The action taken is implementation dependent varying from program termination with an error message (as above) to continuing execution with an incorrect value stored in the variable in question. It is up to the programmer to prevent **undefined behaviour**, i.e.:

During the analysis and design phase: by careful analysis of the program data in terms of its precision and range and then selecting appropriate data types to store the data.

During implementation: when information from <limits.h> and <float.h> can be used to determine the precision and range of real data types and run-time action taken and/or messages printed if undefined behaviour is likely to result.

Exercise 10.1 (see Appendix B for sample answer)

Enter Program 10.1. Compile and generate an assembly listing, e.g.:

Turbo C: use tcc -A -S -f287 filename.c to generate an assembly listing filename.asm
Microsoft C: use cl /W4 /Za /Fc /Od /FPi87 filename.c to generate listing filename.cod

Examine the assembly listing to see if the conversions are as expected. Make sure the compiler is generating ANSI standard C (/Za with Microsoft C) and that optimisation is off (/Od with Microsoft C) otherwise the code may be optimised out of all recognition.

10.3 Increment and decrement operators

Adding one to or subtracting one from the value of a variable is a very common programming requirement (many machines have special instructions for this purpose). In C the increment operator ++ adds one and the decrement operator -- subtracts one and can either prefix or postfix the operand (Table 9.1 and Appendix E shows the precedence and associativity of these operators). Thus the following statements increment i by 1:

```
i = i + 1;
i++;
++i;
```

In these increment statements it does not matter if prefix or postfix is used but in more complex expressions it is critical and the following rules are used:

postfix (e.g. i++ or i--) the value of the operand is used in the expression then it is incremented or decremented.

prefix (e.g. ++i or --i) the value of the operand is incremented or decremented and the new value used in the expression.

For example, assuming i = 10 consider the statements:

k = i++; after assignment k would = 10 and i = 11
k = ++i; after assignment k would = 11 and i = 11

Now, assuming i = 10 and j = 2 consider the expressions (which may be part of a larger expression):

i * j++   result = 20, j = 3 (incremented after evaluation)
i * ++j   result = 30, j = 3 (incremented before evaluation)
i * j--   result = 20, j = 1 (decremented after evaluation)
i * --j   result = 10, j = 1 (decremented before evaluation)

Remember, in addition to the expression being evaluated, the value of the variable in memory is altered (this is called a *side effect*, see Chapter 21.11). **Do not** use a variable more than once in an expression if one (or more) of the references has one of these operators attached to it. The standard does not specify the order in which the operands of an operator are evaluated and there is no guarantee when an affected variable will change its value. Consider:

(i * j++) + (i * j)

will the value of j in (i * j) be that before or after the increment in (i * j++) ?

```
 1 /* Program 10.2 - test increment and decrement operators */
 2
 3 #include <stdio.h>
 4
 5 int main(void)
 6 {
 7     int i = 10, j;
 8
 9     j = 2;  printf(" i = %d, j = %d, i * j++ = %d \n", i, j, i * j++);
10     j = 2;  printf(" i = %d, j = %d, i * ++j = %d \n", i, j, i * ++j);
11     j = 2;  printf(" i = %d, j = %d, i * j-- = %d \n", i, j, i * j--);
12     j = 2;  printf(" i = %d, j = %d, i * --j = %d \n", i, j, i * --j);
13     j = 2;  printf(" (i * j++) + (i * j)  = %d \n", (i * j++) + (i * j));
14     j = 2;  printf(" (i * j)  + (i * j++) = %d \n", (i * j) + (i * j++));
15     j = 2;  printf(" (i * j++) + (i * j--) = %d \n", (i * j++) + (i * j--));
16     j = 2;  printf(" (i * j--) + (i * j++) = %d \n", (i * j--) + (i * j++));
17     j = 2;  printf(" (i * ++j) + (i * j)  = %d \n", (i * ++j) + (i * j));
18     j = 2;  printf(" (i * j)  + (i * ++j) = %d \n", (i * j) + (i * ++j));
19     j = 2;  printf(" (i * ++j) + (i * --j) = %d \n", (i * ++j) + (i * --j));
20     j = 2;  printf(" (i * --j) + (i * ++j) = %d \n", (i * --j) + (i * ++j));
21     return 0;
22 }
```

Program 10.2 Test of increment and decrement operators

Program 10.2 tests some expressions involving increment and decrement operators and prints the results, i.e. in lines:

9-12   expressions containing one reference to the variable altered using + + or --
13-17 expressions containing two references to the variable altered using + + or --

The following are the results from Microsoft C Version 6.00 and Turbo C Version 1.01 on an IBM PC compatible, Whitesmiths Version 3.2 cross compiler executing on a MC68000 based target microcomputer (Bramer 1991) and Apollo DN4500 and Hewlett Packard 700 UNIX based workstations.

IBM PC Microsoft C Apollo DN4500 UNIX C	IBM PC Turbo C MC68000 Whitesmiths C HP 700 UNIX C
i = 10, j = 3, i * j++ = 20	i = 10, j = 3, i * j++ = 20
i = 10, j = 3, i * ++j = 30	i = 10, j = 3, i * ++j = 30
i = 10, j = 1, i * j-- = 20	i = 10, j = 1, i * j-- = 20
i = 10, j = 1, i * --j = 10	i = 10, j = 1, i * --j = 10
(i * j++) + (i * j) = 50	(i * j++) + (i * j) = 50
(i * j) + (i * j++) = 50	(i * j) + (i * j++) = 40
(i * j++) + (i * j--) = 50	(i * j++) + (i * j--) = 50
(i * j--) + (i * j++) = 30	(i * j--) + (i * j++) = 30
(i * ++j) + (i * j) = 60	(i * ++j) + (i * j) = 60
(i * j) + (i * ++j) = 60	(i * j) + (i * ++j) = 50
(i * ++j) + (i * --j) = 40	(i * ++j) + (i * --j) = 50
(i * --j) + (i * ++j) = 40	(i * --j) + (i * ++j) = 30

The order of evaluation of operands in expressions such as (i * ++j) + (i * --j) differed from compiler to compiler giving different results for the same expressions. Also note that in a function call such as in line 9:

```
printf(" i %d, j %d, i * j++ %d \n", i, j, i * j++);
```

the order in which the parameters are evaluated is not specified by the standard. It can be seen that all the compilers have evaluated the third parameter i * j++, before the second j, i.e. the value of j is printed as 3 (after being incremented). The moral is don't write code that is dependent upon the order of evaluation. Break the code down into separate statements so that the order of evaluation will be as required by the specification.

Note that the increment and decrement operators can only be applied to variables, i.e. not constants, expressions, function calls, etc. For example, the following are illegal

```
5++      (i + j)--      ++sqrt(x)                        /* invalid !!! */
```

If incrementing (or decrementing) a variable any of the following can be used:

```
i = i + 1;                              /* add one to i */
i =+ 1;                 /* add one to i, see next section */
++i;                                    /* add one to i */
i++;                                    /* add one to i */
```

Programmers who use more modern languages would tend to use the first and professional C programmers the last. It really does not matter so long as one is consistent.

10.4 The compound assignment operators

C was developed before the days of optimising compilers and contains a number of means by which the programmer could indicate, at the program source code level, possible optimisation. For example, using i++ could enable the compiler to use a fast increment instruction rather than a general add instruction.

The compound assignment operators were another means of improving program performance before the days of optimising compilers. Today they should be restricted as their use can lead to code which is difficult to read (especially for programmers who are not specialists in C).

The compound operators provide a shorthand form when the variable on the left hand side of an assignment is repeated immediately on the left, e.g:

```
i = i + 20;                          /* add 20 to the variable i */
j = j * k;                           /* multiply variable j by k */
x = x / 10.0;                        /* divide variable x by 10.0 */
```

can all be written in short hand form:

```
i += 20;                             /* add 20 to the variable i */
j *= k;                              /* multiply variable j by k */
x /= 10.0;                           /* divide variable x by 10.0 */
```

The compound assignment operators are (the *bitwise* operators << >> & ^ | were covered in Chapter 9.4):

```
+=    -=    *=    /=    %=    <<=    >>=    &=    ^=    |=
```

Thus an expression of the form:

```
variable operator = expression
```

is equivalent to:

```
variable = (variable) operator (expression)
```

Note the (). If variable is an expression it is evaluated only once, e.g. if it is an array index. The () around expression indicates that

```
k *= j + i;        is equivalent to   k = k * (j + i);
```

whereas the 'long-hand' form of writing the expression:

```
k = k * j + i;     is equivalent to   k = (k * j) + i;
```

Use the compound assignment operators sparingly as their use can lead to code which is difficult to read. Modern optimising compilers have reduced the requirement for such shorthand techniques and program readability and maintainability is of paramount importance.

Problem for Chapter 10

Enter program 10.2. Using as many C systems as possible compile, link and execute the program. Compare the results !

11

The *if* statement

Although program flow is normally sequential it is often necessary to select alternate paths through a program. This is achieved by the use of the if statement which is described in this chapter, together with related topics.

11.1 The *if* statement

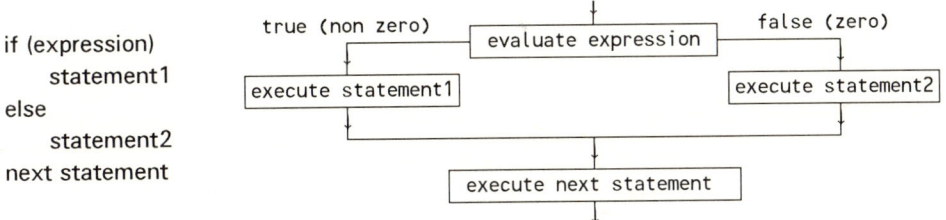

```
if (expression)
    statement
next statement
```

(a)   (b)

Fig. 11.1 The *if* statement

Fig. 11.1 (a) shows the first form of the if statement in which an expression is evaluated and if it is *true* (non-zero) a statement is executed otherwise the statement is skipped. After the if, execution continues with next statement. Fig. 11.1 (b) is a diagrammatic representation of the statement.

```
if (expression)
    statement1
else
    statement2
next statement
```

Fig. 11.2 *if* statement with *else*

Fig. 11.2 shows the second form of if statement in which an expression is evaluated and if it is *true* (non-zero) statement1 is executed otherwise statement2 is executed. After the if, execution continues with next statement.

The if statement is used extensively in programs to test for particular conditions such as an input/output error. The function getchar (see Chapter 7.2) reads a character from the standard input stream **stdin** and returns it as an int function result. In addition to normal characters getchar can return an *End of File* indicator, the value of which is defined in <stdio.h> as the symbolic constant EOF (symbolic constants are covered in Chapter 17.9).

When a program is reading a sequence of characters using getchar it should test each character for being EOF and, if found, terminate the input.

```
 1 /* Program 11.1 - read a character and check for EOF (end of file) */
 2
 3 #include <stdio.h>
 4
 5 int main(void)
 6 {
 7     int ch;
 8
 9     printf("Please enter a character ? ");
10     ch = getchar();
11     if (ch == EOF)
12         printf("\n end of file found \a\n");
13     else
14         printf("\n Character %c, character code %d \n", ch, ch);
15     return 0;
16 }
```

Program 11.1 Read a character and check for EOF (end of file)

Program 11.1 (a modification of Program 7.1) reads a character using getchar and tests it, using an if statement, for being EOF (the == is the *relational operator* which tests for equality - see next section). If EOF is found an appropriate message is printed (line 12, \a is the *bell character*) otherwise the character is printed, together with its character code in decimal (line 14).

Note the ; on the end of line 12 which is required to terminate the printf statement and, if missed, will generate an error, e.g. using Microsoft C:

```
    13     else
***** P11_1.C(13) : error C2143: syntax error : missing ';' before 'else'
```

The indentation of the statements within the if in Program 11.1 is to show the logical structure of the program to the reader, e.g. lines 11 to 14 could be written as follows (which is not quite so readable):

```
    if (ch == EOF) printf("\n end of file found \n");
    else            printf("\n Character %c, character code %d \n", ch, ch);
```

It is very important to lay out the code such that the logical structure of the program is visible to the reader. Within certain restrictions, see Chapter 6, the compiler does not care how the code is positioned on the page, but poorly laid out code is very difficult to maintain in terms of finding errors and upgrading facilities.

Exercise 11.1 (*see Appendix B for sample answer*)

Enter Program 11.1, compile, link and execute it with various data (*end of file* is CTRL/Z or CTRL/Z followed by newline under MS-DOS or newline followed by CTRL/D under UNIX). Remove the ; on the end of line 12, what happens when compiled ?

Replace the == operator in line 11 of Program 11.1 with the = operator, what happens when the program is compiled, linked and executed ? This is discussed in section 11.3.

11.2 Compound statements

```
 1 /* Program 11.2 - read radius of circle from the keyboard and if OK  *
 2  *                  calculate circle area and check radius            */
 3
 4 #include <stdio.h>
 5 #include <math.h>
 6
 7 int main(void)
 8 {
 9     float radius;                                  /* radius of circle */
10     int success_indicator = -1;        /* success/fail indicator, assume fail */
11
12     printf("Enter radius of circle (real number) ? ");
13     if (scanf("%f", &radius) != 1)                      /* read radius */
14         printf("data entry error !! \a\n");            /* read error ! */
15     else
16         {                                          /* radius read OK */
17         const float pi = 3.1415926f;            /* internal constant */
18         float area, radius_check;              /* internal variables */
19
20         area = pi * radius * radius;             /* calculate area */
21         printf("radius = %f, area = %f", radius, area);
22         radius_check = sqrt(area / pi);          /* calculate radius */
23         printf(", radius check = %f \n", radius_check);
24         success_indicator = 0;                      /* return success */
25         }
26     return success_indicator;                 /* return success/fail */
27 }
```

Program 11.2 Using an *if* to check conversion from *scanf* input

The simple programs presented so far have consisted of individual program statements which are executed sequentially. However, it is often necessary to group a number of statements together into a *compound statement*, e.g. to be executed under some condition as part of an if statement. In C a compound statement is enclosed in {} thus:

```
{
  declarations (optional)
  statement
  statement
   ....
  statement
}
```

A compound statement **may** declare *internal* types (using *typedef*), constants and variables (more details in Chapter 17) which are created on entry to the statement and lost on exit (permanent internal storage may be allocated using *static* variables, see Chapter 17.5). When declared, internal variables may be initialised, otherwise the value is *undefined*. In general anywhere where a statement may be used a compound statement may be used.

The scanf function (see Chapter 5.3) returns an int function result which reports the number of successful conversions. This value should be checked by the program and if an error occurred appropriate action taken. Program 11.2 (a modification of Program 5.3) uses scanf to read a real number from the keyboard into variable radius. If data entry is correct the function result of scanf would be 1. The if statement in line 13 checks this:

```
if (scanf("%f", &radius) != 1)                    /* read radius */
```

!= is the *relational operator* which tests for inequality - see next section. If the function result of scanf is not 1 an error message is printed otherwise the circle area is calculated.

In Program 11.2 lines 16 to 25 are a compound statement executed if scanf successfully converts one number. Note the declaration of the internal constant pi and internal variables area and radius_check which exist only within the compound statement. The compound statement is shown indented to emphasise the logical structure of the code. The position of the {} is not critical so long as one is consistent and the program code is readable (but placing them on separate lines makes them more visible). Variable success_indicator is used to return an success/fail indicator to the operating system.

11.3 Relational operators

Unlike more modern languages C has no separate boolean or logical data type with its own rules. Logical expressions are evaluated using integral data types and *true* and *false* are represented by non-zero and zero respectively, i.e:

```
if (expression) statement
```

if the value of expression is non-zero it is treated as *true* and statement executed otherwise if it is zero it is *false* and statement is skipped.

operator	condition tested	example	testing
==	equal	z == 1	is the value of z equal to 1 ?
!=	not equal	ch != '0'	ch not equal to the character '0' ?
<	less than	x < 1.0	x less than 1.0 ?
>	greater than	x > y	x greater than y ?
<=	less than or equal	x <= 1.0	x less than or equal to 1.0 ?
>=	greater than or equal	x >= y	x greater than or equal to y ?

Table 11.1 Relational operators

Table 11.1 presents a list of the *relational operators* (see Table 9.1 or Appendix E for their precedence and associativity) which compare two operands and produce an int result:

   0   if the relationship was *FALSE*
   1   if the relationship was *TRUE*

Note the use of operator == in line 11 of Program 11.1, i.e. if (ch == EOF). A common mistake is to use a single = which changes the expression to an assignment operation, i.e.:

```
if (ch = EOF)
```

The expression assigns the value EOF to the variable ch, thus overwriting the value read from the keyboard. The result of the expression, ch = EOF, is then used for the if conditional test and being none zero is taken as *true* and the printf statement in line 12 executed. Such errors can be very difficult to find. Modern compilers, however, will issue a warning if an assignment is found within a conditional, e.g. Microsoft C:

```
    11      if (ch = EOF)
***** X.C(11) : warning C4206: assignment within conditional expression
```

11.4 Nested *if* statements

The statements which make up the body of an if can be any C statement including other if statements. For example, Program 11.3 (next page), which reads an integer number and prints information indicating if an error occurred, or the number was zero, or greater than or less than zero. Program 11.3 contains three if statements in the following structure:

```
if (expression1)
    if (expression2)
        statement1
    else
        if (expression3)
            statement2
        else
            statement3
else
    statement4
```

This structure was deliberately made quite complex with a number of else scattered around. For example, does the first else belong to the first or second if ? The indentation of the code suggests the second but program layout means little to the compiler. In fact this is correct because the rule which C uses is that an else belongs to the closest preceding if which has not got a corresponding else. Thus using this rule:

1   the first else belongs to the second if
2   the second else belongs to the third if
3   the third else belongs to the first if

Program 11.3 is short and it is fairly easy to sort out the flow of the code. However, an if may contain quite long compound statements and it could be very difficult to sort out the flow if the corresponding else was on another page of code. Although one would use functions to break up a large section of code (see Chapter 15) a simple change in the program logic and layout can often improve the readability.

Program 11.3a is a modification of Program 11.3 with the layout improved. The relational operator of the first if has been changed from == to != thus enabling the corresponding else to be moved up the code so that it immediately follows the if. This slight modification of the layout makes the flow of the program much easier to follow and improves the overall readability.

The general rule that an else belongs to the first if above which has not got a corresponding else can be overridden by 'hiding' an if inside a compound statement, e.g.:

```
if (expression1)
    {
    if (expression2)
        statement2
    }
else
    statement3
```

The second if is inside a compound statement therefore the else is associated with the first if. The use of 'extra' {} around complex structures can also aid readability, i.e. {} which are not needed by the compiler to sort out the logic but aid the reader in grouping logical sections of code. In addition, good commenting helps, e.g. a note alongside an else showing the conditions which cause execution of the else statement.

```
 1 /* Program 11.3 - read a number and test for zero, greater or less than zero */
 2
 3 #include <stdio.h>
 4
 5 int main(void)
 6 {
 7     int i;
 8
 9     printf("Please enter a number ? ");
10     if (scanf("%d", &i) == 1)                              /* read data */
11         if (i == 0)
12             printf("\n value %d was zero \n", i);          /* i = 0 */
13         else
14             if (i > 0)
15                 printf("\n value %d was greater than zero \n", i);   /* i > 0 */
16             else
17                 printf("\n value %d was less than zero \n", i);      /* i < 0 */
18     else
19         printf("\n Data input error \a\n");               /* error */
20     return 0;
21 }
```

Program 11.3 Read a number and test for zero, greater or less than zero

```
 1 /* Program 11.3a - read a number and test for zero, greater or less than zero */
 2
 3 #include <stdio.h>
 4
 5 int main(void)
 6 {
 7     int i;
 8
 9     printf("Please enter a number ? ");
10     if (scanf("%d", &i) != 1)                              /* read data */
11         printf("\n Data input error \a\n");               /* error */
12     else
13         if (i == 0)
14             printf("\n value %d was zero \n", i);          /* i = 0 */
15         else
16             if (i > 0)
17                 printf("\n value %d was greater than zero \n", i);   /* i > 0 */
18             else
19                 printf("\n value %d was less than zero \n", i);      /* i < 0 */
20     return 0;
21 }
```

Program 11.3a Restructured version of Program 11.3 (above)

11.5 Logical operators

Logical expressions such as `ch == EOF` may be combined using the logical operators AND `&&` and OR `||` both of which are binary operators:

logical operation	C operator	sample use	operation performed
AND	&&	a && b	if a AND b are true (non-zero) result is true
OR	||	a || b	if a OR b is true (non-zero) result is true
NOT	!	!a	unary operator performs logical inversion

The logical NOT operator `!` can be used to invert the result of a logical expression. Unlike arithmetic operators (see Chapter 9.3) the ANSI standard guarantees that the operands of binary logical operators are evaluated from **left to right** (after any precedence), i.e. in the above table the operand a will be evaluated first. In addition, if the final result of the expression can be determined from the value of a the operand b is not evaluated, i.e.:

    a && b   if a is *false* (zero) b is not evaluated
    a || b   if a is *true* (non-zero) b is not evaluated

Consider the following expressions (see also the sample answer to Exercise 12.2):

```
if (sqrt(x) > y) ......
if (i/j <= k) ....
```

A run-time error would occur in the first statement if x was less than 0 and in the second statement if j was zero, The statements could be rewritten thus:

```
if ((x >= 0) && (sqrt(x) > y)) ......
if ((j != 0) && (i/j <= k)) ....
```

In both cases the second operand would not be evaluated if the first was *false*, i.e. x was less than 0 or j was 0. Note than the above statements could have been written:

```
if (x >= 0 && sqrt(x) > y) ......
if (j != 0 && i/j <= k) ....
```

because the relational operators have a higher precedence than `&&` and `||` (Table 9.1). However, the extra parenthesis in the first example make the expressions more readable. It is very easy to write logical expressions which are very difficult to read. In practice write expressions in a way that is natural to the application and achieves the most readable code.

Program 11.4 (next page) reads an ASCII character via `getchar` and checks for *end of file*, newline, a control character, a digit or a lower or upper case letter and prints an appropriate message. Consider line 24:

```
if ((ch >= 'A') && (ch <= 'Z'))
```

This is valid if the character codes for upper case letters are contiguous in the range 'A' to 'Z', i.e. it will work for the ASCII character code where 'A' is 65, 'B' is 66, 'C' is 67, etc. up to 'Y' is 89 and 'Z' is 90. The program will not work if the codes are non contiguous, e.g. EBCDIC. To overcome the problem of different character codes the library `<ctype.h>` contains a range of useful functions (see section 11.7) including tests for upper (`isupper`) or lower (`islower`) case letters. The character to be tested is passed as an `int` parameter and the `int` function result indicates *true* (non zero) or *false* (zero). Note that *true* is non zero **not** 1 (the relational and logical operators return 1 for *true*).

```
 1  /* Program 11.4 - read an ASCII character and check for          *
 2  *      EOF (end of file), newline, digit, lower or upper case, etc.   */
 3
 4  #include <stdio.h>
 5
 6  int main(void)
 7  {
 8      int ch;
 9
10      printf("Please enter a character ? ");
11      ch = getchar();
12      if (ch == EOF)
13          printf("\n end of file found \n");
14      else
15          if (ch == '\n')
16              printf("\n newline character \n");
17          else
18              if (ch < ' ')
19                  printf("\n control character %d \n", ch);
20              else
21                  if ((ch >= '0') && (ch <= '9'))
22                      printf("\n Character %c is a digit \n", ch);
23                  else
24                      if ((ch >= 'A') && (ch <= 'Z'))
25                          printf("\n Character %c is upper case \n", ch);
26                      else
27                          if ((ch >= 'a') && (ch <= 'z'))
28                              printf("\n Character %c is lower case \n", ch);
29                          else
30                              printf("\n Other printable character %c\n", ch);
31      return 0;
32  }
```

Program 11.4 Read character and check for EOF, newline, digit, lower/upper case, etc.

11.6 The conditional operator *?*

The condition operator ? is a ternary operator (it has three operands) in which the operands are three expressions. It takes the following general form:

```
    expression1 ? expression2 : expression3
```

First expression1 is evaluated and if it is:

      true (non zero) expression2 is evaluated and that is the value of the whole expression
else **false** (zero)   expression3 is evaluated and that is the value of the whole expression

For example, consider the following if statement:

```
    if (x >= 0)  z = cos(x);
    else         z = sin(x);
```

It may be written:

```
    z = (x >= 0) ? cos(x) : sin(x));
```

The conditional operator may be used in an expression just like any other operator. For example, consider a variable bit_value which holds the value of a binary bit (0 or 1) and which is to be printed using putchar. It may be written:

```
if (bit_value == 0) putchar('0');
else                putchar('1');
```

or `putchar( (bit_value == 0) ? '0' : '1');`

or `putchar('0' + bit_value);`

Use the conditional operator with care; excessive use can lead to code which is difficult to follow and maintain. In general an if statement will be more readable, and sometimes a little more thought will (as in the final example above) give a more elegant solution.

11.7 The standard library <ctype.h>: functions to test characters

The standard library <ctype.h> (see Appendix C.2) contains a range of useful functions which test a character for being within a particular set or sets. The character to be tested is passed as an int parameter and the int function result indicates *true* (non zero) if the character is in the set otherwise *false* (zero). Note that *true* is non zero **not** 1 (the relational and logical operators return 1 for *true*). The functions include (for a full list see Appendix C.2):

```
isalpha(character)       /* a letter of the alphabet 'a' to 'z' or 'A' to 'Z' */
isupper(character)                     /* an upper case letter 'A' to 'Z'*/
islower(character)                     /* a lower case letter 'a' to 'z' */
isdigit(character)                           /* a digit '0' to '9' */
isxdigit(character)      /* a hexadecimal digit '0' to '9', 'a' to 'f', 'A' to 'F' */
isspace(character)       /* white space: space, newline, carriage return and tabs */
ispunct(character)          /* printing character except space, letter or digit */
iscntrl(character)                       /* a control character */
```

In addition <ctype.h> contains functions which convert to upper or lower case:

```
toupper(character)           /* if lower case letter convert to upper case */
tolower(character)           /* if upper case letter convert to lower case */
```

Exercise 11.2 (see Appendix B for sample answer)

Enter Program 11.4, compile, link and execute. Does it work ?
Modify the program to use functions from the library <ctype.h> to check for printable characters (isprint), digits (isdigit) and upper (isupper) and lower (islower) case letters.

Problem for Chapter 11

The Problem for Chapter 9 implemented a program to find the roots of the quadratic equation $ax^2 + bx + c = 0$. Extend the program to check for $(b^2 - 4ac) < 0$ and evaluate the roots as complex numbers. For example, try the following data:

```
a = 2.0     b = -6.0     c = 4.0     roots = 2.0 and 1.0
a = 61.0    b = 159.0    c = 87.0    roots = -0.781449 and -1.825108
a = 1.0     b = 2.0      c = 5.0     roots = -1.0 ± i2.00
a = 61.0    b = 2.0      c = 87.0    roots = -0.016393 ± i1.194136
a = 1.0     b = 0.0      c = 1.0     roots = ± i1.0
a = 10.0    b = 99.0     c = 98.0    roots = -1.115616 ± i8.784384
```

12

The *while* and *do* statements

12.1 The *while* statement

The *while* (and *do*, see next section) statement enables a sequence of statements to be executed a number of times depending upon the value, *true* or *false*, of some expression.

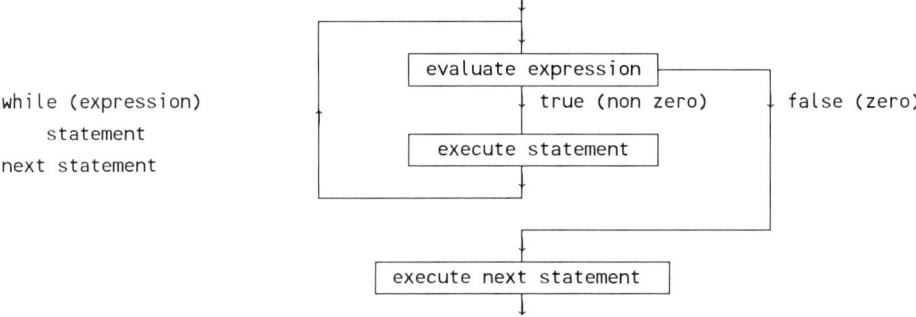

```
while (expression)
    statement
next statement
```

In the while statement the statement is executed while expression is *true* (non zero), i.e.:

1   expression is evaluated
2   if the result of expression is
        true (non zero) statement is executed and then control returns to step 1
    or *false* (zero) the while terminates and execution continues with next statement

If, on entry to the while, the expression is *false* (zero) the statement is never executed.

Program 12.1 (next page) reads a stream of characters from **stdin** and prints the character and its character code. It terminates when EOF (end of file) is found:

line
10   ch = getchar(); reads the next character from **stdin** and assigns it to ch
11   while (ch != EOF) if the character is EOF the while terminates
13   prints the character and its character code
14   ch = getchar(); reads the next character into ch, then control returns to line 11

A general rule of C is that anywhere where it is permissible to use the value of a variable (of some type) an expression (of the same type) may be used. Hence it is possible to replace lines 10 to 15 of program 12.1 with:

```
while ((ch = getchar()) != EOF)
    printf("\n Character %c, character code %d \n", ch, ch);
```

The expression ch = getchar() reads the next character and assigns it to variable ch. The result of the expression (the character read) is then compared with EOF to control the while. Hence the two calls to getchar in Program 12.1 have been reduced to one and the overall code shortened. Unfortunately the resultant code is not so readable to non C programmers.

```
1 /* Program 12.1 - read characters until EOF (end of file) found
2
3 #include <stdio.h>
4
5 int main(void)
6 {
7     int ch;
8
9     printf("Please enter characters (EOF to terminate) ? ");
10    ch = getchar();
11    while (ch != EOF)
12        {
13        printf("\n Character %c, character code %d \n", ch, ch);
14        ch = getchar();
15        }
16    return 0;
17 }
```

Program 12.1 Read characters until EOF (end of file) found

A run of Program 12.1 on an IBM PC compatible under Microsoft C was (user input in bold and the newline character is shown as ↓):

```
Please enter characters (EOF to terminate) ?  abc ↓
 Character a, character code 97
 Character b, character code 98
 Character c, character code 99
 Character
, character code 10
1234 ↓
 Character 1, character code 49
 Character 2, character code 50
 Character 3, character code 51
 Character 4, character code 52
 Character
, character code 10
^Z ↓
```

Remember that text streams operate on a line by line basis (see Chapter 5.3.1) with characters entered being placed in an input buffer until newline (or *end of file*) is entered. In the above the characters abc were typed followed by newline. The function getchar reads each character in turn and the character and character code is printed (the ASCII character code for newline is 10). When the input is exhausted the next line is read from the keyboard (characters 1234) and the values printed. Input terminated when CTRL/Z followed by newline was entered. If, when using Microsoft or Turbo C, the call to getchar was replaced with a call to getche (declared in header file <conio.h>) the character would be read directly from the keyboard and the information printed on a character by character basis.

```
 1 /* Program 12.2 - read and count characters until EOF (end of file) found */
 2
 3 #include <stdio.h>
 4 #include <ctype.h>
 5
 6 int main(void)
 7 {
 8     int digits = 0, upper = 0, lower = 0, other = 0, ch;
 9
10     printf("Please enter characters (EOF to terminate) ? ");
11     while ((ch = getchar()) != EOF)           /* read char & if EOF terminate */
12         if (isdigit(ch)) digits ++;                        /* count digits */
13         else
14             if (isupper(ch)) upper++;                  /* count upper case */
15             else
16                 if (islower(ch)) lower++;              /* count lower case */
17                 else            other++;          /* count other characters */
18     printf("\nDigits %d, upper case %d, lower case %d and other %d\n",
19                     digits, upper, lower, other);
20     return 0;
21 }
```

Program 12.2 Read and count characters until EOF (end of file) found

Program 12.2 counts digits, upper and lower case and other characters using a `while` and a sequence of `if` statements. Note the parentheses in the expression in line 11:

    while ((ch = getchar()) != EOF)

If the line had been written:

    while (ch = getchar() != EOF)

the program would not work. The relational operator `!=` has a higher priority than the assignment operator `=` therefore the order of evaluation would be:

    while (ch = (getchar() != EOF))

The expression `getchar() != EOF` reads the next character and compares it with `EOF`. The result of the comparison (1 or 0) would be assigned to `ch` (and the character read lost).

Braces `{}` are not required around the sequence of `if` statements (lines 12 to 17) which appear to the `while` as a single statement, but may be added to improve readability. Note that lines 16 and 17 could be replaced with one line using the conditional operator `?` thus:

    (islower(ch)) ? lower++ : other++;

Don't, however, get carried away using these (and other) techniques and compress a page of code down to a few lines which are totally unreadable (in fact lines 12 to 17 can be coded using a sequence of three conditional operators). In practice one should aim to produce efficient code but not at the expense of readability.

Exercise 12.1 (*see Appendix B for sample answer*)

Implement and test a program which reads a sequence of digit characters from the keyboard and converts it into a decimal number to be stored in an `int` variable. Terminate the numeric input when a non digit character is entered.

12.2 The *do* statement

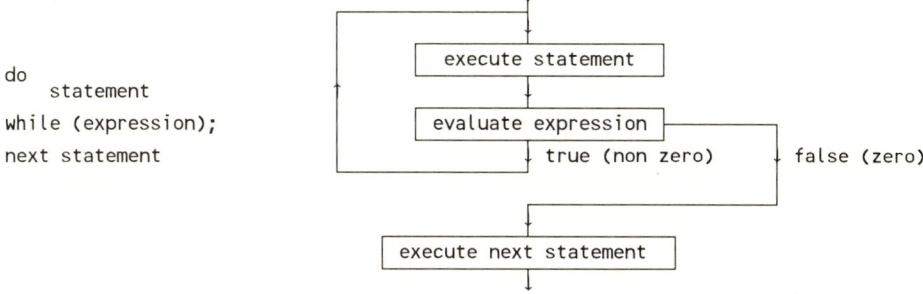

```
do
    statement
while (expression);
next statement
```

The sequence of events in the do statement is:

1   statement is executed
2   expression is evaluated
3   if the result of expression is
       true (non zero) then control returns to step 1
    or *false* (zero) the do terminates and execution continues with next statement

Thus statement is executed at least once (in the case of while if expression is *false* (zero) on entry the statement is never executed). Note the ; on the end of the do statement, it is required to terminate the statement.

The choice between the use of a while or a do statement is dependent upon the algorithm being implemented; in particular whether it is natural to test before or after executing statement for the first time. For example, if the evaluation of statement produces something used in expression the do would be the natural choice, e.g. the summation of the sine series (see Chapter 16.2). Consider a situation where a stream of characters is being read and processed by a function process_character where the stream is terminated by the $ character. It may be implemented as a while or a do statement thus:

```
while ((ch = getchar()) != '$')          do
    process_character(ch);                {
                                              ch = getchar();
                                              process_character(ch);
                                          }
                                          while (ch != '$');
```

The difference between these is that the terminating $ is not processed in the while whereas it is in the do. This seems inconsequential but could have a major effect if the terminating $ was or was not part of the data stream to be processed by process_character.

Exercise 12.2 (see Appendix B for sample answer)

Implement and test a program which reads a sequence of signed decimal numbers from the keyboard until *end of file* is entered. Each decimal number should be read as a sequence of digit characters which may be preceded by a + or - sign. Terminate the number when **white space** is entered (test using function isspace) and ignore invalid characters, e.g.:

```
10  678  -87  78 -67887
999 -999 7865 -98 0 67
EOF
```

12.3 The *null* or empty statement

The *null* or empty statement takes the form:

    ;   /* null statement */

Often time delays are required during program execution, e.g. to display a message on the screen for ten seconds and then continue. In Program 12.3 a delay of ten seconds is generated using the function clock() from library <time.h> (see Appendix C.15). Function clock() returns the number of processor clock 'ticks' since the start of program execution. The header <time.h> contains the symbolic constant CLOCKS_PER_SEC which defines the number of processor clock 'ticks' per second. The program sequence is:

8   declare clock_start to be of type clock_t (the type returned by the function clock)

11   assign the current time to variable clock_start

12-13   a while statement which loops for ten seconds, i.e. the following calculates the number of seconds since the value of clock_start was assigned (in line 11)

             (clock() - clock_start) / CLOCKS_PER_SEC

          when ten seconds have elapsed the while terminates

Note that the body of the while statement (line 13) is a *null statement* which is on a separate line and commented so that it is clearly visible. If the ; was put on the end of the while (in line 12) it may be missed when reading the program and the code on following lines thought to be under the control of the while.

```
 1 /* Program 12.3 - a ten second time delay using library routines */
 2
 3 #include <stdio.h>
 4 #include <time.h>
 5
 6 int main(void)
 7 {
 8     clock_t  clock_start;                    /* holds clock start time */
 9
10     printf("\ndelay ten seconds using library routine clock()/n");
11     clock_start = clock();
12     while (((clock() - clock_start) / CLOCKS_PER_SEC) < 10)
13         /* null statement */ ;
14     putchar('\a');
15     return 0;
16 }
```

Program 12.3 Program to delay ten seconds and sound the alarm

Problem for Chapter 12

Implement and test a program which reads a sequence of signed real numbers from the keyboard (along the lines of Exercise 12.2 which read integer numbers). The real number should be read as a sequence of characters in the form ±mmm.ddd where mmm is the whole number component and ddd is the fractional component, e.g. 125.76. Ignore invalid characters and terminate the number when **white space** is entered. Extend the program to accept a signed exponent, e.g. 1.345e4 (the maths function pow(x, y) returns x^y)

13

The *for* statement

13.1 The *for* statement

A common program requirement is to have a loop in which a control variable is incremented from an initial value to a terminal value with some statement being evaluated on each iteration. Although the for statement can be used for this purpose it is far more flexible being a shorthand way of writing a while statement.

```
for (expression1; expression2; expression3)
    statement
next statement
```

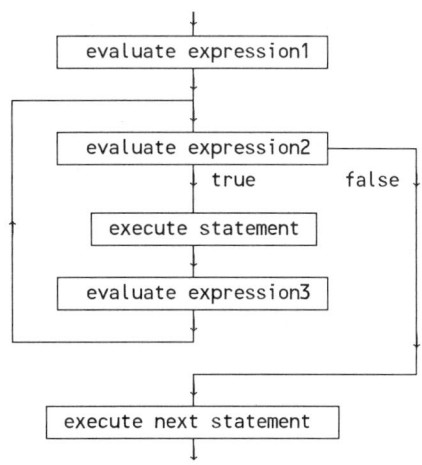

The sequence of events in the for statement is:

1   expression1 is evaluated
2   expression2 is evaluated
3   if the result of expression2 is
       true statement is executed followed by expression3 then control returns to step 2
    or *false* the for terminates and execution continues with next statement

Hence the above for statement can be considered equivalent to:

```
expression1;
while (expression2)
    {
    statement
    expression3;
    }
next statement
```

The choice of when to use a for or a while is dependent upon complexity of the algorithm. The general recommendation is that once the for (expression1; expression2; expression3) structure is longer than a single line a while should be used. Otherwise one can get for statements spreading over several lines leading to unreadable code (this is particularly the case when the sequence operator , (comma) is used, see section 13.4).

13.2 Program to find prime numbers

```
 1 /* Program 13.1 - Search positive integers for prime numbers          *
 2  *   A prime integer is > 1 and is divisible only by itself and 1      *
 3  *     e.g. 2 3 5 7 11 13 17 19 23 29 31 37 41 43 47 53 59 61 67 etc.   *
 4  *   This program uses a for loop searching from 3 and ignores even numbers */
 5
 6 #include <stdio.h>
 7 #include <limits.h>
 8
 9 int main(void)
10   {
11      unsigned long int maximum,                    /* number to search up to */
12                        n,              /* outer loop counter n = 3 upto maximum */
13                        i;              /* inner loop counter checking for a prime */
14
15      printf("\nFind prime numbers up to ? ");
16      scanf("%ld", &maximum);
17      /* search odd unsigned integers from 3 to maximum */
18      for (n = 3 ; n <= maximum ; n = n + 2)
19         {
20         /* attempt to divide number n by odd integer i ranging from 3 to n/2  *
21          *   exit if division occurs without remainder or when i >= n/2        */
22         for (i = 3 ; (n % i != 0) && (i < (n/2)) ; i = i + 2)
23             /* null statement */;
24         if (i >= n/2)                              /* n is a prime if i >= n */
25             printf("\n %lu is a prime ", n);
26         else
27             printf("\n %lu is not prime, divisible by %lu ", n, i);
28         }
29      return 0;
30 }
```

Program 13.1 Program to search positive integers for prime numbers

A prime number is greater than 1 and is divisible only by itself and 1. Program 13.1 uses two for statements to search for prime numbers up to some specified maximum:

lines

18-28   for (n = 3; n <= maximum ; n = n + 2)

Is a for statement which increments the number n from 3 to maximum in steps of 2 (the numbers 1 and 2 are ignored and even numbers cannot be prime because they can be divided by 2), i.e. 3 5 7 9 11 13 etc.

22-23   for (i = 3 ; (n % i != 0) && (i < (n/2)) ; i = i + 2)

Is a for statement which divides the number n by all the odd integers in the range 3 to n/2 (there is no need to go beyond n/2), i.e.

(a) i (which is divided into n) is initialised to 3

(b) if the remainder of n/i is zero the for terminates (n is not a prime)

(c) if i >= n/2 the loop terminates

(d) otherwise i is incremented by 2

24-27   prints a message indicating if the number n was a prime or not

13.3 Program to evaluate the factorial of an integer number

```
 1 /* Program 13.2 - Calculate the factorial of an integer number, i.e.  *
 2  *     N! = N * (N -1) * (N - 2) ..... 1                                 */
 3
 4 #include <stdio.h>
 5
 6 int main(void)
 7 {
 8     int scan,                           /* holds number of scanf conversions */
 9         n;                              /* holds number */
10
11     /* read an integer number, terminate on EOF */
12     printf("\nEnter number > 0 ? ");
13     while((scan = scanf(" %d", &n)) != EOF)
14         {
15         /* if error occurred print an error message */
16         if (scan != 1)                          /* one number read ? */
17             printf("\a Illegal character '%c' try again\n", getchar());   /*no*/
18         else
19             if (n <= 0)                          /* number OK ? */
20                 printf("\a Number %d <= 0 !, try again\n", n);        /*no*/
21             else
22                 {                               /* number is OK */
23                 int factorial_n,          /* holds factorial of number */
24                     i;                    /* holds 'for' loop variable */
25
26                 /* calculate factorial by decrementing i from n to 1 */
27                 factorial_n = 1;                /* initialise factorial */
28                 for (i = n ; i > 1 ; i--)       /* loop i = n downto 1 */
29                 factorial_n = factorial_n * i;  /* N! = N * !(N-1) * .. */
30
31                 printf(" number = %d,  factorial = %d \n", n, factorial_n);
32                 }
33         printf("\nEnter number > 0 ? ");
34         }
35     return 0;
36 }
```

Program 13.2 Evaluate the factorial of an integer number

Program 13.2 evaluates the factorial of an integer number, i.e.:

$$N! = N * (N -1) * (N - 2) ..... 1 \qquad\qquad N > 0$$

When data is being read from the keyboard (or anywhere else) it should be verified for correctness and if an error occurs appropriate action taken. In Program 13.2 the input is being verified in three ways:

1   If *end of file* is entered the program terminates.
2   That scanf converts one integer correctly.
3   That the number entered is > 0, i.e. factorial cannot be calculated if the number is less than or equal to 0.

In Program 13.2 lines 13 to 34 is a while which attempts to read an integer number into variable n and terminates when *end of file* is entered. The program sequence is:

lines

12   prompts the user to enter an integer number > 0

13   while((scan = scanf(" %d", &n)) != EOF)

           (a) scanf attempts to read an integer from **stdin** into variable n

           (b) the number of successful conversions is assigned to variable scan

           (c) if this value is equal to EOF the while terminates

16-17   tests the value of scan (set in line 13) and if scanf failed to convert one integer an error message is printed together with the character in error

else

19-20   tests the value of n to ensure that it is > 0, if not an error message is printed

else

22-32   is a compound statement which evaluates the factorial of n

23-24   declare internal variables factorial_n and i

27   initialise factorial_n to 1 (otherwise it would be undefined when used in line 29)

28-29   is a for statement which evaluates !n (see below)

31   prints the result of factorial

33   prompts the user to enter an integer number > 0

Note than if a scanf conversion fails the character in error is left in the input stream. This character must be removed before attempting to call scanf again (Program 13.2 calls getchar to remove the character in line 17). Once the integer number has been read and verified a for statement is used to calculate the factorial, i.e. lines 27 to 29:

```
factorial_n = 1;                        /* initialise factorial */
for (i = n ; i > 1 ; i--)               /* loop i = n downto 1 */
    factorial_n = factorial_n * i;      /* N! = N * !(N-1) * .. */
```

This is a shorthand way of writing the following while statement:

```
factorial_n = 1;                        /* initialise factorial */
i = n;                                  /* initialise i to n */
while (i > 1)
    {
    factorial_n = factorial_n * i;      /* N! = N * !(N-1) * .. */
    i = i - 1;                          /* decrement n */
    }
```

The variable i is decremented from n to 1 and on each iteration calculates the next term of factorial series, i.e.:

1   factorial_n is initialise to 1

2   i is initialised to n

3   if i is <= 1 the for terminates

4   the value of the next term of n! is calculated

5   i is decremented

Care must be taken with algorithms such as factorial to see that the result does not exceed the range of the variables, i.e. Program 13.2 fails when n > 7 if int variables are stored as 16-bit numbers (factorial 8 is too large to be held in a signed 16-bit number). If a 32-bit long int is used the program then fails when n > 16 (see Program 13.3).

13.4 The sequence operator , (comma)

The , (comma) or sequence operator is a binary operator which has the lowest precedence and associates from left to right:

```
expression1 , expression2
```

first (a) expression1 is evaluated,
then (b) expression2 is evaluated,
and (c) the overall expression has the value and type of the right hand operand.

Thus a new expression may be formed from a sequence of other expressions separated by the , (comma) operator:

```
expression , expression , expression , expression , expression , expression
```
→   ↑
order of evaluation   value of whole expression

The expressions are evaluated from left to right and the type and value of the whole expression is the type and value of the right-most one. The main use for the comma operator is in while and for statements, e.g.:

```
for (expression1; expression2; expression3)
        statement
```

The expressions expression1, expression2, expression3 may be sequences of expressions separated by the comma operator. For example, in the following for statement, from Program 13.3 (on the next page), expression1 consists of two expressions separated by the comma operator:

```
for (factorial_n = 1 , i = n ; i > 1 ; i--)
        factorial_n = factorial_n * i;        /* N! = N * !(N-1) * .. */
```

The expression factorial_n = 1 , i = n assigns the variables factorial_n and i the values 1 and n respectively. The remainder of the for statement is then as in Program 13.2.

The above use of the comma operator in Program 13.3 gives little or no advantage over Program 13.2 (in this case being a matter of programming style). Program 13.3, however, makes more effective use of the comma operator in line 12:

```
while(printf("\nNumber > 0 ? ") , (scan = scanf(" %d", &n)) != EOF)
```

the expression:

```
printf("\nNumber > 0 ? ") , (scan = scanf(" %d", &n))
```

consists of two subexpressions evaluated so:

(a) printf("\nNumber > 0 ? ") prints a prompt on the screen (the function result returned by printf is discarded)
then (b) (scan = scanf(" %d", &n)) != EOF)
     (i) scanf attempts to read an integer from **stdin** into variable n
     (ii) the number of successful conversions is assigned to variable scan
     (iii) this value is compared using the != operator with EOF

The result of the comparison in (b) (iii) is the result of the whole expression and controls the while, i.e. if EOF is entered the while terminates. Thus the two calls to printf in Program 13.2 (lines 12 and 33) have been reduced to one in Program 13.3 (line 12).

At each , operator is a *sequence point* where the preceding expression, including possible side effects, will have been fully evaluated (see Chapter 21.11).

```
1 /* Program 13.3 - Calculate the factorial of an integer number, i.e.   *
2 *       N! = N * (N -1) * (N - 2) ..... 1                                */
3
4 #include <stdio.h>
5
6 int main(void)
7 {
8      int scan,                              /* holds number of scanf conversions */
9          n;                                 /* holds number */
10
11     /* read an integer number, terminate on EOF */
12     while(printf("\nNumber > 0 ? ") , (scan = scanf(" %d", &n)) != EOF)
13         {
14         /* if error occurred print an error message */
15         if (scan != 1)                                 /* one number read ? */
16             printf("\a Illegal character '%c' try again\n", getchar());   /*no*/
17         else
18             if (n <= 0)                                /* number OK ? */
19                 printf("\a Number %d <= 0 !, try again\n", n);            /*no*/
20             else
21                 {                                      /* number is OK */
22                 long int factorial_n;      /* holds factorial of number */
23                 int i;                     /* holds 'for' loop variable */
24
25                 /* calculate factorial by decrementing i from n to 1 */
26                 for (factorial_n = 1 , i = n ; i > 1 ; i--)
27                     factorial_n = factorial_n * i;       /* N! = N * !(N-1) * .. */
28
29
30                 printf(" number = %d,  factorial = %ld \n", n, factorial_n);
31                 }
32         }
33     return 0;
34 }
```

Program 13.3 Factorial program using the , or sequence operator

It should be emphasised that the vast majority of commas in programs are not comma operators, i.e. the commas used to separate variable names in declarations and expressions in the parameter list of a function. If the comma operator is used in a place where confusion may occur enclose the expression in brackets, e.g.:

```
angle = 0.25;
print("%f", cos(angle));
```

could be written:

```
print("%f", (angle = 0.25, cos(angle)));
```

printf is called with two arguments not three. The expression (angle = 0.25, cos(angle)):

(a) assigns the variable angle the value 0.25,

then (b) evaluates cos(angle).

the result of (b) is the overall result of the expression and this is the value printed.

The general recommendation is to use the comma operator sparingly and only in situations where it fits naturally and simplifies the code. Extensive use of comma operators in for statements that stretch over many lines leads to unreadable code.

13.5 Plotting a sine wave on a text display screen

A common programming requirement is to display information on the screen in pictorial or graphical form. Program 13.4 (next page) plots a sine wave on the screen using ordinary character output (the following was printed when run on an IBM PC compatible computer):

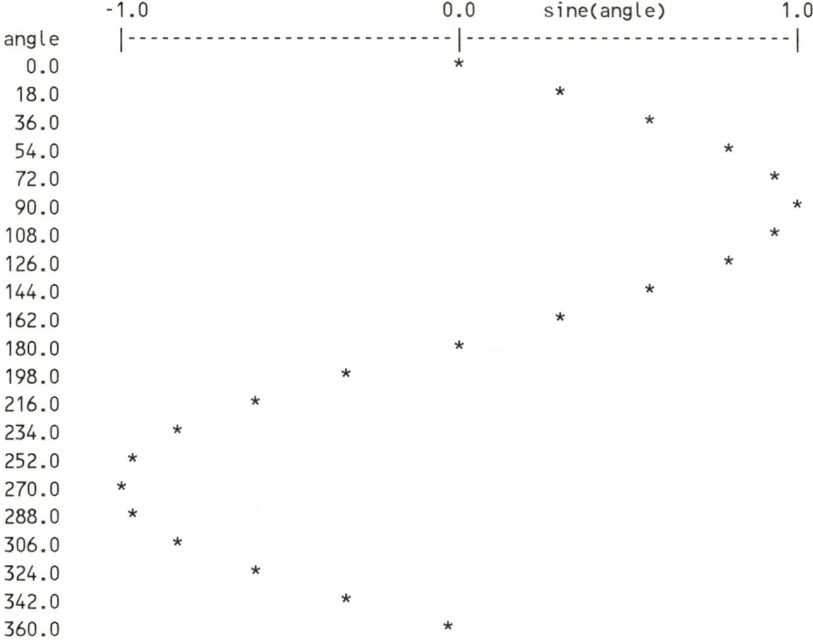

One of the most difficult parts of the design of a graph plotting program (such as Program 13.4) is 'mapping' the values generated onto the drawing area (the normal text display screen in this case). The above plot of sine was designed as follows:

1 The angle is from 0 to 360 degrees inclusive, which is 'mapped' onto 21 lines on the screen, i.e. each line represents a change in the angle of 18 degrees
2 The value of sine varies from -1.0 to +1.0, which is mapped across the screen starting at character position 11 and finishing at character position 71 (the sine wave is 60 characters across from -1.0 to +1.0).

Hence the sine wave (as shown above) is 21 lines high. In Program 13.4 the variable x is used as a line count, being incremented (in line 16) from 0 to 20. This value is used (in line 18) to calculate the corresponding angle, i.e. x = 0 is an angle of 0 degrees and x = 21 is an angle of 360 degrees with angle being incremented by $2\pi / 20$ on each line. The value of the sine of angle is calculated (variable sin_angle) and this is used to calculate the number of spaces (in variable y) to display on the screen (the sine wave is 60 characters wide with the centre offset by 35 spaces from the printed value of angle). The spaces are then printed followed by an *.

```
 1 /* Program 13.4   Display a sine wave on the screen */
 2
 3 #include <stdio.h>
 4 #include <math.h>
 5
 6 int main(void)
 7 {
 8     const float two_pi = 2.0f * 3.1415926f;                    /* value of 2 pi */
 9     int x, y, y_count;                                    /* x and y coordinates */
10     float angle, sin_angle;                                /* angle and its sine */
11
12     /* display a sine wave from angle = 0 to 2pi radians (0 to 360 degrees) */
13     printf(
14     "           -1.0                      0.0      sine(angle)              1.0\n"
15     "angle      |-----------------------------|-----------------------------|");
16     for (x = 0 ; x <= 20 ; x++)                              /* print 21 lines */
17         {
18         angle = x * two_pi / 20;                            /* calculate angle */
19         sin_angle = sin(angle);                        /* calculate sin(angle) */
20         y = 35 + 30 * sin_angle;                       /* y offset screen edge */
21         printf("\n%5.1f", angle * 360.0 / two_pi);              /* print angle */
22         for (y_count = 0 ; y_count < y ; y_count++)           /* print spaces */
23             putchar(' ');
24         putchar('*');                                        /* and then * */
25         }
26     return 0;
27 }
```

Program 13.4 Display a sine wave on the screen

The sequence of statements in Program 13.4 is:

8   declare two_pi (const qualified) and initialise its value to 2π
9   declare variables x, y and y_count to hold drawing coordinates
10   declare variables angle and sin_angle to hold an angle and the sine of the angle
13-15   draw heading at the top of the plot (remember adjacent strings are concatenated)
16-25   a for statement incrementing x from 0 to 20 (the sine wave is 21 lines long)
        18   calculate angle from the current x coordinate
        19   call function sin to evaluate the sine of angle
        20   calculate y offset across the screen
        21   print the angle in degrees
        22-23   a for statement which prints y spaces on the screen
        24   print an *

Note that lines 21 to 24 can be written:

        printf("\n%5.1f %*c ", angle * 360.0 / two_pi, y, '*');

the printf *control string* "\n%5.1f %*c " prints the following:

1   the %5.1f prints the value of the second parameter angle * 360.0 / two_pi
2   the %*c prints the fourth parameter '*' using a field width specified by the third
     parameter y (the * uses the next parameter as the field width). Thus the '*' is printed
     preceded by y - 1 spaces.

13.6 Plotting a sine wave on a graphics display screen

The main problem with using character based output to plot pictorial information is that the quality of the result is very poor and lacks detail. The alternative is to use the pixel based graphics facilities available on the majority of modern microcomputers and workstations. Such facilities enable the drawing of lines, plotting of points, etc. at a much higher quality than is possible when using characters.

Program 13.5 uses the Turbo C graphics library <graphics.h> (Turbo C 1991) to draw a sine wave on the screen of an IBM PC compatible computer. In this case the sine wave is drawn with the angle varying along the x axis, rather than along the y axis as in Program 13.4, e.g.:

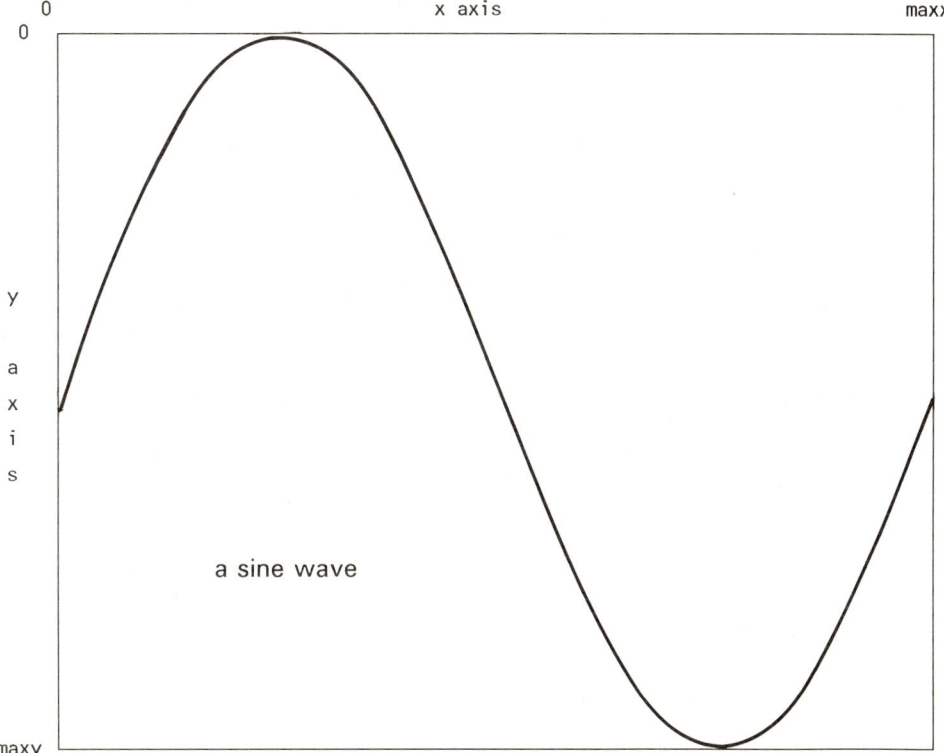

The 'mapping' of the above plot onto the screen was designed as follows:

1   The display screen size is such that the x axis varies from 0 to maxx horizontally across the screen and the y axis from 0 to maxy vertically down the screen (the position 0 0 is the top left hand corner). The values of maxx and maxy are obtained either from graphics package functions (see Program 13.5) or from a knowledge of the screen size.

2   The angle is from 0 to 360 degrees inclusive, which is 'mapped' to x, varying from 0 to maxx, i.e. each change in x represents a change in the angle of 360 / maxx degrees.

3   The value of sine(x) varies from -1.0 to +1.0, which is mapped to y, varying from maxy to 0 (the origin of the screen is the top left hand corner so the sine wave is drawn upside down in terms of y coordinates).

The sequence of statements in Program 13.5 is:

3-5   include <graphics.h> (Turbo C graphics library) plus standard library headers

9   declare two_pi (const qualified) and initialise it to the value of 2π

10   declare variables used by initgraph and initialise graphdriver to DETECT

11   declare variables x and y to hold drawing coordinates

12   declare variables to hold the maximum x and y screen coordinates and half maximum y coordinate

13   declare variables angle and sin_angle to hold an angle and the sine of the angle

16   call initgraph to initialise the graphics system (see below)

17-21   if the result of graphresult was not grOK (graphics OK) display error report

   19 print error message returned from function grapherrormsg(graphdriver)

   20 return to operating system indicating failure

24-26   get the maximum x and y coordinates and calculate half of the y maximum

27   set the colour to WHITE (defined in <graphics.h>)

28   draw a box around the edges of the screen

29   display the text a sine wave

32   move to the start coordinates of the sine wave

33-39   a for statement incrementing x from 0 to maxx

   35 calculate angle from the current x coordinate

   36 call function sin to evaluate the sine of angle

   37 calculate y offset from the x axis (which divides the screen in two)

   38 draw a line to the new x and y positions

     y is subtracted because y = 0 is the top left hand corner

41   the sine wave is now drawn on the screen, prompt user to terminate the program

42   wait for the user to hit the return key

43-44   close the Turbo C graphics system and terminate the program

The screen size, maxx by maxy, is determined in lines 24 and 25. On each loop (line 33) x is incremented by one screen position and the angle calculated such that the range of x from 0 to maxx (the maximum x value) covers the angle 0 to 2π radians (0 to 360 degrees). The value of the sine of angle is calculated (variable sin_angle in line 36) which is then used to calculate the y coordinate (line 37), i.e. the range of sine -1.0 to +1.0 is mapped to the y coordinates 0 to maxy. The function lineto is then called to draw a line from the last drawing position to the coordinate specified by x and y (line 38). The way the x and y coordinates are evaluated in lines 33 to 39 has been broken down into a number of statements to aid clarity They could be written:

```
for (x = 0 ; x <= maxx ; x++)
    lineto(x, half_maxy * (1.0f - sin(x * two_pi / maxx)));
```

In line 16 initgraph initialises the graphics system. The first parameter, graphdriver, specifies the graphics driver to use and the second parameter, graphmode, the mode of the driver. In the above example graphdriver is set to DETECT (defined in <graphics.h>) which will automatically detect what type of graphics card is fitted (graphmode is not used in this case). The third parameter is the pathname to the directory where the Turbo C graphics driver files are stored (in a string constant \\ is converted to \ hence the string "c:\\tc\\bgi" refers to the subdirectory c:\tc\bgi). In line 17 the function graphresult is called to check that the graphics was initialised correctly. If so graphresult returns the value grOk otherwise an error message is displayed (line 19) and the program terminates (line 20). In line 19 the function grapherrormsg(graphdriver) returns a pointer to a string containing an error message (which is printed by scanf using the %s conversion specification). Refer to the Turbo C manuals (Turbo C 1991) and on-line help system for full details of the function initgraph, moveto, lineto, outtextxy, setcolor, etc.

```
 1 /* Program 13.5  Display a sine wave on the screen using Turbo C++ graphics   */
 2
 3 #include <graphics.h>                    /* Turbo C graphics library functions */
 4 #include <stdio.h>
 5 #include <math.h>
 6
 7 int main(void)
 8 {
 9     const float two_pi = 2.0f * 3.1415926f;                /* value of 2 pi */
10     int graphdriver = DETECT, graphmode;                 /* for initgraph */
11     int x, y,                                       /* x and y coordinates */
12         maxx, maxy, half_maxy;                         /* screen size */
13     float angle, sin_angle;                        /* angle and its sine */
14
15     /* Initialise graphics system */
16     initgraph(&graphdriver, &graphmode, "c:\\tc\\bgi");
17     if (graphresult() != grOk)
18         {
19         printf("initgraph failed: %s ", grapherrormsg(graphdriver) );
20         return 1;                                    /* failed, return */
21         }
22
23     /* get the size of the screen and draw a box around the edges */
24     maxx = getmaxx();
25     maxy = getmaxy();
26     half_maxy = maxy / 2;
27     setcolor(WHITE);                                 /* set colour white */
28     rectangle(0, 0, maxx, maxy);               /* draw box around screen */
29     outtextxy(100, maxy * 3 / 4, "a sine wave");       /* display message */
30
31     /* display a sine wave from angle = 0 to 2pi radians (0 to 360 degrees) */
32     moveto(0, half_maxy);                            /* start of sine wave */
33     for (x = 0 ; x <= maxx ; x++)
34         {
35         angle = x * two_pi / maxx;                  /* calculate angle */
36         sin_angle = sin(angle);                /* calculate sin(angle) */
37         y = half_maxy * sin_angle;             /* y offset from x axis */
38         lineto(x, half_maxy - y);                   /* draw next line */
39         }
40
41     printf("\nHit return to terminate program");
42     x = getchar();                              /* wait for keyboard hit */
43     closegraph();                              /* close graphics system */
44     return 0;
45 }
```

Program 13.5 Display a sine wave on the screen using Turbo C graphics

13.7 Infinite loops

The are situations where one wishes to lock the program into an infinite loop. For example, in a control system the program may loop continuously reading control values and taking actions. In such a situation the program cannot stop itself, this being done externally by an operating system killing the process or by hitting a hardware reset button to reboot the program. Infinite loops may be achieved in a number of ways:

```
while (1)              do                  for (;;)
    statement             statement            statement
                      while (1);
```

In all the above cases statement is executed until the program is stopped by some external agency (operating system or hardware reset). If the condition is omitted (as in the for statement) it is assumed to be true.

Exercise 13.1 (*see Appendix B for sample answer*)

Using a suitable graphics library write a program to bounce a ball around the display screen, e.g.:

1   Initialise the graphics system.
2   Determine the minimum and maximum screen coordinates in the x and y directions.
3   Draw a box around the edges of the screen.
4   Loop:
    (a) draw ball at current x and y coordinates in white, e.g. draw a circle,
    (b) calculate new x and y coordinates,
    (c) redraw ball at old coordinates in black (to erase old ball).

Either loop forever or terminate the loop when a key is hit. You will need to consult the C manuals to determine how to use the graphics library (e.g. Program 13.5 used the Turbo C graphics library).

Problem for Chapter 13

Amend Exercise 13.1, bouncing ball, to have a box in the middle of the screen (length and height one third screen size would be suitable). Bounce the ball around between the edges of the screen and the edges of the box.

14

Further control statements

The vast majority of control structures required in program implementation can be satisfied by the if, while, do and for statements covered in the previous chapters. This chapter will describe some control statements which can be very useful in particular circumstances.

14.1 The *continue* statement

The continue statement is used within while, do and for statements. Executing a continue starts the next iteration of the smallest enclosing while, do or for. For example, if a condition occurs when the remaining statements of a loop are to be skipped and execution continued with the next loop, e.g.:

```
while (i < 10)
    {
    ......
    if ((ch = getchar()) == '\n') continue;
    ......                                      /* statements skipped if ch == '\n' */
    }
```

which could be better written:

```
while (i < 10)
    {
    ......
    if ((ch = getchar()) != '\n')
        ......                                  /* statements executed if ch != '\n' */
    }
```

Use continue with care and only after consideration of alternatives (such as that shown above). If used, comment it clearly otherwise it may be missed when reading the code.

14.2 The *break* statement

The break statement is used within while, do, for and switch (see section 14.4) statements. Executing a break terminates the statement and transfers control to the statement immediately following the body of the while, do, for or switch. For example, if an error condition occurs and the execution of a loop is to be aborted, e.g.:

```
while (i < 10)
    {
    ......
    if ((ch = getchar()) == EOF) break;        /* abort loop if EOF entered */
    ......
    }
```

See the sample answer to Exercise 27.2 (in Appendix B) for an example of the use of while and break. Again use break with great care and comment it clearly.

14.3 The *goto* statement

The goto statement takes the following general form:

```
goto label;
```

Control is transferred to the statement labelled with the name label, e.g.:

```
label: statement
```

A label is an identifier followed by a colon. The identifier only exists within the body of the particular function (Chapter 15 discusses functions) so the same name can be used in different functions. Labels have their own *name space* so the same name can be used for labels, variables and function names.

Tutors frown upon the excessive of use goto statements, sometimes to the extent of banning their use altogether (the reliance of early languages on the goto statement lead to unstructured and unreadable code). There are, however, rare situations where the use of a goto will simplify the overall structure of a program. For example, consider a program which consists of a number of nested loops where an error condition within the innermost loop should abort all the loops (a break would only abort the loop containing the break):

```
while (.....)
    {
    ......
    while (.....)
        {
        .....
        if ((ch = getchar()) == EOF) goto abort;        /* abort on EOF */
        ......
        }
    ......
    }
......
abort: ....                                             /* come here on EOF */
......
```

goto should only be used after careful consideration of the alternatives.

14.4 The *switch* statement

A common programming requirement is to select one of a sequence of statements depending upon the value of some integer variable, e.g.:

```
if (i == 1)
    statement1
else
    if (i == 2)
        statement2
    else
        if (i == 3)
            statement3
        ....
        else default_statement
```

For example, a particular function is executed depending upon the value of a control character read from the keyboard (remember characters are treated as integers in expressions), e.g.:

```
if ((ch = getchar()) != EOF)                    /* read command character */
    if (ch == 'r')
        read_data();                            /* r = read data */
    else
        if (ch == 'p')
            print_data();                       /* p = print data */
        else
            if (ch == 'x')
                exit(0);                        /* x = exit program */
    . . . . .
```

The `switch` statement, which provides a more elegant means of carrying out such a selection, takes the following general form:

```
switch (expression)
    {
    case constant1: statement1
    case constant2: statement2
    case constant3: statement3
    case constant4: statement4
    . . . . . .
    default: default_statement
    }
```

where *expression* should evaluate to an integral value (using a cast if necessary) and *constant1*, *constant2*, etc. should be integral constant expressions, i.e. which evaluate to an integral constant at compile time. The `switch` statements operates as follows:

evaluate `expression` and if its value equals:

> *constant1* execution continues with the statement following the associated `case` label
> *constant2* execution continues with the statement following the associated `case` label
> *constant3* execution continues with the statement following the associated `case` label
> *constant4* execution continues with the statement following the associated `case` label
> etc.

else

> the default is executed (if it does not exist the `switch` terminates)

Notes:

1   The `expression` is used to select an entry point into the body of the `switch` statement. When a `case` label is selected all the following statements will be executed in turn (including the default) unless the `break` statement is used to terminate the `switch`.

2   The `case` labels do not have to appear in any order.

3   Several labels can be in front of a single statement, e.g. `case 1: case 2: statement`.

4   Several statements can be placed after a label, i.e. it need not be a compound statement.

5   The `default` label can be placed anywhere (it does not have to be last).

```
1 /* Program 14.1 - use of the switch and break statements */
2
3 #include <stdlib.h>
4 #include <stdio.h>
5
6 int main()
7 {
8     char ch;                        /* command character read from keyboard */
9     int i = 1;                      /* integer value being read and printed */
10
11    while (printf("\nCommand ? "), scanf(" %c", &ch) != EOF)      /* read ch */
12        switch (ch)
13            {
14            case 'r': printf("\n Enter value of i ? ");     /* r = read data */
15                      scanf(" %d", &i);
16                      break;
17            case 'p': printf("\n value of i = %d ", i);     /* p = print data */
18                      break;
19            case 'x': printf("   Program terminated\n");
20                      exit(0);                              /* x = exit program */
21            default: printf("   illegal character %c (%#x) ", ch, ch);
22            }
23        printf("program terminated on EOF\n");
24        return 0;
25 }
```

Program 14.1 Command selection using switch and break statements

In Program 14.1 switch is used to select the execution of a group of statements via a command character read from the keyboard. The program sequence is:

11-22   a while which prompts the user for input and reads the command character ch
         (the while terminates when EOF is entered)
12-22   a switch statement which selects statements to execute under the control of ch
         14-16   executed if ch == 'r', reads a new value into i
         17-18   executed if ch == 'p', prints the value of i
         19-20   executed if ch == 'x', terminates the program (see below)
         21   else default prints a message indicating invalid character
23-24   terminates the program if EOF was entered

The break statements terminate the switch after the statement(s) associated with a particular command have been executed. For example, if the break statements in lines 16 and 18 had been omitted and 'r' was entered lines 14, 15, 17, 19 and 20 would be executed in turn and the program terminated. The function exit from <stdlib.h> terminates the program and returns the parameter as a program success/failure indicator to the operating system.

Note the use of the comma operator in line 11 (which is similar to its use in Program 13.3):

```
while (printf("\nCommand ? "), scanf(" %c", &ch) != EOF)      /* read ch */
```

The call to scanf reads a character into ch. In " %c" the space before the %c causes any **white space** (spaces, tabs, newlines, etc.) in the input stream to be skipped.

Many library functions return information in the form of integer values indicating success or failure. For example, the Turbo C graphics library (Turbo C 1991) is initialised by calling the function initgraph (see Program 13.5 for more details):

```
int graphdriver = DETECT, graphmode;

initgraph(&graphdriver, &graphmode, "c:\\tc\\bgi");
```

If successful, an integer value indicating the type of graphics card found is returned in parameter graphdriver. This could be displayed on the screen as an integer number and the user would look up (in manuals) the meaning of the value to determine what graphics card is fitted. A preferable alternative is to print a meaningful message on the screen:

```
initgraph(&graphdriver, &graphmode, "c:\\tc\\bgi");      /* initialise graphics */
switch (graphdriver)                                      /* and print driver */
   {
   case CGA: printf("\n  CGA graphics initialised"); break;
   case EGA: printf("\n  EGA graphics initialised"); break;
   case VGA: printf("\n  VGA graphics initialised"); break;
   }
```

the *symbolic constants*, CGA, EGA and VGA are defined in <graphics.h> as integral constants corresponding to the values which may be returned in graphdriver.

Problem for Chapter 14

The *soundex* code phonetically groups characters as follows:

group 0: A E I O U H W Y plus all non-alphabetic characters
group 1: B F P V
group 2: C G J K Q S X Z
group 3: D T
group 4: L
group 5: M N
group 6: R

A sequence of characters is encoded as follows:

1 each character is replaced by its group digit, i.e. SMIT becomes 2503, SMITH becomes 25030 and SCHMIDT becomes 2205033
2 consecutive similar digits are replaced by a single digit, i.e. SMIT remains 2503 and SMITH and SCHMIDT become 20503
3 zeros are removed and SMIT, SMITH and SCHMIDT become 253

Hence the technique can be used to encode names in such a way that the effect of slight variations in spelling are reduced. For example, it could be used when taking customer orders over a noisy telephone line where the generated codes are used to key into a computer database. As each code is generated (surname, first name, house number, street name, city name, post code, etc.) it narrows down to the information on a particular customer.

Implement and test a program which reads a sequence of characters from the keyboard and generates the *soundex* code. Use the library function toupper (from <ctype.h>) to convert the characters to upper case then use a switch statement to select the group. Remember that several case labels can be in front of a single statement, e.g.:

```
case 'D': case 'T': group = 3;
```

15

Functions

There are three major reasons for breaking a program down into *functions*:

    (a) to break a large program down into manageable modules,
    (b) to provide libraries of common modules,
and (c) to save repeating the same code many times in the program.

For example, the Problem for Chapter 12 was to implement a program to read a real number from the keyboard in the form ±mmm.ddde±xxx where mmm is the whole number component, ddd is the fractional component and xxx is the exponent, e.g. $1.76e^4$. The program effectively reads two signed integer numbers mmm and xxx (the code for the factional component ddd would be similar). It is possible at each point to repeat the identical sequence of instructions (to read the two integer numbers) but this is wasteful and error prone. By using a *function* the sequence of instructions can be written once and then *called* as required, i.e. once each to read mmm and the exponent. If a function has a wider context it may be placed in a library to be accessed by other programs (possibly written by other programmers) in a way similar to the standard C libraries.

15.1 Function *definition*

The function *definition*, where the body of the function is defined, takes the following general form:

```
result_type function_name(parameter_list)
{
   declarations
   statements
}
```

where:

  the function *header*, `result_type function_name(parameter_list)`, specifies:

    (a) `result_type`   the type of the function result, e.g. int, double, etc.
    (b) `function_name`   the name or identifier of the function,
    (c) `parameter_list`   a list of parameters (see next section).

    { indicates the start of the function `function_name`

      declarations is a list of functions and *variables* (internal to `function_name`)

      statements   specify the computing operations to be carried out in `function_name`

    } matches the { and indicates the end of `function_name`

The body of the function, enclosed in {} is a *compound statement*. Internal variables are created on entry to the function and lost on exit and may not be accessed by other functions unless passed as parameters to another function (permanent internal storage may be allocated using *static* variables, see Chapter 17.5). When declared internal variables may be initialised, otherwise the value is *undefined*.

Although some functions are 'stand alone', in that no data is passed in or out, the majority:

(a) require data from the calling function in the form of parameters (see next section), and (b) return a *function result*, e.g. the square root of a number (passed as an parameter).

Functions return the *function result* to the calling function via the function_name (introduced in Chapter 4.6). The result_type specifies the type returned by the *function result* which may be any type other than an array (see Chapter 18) or a function (although *pointers* to arrays and functions can be returned, see Chapters 24.2 and 29.4). If a function does not return a *function result* result_type should be specified as void, i.e. a function may carry out some task for which no result is returned (e.g. clear the display screen). Specifying a result_type of void indicates to the compiler that no result is returned and it can check that no attempt is made to return a result or that a calling function does not attempt to use a result which does not exist. Note that if the result_type is missing int will be assumed.

15.1.1 The *parameter_list*

The majority of functions require data from the calling function in the form of parameters, e.g. printf requires the *control string* and the values of variables and expressions to print:

The *actual parameters* are the values passed to the function when it is called (sometimes called *arguments*).

The *formal parameters* are the names used inside the function to refer to the *actual parameters*.

The parameter_list is a list of the names of the *formal parameters* with their types:

```
(parameter_type parameter_name, parameter_type parameter_name, ....)
```

If a function has no parameters void is specified as the parameter_list indicating that there are no parameters (if the parameter_list is missing void will be assumed).

When a function is called, the number and types of the *actual parameters* passed to the function must match the number and types as specified by the *formal parameters* (see *function prototypes*, section 15.3). Note that the order in which the *actual parameters* are evaluated before being passed is not specified by the ANSI standard (for example, see the results of Program 10.2) although all the parameters are completely evaluated, including side effects, before the function is called (see Chapter 21.11).

15.2 The *return* statement

The return statement performs two operations:

1   it terminates the function and returns control to the calling function,
2   if followed by an expression it returns a *function result* to the calling function.

For example:

```
return 0;                    /* terminate and return function result of 0 */
return i*j;                   /* terminate and return function result */
return 25.0;                  /* terminate and return function result */
return;                             /* terminate without function result */
return (2.0 * x - sin(y));    /* terminate and return function result */
```

Points to note:

1 The type of expression following `return` must match the `result_type` of the function or be capable of being converted to it.

2 If the function does not have a `return` statement the closing } acts as one.

3 If the `result_type` is other than `void` and a function result is not returned garbage will be passed back to the calling function resulting in *undefined behaviour* (a modern compiler will issue warnings in such a case).

4 A function with a `result_type` of `void` may not return a function result (a modern compiler will issue a warning if an attempt is made to return a result).

5 The expression returned can be enclosed in parenthesis, i.e. to make a complex expression stand out in the program.

In general it is recommended that a function have only one `return` statement at the end of the body of the function. Otherwise, if a large function can `return` at a number of places, it can become very difficult to follow the flow of the code.

15.3 Function *prototypes*

When a function is called the number and types of the *actual parameters* passed to the function must match the number and types expected (as specified by the *formal parameters*) otherwise *undefined behaviour* occurs. To enable the compiler to check that a function call is correct it requires information regarding number and type of parameters and the type of the *function result* returned. The *declarations* at the start of a function should contain *function prototypes* (which provide this information) for all the functions which it calls.

A *function prototype* is effectively a copy of the *header* from the *function definition* plus a terminating ; and has the following general form:

```
result_type function_name(parameter_list);
```

For example, the *function prototype* for `sqrt` specifies that it has one parameter of type `double` (double precision real) and returns a function result of type `double`:

```
double sqrt(double x);
```

When a function is called the compiler uses the *function prototype* to:

1 Check that the number of parameters is correct, i.e. `sqrt` has one parameter.

2 If necessary, convert the types of the *actual parameters* to those required by the *formal parameters*, e.g. in Program 5.1 the `float` parameter to `sqrt` would be converted to a `double`. The conversion is carried out as though the *formal parameter* is assigned the value of the *actual parameter* using the *assignment operator* = (see Chapter 10.2).

3 If necessary, convert the type returned by the *function result* to that required by the calling function, e.g. in Program 5.1 the `double` result returned by `sqrt` is assigned to a `float` variable.

If a prototype is not available when a function is called integral parameters undergo integral promotion and `float` parameters are converted to `double` (other types are passed as they are) and any function result is assumed to be of type `int`. Undefined behaviour occurs if the number or types of the actual parameters disagrees with the formal parameters.

The standard header files contain *function prototypes* for the library functions, e.g. `<math.h>` contains the *function prototypes* of all the mathematical functions.

15.4 Function to raise a *float* to an *integer* exponent

```
 1  /* Program 15.1 - call function to raise a float to an integer exponent */
 2
 3  #include <stdio.h>
 4
 5  int main(void)
 6  {
 7      float power(float number, int exponent);          /* function prototype */
 8
 9      float x, result;                                  /* internal variables */
10      int exp;
11
12      printf("\n Enter real number and integer exponent ? ");
13      while (scanf("%f%d", &x, &exp) == 2)              /* read data */
14          {
15          result = power(x, exp);                       /* call function */
16          printf("\n%f to the exponent %d = %f ", x, exp, result);
17          printf("\n\n Enter real number and integer exponent ? ");
18          }
19      return 0;
20  }
21
22  /*-------------------------------------------------------------*
23   * Function to raise a float to an integer exponent            *
24   * Parameters in: number (float) value to be raise to exponent *
25   *                exponent (int) the value of the exponent     *
26   * Function result: number raised to exponent                  *
27   *-------------------------------------------------------------*/
28  float power(float number, int exponent)               /* function header */
29  {
30      int i;                                            /* loop counter */
31      float result;                                     /* holds result */
32
33      for (result = i = 1; i <= exponent; i++)   /* loop i from 1 to exponent */
34          result = result * number;              /* number to the exponent i */
35      return result;                             /* return function result */
36  }
```

Program 15.1 Function to raise a float to an integer exponent

Program 15.1 contains the functions main and power, which evaluates number^{exponent} where number is a float and exponent is an int, e.g. 3.6^4. The function main consists of:

7	float power(float number, int exponent); *prototype* for the function power
9-10	declare variables which are internal to main
12	prompts the user to enter a real number and an integer exponent
13-18	a while statement executed while scanf successfully converts two numbers
	15 result = power(x, exp);
	call power, parameters x and exp and result assigned to result
	16-17 print results and prompt for next input

The function power (lines 22 to 36) consists of:

line

28   float power(float number, int exponent) is the function header

30-31   internal variables used within in the function power

33-34   a for statement to evaluate number^{exponent}

35   return result; returns control to main together with the function result

The program terminates when scanf fails to convert two numbers. The function prototype in line 7 tells the compiler that function power has two parameters of types float and int respectively and returns a function result of type float. In the call to power in line 15 there is no need for conversion but if it had been called with two int parameters the compiler would know to convert the first to a float before passing it. The *function prototype* need only specify the types of the parameters (the names being unnecessary), i.e. line 7 of Program 15.1 could be written:

    float power(float, int);   /* function prototype */

The name used within a function for a *formal parameter* has no relationship with the name of the corresponding *actual parameter* when the function is called, i.e. they may be the same or not. The critical thing is that the **types** correspond, with each *formal parameter* taking the value of the corresponding *actual parameter* (see next section). In addition, variables declared within functions are *internal* and are not accessible outside the function (unless passed as parameters to other functions), e.g. result declared in main in line 9 is a totally distinct variable from result declared in power in line 31 (more on internal variables in Chapters 17 and 21). When a function terminates, any internal variables are lost and recreated when it is called again (see Chapter 17.5 on *static* internal variables).

Unfortunately, for reasons of compatibility with the original C, ANSI C does not require a *function prototype* when a function is called. For example, if the declaration of the *function prototype* of power in line 7 of Program 15.1 had been missed out:

1   The number of parameters could not be checked and the compiler would assumed that it was called with the correct number.

2   How a particular parameter is passed depends upon its type with integral parameters undergoing integral promotion and float parameters being converted to double (other types are passed as they are). Therefore in the call to power in line 15 the first parameter would be passed incorrectly and the second correctly.

3   The function result would be assumed to be of type int and converted to a float to be assigned to result (this giving an incorrect result).

If incorrect parameter types are passed into a function the behaviour is undefined (the program may crash with a run-time error or at the very least the result of the function would be incorrect). It is therefore unwise to miss out *function prototypes* and considered very bad programming practice. A modern compiler will issue a warning if a *function prototype* is not available when a function is called (see the example in Chapter 6).

If, when the function is defined, the *header* differs from any *prototype* an error message will be generated. For example, if line 28 of Program 15.1 was replaced with:

float power(float number, float exponent)   /* function header */

Turbo C++ Version 1.01 would display the message:

Error p15_1.c 28: Type mismatch in redeclaration of 'power'

15.5 Function declarations in the original C

Function prototypes and the method of function definition described in section 15.1 are new to ANSI C. In the original C the header of function power would be:

```
float power(number, exponent)                    /* function header */
float number;                                    /* first parameter type */
int exponent;                                    /* second parameter type */
{                                                /* start of function power */
```

The () contain a list of the names of the of the formal parameters with the types declared on the following lines (before the opening { of the function compound statement). The declaration of power in a function which calls it would be:

```
float power();                    /* declaration of function power in old 'c' */
```

Only the function result type is specified. It is up to the programmer to ensure that the number and types of parameters are correct.

15.6 Passing parameters using *call by value*

C passes parameters into a function using *call by value*:

1   copies of the *actual parameters* are made in temporary variables and these are passed;
2   the called function can access the **values** of the *actual parameters* via the names of the corresponding *formal parameters*.

Consider line 15 of Program 15.1:

```
result = power(x, exp);
```

When power is called copies of the values of x and exp are made into temporary variables. The function power would then access these values via the names number and exponent as specified in the parameter list in the function header in line 28:

```
float power(float number, int exponent)
```

On entry to the function power the *formal parameters* number and exponent have the same values as x and exp respectively, as passed from the function main. Such *formal parameters* can be considered as *internal* variables which are given an initial value on entry to the function and may then be used like any other variable. *Call by value* prevents code within the function inadvertently accessing the original parameters and corrupting them, i.e. if number in power is changed the value of x in main is not affected. It is therefore possible to modify function power as follows:

```
float power(float number, int exponent)              /* function header */
{
    float result;                                    /* holds result */

    for (result = 1; exponent > 0; exponent--)       /* loop from exponent to 1 */
        result = result * number;                    /* number to the exponent */
    return result;                                   /* return function result */
}
```

$number^{exponent}$ is calculated with the value of exponent decrementing until it reaches 0, when the for statement terminates. The value of exp in main is unaffected. This modification enables the internal variable i in function power of Program 15.1 to be removed. The sample program of Appendix D.1 uses this function in a modified version of Program 5.3.

If a formal parameter should not the altered within the function it should be prefixed with the *type qualifier* const. For example, the header of power could be written:

```
float power(const float number, const int exponent)          /* function header */
```

Indicating that number and exponent are constants and may not be altered within power. The modified version of power would now give an error, e.g. Microsoft C:

```
31      for (result = 1; exponent > 0; exponent--)     /* loop from exponent to 1 */
***** X.C(31) : error C2166: lvalue specifies const object
```

Qualifying parameters using const will ensure that a value is not altered inadvertently within the function (e.g. by mistyping a variable name) and may allow the compiler to perform some optimisation.

Exercise 15.1 (*see Appendix B for sample answer*)

Implement a function which reads a binary number from the keyboard, the function prototype could be:

```
long int read_binary(void);                        /* function prototype */
```

1   terminate the binary number when the character read is not '0' or '1'
2   push the last character read back into the input stream using:
```
        ungetc(ch, stdin);
```
    which pushes one character ch (the maximum) back into the stream stdin
    note that EOF cannot be pushed so push a 0 in its place

Test the function with a suitable main function which should call read_binary and then getchar() (to read the last character entered). If the last character entered was:

1   EOF (indicated by 0) stop the program
2   **white space** the number is correct and it should be printed in decimal, octal and hex.
3   anything else print an error message plus the invalid character

15.7 Passing parameters using *call by reference*

In general programming terms there are two ways of passing a parameter into a function:

call by value: a copy of the value of the parameter is made in a temporary variable and this is passed to the function. Within the function the parameter appears to be an internal variable initialised to the value of the parameter.

call by reference: the address of the parameter is passed to the function. The function can use the address to access and alter the memory allocated to the parameter.

C passes all **actual parameters by value**. It is, however, possible to pass the address of a variable as an actual parameter and inside the function use the address, via the name of corresponding formal parameter, to achieve *call by reference*. For example, scanf needs to use *call by reference* to access the memory allocated to variables to return the values read from the keyboard.

In C *pointers* are used to hold and manipulate addresses, see Chapter 23. It is possible, however, to use pointers to pass function parameters using *call by reference* without fully understanding all the details of *pointers*. The following is therefore presented on an 'as use' basis with further details of *pointers* covered in Chapter 23.

15.7.1 Introduction to *pointers*

A pointer to a particular type of object is declared as follows:

```
type *p_type;                           /* declare a pointer to type */
```

The * prefixing the identifier p_type in the declaration indicates that it is a pointer, i.e. it will contain the address of an object of the specified type. For example:

```
int *p_int;                             /* declare a pointer to an int */
```

declares p_int to be a pointer which can point to (hold the address of) an int variable.

The address operator &, which returns the *address of* an operand, is used to set up a pointer, e.g.:

```
int *p_int;                             /* declare a pointer to an int */
int number;                             /* declare an int variable */

p_int = &number;                        /* point p_int at variable number */
```

The statement p_int = &number; assigns the *value of the address* of variable number to pointer p_int, i.e. when the identifier p_int is used in an expression the contents of the pointer itself (an address) is accessed.

To access the object which a pointer points to (holds the address of), the pointer is prefixed by the indirection operator *, e.g.:

```
int *p_int;                             /* declare a pointer to an int */
int number;                             /* declare an int variable */

p_int = &number;                        /* point p_int at variable number */
*p_int = 10;                   /* assign the int pointed at by p_int the value 10 */
```

The last statement assigns the value 10 to the variable number, i.e. *p_int = 10; assigns 10 to the variable pointed at by p_int, which in this case points at variable number, therefore 10 is assigned to number. Which is equivalent to:

```
number = 10;                  /* assign of the value 10 to the variable number */
```

To differentiate pointers from other types it is wise to use some naming convention, e.g. use p_ to start pointer names.

15.7.2 Using *pointers* to achieve *call by reference*

To pass an object into a function using *call by reference* the address of the object is passed as the actual parameter (using the address operator &) and the corresponding formal parameter is declared as a pointer to the correct type. Inside the function the name of the formal parameter is prefixed with the indirection operator * which will then access the memory allocated to the original object. Consider the following function which swaps the contents of a pair of int parameters:

```
void swap_int(int *p_int1, int *p_int2)
{
    int temporary;                              /* temporary storage */

    temporary = *p_int1;            /* copy first variable into temporary */
    *p_int1 = *p_int2;               /* copy second variable into first */
    *p_int2 = temporary;            /* copy temporary variable into first */
}
```

The formal parameters p_int1 and p_int2 are pointers to type int. The function would be called (where x and y are variables of type int):

        swap_int(&x, &y);

The address operator & will pass the addresses of x and y to the function swap_int (not a copy of their values). Function swap_int can then access x and y:

        *p_int1 will access the memory allocated to variable x

and *p_int2 will access the memory allocated to variable y

Hence the following statements:

```
        temporary = *p_int1;              /* copy first variable into temporary */
        *p_int1 = *p_int2;                   /* copy second variable into first */
        *p_int2 = temporary;           /* copy temporary variable into first */
```

swaps the contents of variables x and y by:

        (a) assigning the value of x to temporary
        (b) assigning the value of y to x
and (c) assigning the value of temporary (old value of x) to y

15.8 Function to swap the values of two variables

```
 1 /* Program 15.2 - calling a function using 'call by reference' */
 2
 3 #include <stdio.h>
 4
 5 int main(void)
 6    {
 7    int x = 1, y = 2;                                /* local variables */
 8    void swap_int(int *const p_int1, int *const p_int2);      /* prototype */
 9
10    printf("\n x = %d and y = %d ", x, y);                /* print x and y */
11    swap_int(&x, &y);                                    /* swap x and y */
12    printf("\n x = %d and y = %d ", x, y);               /* print x and y */
13    return 0;
14    }
15
16 /*----------------------------------------------------------------------*
17  * Function swap_int: to swap the values of two int parameters          *
18  * Parameters in/out: p_int1 (pointer to int) address of first variable  *
19  *                    p_int2 (pointer to int) address of second variable *
20  * Function result: none                                                 *
21  *----------------------------------------------------------------------*/
22 void swap_int(int *const p_int1, int *const p_int2)
23 {
24    int temporary;                                /* temporary storage */
25
26    temporary = *p_int1;              /* copy first variable into temporary */
27    *p_int1 = *p_int2;                   /* copy second variable into first */
28    *p_int2 = temporary;           /* copy temporary variable into first */
29 }
```

Program 15.2 Calling a function using *call by reference*

Program 15.2 contains a slightly enhanced version of the swap_int function discussed in the previous section. The sequence of statements is:

7   declare int variables x and y and initialise them

8   function prototype for swap_int

10   print values of variables x and y

11   swap_int(&x, &y); call swap_int to swap the values of variables x and y

12   print the new values of variables x and y

22   void swap_int(int *const p_int1, int *const p_int2)
      function header with two formal parameters which are pointers to type int (see below)

24   internal variable used for swapping

26   assign contents of int pointed to by p_int1 (x in this case) to temporary

27   assign contents of int pointed to by p_int2 (y in this case) to int pointed to by p_int1 (x in this case)

28   assign contents of temporary to int pointed to by p_int2 (y in this case)

Note that in the function header of swap (line 22) the formal parameters are const qualified pointers to int, i.e. the pointer values may not be changed inside the function (although the object pointed to may be). For example, the following would generate a warning or error:

```
p_int1 = &temporary;                    /* point p_int1 at temporary */
```

15.9 Summary: *call by reference*

In C actual parameters are passed into a function using *call by value*, i.e. copies of the *actual parameters* are made in temporary variables and these are passed. To achieve *call by reference* the programmer explicitly passes the address of an object as the actual parameter (using the address operator &) to the function. Within the function a pointer is used to access the memory allocated to the object (using the indirection operator *). In fact, C is still passing the actual parameter by value but it is the value of the address of the object that is passed, not a copy of the value of the object itself. The function then uses the value of the address (via a pointer) to access the memory allocated to the object.

If parameters are to be passed using *call by reference* both the calling and called functions must agree which parameters are to be passed using *call by value* and which using *call by reference*. When a parameter is to be passed using *call by reference*:

1   The calling function must remember to prefix the name of the object with the address operator & when calling the function.

2   The called function must:
        (a) declare the corresponding formal parameter to be a pointer to the type of object.
    and (b) prefix the name of the corresponding formal parameter with the indirection operator * to access the memory allocated to the object.

The use of function prototypes, introduced by ANSI C, enables compilers to check that an address is passed as an actual parameter when the corresponding formal parameter is a pointer. In addition a modern compiler will issue errors or warnings if a pointer is used in a dubious way, e.g. by forgetting to prefix the name of the formal parameter with the indirection operator *.

Exercise 15.2 (*see Appendix B for sample answer*)

Modify read_binary of Exercise 15.1 to return the value read using *call by reference*, e.g.:

```
int read_binary(long int *const number);            /* function prototype */
```

The function result should indicates success or failure, e.g. return the following:

1	number was OK (terminated by **white space**)
0	invalid character entered (leave character in the input stream)
EOF	EOF entered

Problem for Chapter 15

Implement and test a function which reads an unsigned decimal integer number, e.g.:

```
long int read_decimal(void);                        /* function prototype */
```

1 terminate the number when the character read is not a digit, i.e. in range '0' to '9'
2 push the last character read back into the input stream using ungetc(ch, stdin)

Implement a function to read a signed real number in the form ±mmm.ddde±xxx where mmm is the whole number component, ddd is the fractional component and xxx is the exponent of ten, e.g. 2, 1.2, -3.6, $3.0e^4$, $5.6e^{-7}$, $5e^6$, etc. ($5.6e^6$ being equal to $5.6 * 10^6$), e.g.:

1 Skip any leading **white space**.
2 Check the first character for a leading sign + or - (if not found push the character back into the input stream ready for the next read).
3 Call read_decimal (above) to read the whole number component terminated with:
  (a) **white space** terminates the real number
  (b) a . indicating that the fractional component follows
  (c) an **e** indicating that the exponent follows
  (d) anything else is an error
4 If the whole number component terminated in a . read the fractional component terminated with:
  (a) **white space** terminates the real number
  (b) an **e** indicating that the exponent follows
  (c) anything else is an error
5 If the whole number or fractional component terminated in an **e**:
  (a) check for a - or + sign
  (b) call read_decimal to read the exponent (terminated with **white space**)
6 Push the last character read back into the input stream (EOF as 0).
7 Evaluate the complete number and return as a function result (the maths function pow(x, y) returns x^y).

Implement a function main to test the function. The program should call read_float and then getchar() to read the last character. If the last character was:

1 **white space** the number is correct and it should be printed using printf.
2 EOF (indicated by 0) stop the program
3 anything else print an error message plus the invalid character

Test the program with suitable data including 0, 2, 1.2, -3.6, $3.0e^4$, $5.6e^{-7}$, $5e^6$, etc.

16

Evaluating mathematical series

The summation of an infinite series or the evaluation of algorithms which involve an infinite number of iterations are common in many mathematical, scientific and engineering applications. The chapter introduces programming techniques for solving such problems.

16.1 Truncating infinite series

Consider the Taylor series for the sine function $\sin(x)$ (where x is an angle in radians):

$$\sin(x) = x - \frac{x^3}{3!} + \frac{x^5}{5!} - \frac{x^7}{7!} + \frac{x^9}{9!} \cdots \cdots \qquad\qquad x^2 < \infty$$

Although the series is infinite, in practice it is terminated after calculating a certain number of terms (five or ten or fifty or ten thousand) when it is deemed (somehow) that the summation has achieved a value which is sufficiently accurate. The terms omitted (which are infinite in number) introduce an error into the result caused by the truncation of an infinite process. This is acceptable so long as the contribution from the remaining terms in the truncated series is less than the required accuracy.

Series such as the sine function are well suited to evaluation using while, do or for statements (the choice depends upon the algorithm being evaluated). The problem facing the programmer is when to terminate the iterative process. For example, using a simple for statement with one hundred loops could either result in doing too many loops (if the result is sufficiently accurate after ten iterations) or too few (the series needs to be summed for ten thousand loops). A technique commonly used is to terminate the iterative process is when the absolute value of a particular term becomes less than the accuracy required, i.e.:

| value of n'th term | < accuracy   terminate the iteration

When evaluating the sine series, the iterative process is terminated when the contribution of x^n / n! becomes so small that it can be ignored (typically accuracy is between 10^{-6} and 10^{-9}). This technique is suitable for terminating the sine series where the result is in the range -1.0 to +1.0. Problems can occur, however, when the summation results in a very small number (the result is of the same order of magnitude as accuracy) or a very large number (looking for changes of 10^{-6} in a figure of 10^9). An alternative technique is to examine the contribution of the current term relative to the summation so far:

$$\left| \frac{\text{value of n'th term}}{\text{sum of series so far}} \right| < \text{accuracy} \qquad \text{terminate the iteration}$$

This, however, will fail if the sum of the series becomes zero, i.e. division by 0 occurs. A more exacting requirement may be that one of the above criteria is satisfied for a minimum of ten (or more) iterations, then the process terminates. The precise techniques used depend on how well conditioned and convergent the formulas are; refer to a text on numerical methods for a full discussion (Dorn & McCraken 1972, James & Riba 1992).

16.2 Program to evaluate the sine function sin(x)

```
 1 /* Program 16.1 - test sin(x) function */
 2
 3 #include <stdio.h>
 4 #include <math.h>
 5
 6 int main()
 7 {
 8     float sinf(const float x);                    /* function prototype of sinf */
 9     float x;                                      /* evaluate sin(x) */
10
11     while (printf("\nAngle (radians) ? ") , scanf("%f", &x) == 1)
12         printf("  sin = %20.8f, library = %12.8f ", sinf(x), sin(x));
13     return 0;
14 }
15
16 /*----------------------------------------------------------------*
17 /* Function to evaluate sin(x) by summing the series (** is power):    *
18  *   sin(x) = x - (x**3 / 3!) + (x**5 / 5!) - (x**7 / 7!) + ..         */
19 float sinf(const float x)
20 {
21     const float accuracy = 1.0e-8f;               /* accuracy required */
22     float xsq = x * x,                            /* x squared */
23           sin_x = x,                              /* sum of sin(x) series */
24           n = 3.0f,                               /* start iterations at 3rd term */
25           term_n = x;                             /* value of n'th term of series */
26
27     /*printf("                 n                    term_n                sin_x ");*/
28     do
29         {
30         term_n = -(term_n * xsq / (n * (n - 1)));   /* evaluate n'th term */
31         sin_x = sin_x + term_n;                     /* add term  */
32         n = n + 2;                                  /* next n */
33         /*printf("\n sin(%6.1f) %3d %24f %20f", x, n, term_n, sin_x);*/
34         }
35     while (fabs(term_n) > accuracy);              /* finished ? */
36     return sin_x;                                 /* yes, return result */
37 }
```

Program 16.1 Program to evaluate sin(x) and check using the library function

Program 16.1 evaluates the sine series:

$$sin(x) = x - \frac{x^3}{3!} + \frac{x^5}{5!} - \frac{x^7}{7!} + \frac{x^9}{9!} \cdots \cdots \qquad x^2 < \infty$$

where n! is factorial n, see Program 13.2. Although each term of the series could be calculated independently, use can be made of the fact that each term has a simple relationship to the previous, i.e.:

$$term_n = \pm \frac{x^n}{n!} = -term_{n-1} * \frac{x^2}{n*(n-1)}$$

In function `sinf` the following `float` (single precision real) variables are used:

xsq   holds the value of x^2
sin_x   holds the current value of the sum of the series sin(x)
n   holds the number of the term being calculated
term_n   holds the value of the n'th term of the series

The sequence of statements in Program 16.1 is:

line
8   prototype for the function `sinf`
11-12   prompt the user to enter angle, read the value into variable x, if converted OK
         12   call `sinf` and the maths library function `sin` to evaluate sin(x)
19   header for function `sinf`, one `float` parameter and returns a `float` function result
21   declare accuracy (`const` qualified) and initialise its value to required accuracy
22   declare xsq and initialise its value to x^2 (which is used in every term and is constant within the iteration loop; evaluating x^2 outside the loop makes the code more efficient - a good optimising compiler would do a similar thing)
23   declare sin_x and initialise its value to x (the value of the first term of the series)
24   declare n and initialise its value to 3 (the next term to be calculated)
25   declare term_n and initialise its value to x (the value of the first term of the series)
27   a `printf` statement used for debugging (commented out)
28-35   a do statement which sums the series sin(x)
         30   `term_n = -(term_n * xsq / (n * (n -1)))`
                  calculates the value of the n'th term in the series
         31   `sin_x = sin_x + term_n` adds the n'th term to the sum of the series
         32   `n = n + 2;` increments n by 2 ready to calculate the next term
         33   a `printf` statement used for debugging (commented out)
                     prints x, n, term_n and sin_x (the sum of the series so far)
         35   `while (fabs(term_n) > accuracy);` terminates the sum - see below
36   return function result

The summation of the series is stopped (in line 35) when the absolute value of a particular term becomes less than or equal to the accuracy required:

```
while (fabs(term_n) > accuracy);                            /* finished ? */
```

The maths function `fabs` is used to determine the absolute value of term_n (the absolute value is required because negative values may be evaluated).

   The value of accuracy can be set to give the required accuracy for the application. Line 33 prints information to enable the convergence of the series to be viewed while executing the program (commented out in this version).

   Below is shown a sample run of the program (using Microsoft C Version 6.00). From the results it can be seen that when the angle is below 5.0 radians the value returned by `sinf` is the same as that returned by the maths function sin(x) to approximately six or seven figures. When the angle is 10 radians the accuracy of the sum is approximately 2 to 3 figures and when the angle is above 20 radians the results are complete nonsense ! The series is valid for all angles assuming that the calculations are performed to infinite accuracy and the problem with the above results is due to rounding errors in floating point calculations (which will be discussed in the next section).

```
Angle (radians) ? .5  sin =          0.47942552, library =    0.47942554
Angle (radians) ? 1   sin =          0.84147096, library =    0.84147098
Angle (radians) ? 2   sin =          0.90929741, library =    0.90929743
Angle (radians) ? 5   sin =         -0.95892441, library =   -0.95892427
Angle (radians) ? 10  sin =         -0.54420567, library =   -0.54402111
Angle (radians) ? 15  sin =          0.66512936, library =    0.65028784
Angle (radians) ? 20  sin =          1.52592909, library =    0.91294525
Angle (radians) ? 25  sin =         -5.36588192, library =   -0.13235175
Angle (radians) ? 30  sin =      -24048.72656250, library =   -0.98803162
Angle (radians) ? 40  sin =   523443136.00000000, library =    0.74511316
Angle (radians) ? 50  sin = -8887603298304.00000000, library =   -0.26237485
```

16.3 Rounding errors

In C real numbers are stored in floating point form, i.e. a fractional part and an exponent. For example, decimal floating point numbers are in the form $f*10^e$ where f is the fraction in the range $0.1 \leq f < 1.0$ and e is the exponent, e.g. 7392.0 would be $0.7392 * 10^4$ and 0.0007392 would be $0.7392 * 10^{-3}$. Note, however, that computer systems tend to use base 2 or 16 for floating point numbers, e.g. $f*2^e$, but the following discussion still applies.

When computation is being carried out the fractional part of a decimal floating point must be within the range $0.1 \leq f < 1$ and if at any time the leading digit becomes 0 then the fractional part is shifted one place left and the exponent decremented, e.g. $0.0023*10^4$ becomes $0.23*10^2$. This process of getting the fractional part in the correct range is called **normalisation**.

Now suppose that two floating point numbers which are accurate to four significant figures are to be added:

$$z = 1.246 + 0.03290 = 0.1246*10^1 + 0.3290*10^{-1}$$

Before the add can take place the floating point number exponents must be aligned, i.e. one of the numbers unnormalized:

$$z = 0.1246*10^1 + 0.00329*10^1$$

This gives the result $0.1278*10^1$ assuming four figure accuracy. Note that the digits of the fraction shifted out of the capacity of the system have been lost. Furthermore, no rounding was carried out when the digits were lost. Many computer systems do not round in this situation so it is a likely source of error in the program. Now consider subtraction:

$$z = 26.31 - 19.76 = 0.2631*10^2 - 0.1976*10^2 = 0.0655*10^2$$

this has resulted in a leading zero so it will be shifted:

$$z = 0.6550*10^1$$

Notice two things:

1 The last digit of the result has no significance whatever. The zero has been inserted in the shifting process because something has to be placed in that position in storage.

2 There can easily be more than one leading zero in such sums. For example if $0.3471*10^5$ is subtracted from $0.3472*10^5$ the answer is $0.0001*10^5$ which when normalised is $0.1000*10^2$. The last three digits have no meaning.

Thus when subtracting it is possible to end up with numbers with far less significant figures than the calculation started with. However, succeeding operations will act on these results as though all the figures were significant. This is a major source of run-time errors.

Now consider Program 16.1 which evaluates $\sin(x)$. As the signs of the terms alternate rounding errors can result from the subtraction process (as described above). In addition, if x is large the values of x^n can become a very large number. Below is a listing of a run of Program 16.1 for an angle of 25.0 radians with the comments in lines 27 and 33 removed (so that the results of each iteration is printed):

```
Angle (radians) ? 25
                    n                  term_n                   sin_x
 sin( 25.0)   5            -2604.166748            -2579.166748
 sin( 25.0)   7            81380.210938            78801.046875
 sin( 25.0)   9         -1211015.000000         -1132214.000000
 sin( 25.0)  11         10512283.000000          9380069.000000
 sin( 25.0)  13        -59728880.000000        -50348812.000000
 sin( 25.0)  15        239298400.000000        188949584.000000
 sin( 25.0)  17       -712197632.000000       -523248064.000000
 sin( 25.0)  19       1636483584.000000       1113235456.000000
 sin( 25.0)  21      -2990649856.000000      -1877414400.000000
 sin( 25.0)  23       4450371584.000000       2572957184.000000
 sin( 25.0)  25      -5497000448.000000      -2924043264.000000
 sin( 25.0)  27       5726042112.000000       2801998848.000000
 sin( 25.0)  29      -5097971712.000000      -2295972864.000000
 sin( 25.0)  31       3923931392.000000       1627958528.000000
 sin( 25.0)  33      -2637050624.000000      -1009092096.000000
 sin( 25.0)  35       1560754432.000000        551662336.000000
 sin( 25.0)  37       -819723968.000000       -268061632.000000
 sin( 25.0)  39        384630240.000000        116568608.000000
 sin( 25.0)  41       -162209104.000000        -45640496.000000
 sin( 25.0)  43         61817492.000000         16176996.000000
 sin( 25.0)  45        -21393096.000000         -5216100.000000
 sin( 25.0)  47          6752871.000000          1536771.000000
 sin( 25.0)  49        -1952148.125000         -415377.125000
 sin( 25.0)  51          518746.843750          103369.718750
 sin( 25.0)  53         -127143.835938         -23774.117188
 sin( 25.0)  55           28833.417969           5059.300781
 sin( 25.0)  57           -6067.638672          -1008.337891
 sin( 25.0)  59            1188.055786            179.717896
 sin( 25.0)  61            -216.988571            -37.270676
 sin( 25.0)  63              37.054058             -0.216618
 sin( 25.0)  65              -5.929029             -6.145647
 sin( 25.0)  67               0.890780             -5.254867
 sin( 25.0)  69              -0.125902             -5.380769
 sin( 25.0)  71               0.016771             -5.363998
 sin( 25.0)  73              -0.002109             -5.366107
 sin( 25.0)  75               0.000251             -5.365856
 sin( 25.0)  77              -0.000028             -5.365884
 sin( 25.0)  79               0.000003             -5.365881
 sin( 25.0)  81              -0.000000             -5.365882
 sin( 25.0)  83               0.000000             -5.365882
 sin( 25.0)  85              -0.000000             -5.365882
   sin =        -5.36588192, library =  -0.13235175
```

The final value of the sin of an angle must be in the range -1.0 to 1.0 but the above listing shows values as large as 5726042112.0. As the float calculations are only carried out to 6 or 7 figures of accuracy the last four figures of the number are meaningless. We are therefore attempting to get a result in the range -1.0 to 1.0 using values that are not accurate to hundreds or even thousands.

16.3.1 Using higher precision types to overcome rounding errors

One way to *reduce* the effect of rounding errors is to increase the precision and range of the variables and constants used. This, however, has an overhead in that the extra computation involved increases the run-time of the program. In many applications there is often a trade-off between the accuracy desired and the run-time acceptable.

Increasing precision, however, only reduces the problem; it does not eliminated it. Consider the following results produced using float, double and long double versions of the sin(x) function of Program 16.1 (under Turbo C). In may be seen that even long double (19 decimal digits of precision) is only effective up to about 30 radians.

angle x	sin(x) =	float	double	long double	library
1.0		0.841471	0.841471	0.841471	0.841471
2.0		0.909297	0.909297	0.909297	0.909297
5.0		-0.958924	-0.958924	-0.958924	-0.958924
10.0		-0.544206	-0.544021	-0.544021	-0.544021
15.0		0.665129	0.650288	0.650288	0.650288
20.0		1.525929	0.912945	0.912945	0.912945
25.0		-5.365882	-0.132351	-0.132352	-0.132352
30.0		-24048.726562	-0.988053	-0.988032	-0.988032
40.0		523443136.000000	-0.605842	0.744634	0.745113
50.0		-8887603298304.000000	9991.828290	13.111824	-0.262375

16.3.2 Modification of the algorithm to overcome rounding errors

A change to the algorithm may be possible, e.g.:

1   Modify the way that the mathematical equation is mapped into program code. For example, try to avoid situations where numbers with similar values are subtracted.
2   Using different mathematical equations and/or algorithms over different ranges of the input values.

For example, because the sin(x) function is periodic, a simple approach is to subtract 2π from the angle until its value is in the range 0 to 2π (for angles greater than 0), e.g. assuming an angle x in radians and two_pi equals 2π:

```
x = x - two_pi * (int) (x / two_pi);        /* get x in range 0 to 2pi */
```

The expression (int) (x / two_pi) evaluates, as an integer, how many times 2π goes into the angle x. This integer value is then multiplied by 2π and subtracted from the angle x; the result being an angle in the range 0 to 2π. The problem is that casting the floating result of x / two_pi to an int may result in integer overflow. This can be overcome by using the maths library function floor:

```
double floor(double x);        /* returns the largest integer below x */
```

which returns as a double function result the largest integer below x (the effect is similar to an int cast but avoids the danger of overflow). Hence the statement can be rewritten (and it also works for negative angles):

```
x = x - two_pi * floor(x / two_pi);                    /* get x in range 0 to 2pi */
```

Fig. 16.1 shows a modified version of the sinf function of Program 16.1 using the above technique.

```
 1 float sinf(float x)
 2 {
 3     const float accuracy = 1.0e-8f;                        /* accuracy required */
 4     const float two_pi = 2.0f * 3.14159265358979323846264343f;   /* constant 2pi */
 5     float xsq,                                             /* x squared */
 6           sin_x,                                    /* sum of sin(x) series */
 7           n = 3.0f,                              /* start iterations at 3rd term */
 8           term_n;                              /* value of n'th term of series */
 9
10     x = x - two_pi * floor(x / two_pi);               /* get x in range 0 to 2pi */
11     xsq = x * x;                                     /* calculate x squared */
12     sin_x = x;                                     /* initialise sin(x) */
13     term_n = x;                                   /* initialise term */
14     /*printf("                n                      term_n                 sin_x ");*/
15     do
16         {
17         term_n = -(term_n * xsq / (n * (n - 1)));        /* evaluate n'th term */
18         sin_x = sin_x + term_n;                              /* add term   */
19         n = n + 2;                                          /* next n */
20         /*printf("\n sin(%6.1f) %3d %24f %20f", x, n, term_n, sin_x);*/
21         }
22     while (fabs(term_n) > accuracy);                      /* finished ? */
23     return sin_x;                                  /* yes, return result */
24 }
```

Fig. 16.1 Modified version of sin(x) to cope with large angles

The following results were produced using float, double and long double versions of Fig. 16.1:

angle x	sin(x) =	float	double	long double	library
10.0		-0.544021	-0.544021	-0.544021	-0.544021
50.0		-0.262379	-0.262375	-0.262375	-0.262375
100.0		-0.506368	-0.506366	-0.506366	-0.506366
1000.0		0.826864	0.826880	0.826880	0.826880
10000.0		-0.305349	-0.305614	-0.305614	-0.305614
100000.0		0.038530	0.035749	0.035749	0.035749
1000000.0		-0.375923	-0.349994	-0.349994	-0.349994

It can be seen that the double and long double results are as accurate as the maths library function to the six figures displayed. The error in the float is due to rounding errors in the evaluation of the angle in the range 0 to 2π (line 10 of Fig. 16.1).

The above discussion has necessarily been very brief; refer to a text on numerical methods for a full discussion of such problems and the techniques used to overcome them (Dorn & McCraken 1972, James & Riba 1992).

16.4 Evaluation of square root using Newton-Raphson method

```
 1 /* Program 16.2 - test sqrt(x) function */
 2
 3 #include <stdio.h>
 4 #include <math.h>
 5
 6 int main()
 7 {
 8     double sq_root(const double x);                 /* function prototype */
 9     double number;                        /* hold number to find square root of */
10
11     while (printf("\nNumber > 0 ? ") , scanf("%lf", &number) == 1)
12         printf(" square root = %20.8f, library = %12.8f ",
13                 sq_root(number), sqrt(number));
14     return 0;
15 }
16
17 /*------------------------------------------------------------------*
18 /* Function: square root using Newton-Raphson method of successive   *
19  *      approximations, i.e. next approximation = x - f(x) / f'(x)   *
20  * For sqrt(number)  f(x) = x ** 2 - number   and f'(x) = 2 * x      *
21  *    thus f(x) / f'(x) = (x - number / x) / 2                       */
22 double sq_root(const double x)
23 {
24     const double accuracy = 1.0e-8;                 /* accuracy required */
25     double root,                        /* holds calculated value of square root */
26            term;                             /* holds f(x)/f'(x) term */
27
28     root = x;                            /* initial 'guess' at root */
29     do
30         {
31         term = (root - (x / root)) / 2.0;          /* f(x) / f('(x) */
32         root = root - term;                         /* new root */
33         }
34     while (fabs(term/root) > accuracy);             /* finished ? */
35     return root;                                    /* return result */
36 }
```

Program 16.2 Evaluation of the square root of a number using Newton-Raphson method

Program 16.2 evaluates the square root of a real number using the Newton-Raphson method of successive approximations, i.e. to find the root of the equation $f(x) = 0$:

$$x_{n+1} = x_n - \frac{f(x_n)}{f'(x_n)}$$

where x_n is the last approximation of the root

        x_{n+1} is the next approximation of the root

        $f(x_n)$ is the value of the function $f(x)$ at x_n

        $f'(x_n)$ is the value of the first derivative of $f(x)$ at x_n

A do statement is very suitable for solving an iterative problem such as this (this is often the technique used by the library routine sqrt):

1   An informed 'guess' of the initial value of x_n is made (how, depends upon f(x) and one would usually refer to a mathematical text).

2   The next approximation $x_{n+1} = x_n - f(x_n) / f'(x_n)$ is evaluated

3   The value of x_n is replaced with x_{n+1} and step 2 repeated

Steps 2 and 3 are repeated until the value of x_{n+1} is sufficiently accurate when the iteration is terminated.   Like the initial 'guess' of x_n, the method for terminating the iterations depends upon f(x) and how well the process converges.   The techniques described in section 16.1 are suitable, i.e. terminate the iteration when the absolute value of $f(x_n)$ / $f'(x_n)$ becomes less than some value of accuracy:

   $| f(x_n) / f'(x_n) |$ < accuracy   then terminate the iteration

This will fail if f'(x) becomes zero. An alternative is to use a value relative to x_n:

$$\left| \frac{f(x_n) / f'(x_n)}{x_{n+1}} \right| < accuracy \qquad \text{then terminate the iteration}$$

This, however, will fail if f'(x) or x_{n+1} become zero, i.e. division by 0 occurs.

To solve a problem such as finding the square root of number, i.e. $x = (number)^{1/2}$, the equation must be in the form:

   f(x) = 0

Thus to determine square root $x = (number)^{1/2}$ the form of f(x) is:

   $f(x) = x^2 - number = 0$

hence   f'(x) = 2 * x

In this case $f(x_n)$ / $f'(x_n)$ can be rewritten as:

   $f(x_n) / f'(x_n) = \frac{1}{2} (x - (number / x))$

The sequence of events in Program 16.2 is:

6-15   function main
8   declare prototype of function sq_root
9   declare variable number which will hold the value whose square root is required
11-13   prompt the user to enter a number > 0, read the value into variable number,
            12-13   call sq_root and the maths library function sqrt and print results

22-36   function sq_root: evaluates the square root of a double parameter, returns a double
22   function header indicating one double parameter x, returns a double function result
24   declare accuracy (const qualified) and initialise its value to 1.0e-8
25   declare variable root which will hold the value of x_n
26   declare variable term which will hold the value of $f(x_n)$ / $f'(x_n)$
28   assign root = x; the initial 'guess' at the root
29-34   is a do statement evaluating successive approximations of root
            31   evaluate $f(x_n)$ / $f'(x_n)$ and assign the result to variable term
            32   evaluate next approximation of root
            34   terminate the do when absolute value of term/root is ≤ accuracy
35   return the function result

Program 16.2 will fail if a negative value is entered for number, i.e. the square root of a negative number has imaginary components. The input should therefore be verified as a positive number (Program 13.2 shows a method).

Chapter 29.3 (Advanced use of functions), Program 29.2, contains a generalised function newton which uses the Newton-Raphson method of successive approximation to determinate the root of a function $f(x) = 0$. Pointers to the functions $f(x)$ and $f'(x)$ are passed to newton which then calls them as required. The function main calls newton twice to find the roots of $f(x) = \cosh(x) + \cos(x) - 3 = 0$ and $f(x) = x^2 - 25 = 0$.

Problems for Chapter 16

Problem 16.1 Implement and test a program which evaluates e^x using the following series:

$$e^x = 1 + x + \frac{x^2}{2!} + \frac{x^3}{3!} + \frac{x^4}{4!} + \frac{x^5}{5!} + \ldots \cdot \frac{x^n}{n!} \qquad x^2 < \infty$$

Test the program with various data including large values of x.

Notes that each term has a simple relationship to the previous, i.e.:

$$term_n = \frac{x^n}{n!} = term_{n-1} * \frac{x}{n}$$

The value of e^x can become very large so terminate the summation when:

$$\left| \frac{value\ of\ n'th\ term}{sum\ of\ series\ so\ far} \right| < accuracy \qquad terminate\ the\ iteration$$

Problem 16.2 Implement and test a program which evaluates $\log_e(x)$ using the series:

$$\log x = 2 \left[\frac{(x-1)}{(x+1)} + \frac{(x-1)^3}{3(x+1)^3} + \frac{(x-1)^5}{5(x+1)^5} \cdots \right] \qquad x > 0$$

Check that the relationship $x = e^{\log(x)}$ is true.

Problem 16.3 Implement and test a program which evaluates $\sin^{-1}(x)$ using the series:

$$\sin^{-1}(x) = x + \frac{x^3}{2.3} + \frac{1.3x^5}{2.4.5} + \frac{1.3.5x^7}{2.4.6.7} + \frac{1.3.5.7x^9}{2.4.6.8.9} \qquad x^2 < 1$$

which returns an angle in radians $-\pi/2 < \sin^{-1}(x) < \pi/2$.

Problem 16.4 Implement and test a program using the Newton-Raphson method to evaluate the root of:

$$f(x) = \cosh(x) + \cos(x) - 3 = 0$$

where:

$$f'(x) = \sinh(x) - \sin(x)$$

Start with an initial 'guess' of $x = 1.0$ and when the root has been evaluated print the value of the root together with the value of $f(x)$ at the root (which should be zero). Note that the root of the above equation is 1.85792.

17

Towards larger programs

A large program can consist of hundreds of functions and attention must now be paid to the problems of managing data storage and the flow of information between functions.

17.1 Data hiding

An important concept in Software Engineering is *data hiding*, i.e. program modules are kept as independent as possible by controlling the passage of information between modules and only allowing an individual module access to data that it actually uses. Different programming languages have different techniques to facilitate modular programming and data hiding, e.g. a modern language such as Modula 2 has more effective means than older languages such as Fortran, C and Pascal.

17.2 The scope of identifiers

The scope of a particular identifier determines where it may be used. For example:

1   Within a compound statement *internal* objects such as variables, arrays (see Chapter 18), etc., may be used from the point of declaration up to the end of the compound statement in which they are declared (such internal variables are called *automatics*).
2   The *formal parameters* of a function may be used from the point of declaration up to the end of the compound statement which forms the body of the function.

Although the same identifier may be declared in different compound statements the identifiers are distinct and do not refer to the same variable or object. An identifier declared within a compound statement will 'hide' any identifier with the same name declared outside.

17.3 External identifiers

External identifiers are function names and the names of objects declared outside functions. Their scope is from the point of declaration to the end of the file in which they are declared. In addition external identifiers may also be accessed from other files (see Chapter 21). A formal parameter declared in a function header or an internal identifier declared within a compound statement will 'hide' any external identifier of the same name. Because external identifiers may be accessed by any function which follows the declaration in the file they must be used with care if the concept of *data hiding* is to be maintained.

External variables are allocated storage and initialised prior to the start of program execution and maintained until the program terminates. They may be initialised with the proviso that the initial values are constants (simple internal variables may be initialised using expressions, e.g. line 22 of Program 16.1). External variables not explicitly initialised are initialised to zero when program execution starts.

```
 1 /* Program 17.1 - examples of scope of internal and external variables */
 2 #include <stdio.h>
 3
 4 float a = 2, b = 10;                         /* external variables a and b */
 5 const float pi = 3.14159f;              /* external const qualified variable */
 6
 7 int main(void)
 8 {
 9     int test(float, int);                        /* function prototype */
10     int i, x = 5;                          /* variables internal to main */
11     /* can use external a, b and pi and internal i and x */
12
13     for (i = 1 ; i < b ; i++)
14         {
15         int x = 2, y =10;
16         /* can use external a, b and pi, internal i and own internal x & y */
17
18         printf("\ni = %d, a = %f, b = %f, pi = %f, x = %d, y = %d, test = %d ",
19                 i, a, b, pi, x, y, test(a, x));
20         }
21     return 0;
22 }
23
24 int i = 2;                                    /* external variable i */
25
26 int test(float b, int j)                  /* formal parameters b and j */
27 {
28     /* can use external a, pi and i and formal parameters b and j */
29     a = a + j;                      /* altering value of external variable */
30     return (b * i);                              /* function result */
31 }
```

Program 17.1 Examples of scope of internal and external variables

Program 17.1 shows some simple examples of the scope of internal and external variables:

4	declare external variables a and b and assign initial values
5	declare external const qualified variable pi and assign it the value 3.14159f
7	start of function main
9	declare prototype for function test
10	declare variables internal to main
11	at this point external a, b and pi and internal i and x can be used
13-20	a for statement executed while i < b
	15 declare internal x and y (x declared in line 10 is now 'hidden')
	18-19 print various values including result of a call to function test
24	declare external variable i
26	function header for test with formal parameters b and j (the formal parameter b 'hides' the external variable b)
29	Assigns a new value to the external variable a
30	return a function result

Fig. 17.1 is a diagrammatic representation of the scope of identifiers in Program 17.1.

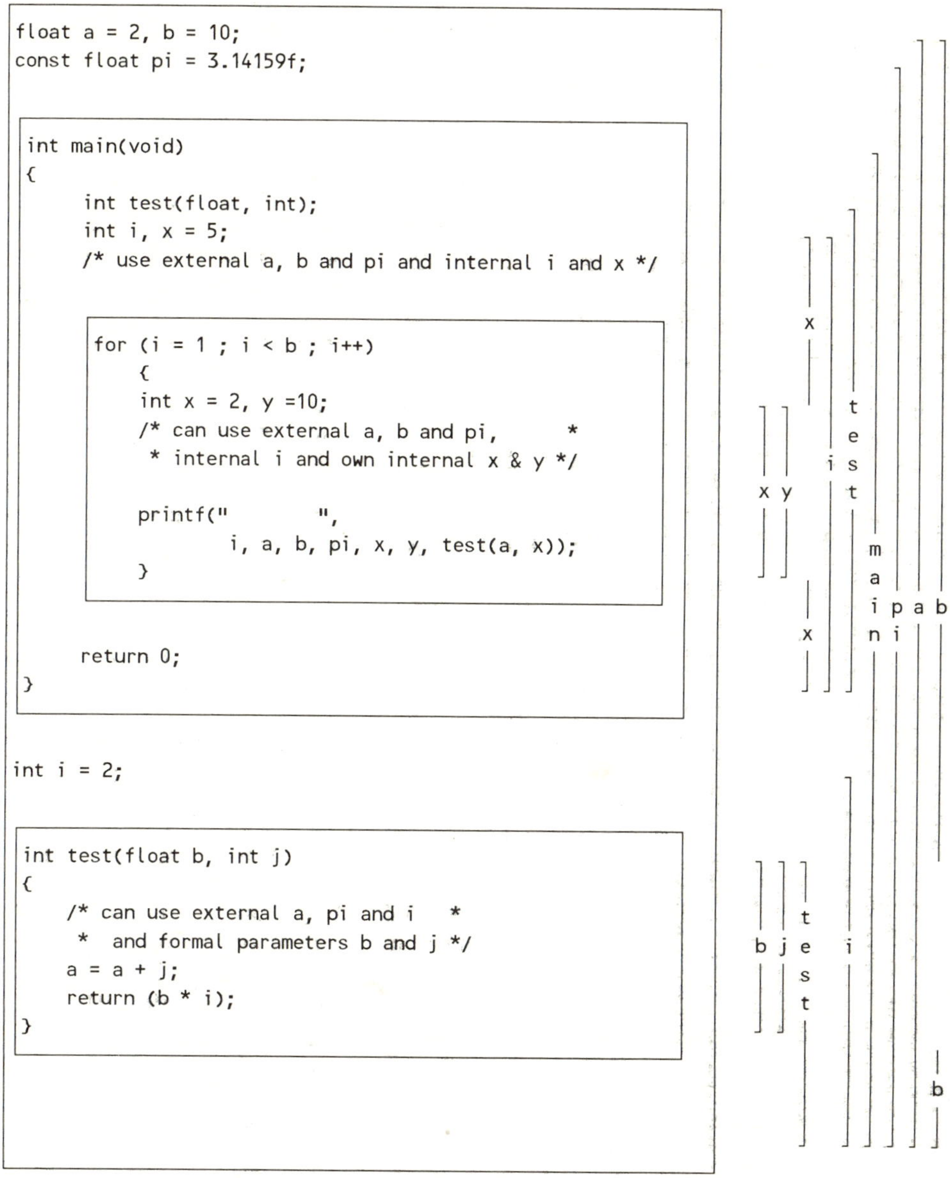

```
float a = 2, b = 10;
const float pi = 3.14159f;

int main(void)
{
        int test(float, int);
        int i, x = 5;
        /* use external a, b and pi and internal i and x */

                for (i = 1 ; i < b ; i++)
                {
                        int x = 2, y =10;
                        /* can use external a, b and pi,      *
                         * internal i and own internal x & y */

                        printf("        ",
                                i, a, b, pi, x, y, test(a, x));
                }

        return 0;
}

int i = 2;

int test(float b, int j)
{
        /* can use external a, pi and i     *
         *  and formal parameters b and j */
        a = a + j;
        return (b * i);
}
```

Fig. 17.1 Diagram showing the scope of internal and external variables in Program 17.1

Note:

1   The variable x declared in line 10 cannot be accessed from within the compound statement in lines 14 to 20 because it is 'hidden' by the declaration of x in line 15, i.e. any references within the compound statement will access the x declared in line 15. The variable x (and y) declared in line 15 will be lost when the compound statement finishes and any further references will access the x declared in line 10.

2   The formal parameter b declared in the header of function test 'hides' the external variable b declared in line 4.

Note that the external variable a which is an actual parameter to the call of function test in line 19 is altered within test in line 29. Such alterations to external variables can give rise to unforeseen *side effects* if great care is not taken and is therefore not recommended (see Chapter 21.10 for a discussion of side effects), e.g. work out on paper what the results of the program should be and then run the program; compare the results !

It can be seen that the same identifiers may refer to different things in different parts of the program. Program 17.1 purely shows the effect of identifier scope and it is not recommended practice to use the same name to mean several different things. If one forgets to declare a variable which is to be internal to a compound statement (e.g. variable x in line 15) and the same name is already declared, run time errors will occur which can be very difficult to find.

17.4 Evaluating pseudo random numbers using *external* variables

Internal variables within compound statements (such as function bodies) are created on entry and lost on exit, i.e. storage allocated and initialised on entry to the statement and deallocated on exit. There are occasions, however, when a function needs to store information between successive calls or where two or more functions need to access a common data set which should be 'hidden' from the calling function.

Consider a function which on successive calls returns the next number in a sequence of random numbers (such *random number generators* are often used in computer simulations of real life systems). The most common way to generate random numbers is the *linear congruential method* in which each number in a random sequence is calculated from its predecessor (MOD is the modulus operation, % in C):

$$number_{n+1} = (\text{multiplier} * number_n + \text{increment}) \text{ MOD } modulus$$

The sequence of numbers generated by this formula is not truly random in that given a particular starting value of $number_n$ (called the *seed*) the sequence generated is always the same. In general such a sequence is called a *pseudo-random sequence* and functions using it *pseudo-random* number generators. The start value of the sequence is called the *seed* and is usually supplied by the user or generated using some other 'random' technique (see below). For example, the standard library <stdlib.h> contains the following functions:

```
void srand(unsigned int seed);          /* set seed for random number sequence */
int rand(void);                          /* return random number in range 0 to RAND_MAX */
```

The function srand may be called to initialise the seed (default seed is 1) and then rand is called as often as required to get the next number in the sequence.

If the library function is not available the *linear congruential method* can be used with the following values:

$$number_{n+1} = (25173 * number_n + 13849) \text{ MOD } 65536$$

This will generate pseudo random numbers in the range 0 to 65535 (unsigned 16-bit numbers) and will not cause overflow so long as 32-bit numbers are used in the calculation. The seed $number_n$ is given an initial value and the algorithm will generate 65536 random numbers before repeating itself. To implement such an algorithm as a C function the value of the seed must be stored between successive calls to the function and this can be achieved in a number of ways:

1   The calling function could store the seed and pass the value to the random number function when it is called. This causes problems if the function is at the end of a long sequence of function calls or is called from a number of different functions.

2   The value could be stored in an external variable.

3   The value could be stored in a *static* internal variable (see next section).

```
 2
 3 #include <stdio.h>
 4 #include <time.h>
 5
 6 int main(void)
 7 {
 8     void random_initialise(void);                    /* function prototypes */
 9     unsigned int random_number(void);
10     int i;
11
12     random_initialise();                             /* initialise seed */
13     for (i=0; i < 10 ; i++)
14         printf("\n %10u", random_number());          /* print next number */
15     return 0;
16 }
17
18 /*-------------------------------------------------------------------*
19  * Pseudo random number generator functions                         */
20
21 unsigned int random_seed;      /* external variable holds random number seed */
22
23 /* Function to initialise pseudo random number generator             */
24 void random_initialise(void)
25 {
26     /*  To start with a 'random' seed set seed to the calender time */
27     random_seed = (unsigned int) time(NULL);
28 }
29
30 /* Function to return pseudo random number (set_random must be called first)  */
31 unsigned int random_number(void)
32 {
33     /* calculate next value of seed and return value */
34     random_seed = (unsigned int) ((25173UL * random_seed + 13849UL) % 65536UL);
35     return random_seed;
36 }
```

Program 17.2 Pseudo random number generator using external variables

Program 17.2 consists of function `main` plus:

```
void random_initialise(void);                    /* initialise seed */
unsigned int random_number(void);                /* return next random number */
```

An external variable `seed` is used to pass information between the functions and store information between successive calls of `random_number`. The program sequence of function `main`, lines 6 to 16 is:

lines

8-9   function prototypes random_initialise and random_number
12   call random_initialise to initialise the value of seed
13-14   a for statement which calls random_number ten times and prints the result

Line 21 declares the variable random_seed which, being declared outside a function body, is external. The sequence of events in function random_initialise, lines 24 to 28, is:

lines

24   function header indicating no parameters and no function result
27   initialise seed with the current time; the function time (defined in <time.h>, see Appendix C.15) returns the calendar time using type time_t (typically long int) and the cast converts it to unsigned int (discarding any high-order bits)

Thus seed is initialised from the current time and successive runs of the program will start with different values of seed (unless run within the same second). The sequence of statements in function random_number, lines 31 to 36, is:

lines

31   function header, no parameters and returns an unsigned int function result
34   calculate the next value of seed (UL makes the constants unsigned long int)
35   return the function result, i.e. the next pseudo random number in the sequence

In line 34 the calculation is performed using unsigned long int arithmetic (minimum 32-bit numbers to avoid overflow; see discussion of algorithm above) and the result cast to unsigned int (the function returns a number in the range 0 to 65535; an unsigned 16-bit number). These requirements are satisfied by the minimum range the ANSI C standard specifies for unsigned int and unsigned long int (see Chapter 7.1).

17.5 *Static* internal variables

The major problem with Program 17.2 is that other functions apart from random_initialise and random_number have access to the external variable seed and may corrupt its value. If only one function needs to maintain the values of variables between successive calls *static* internal variables are more suitable. *Static* internal variables have the same scope as automatic internal variables but are allocated storage and initialised prior to the start of program execution and maintained until the program terminates, i.e. the permanent information is 'hidden' within the function. The variables can be explicitly initialised (using constants, not expressions, as in line 22 of Program 16.1) and if not are initialised to zero. The values stored in *static* internal variables can be changed during program execution with the updated values available when the statement is reentered.

17.6 Evaluating Fibonacci numbers using *static* internal variables

The Fibonacci numbers (0 1 1 2 3 5 8 13 21 34 55 89 144 233 377 610 987 etc.) are evaluated using the following relationship:

$$F_0 = 0 \text{ and } F_1 = 1 \text{ then } F_{n+2} = F_{n+1} + F_n$$

A function which evaluates the numbers needs to the store values of F_n and F_{n+1} between successive calls and *static* internal variables are the simplest way to do this. For example, the function fibonacci, in Program 17.3, contains the following (line 23):

```
static long int fn_plus1 = 0, fn_plus2 = 1;     /* initialise f(0) & f(1) */
```

The variables declared are internal to the function but because the type is prefixed with the keyword static they are made permanent and initialised with the values of the first two Fibonacci numbers:

fn_plus1 holds the next value of F_n to be returned by the function

fn_plus2 holds F_{n+1}

On successive calls to fibonacci the variables are updated with the next values in the sequence, i.e.:

26 fn = fn_plus1; copy current value of F_n to local variable (will be the function result)
27 fn_plus1 = fn_plus2; evaluate F_{n+1}
28 fn_plus2 = fn + fn_plus1; evaluate F_{n+2}
29 return (fn); return current value of F_n

Because fn_plus1 and fn_plus2 are static internal variables the updated values are available on the next call to the function.

```
 1 /* Program 17.3 -Evaluating Fibonacci numbers using static internal variables */
 2
 3 #include <stdio.h>
 4
 5 int main(void)
 6 {
 7     long int fibonacci(void);                  /* function prototype */
 8     long int counter;
 9
10     for (counter = 1; counter < 20 ; counter++)       /* print 20 numbers */
11         printf("%ld ", fibonacci());
12     return 0;
13 }
14
15 /*----------------------------------------------------------------*
16  * Function to return Fibonacci numbers, i.e.: 0 1 1 2 3 5 8 13 etc.        *
17  *   evaluated thus: f(0) = 0, f(1) = 1,   f(n+2) = f(n+1) + f(n)           *
18  * Function result: on successive calls return next Fibonacci number        *
19  *----------------------------------------------------------------*/
20 long int fibonacci(void)
21 {
22     /* declare Fibonacci numbers in static internal variables */
23     static long int fn_plus1 = 0, fn_plus2 = 1;    /* initialise f(0) & f(1) */
24     long int fn;
25
26     fn = fn_plus1;                             /* set up f(n) */
27     fn_plus1 = fn_plus2;                       /* set up next f(n+1) */
28     fn_plus2 = fn + fn_plus1;                  /* set up next f(n+2) */
29     return (fn);                               /* return current f(n) */
30 }
```

Program 17.3   Evaluation of Fibonacci numbers (using static internal variables)

17.7 Summary: internal and external variables

automatic internal variables are allocated storage (and optionally initialised) on entry to a
compound statement and deallocated on exit from the compound statement (any
contents are then lost).   Automatic internal variables may be initialised with any
meaningful expression (every time the statement is reentered the automatic variables
are recreated and reinitialised).   The contents of automatic internal variables not
explicitly initialised will be *undefined*. These are the 'normal' working variables of
the program.

Static internal variables are allocated storage (and initialised) prior to the start of program
execution and maintained until the program terminates. The variables can be explicitly
initialised (using constants, not expressions) and if not are initialised to zero.   The
values stored in *static* internal variables can be changed during program execution with
the updated values available when the statement is reentered. These are generally used
when a single function needs to retain information between successive calls and the
information should be 'hidden' within the function and not accessible from outside.

external variables are allocated storage and initialised prior to the start of program
execution and maintained until the program terminates. The variables can be explicitly
initialised (using constants, not expressions) and if not are initialised to zero. These
are used when a number of functions need to access a common data set; such functions
would be placed in a separate file which forms a module within the complete program
(multi-file programs are discussed in Chapter 21).

Exercise 17.1 (see Appendix B for sample answer)

Modify Program 17.2 replacing the functions random_initialise and random_number with a
single function which returns a float pseudo random number in the range 0 to 1.0, e.g.:

```
float random_number(void);                            /* function prototype */
```

The seed should be stored within random_number as a static internal variable which is
initialised on the first call to the function (from the current time as in Program 17.2). It is
suggested that the calculations are performed using unsigned long int and the result
converted to a float in the return statement.

17.8 Defining new type names using *typedef*

The keyword *typedef* enables the creation of new data type names, e.g.:

```
typedef float object_area_t;
typedef float object_volume_t;
typedef int   loop_counter_t;
```

The identifiers object_area_t and object_volume_t are synonyms or alternative names for
the type float and loop_counter_t is a synonym for int. Once a new type name has been
specified it can be used to declare variables, e.g.:

```
object_area_t    circle_area, sphere_area, cylinder_area;
object_volume_t  sphere_volume, cylinder_volume;
loop_counter_t   counter_1, counter_2;
```

It must be emphasised, however, that *typedef* does not create a new type, just an alternative name. The variables `circle_area`, `sphere_area`, etc. are variables of type `float`, having the same properties and obeying the same rules as other `float` variables. It can, however, help the overall semantics and readability of the program to use meaningful names such as `object_area_t` and `object_volume_t` instead of `float`. Enumeration types (see Chapter 7.4) may also be defined using *typedef*, e.g.:

```
typedef enum {Bolt, Washer, Nut, Lock_nut, Nylon_nut} component_t;
component_t component_1, component_2;

scanf("%d", &component_1);
if (component_1 == Washer)
    printf("\n component %d is a washer", component_1);
component_2 = Lock_nut;
```

A new integral type `component_t` is defined together with its set of enumerators. Variables of the type are then declared and used (note that `scanf` reads an integer number not 'washer').

The keyword *typedef* obeys the same scope rules as declarations therefore new type names may be specified within compound statements or a program source file may start with the specification of new types that will be used within the functions in the file.

To make type identifiers stand out in a program it is wise to have a convention for assigning names, e.g. in the above the names are terminated with _t.

17.9 The preprocessor *#define* directive

The preprocessor *#define* directive takes the following general form:

```
#define IDENTIFIER  replacement_text
```

Being a preprocessor directive the `#define` statement should be on a separate line and not terminated with a `;`. The preprocessor, when it reads the program source code file replaces all occurrences of `IDENTIFIER` with the `replacement_text`. For example:

```
#define ARRAY_SIZE 100
#define MAX_TEMPERATURE 50.0
```

The identifiers `ARRAY_SIZE` and `MAX_TEMPERATURE` are called *symbolic constants* and by convention are in upper case. When the preprocessor reads the program file all occurrences of the symbolic constants are replaced with the corresponding `replacement_text` using literal substitution. For example, all occurrences of `MAX_TEMPERATURE` are replaced with 50.0:

```
#define MAX_TEMPERATURE 50.0f
    if (temperature > MAX_TEMPERATURE)
    ........
```

After preprocessing the compiler would get:

```
    if (temperature > 50.0f)
    ........
```

Hence the compiler knows nothing about symbolic constants. Remember that the preprocessor performs literal substitution and an error in a preprocessor directive will appear at compile time in a line of code that may look perfectly OK. For example, if a `;`

has been typed on the end of the #define by mistake:

```
#define MAX_TEMPERATURE 50.0f;
    if (temperature > MAX_TEMPERATURE)
        ........
```

After preprocessing the compiler would get:

```
    if (temperature > 50.0;)
        ........
```

and generate an error due to the ; being in the wrong place. For example, Microsoft C Version 6.00 generated the following error messages:

```
    6        if (temperature > MAX_TEMPERATURE)
***** X.C(6) : error C2143: syntax error : missing ')' before ';'
***** X.C(6) : error C2143: syntax error : missing ';' before ')'
```

The problem is that the line of code where the error was found (line 6 in this case) looks correct; the error being in the #define directive. Such errors can be quite difficult to find especially when #define is used to generate macros with parameters (see Chapter 26.1). Most compilers provide some means of examining the output of the preprocessor to track down such errors, e.g. the /P option of the Microsoft C version 6.00 compiler CL.EXE.

The #define directives are normally placed at the start of a file following the #include directives, and have file scope, i.e. from the #define to the end of the current file. However, the #undef directive may be used to 'undefine' an identifier.

The #define directive is used extensively in header files to define symbolic constants relevant to the library concerned, e.g. symbolic constants such as INT_MIN, INT_MAX, etc. in <limits.h>. Symbolic constants can be used to improve program maintainability and readability by using relevant names for constants within the program. It must be emphasised, however, that the compiler knows nothing about symbolic constants and can perform no optimisation (unlike const qualified objects which the compiler knows about).

An alternative to using the preprocessor #define directive when defining int constants is to use the enumerative type, e.g.:

```
    enum {Max_temperature = 50, Array_size = 100};
    if (temperature > Max_temperature)
        ........
```

There are two advantages to using this technique:

1   The enumerative type obeys the same scope rules as declarations (not file scope as #define) and the constants can therefore be internal to a compound statement.
2   Because the compiler knows about the enumerations it can generate information to enable a debugger to print the values in symbolic form (#define is a preprocessor directive and the compiler knows nothing about the symbolic constants, only the equivalent constants).

There will be further discussion on these points when the specification of array sizes is discussed in the next chapter.

Problem for Chapter 17

Modify line 9 of Program 5.3 to use a #define directive instead of a const qualified variable. Preprocess the file and examine the resultant output.

18

One dimensional arrays

Many applications require the storing and processing of large sequences of data elements. For example, an experiment may require the sampling of the temperature and pressure of a liquid over a period of ten seconds with readings taken every tenth of a second. If the data from the experiment is to be processed by a computer a means is required to store two hundred values (one hundred of each of temperature and pressure). It would be possible to declare two hundred separate identifiers:

```
int temperature_1, temperature_2, temperature_3 etc.
int pressure_1, pressure_2, pressure_3 etc.
```

which although possible is very clumsy and long winded. The C programming language provides three ways of grouping basic types into data structures:

An array   a fixed sized group in which the elements are of the same type
A structure   a fixed sized group in which the elements are of dissimilar types
A union   an overlap of different structures

18.1 Declaring and initialising arrays
The declaration of an array has the following general form:

```
array_type   array_name[array_size];
```

where:

```
array_type   is the type of the array elements
array_name   is the identifier or name of the array
array_size   is an integer constant which specifies the number of elements in the array
```

For example:

```
int temperatures[100], pressures[100];
```

This declares two arrays temperatures and pressures both of size one hundred int elements. Arrays may be declared along with simple variables of that type, e.g.:

```
int temperature, temperatures[100], min_temperature, max_temperature;
```

In the above declaration only temperatures is an array, the others are simple int variables. It is also possible to use *typedef* to define a new array type and then declare variables, e.g.:

```
typedef int data_array_t[100];                    /* define a new type */
data_array_t temperatures, pressures;             /* and declare variables */
```

It is very important to note that when declaring arrays the size or dimension of the array must be a positive integer specified by an **integer constant** or a **constant expression** which yields an integer type, e.g.:

```
int temperatures[100], pressures[100 * 2];
```

In this case temperatures has one hundred elements and pressures two hundred, e.g. in an experiment the pressure may be sampled twice as often as the temperature (*#define* and *enum* can be used to define integer constants which can be used to specify array size, see section 18.7). It is not possible to declare dynamic arrays although dynamic arrays can be created at run time using the `calloc` and `malloc` functions (see Chapter 28).

18.1.2 Array initialisation

The contents of an array may be initialised when it is declared:

```
float voltages[5] = {3.6, 56.0, 5.0e-6, 2.0e4, 95.0};
int test_data[10] = {2, 5, 78, -9, 67, -3, 34, -9};
```

The initial values must be constants (simple internal variables may be initialised using expressions, e.g. Program 16.1 line 22). The second example initialises the first eight of the ten array elements. Any elements not explicitly initialised will be initialised to 0. If an array is not initialised the element values are *undefined* if it is internal or zero if it is external or a static internal. A simple way to initialise all the elements of an array to 0 is:

```
float array[20] = {0}                       /* initialise all elements to 0 */
```

element `array[0]` is explicitly initialised to 0 and the remainder zeroed automatically.

If the size of the array is not specified the number of initialisers will be used to determine its size, e.g. in the following the array `Fibonacci` has fifteen elements:

```
int Fibonacci[] = {0, 1, 2, 3, 5, 8, 13, 21, 34, 55, 89, 144, 233, 377, 610};
printf("%d %d \n", sizeof(Fibonacci), sizeof(Fibonacci[0]));
```

This fragment of code shows the use of the `sizeof` operator with arrays, i.e. `sizeof(Fibonacci)` returns the number of bytes used to store the whole array and `sizeof(Fibonacci[0])` returns the number of bytes required to store one element.

18.2 Accessing the elements of an array

The elements of an array are accessed using an integer subscript or index which ranges from 0 to array_size - 1, e.g.:

```
int array_index, temperatures[100], pressures[100];

temperatures[0] = 0;                /* zero first element of the array */
temperatures[4] = 20;               /* assign 20 to the fifth element */
value = temperatures[99];           /* assign the value of the last element */
printf(temperatures[10]);           /* print the eleventh element */
```

The size of array `temperatures` is 100 elements hence the value of the index range is 0 to 99. Because the index starts from 0, the first element is `temperatures[0]`, second `temperatures[1]` and last `temperatures[99]`. A for statement can be used to zero all the elements of the array:

```
for (array_index = 0 ; array_index < 100 ; array_index++)
    temperatures[array_index] = 0;
```

It is very important to note that the array index starts at 0; a common error is to use the Fortran convention where the index range is 1 to array_size. C performs no array bound checking so an invalid index will access memory outside the array. This can lead to the corruption of memory contents (program or data) or a run time error where the program may halt with a message such as 'memory segmentation error'. Such faults can be very difficult to find, e.g. when the corruption of data shows up much later in a different function which has nothing to do with the original array.

A difference between arrays and all other types is that the name of an object generally refers to the contents of the object whereas the name of an array refers to the address of the first element in memory (in fact the name of an array is a *pointer* to the first element). This may appear to be a rather subtle point but it has major implications in the way arrays are treated, in particular how arrays are passed to functions (discussed in section 18.4). Consider the following assignment statement where x and y are float variables:

```
x = y;                                    /* assign the value of y to x */
```

The equivalent statement for arrays is not allowed:

```
pressures = temperatures;                  /* illegal for arrays */
```

If pressures and temperatures are arrays the names refer to address of the first elements and the statement is therefore illegal, i.e. the start address of array pressures cannot be assigned the value of the start address of array temperatures. To assign the contents of one array to another the arrays must be copied element by element, e.g.:

```
for (array_index = 0 ; array_index < 100 ; array_index++)
      pressures[array_index] = temperatures[array_index];
```

18.3 Program to calculate the average of a sequence of real numbers

Exercise 9.2 implemented a program to calculate the average of a sequence of up to six real numbers. The sample answer (see Appendix B) declared six variables x1, x2, x3, x4, x5 and x6 which held the numbers read. Program 18.1 (next page) calculates the average of a sequence of real numbers using an array to hold the values. The average is evaluated by summing the elements of the array and dividing by the number of elements, i.e.:

$$\text{average of array } x = \sum_{i=1}^{n} x_i \, / \, n$$

Where Σ indicates summation, x_i are the elements of the array and n is the number of elements. The specification of the program is:

1   The program will terminate when EOF is entered.
2   A maximum of up to ten numbers will be processed on a line by line basis:
    (a) less than ten numbers will be terminated by a newline,
    (b) if more than ten numbers are entered on a line they will be summed in groups of up to ten,
    (c) invalid characters will be reported and the program will then continue.

The sequence of statements in Program 18.1 is:

14   prompt the user for input
15   initialise index to zero (to index first element of array data)
16-36   a while statement calling scanf to read one real number into element data[index]
               (the while terminates when EOF is entered)
     17-18   if scanf failed to convert one number print message and character in error
    else

21	echo number and increment index to index next element of array data
22-23	removes any space characters from the input stream
24	push the last character (read by line 23) back into the input stream (ready for the next call of scanf)
27	if the last character was \n (newline) or the array index == 10
29-30	sum the contents of the array data from 0 to index - 1
31-32	print the average
33-34	prompt for next input and reset index to start of array data

Line 27 ensures that the array bounds are not exceeded, i.e. if ten numbers have been entered the average of the ten is calculated and then scanf called again.

```
 1 /* Program 18.1  - to calculate the average of a sequence of real  numbers    *
 2  * (a) a sequence of numbers is terminated with newline <CR>                   *
 3  * (b) a maximum of ten numbers may be processed at one time                   *
 4  * (c) report invalid character and terminate program on EOF                   */
 5
 6 #include <stdio.h>
 7
 8 int main(void)
 9 {
10     float average, data[10];
11     int converted, ch, index, i;
12
13     /* read one real number, terminate on EOF */
14     printf("\nEnter up to ten numbers (<CR> to end) \n    ? ");
15     index = 0;
16     while ((converted = scanf("%f", &data[index])) != EOF)
17         if (converted != 1)                                   /* read error */
18             printf("\n illegal character %c in input, try again\n", getchar());
19         else
20             {                                             /* number read OK */
21             printf("%6.1f ", data[index++]);
22             while ((ch = getchar()) == ' ')               /* remove spaces */
23                 /* null statement */;
24             ungetc(ch, stdin);                        /* push last character */
25
26             /* if newline or index = 10 calculate average */
27             if ((ch == '\n') || (index == 10))
28                 {
29                 for (average = i = 0 ; i < index ; i++)
30                     average = average + data[i];
31                 printf("\n  Average of %d numbers = %f ",
32                                     index, average / index);
33                 printf("\n\nEnter up to ten numbers (<CR> to end) \n    ? ");
34                 index = 0;
35                 }
36             }
37     return 0;
38 }
```

Program 18.1 Calculate the average of a sequence of real numbers

18.4 Arrays as function parameters

In C, all *actual parameters* are passed to a function using *call by value*, i.e. copies of the *actual parameters* are made in temporary variables and these are passed.   Arrays, however, *appear* to be an exception in that they are passed using *call by reference*.

Section 18.2 explained that the name of an array refers to the address of the first element. Hence, when an array name appears in a function call the actual parameter is the address of the first element and this is passed to the function (not a copy of the values stored in the array). Within the function the address is then used to access the memory allocated to the original array. Consider a function array_write which prints the contents of a five element float array to the screen. The code in the calling function could be:

```
void array_write(float array[5]);            /* function prototype */
float data[5] = {1.0, 2.0, 3.0, 4.0, 5.0};   /* initialised array */

array_write(data);                           /* call function */
```

The function prototype tells the compiler that array_write has one parameter which is an array of type float. When the function is called the compiler can check that there is one parameter and that it is an array of the correct type (because arrays are passed using *call by reference* there can be no conversion of types). The statement:

```
array_write(data);                           /* call function */
```

passes the address of the first element of array data as the first (and only) actual parameter. The function can then use the address to directly access the contents of array data.   An example of the function code is:

```
/ * function to print an array of 5 elements */
void array_write(float array[5])
{
    int index;
    for (index = 0 ; index < 5 ; index++)
        printf("%f ", array[index]);
}
```

The [5] following the name array declares that the first formal parameter is an array (otherwise it would be a variable). Inside the function the name of the formal parameter is a synonym for the name of the array in the calling function, i.e. when function array_write uses the name array it accesses the memory allocated to array data in main.

In the above example the array size was specified in the function header. In practice it can be specified or not; it makes no difference because C does no array bound checking and the function could be called with arrays of different sizes. It is up to the programmer to ensure that the bounds of the array are not exceeded. In this case the programmer must ensure that array_write is called with arrays of five elements or greater (only the first five elements will be printed). If the function is to process arrays of different sizes the size of the array must be passed into the function, see Program 18.2.

The important thing to remember is that arrays are passed using *call by reference* and the called function has access to memory allocated to the original array. An array may be passed as a parameter through a sequence of function calls and the final function will still have access to the original array.

In addition, because an array name refers to the address of the first element, not the contents, **arrays cannot be returned as function results**.

18.5 Functions to read, write and manipulate arrays

```
 1  /* Program 18.2 - Array read, write & reverse.  Find maximum & minimum values */
 2
 3  #include <stdio.h>
 4
 5  int main(void)
 6  {
 7      int array_read(float array[], const int max_index);         /* prototypes */
 8      void array_write(const float array[], const int number);
 9      int array_maximum(const float array[], const int number);
10      int array_minimum(const float array[], int number);
11      void array_reverse(float array[], const int number);
12
13      float  data[10] = {0};                                /* data array */
14      int index;                                /* number of elements in data */
15
16      while ((index = array_read(data, 10)) > 0)   /* read array, exit on EOF */
17         {
18         array_write(data, index);                           /* write array */
19         printf("\n maximum %f", data[array_maximum(data, index)]); /* maximum */
20         printf("\n minimum %f", data[array_minimum(data, index)]); /* minimum */
21         data[array_maximum(data, index)] = 100;          /* replace maximum */
22         data[array_minimum(data, index)] = -100;         /* replace minimum */
23         array_reverse(data, index);                       /* reverse array */
24         array_write(data, index);                           /* write array */
25         }
26      return 0;
27  }
28
29  /*-----------------------------------------------------------------*
30   * function to read up to max_number values into array,            *
31   *    return  number of values read or 0 for EOF                   */
32  int array_read(float array[], const int max_number)
33  {
34      int converted, index = 0, ch = 0;
35
36      printf("\n\nEnter up to %d numbers (<CR> to end) \n   ? ", max_number);
37      while ((converted = scanf("%f", &array[index])) != EOF)
38         if (converted != 1)                              /* read error ? */
39            printf("\n illegal character %c in input, try again\n", getchar());
40         else
41            {
42            while ((ch = getchar()) == ' ')     /* get next non space character */
43               /* null statement */;
44            ungetc(ch, stdin);                     /* push last character back */
45            if ((++index == max_number) || (ch == '\n'))
46               return index;                                 /* return OK */
47            }
48      return 0;                                  /* return EOF indicator */
49  }
```

Program 18.2 Functions to read, write and manipulate arrays (continued on next page)

```
50
51 /*--------------------------------------------------------------------*
52  * function to print an array of number elements, print five values per line  */
53 void array_write(const float array[], const int number)
54 {
55     int index;
56
57     for (index = 0 ; index < number ; index++)
58         printf("%c%10.3f", (index % 5) ? ' ' : '\n', array[index]);
59 }
60
61 /*--------------------------------------------------------------------*
62  * function to find the maximum value in an array of number elements      *
63  *  function result: return index to element with maximum value          */
64 int array_maximum(const float array[], const int number)
65 {
66     int index,                              /* general array index */
67         index_max = 0;                      /* index to maximum, initialise to 0 */
68
69     for (index = 1 ; index < number ; index++)
70         if (array[index] > array[index_max])        /* new maximum value ? */
71             index_max = index;                       /* if so note index */
72     return index_max;
73 }
74
75 /*--------------------------------------------------------------------*
76  * function to find the minimum value in an array of number elements      *
77  *  function result: return index to element with minimum value          */
78 int array_minimum(const float array[], int number)
79 {
80     int index_min = 0;                  /* index to minimum, initialise to 0 */
81
82     for (number-- ; number > 0 ; number--)
83         if (array[number] < array[index_min])       /* new minimum value ? */
84             index_min = number;                      /* if so note index */
85     return index_min;
86 }
87
88 /*--------------------------------------------------------------------*
89  * function to reverse the contents of an array                          */
90 void array_reverse(float array[], const int number)
91 {
92     int up, down;                           /* up and down array index values */
93     float value;                            /* temporary data store */
94
95     for (up = 0, down = number-1 ; up < down ; up++, down--)
96         (value = array[up], array[up] = array[down], array[down] = value);
97 }
```

Program 18.2 Functions to read, write and manipulate arrays

Program 18.2 contains six functions:

main	a test program calling the other functions
array_read	which reads real numbers into a float array
array_write	which prints the contents of a float array
array_maximum	which returns the index to the element with the maximum value
array_minimum	which returns the index to the element with the minimum value
array_reverse	which reverses the elements of an array

The sequence of statements in function main, lines 5 to 27, is:

lines
7-11	declare function prototypes
13	declare array data initialised to 0
14	declare index which will hold number of elements in the array data
16-25	a for statement which reads an array and processes it

    16   call array_read to read the array, terminate for on EOF
    18   write the contents of array data
    19   call array_maximum to find maximum value in array
    20   call array_minimum to find minimum value in array
    21   replace maximum value with 100
    22   replace minimum value with -100
    23   call array_reverse to reverse the contents of the array
    24   print array contents again
26   terminate program

The functions array_maximum and array_minimum are both called twice which is inefficient. A modification would be to assign the index value returned to a variable and then use that.

    The function array_read will read up to max_number real values into array terminating when EOF or *newline* is entered or when the array contains max_number values. The function returns, as a function result, the number of values in the array, or 0 for EOF. The sequence of statements in function array_read, lines 32 to 49 is:

32   int array_read(float array[], const int max_number)
        is the function header specifying that:
        (a) it returns a int function result (the number of values read or 0 for EOF)
        (b) it has two parameters, the array and max_number
36   prompts the user to enter up to max_number numbers
37-47   a while statement which terminates when EOF is entered
    37   call scanf to read one number (terminate the while on EOF)
    38   if scanf failed print error message and character in error
    else
    42-43 read **stdin** input stream looking for next non-space character
    44   ungetc last character (ready for next scanf call)
    45   if array is full (index == max_number) **or** last character was *newline*
        46   return to calling function, index contains the number of values entered
48   EOF has been entered, return 0 to indicate EOF

Now consider the function header, line 32:

```
int array_read(float array[], const int max_number)
```

The [] following the name array tells the compiler that the first formal parameter is an array (otherwise it would be a variable).

In the function main the prototype for function array_read is declared in line 7 and it is called in line 16:

```
while ((index = array_read(data, 10)) > 0)    /* read array, exit on EOF */
    {
    ...
    }
```

the function array_read is called with the actual arguments:

data   the array to be passed
10   the size of the array data

The value of the address of the first element of data is passed to the function array_read (the function prototype enables the compiler to check that the first formal parameter is an address). The function returns either the number of values read or 0 for EOF. Because arrays are passed using *call by reference* the values read from the keyboard by array_read are placed directly in array data declared in the function main.

The function array_write, lines 53 to 59, prints the contents of an array on the display screen. The sequence of statements is:

53   `void array_write(const float array[], const int number)`
            is the function header specifying:
            (a) it does not return a function result
            (b) it has two parameters, the array and the number of elements
57-58   a for statement printing the elements of array from index 0 to number-1

Note the use of the conditional operator ? in line 58:

```
printf("%c%10.3f", (index % 5) ? ' ' : '\n', array[index]);
```

The function array_write prints five numbers to a line. The scanf control string "%c%10.3f" converts a character (calculated from index) and a float (array[index]). The condition operator ? selects the character, i.e. if index % 5 is non zero a space is printed otherwise a *newline* is printed.

The function array_maximum, lines 64 to 73, scans an array looking for the maximum value. The sequence of statements is:

64   `int array_maximum(const float array[], const int number)`
            is the function header specifying that:
            (a) it returns an int function result (index to the maximum value found)
            (b) it has two parameters, the array and the number of elements
67   declare index_max and initialise it to 0 (assuming array[0] contains is the maximum)
69   a for statement scanning the array for the maximum value
            index is incremented from 1 to number-1 when the for terminates
        70   if the value of array element array[index] is greater than array[index_max]
                71   set index_max to index
72   return index_max as the function result (index to the element with the maximum value)

The function array_minimum, lines 78 to 86, scans an array looking for the minimum value. Although it could be written in a similar manner to array_maximum the algorithm used is different:

78   int array_minimum(const float array[], int number) the function header
80   declare index_min and initialise it to 0 (assuming array[0] contains the minimum)
82   a for statement scanning the array for the minimum value
    number is decremented from its initial value - 1 to 0 when the for terminates
      83   if the value of array element array[number] is less than array[index_min]
          84   set index_min to number (the current index)
85   return index_min as the function result (index to the element with the minimum value)

Note that the formal parameter number is used as the array index (hence it is not const qualified as in the header of function array_maximum). In line 82 the for statement is initialised by decrementing number so that it indexes the last element of the array (number is then decremented to 0 when the for terminates).

The function array_reverse, lines 90 to 97, reverses the elements of an array, the sequence of statements is:

90   void array_reverse(float array[], const int number) is the function header
92   int up, down; two array indices, i.e.:
    up increments up the array and down decrements down the array
95   a for statement which:
    (a) increments up from 0
    (b) decrements down from number-1
    (c) terminates when up = down
    (d) increments up and decrements down on each iteration
96   swaps the two array elements array[up] and array[down]

Note the use of the comma or sequence operator in lines 95 and 96:

```
for (up = 0, down = number-1 ; up < number/2 ; up++, down--)
    (value = array[up], array[up] = array[down], array[down] = value);
```

Line 95, in particular, is a very good example of its use where there are two array indices, up indexing up the array and down indexing down the array. Line 96 is a single statement using the comma operator which could have been written as the compound statement:

```
{
value = array[up];
array[up] = array[down];
array[down] = value);
}
```

Which is used is a matter of programming style but use the comma operator with restraint because excessive use can lead to code which is difficult to read and maintain.

The majority of the formal function parameters in Program 18.2 are const qualified, i.e. if the function attempts to alter a value a warning or error will be issued. This is particularly important with arrays because the function has access to the memory allocated to the array, not just a copy of its value. Only functions array_read and array_reverse need to alter the array values and the corresponding formal parameter is not const qualified.

18.6 Summary: arrays as function parameters

A difference between arrays and all other types is that the name of an object generally refers to the contents of the object whereas the name of an array refers to the address of the first element in memory (the name is a *pointer* to the first element). One of the effects of this is that arrays are passed using *call by reference* in that when an array name appears in a function call the *actual parameter* is the address of the first element and this (not a copy of the values stored in the array) is passed to the function. Within the function the address is used to access the memory allocated to the original array, e.g. line 18 of Program 18.2:

```
array_write(data, index);                                    /* write array */
```

The array name data, represents the memory address of the first element, and **the value of this address** is passed to the function. In the function header of array_write the first formal parameter is specified as an array therefore the function will expect an address and be able to access the memory allocated to the array via the name of the formal parameter.

When an array name is followed by a subscript enclosed in [] operators the complete expression refers to the contents of the specified element, e.g. line 58 of Program 18.2:

```
printf("%c%10.3f", (index % 5) ? ' ' : '\n', array[index]);
```

The expression array[index] refers to the contents of an element of the array and its **value** is passed to printf.

In C arrays and pointers have a very close relationship and the function header of array_write can generally be written using pointer notation without any other modification:

```
void array_write(const float *array, const int number)
```

The first formal parameter is a 'pointer to an object of type float'. Inside the function the name array can be used with subscripts as normal. The use of pointer notation in function headers is common in particular in the descriptions of library functions. There will be more discussion when pointers are described in Chapters 23 and 24. Note that when using pointer notation (as above) there is no way to tell if array is a pointer to a simple float variable or to an array of float (further discussion in Chapter 24.5)

To summarise, when an array name is an actual parameter in a function call it is the value of the address of the first element which is passed. The address is used inside the function to access the original array. Thus although the actual parameter is passed using *call by value* the overall effect is that arrays are passed using *call by reference*. If the contents of an array should not be altered the formal parameter should be const qualified.

Note that library <string.h> contains functions to manipulate arrays, e.g. memset to set all elements to a value, memcpy to copy an array, memchr and memcmp to search an array, etc.

18.7 Using *#define* and *enum* to specify the array size

Programs should be as portable as possible and the size of particular arrays may be dependent upon the target application. To have to edit a large program changing dozens of array sizes in declarations would be a time consuming and error prone task and some method is therefore required of associating a name with an integer constant and then using the name in declarations. The are two methods of doing this:

1 Using the preprocessor #define directive to define a *symbolic constant* (see Chapters 17.9 and 26.1.
2 Using the enumerative type to define an integer constant (see Chapter 7.4).

For example, using #define:

```
#define ARRAY_SIZE 100
    int temperatur‑s[ARRAY_SIZE], pressures[ARRAY_SIZE];
```

The #define is a preprocessor directive (it is on a line by itself and not terminated by a ;) which replaces every occurrence of ARRAY_SIZE with 100 using literal substitution (see Chapter 17.9). After preprocessing the compiler then gets the result:

```
    int temperatures[100], pressures[100];
```

The compiler knows nothing about the symbolic constant ARRAY_SIZE, it having been replaced by the preprocessor with the replacement text 100. When transporting the program the #define directives are edited and the program recompiled. A problem with using #define is that once a symbolic constant has been defined it remains in existence for the remainder of the file (unless undefined using #undef) and functions following will have access to it (which may be acceptable or not, depending upon the program).

An alternative is to use the enumerative type to define an integer constant, for example:

```
    enum {Array_size = 100};
    int temperatures[Array_size], pressures[Array_size];
```

The identifier Array_size is an integer constant which is used to specify the array sizes. There are two advantages of using this technique:

1 The identifier Array_size has the same scope as the declarations, i.e. within the compound statement where it is defined.
2 Because the compiler knows about the enumerations it can generate information to enable a debugger to print the values in symbolic form (#define is a preprocessor directive and the compiler knows nothing about the symbolic constants, only the equivalent constants).

The value of a const qualified int may not be used to specify an array size, e.g. Turbo C:

```
    6       const int array_size = 100;
    7       int temperatures[array_size];
***** X.C(7) : error C2057: expected constant expression
***** X.C(7) : error C2133: 'temperatures' : unknown size
```

const is a type qualifier indicating that the object concerned has special properties; array_size is a non-modifiable variable, **not** an integer constant. Note, however, that the above is legal in C++.

Exercise 18.1 (*see Appendix B for sample answer*)

Enter Program 18.2 and test it with suitable data. Extend the program to sort the values stored in the array into ascending order. Use a simple linear sort algorithm, e.g.:

```
    FOR   index_1 = 0   TO   array_size-2
        minimum = array[index_1]
        FOR   index_2 = index_1 + 1   TO   array_size - 1
            IF   array[index_2] < minimum
                minimum = array[index_2]
                SWAP   array[index_2] and array[index_1]
```

Problems for Chapter 18

Problem 18.1   Extend Program 18.2, implementing and testing functions to return the average and standard deviation of the values stored in the array.   Standard deviation is evaluated thus:

$$\text{standard deviation} = \left(\sum_{i=1}^{n} x_i^2 \ / \ n \ - \ \left(\sum_{i=1}^{n} x_i \ / \ n \right)^2 \right)^{\frac{1}{2}}$$

where x_i are the elements of the array and n is the number of elements in the array, i.e. $\Sigma x \ / \ n$ is the average of the array.   For example, if an array contained the values 12, 6, 7, 3, 15, 10, 18 and 5 the average would be 9.5 and the standard deviation 4.87.

Problem 18.2   Implement and test a program which uses Aristosthenes method of finding prime numbers in the range 2 to n:

1   Construct an array from 2 to n zeroing all elements.
2   Starting from 2 examine each element in turn:
      (a) if zero it is prime, print the index and mark all multiples of it,
   or   (b) if marked (from a previous prime) it is not a prime.

Problem 18.3   The number 2 is the only even prime;   hence half the space in the array of Problem 18.2 is effectively wasted (once 2 has been found all other even numbers can be ignored).   Rewrite the program only considering odd numbers and utilising all elements of the array, i.e. the length of the array can be n / 2.

Problem 18.4   The simple linear sort described in Exercise 18.1 is very inefficient. Implement and test a program which sorts the elements of an array into ascending order using a bubble sort, e.g. assuming an array of number elements:

1   scan through the array:
      (a) if array[1] > array[0] swap the values
      (b) if array[2] > array[1] swap the values
      (c) if array[3] > array[2] swap the values
   etc. up to:
      (d) if array[number-1] > array[number-2] swap the values
   array[number-1] now holds the largest value
2   repeat 1 terminating at number-2
3   repeat 1 terminating at number-3

The process stops at array[0].   A pseudo-code version would be :

```
FOR   end_index = number - 1  DOWNTO  1
     FOR   index = 0  TO end_index - 1
          IF array[index + 1] < array[index]
               SWAP  array[index] and [array[index+1]
```

Chapter 29.1, Exercise 29.1, describes the quicksort algorithm and its implementation using a recursive function.

19
Strings and arrays of characters

The processing of characters and sequences of characters is of particular importance in commercial data processing applications. It still needs attention in many other application areas if only to control interaction with the user terminal, e.g. display of prompts, menus, reading commands, etc. This chapter will introduce character processing and the manipulation of arrays of characters.

19.1 Character and string constants

In C, a constant enclosed in single quotes ' is a single character and a constant enclosed in double quotes " is a string or an array of char, e.g.:

```
'x'                    /* a single character constant of type int */
"hello"                  /* a string constant of five characters */
"x"                       /* a string constant of one character */
```

Strings such as "hello" and "x" are arrays of char where the element immediately after the last character is set to the null character '\0'. For example, The following table shows the internal representation of the above constants in the ASCII character code:

constant	type	internal representation (ASCII)
'x'	int	120
"hello"	array of char	104 101 108 108 111 0
"x"	array of char	120 0

Remember that constants such as 'x' are constants of type int, there being no constants of type char (see Chapter 7.2). It is important to note that the constants 'x' and "x" are different, the former being a single character of type int and the latter a two element array of type char. When the C compiler comes across a string constant, such as "hello" or "x", it converts the characters into the equivalent character codes and appends '\0'.

19.2 Declaring and initialising arrays of characters

Arrays of characters may be declared and initialised like any other array, e.g.:

```
char student_name[30];
char today[10] = {'F','r','i','d','a','y','\0'};
```

If the elements of the array are initialised individually (as in the second example above) the programmer is responsible for appending the terminating null. Arrays of char may, however, be initialised with strings and the compiler will append the terminating null, e.g.:

```
char day_of_week[10] = "Tuesday";      /* an initialised character array */
char month_of_year[] = "May"          /* character array of 4 elements */
```

In the first example the character array day_of_week is initialised with the string Thursday and the compiler automatically appends the terminating null '\0' (the array length must allow for the addition of the terminating null). In the second example the array size is not specified so it becomes the number of characters plus one (for the terminating null).

19.3 Assigning and manipulating arrays of characters

Arrays of characters may be assigned and manipulated like any other array. For example, to find the number of characters in an array:

```
for (number = 0 ; array[number] != '\0' ; number++)      /* look for null char */
    /* null statement */;
```

This assumes that the terminating null exists, otherwise unpredictable behaviour will occur (depending upon what is in the array and the memory following it).

There are a large number of functions which can be used to read, write and manipulate strings. For example, the above code which returns the length of a string can be replaced with a call to the following function strlen. The function prototype is:

```
size_t strlen(const char string[]);
```

Returns the length of the string (not including the terminating null) as a function result of type size_t, which is defined in <stdlib.h> (typically an unsigned int). The formal parameter string represents the address of the first element of the array passed as the actual parameter, i.e. arrays are always passed using *call by reference*. The alternative and more common way to write the function prototype of strlen is to use pointer notation:

```
size_t strlen(const char * string)
```

The parameter string is a pointer to (the start address of) an array of characters. Because arrays and pointers are closely related either notation may generally be used. The function could be called as follows:

```
printf(" string length %d", (int) strlen(char_array));
if (strlen(char_array) > 10) .....
```

Note the cast (see Chapter 9.5) to ensure that the second parameter of printf is an int (to suit the conversion specification %d).

Arrays of characters, like any other arrays, cannot be assigned using an assignment statement such as:

```
char_array = "hello John Doe";                              /* not allowed */
```

Although the individual elements may be set up like any other array there is a library function strcpy which performs this operation:

```
strcpy(char_array, "hello John Doe");          /* assign a character array */
strcpy(string1, string2);                /* assign one char array to another */
```

In the first example the string "hello John Doe" is copied into the array char_array, in the second the contents of string2 is copied into string1. The function prototype for strcpy is:

```
char *strcpy(char destination[], const char source[]);
```

the parameters source and destination are source and destination arrays of char. The function returns a pointer to the first character of the destination string which can be used as the parameter to another function (further discussion in Chapter 24.3). When using strcpy it is up to the programmer to ensure that there is sufficient room in the destination array to accept the source string. An alternative function is strncpy:

```
char *strncpy(char destination[], const char source[], size_t n);
```

which copies at most n characters from source to destination. If less than n characters are copied destination is padded with nulls '\0', otherwise, if n characters are copied the terminal null is not appended and it is up to the program to ensure that the destination is terminated correctly, e.g. by placing a null at destination[n].

To concatenate two strings there are the functions strcat and strncat. The function prototypes are:

```
char *strcat(char destination[], const char source[]);
char *strncat(char destination[], const char source[], size_t n);
```

The string source is appended on the end of any existing string in destination. strncat stops if the source contains more than n characters, e.g.:

```
strcpy(char_array, " text to append ");
strncpy(string1, string2, 10);
```

The first example appends string "text to append" on the end of any existing characters in char_array (removing the terminating null) and adds a terminating null on the end of the complete string. The second example appends at most 10 characters from string2 on the end of any characters in string1.

This has been a very brief introduction to string processing routines (full details in Appendix C.14). To use many of the string processing functions (in particular string searching) more knowledge of pointers is required (see Chapters 23 and 24). It is possible, however to perform many basic string operations using normal array manipulation techniques (although not as efficiently as the specialised functions).

19.4 String input and output

Strings may be printed and read using printf and scanf, e.g.:

```
printf("%s", char_array);                          /* print characters */
scanf(" %s", char_array);   /* skip white space then read chars to white space */
```

printf prints characters from a string until a terminating '\0' is found and scanf reads a string of non white space characters and appends the terminating '\0'. In both cases the %s conversion specification expects the corresponding parameter to be an address (because the name of an array refers to the address of the first element an & is not required).

Alternatively strings may be printed and read character by character using getchar and putchar, e.g.:

```
for (index = 0; (array[index] = getchar()) != '\n' ; index++)  /* read until \n */
    putchar(array[index]);                              /* echo character */
array[index] = '\0';                                /* replace \n with \0 */
printf("\n%s ", array);                             /* print the string */
```

Another method is to use the string input/output library functions. For example, gets and puts:

```
char *gets(char string[])
int puts(const char string[])
```

gets reads characters from the standard input stream stdin into the array string until
newline '\n' is entered. The newline character is replaced by '\0' (its effect is similar
to the code using getchar above). It returns a pointer to string or the null pointer NULL
if EOF was entered (don't worry about this at this stage just use NULL to check for EOF).

puts writes the string to stdout and appends a newline. It returns EOF if an error occurres
otherwise some non-negative value.

For example, to terminate the program on EOF the code could be:

```
if (gets(char_array) == NULL)              /* read characters into char_array */
    exit(1);                                   /* failed !, terminate */
```

The main problem with gets is that it performs no array bounds checking and if too many
characters are entered the array bounds will be exceeded, corrupting the program.
Recommended practice is to use fgets which will perform array bounds checking:

```
char *fgets(char string[], int n, FILE *stream)
int fputs(const char string[], FILE *stream)
```

fgets reads at most n - 1 characters from stream (FILE and streams will be described in
Chapter 27) into the array string. If a newline character is found, reading stops and
'\n' is placed into array. A terminating '\0' is appended to the string.

fputs writes string to stream (no terminating newline).

For example, if char_array is a character array of twenty elements a string may be read
from the keyboard and printed on the screen (a maximum of 19 characters being read):

```
if (fgets(char_array, 20, stdin) == NULL)    /* read characters from keyboard */
    exit(1);                                   /* failed !, terminate */
fputs(char_array, stdout);                    /* print characters to screen */
```

The main differences between gets and fgets are:

1   fgets stops reading after number-1 characters
2   fgets includes the newline '\n' in the string (gets does not)
3   fgets can read from any input stream, e.g. a file (gets reads from stdin only)

A point to remember when using fgets is that if number - 1 characters are read reading
stops and a '\0' appended. A newline character '\n' will not be placed in the string and
any characters remaining on the line will be left in the input stream. It is therefore up to
the user to check for this condition if appropriate (see function str_read in Program 19.1).
Similarly puts terminates the string with a newline, fputs does not.

19.5 Program using functions to process strings

Program 19.1 consists of a number of string processing functions

main	lines 5 to 39, a test program
str_length	lines 43 to 50, returns the length of a string
str_copy	lines 52 to 59, copies the contents of one string to another
str_reverse	lines 63 to 70, reverses the contents of a string
str_ch_find	lines 74 to 80, find a character in a string
str_remove_spaces	lines 84 to 100, removes leading and trailing spaces from a string
str_read	lines 108 to 122, reads a string from the keyboard

```
 1 /* Program 19.1 - String processing functions using arrays and subscripts */
 2 #include <stdio.h>
 3 #include <string.h>
 4
 5 int main(void)
 6 {
 7     int str_length(const char string[]);                    /* prototypes */
 8     int str_copy(char string_1[], const char string_2[]);
 9     void str_remove_spaces(char string[]);
10     void str_reverse(char string[]);
11     int str_ch_find(const char string[], const char character, int index);
12     int str_read(const char prompt[], char string[], const int max_length);
13
14     char text_1[20], text_2[20];                    /* internal variables */
15     int index;
16
17     while (str_read("\n\nEnter string ? ", text_1, 20))     /* read string */
18         {
19         printf("read    string length %3d (%3d) |%s| \n",   /* print string */
20                 str_length(text_1), (int) strlen(text_1), text_1);
21         index = str_copy(text_2, text_1);                   /* copy string */
22         printf("copied string  length %3d (%3d) |%s| \n",
23                 index, (int) strlen(text_2), text_2);
24         str_reverse(text_2);                            /* reverse string */
25         printf("reverse string length %3d (%3d) |%s| \n",
26                 str_length(text_2), strlen(text_2), text_2);
27         str_remove_spaces(text_1);                      /* remove spaces */
28         printf("spaces removed length %3d (%3d) |%s| \n",
29                 str_length(text_1), (int) strlen(text_1), text_1);
30         printf("Character 'a' found:");                 /* search for 'a' */
31         index = -1;
32         while((index = str_ch_find(text_1, 'a', index + 1)) >= 0)
33             {
34             text_1[index] = 'x';                    /* replace 'a' with 'x' */
35             printf(" |%s|", &text_1[index]);            /* and print */
36             }
37         }
38     return 0;
39 }
40
41 /*-----------------------------------------------------------------*
42  * function to find length of string, not counting terminating null       */
43 int str_length(const char string[])
44 {
45     int number = 0;                 /* initialise number of characters to 0 */
46
47     while (string[number] != '\0')              /* look for null character */
48         number++;                       /* not null increment character count */
49     return number;                          /* return number of characters */
50 }
```

Program 19.1 String processing functions using arrays and subscripts (continued →)

```
51    * function to copy a string to another, return number of characters copied    */
52  int str_copy(char string_1[], const char string_2[])
53  {
54      int index = 0;
55
56      while ((string_1[index] = string_2[index]) != '\0')        /* copy to null */
57          index++;                                    /* if not null increment index */
58      return index;                      /* return number of characters copied */
59  }
60
61  /*------------------------------------------------------------------*
62   * function to reverse the contents of an array                      */
63  void str_reverse(char string[])
64  {
65      int up, down;                          /* up and down array index values */
66      char value;                                /* temporary data store */
67
68      for (up = 0, down = strlen(string) - 1 ; up < down ; up++, down--)
69          (value = string[up], string[up] = string[down], string[down] = value);
70  }
71
72  /*------------------------------------------------------------------*
73   * function to find character in string starting from position index    */
74  int str_ch_find(const char string[], const char character, int index)
75  {
76      while (string[index] != '\0')                /* look for null character */
77          if (string[index] == character) return index;   /* found character ! */
78          else                          index++;       /* increment index */
79      return -1;                                  /* return -1 for fail */
80  }
81
82  /*------------------------------------------------------------------*
83   * function to remove leading and trailing spaces from a string       */
84  void str_remove_spaces(char string[])
85  {
86      int index,                      /* index to first non space character */
87          index2,                     /* index to next position to copy to */
88          index3;                     /* index to put terminating null */
89
90      /* find first non space character, return position in index */
91      for (index = 0 ; string[index] == ' ' ; index++)
92          /* null statement */;
93
94      index2 = index3 = 0;                      /* set to start of array */
95      /* loop copying characters until null character found */
96      while (string[index] != '\0')
97          if ((string[index2++] = string[index++]) != ' ')    /* copy character */
98              index3 = index2;                /* not space note position in index3 */
99      string[index3] = '\0';                    /* put in terminating null */
100 }
```

Program 19.1 String processing functions using arrays and subscripts (continued →)

```
101
102  /*---------------------------------------------------------------------*
103   * read string using fgets remove terminating \n or characters left in stdin  *
104   * on entry prompt[]   contains prompt string to print                 *
105   *           max_length contains maximum length of string              *
106   * return string read in array string[]                                *
107   * return function result true if all OK else false on EOF             */
108  int str_read(const char prompt[], char string[], const int max_length)
109  {
110      int index;
111
112      printf("%s", prompt);                              /* print prompt */
113      if (fgets(string, max_length, stdin) == NULL)       /* get string */
114          return 0;                                  /* if EOF return false */
115      for (index = 0 ; string[index] != '\0' ; index++)       /* look for \0 */
116          /* null statement */;
117      if (string[--index] == '\n')
118          string[index] = '\0';                      /* replace \n with \0 */
119      else
120          do ; while (getchar() != '\n');      /* else discard characters to \n */
121      return 1;                                    /* all OK return true */
122  }
```

Program 19.1 String processing functions using arrays and subscripts

The sequence of statements in function main is:

7-12	function prototypes of string processing functions
14	declare text_1 and text_2 as arrays of char length 20 elements
15	declare index which is used as a character count and array index
17-37	a while statement which reads strings until EOF is entered

17   call str_read to read a string into text_1 maximum 20 characters
          returns *true* if OK else *false* if EOF was entered

19-20   print the size of the string using string_length and library function strlen
          plus the string enclosed in | (so that the start and end can be seen)

21   call str_copy to copy the contents of text_1 to text_2

22-23   print the number of characters copied and the contents of text_2

24   call str_reverse to reverse the contents of text_2

25-26   print the reversed contents of text_2

27   call str_remove_spaces to remove leading/trailing spaces from text_1

28-29   print the length of text_1 and its contents

30   print heading for character search

31   initialise index to -1 (one before the start of the array)

32-36   a while searching string text_1
          the search starts from position index + 1 for next occurrence of 'a'
          34 replace character 'a' at position index with an 'x'
          35 print remainder of string from position index

Function str_length, lines 43 to 50, returns the length of the string (not counting the terminating null). The sequence of statements is:

43   int str_length(const char string[]) the function header

45   declare number and initialise it to 0 (used to index array and hold character count)

47-48   a while statement searching string for a null

          the while terminates when a null '\0' is found

       48 if the character was not null increment character count (and index) number

49   return number of characters in string

Because C treats 0 as *false* lines 47 and 48 could be written:

```
while (string[number])              /* look for null character */
    number++;                  /* not null increment character count */
```

When '\0' is found ((*false*) the while terminates. The result from this function is printed in main together with the result returned by the library function strlen.

Function str_copy, lines 52 to 59, copies the contents of one string string_2 to another string_1 overwriting any existing contents. It returns the number of characters copied. The sequence of statements is:

52   int str_copy(char string_1[], const char string_2[]) the function header

54   declare index and initialise it to 0 (used to index array and hold character count)

56-57   a while statement copying string_2 into string_1

       the while terminates when a null '\0' is copied

       57 if the character was not null increment index to next character position

58   return number of characters copied

Line 56 copies a character from string_2 into string_1 and terminates the while if the character is a '\0'. As in lines 47 and 48 the != '\0' can be removed but a modern compiler will issue a warning, e.g. Microsoft C:

```
 59      while (string_1[index] = string_2[index])     /* copy to null */
***** P19_1.C(59) : warning C4206: assignment within conditional expression
```

warning that there is an assignment within a conditional statement; which is OK in this case.

The function str_reverse, lines 63 to 70, reverses the characters in a string and is similar to array_reverse in Program 18.2. The sequence of statements is:

63 void str_reverse(char string[]) the function header

65 int up, down; two array indices, i.e.:

      up increments up the array and down decrements down the array

68 a for statement which:

      (a) increments up from 0

      (b) decrements down from strlen(string) - 1 (last character in the string)

      (c) terminates when up = down

69 swaps the two characters string[up] and string[down]

The function str_ch_find, lines 74 to 80, searches string from position index for a character. If the character is found it returns the index, else -1:

74   int str_ch_find(const char string[], const char character, int index) header
76-78   a while statement scanning string for a null, if found the while terminates
    77   if string[index] == character return index (character found)
    78   else increment index to next character
79   character not found, return -1 to indicated fail

The function is called from main, lines 31 to 36, searching for occurrences of the character 'a' in string text_1:

```
index = -1;
while((index = str_ch_find(text_1, 'a', index + 1)) >= 0)
    {
    text_1[index] = 'x';                    /* replace 'a' with 'x' */
    printf(" |%s|", &text_1[index]);            /* and print */
    }
```

On each call one is added to the current value of index to start the search either from the beginning of the string (index is initialised to -1 in line 31) or following the last occurrence of the character (str_ch_find returns -1 if the character is not found). The character indexed by index is replaced and the remainder of the string is printed. Thus str_ch_find works down the string finding each occurrence of the character 'a' and replacing it with 'x'. Note the use of &text_1[index] in line 35 to pass the address of a position within text_1; the remainder of string from position index is printed. This technique can be used to pass parts of arrays into functions, i.e. in the above case the name text_1 is the address of the first element and &text_1[index] is the address of the element at position index. The printf conversion specification %s expects the parameter to be an address.

Function str_remove_spaces, lines 84 to 100, removes leading and trailing spaces from a string. The sequence of statements is:

84   void str_remove_spaces(char string[]) the function header
86-88   declare int indices used in the function
91-92   find first non-space character in the string, return position in index
94   initialise indices index2 and index3 to the start of the array
96-98   a while loop which copies characters until '\0' is found (see notes below)
    97   copies a character (overwriting any leading spaces)
    98   if character copied was not a space note position plus 1 in index3
99   terminate string (index3 contains the position of last non space character plus 1)

Notes:
1   After executing lines 91 to 92 index contains the position of the first non space character in the array.
2   Line 94 positions index2 at the start of the array ready for copying the characters.
3   Line 94 positions index3 at the start of the array in case the string is empty or full of spaces, i.e. line 98 would not be executed to assign a value to index3.
4   Line 97 overwrites any leading spaces by overwriting the character at position index2 with the one from position index.
5   In line 98 index3 is positioned at the last non-space character plus 1 which is then overwritten with '\0' in line 99.

The function str_read, lines 108 to 122, reads a string of maximum length max_length from stdin. It returns *true* if the string was read OK otherwise *false* if EOF was entered. If the length of the string is less than max_length characters the terminating newline is replaced with '\0', otherwise the characters remaining on the line are discarded including the newline:

108   `int str_read(const char prompt[], char string[], int max_length)`
         the function header declaring three parameters:
         prompt[]   an array of char containing a message to print on the screen
         string   an array of char to accept the characters input
         max_length   an int specifying the length of string
112-14   display prompt and call fgets to read a string length max_length - 1 from stdin
         114 if EOF was entered (fgets returned NULL) terminate function with result *false*
115-16   search string for terminating '\0'
117   if previous character (to '\0') was newline
         118 replace '\n' with '\0'
         else 120 discard remaining characters from stdin up to and including newline

Line 118 is executed if the input text contained less than max_length - 1 characters otherwise the input text contained too many characters and line 120 discards them (so that they do not appear when fgets is called again). Line 120 could be written:

```
while (getchar() != '\n')              /* else remove characters to \n */
    /* null statement */;
```

A run of the program was (newline is indicated by ↴):

```
Enter string ? hello abc abc abc ↴
read      string length  17 ( 17) |hello abc abc abc|
copied string  length  17 ( 17) |hello abc abc abc|
reverse string length  17 ( 17) |cba cba cba olleh|
spaces removed length  17 ( 17) |hello abc abc abc|
Character 'a' found: |xbc abc abc| |xbc abc| |xbc|

Enter string ?       test spaces      ↴
read      string length  19 ( 19) |     test spaces  |
copied string  length  19 ( 19) |     test spaces  |
reverse string length  19 ( 19) |  secaps tset     |
spaces removed length  11 ( 11) |test spaces|
Character 'a' found: |xces|

Enter string ? abcdefghijklmnopqrstuvwxyz ↴
read      string length  19 ( 19) |abcdefghijklmnopqrs|
copied string  length  19 ( 19) |abcdefghijklmnopqrs|
reverse string length  19 ( 19) |srqponmlkjihgfedcba|
spaces removed length  19 ( 19) |abcdefghijklmnopqrs|
Character 'a' found: |xbcdefghijklmnopqrs|

Enter string ? ↴
read      string length   0 (  0) ||
copied string  length   0 (  0) ||
reverse string length   0 (  0) ||
spaces removed length   0 (  0) ||
Character 'a' found:

Enter string ? ˉZ ↴
```

The second test shows the removal of leading and trailing spaces (the | show the limits of the string), the third the truncation of the input text at 19 characters and the final test an empty string (it is wise to test string processing functions with an empty string as it can often cause problems).

Exercise 19.1 (*see Appendix B for sample answer*)

Implement and test a function which searches for a string within a string. The function prototype of a string search function could be:

```
int str_search(const char string_1[], const char string_2[], int index);
```

Starting at position `index` search `string_1` for the next occurrence of `string_2`. If found return the index else -1. Test the function (similar to lines 32 to 36 in Program 19.1).

Implement and test a function `str_compare` which compares two strings (similar to `strcmp` in the standard library):

```
int str_compare(const char string_1[], const char string_2[]);
```

the contents of `string_1` is compared with `string_2` and the following result returned:

<0 if `string_1` comes before `string_2` in the sorting sequence
0 if `string_1` equals `string_2`
>0 if `string_1` comes after `string_2` in the sorting sequence

19.6 Array processing functions in < string.h>

Arrays of characters can be processed using the same techniques as any other array with the proviso that special attention has to be paid to the terminating null character '\0'. The library <string.h> (see Appendix C.14) contains functions to process strings (arrays of char terminated by '\0') which give enhanced performance in terms of faster processing. However, many of the functions require a knowledge of pointers (see Chapters 23 and 24).

   Library <string.h> also contains general functions to manipulate blocks of memory as arrays of characters (bytes) which are not null terminated, e.g. memset to set all elements to a value, memcpy to copy an array, memchr and memcmp to search an array, etc. For example, memcmp compares at most number characters of string1 with string2:

```
int memcmp(const void *string1, const void *string2, size_t number);
```

The pointers string1 and string2 can point to any type of data (void * will be discussed in Chapter 23.4) with the comparison being carried out on a byte of byte basis, e.g.:

```
if (! memcmp(x , y, sizeof(x))) printf("arrays are the same");
else                            printf("arrays are different");
```

x and y could be arrays of float, double, int, etc. or arrays of structures (see Chapter 22):

Problem for Chapter 19

Implement and test some string processing functions. For example:

1   Concatenate string_1 with string_2 return result in string_1, e.g.:

```
void str_concat(char string_1[], const char string_2[]);
```

2   Find last occurrence of a character in a string; return index if found else -1, e.g.:

```
int str_r_ch_find(const char string[], const char character);
```

20

Multi-dimensional arrays

20.1 Declaring and accessing multi-dimensional arrays

In C one can have arrays of any type and an array is itself just another type of object. It is therefore possible to define a type which is an array and then an array of that type, e.g.:

```
enum {rows = 2, columns = 3};
typedef float row_t[columns];          /* type row_t is a one dimensional array */
row_t matrix[rows];                     /* matrix is an array of type row_t */
```

The array matrix is made up of 10 elements of type row_t each of which is an array of 10 float elements. Alternatively matrix could be declared:

```
enum {rows = 2, columns = 3};
typedef float matrix_t[rows][columns];          /* a two-dimensional array */
matrix_t matrix;                                 /* declare variables */
```

The contents of an array may be initialised with simple constants when it is declared:

```
enum {rows = 2, columns = 3};
float matrix[rows][columns] = { { 2, -1, 0} ,          /* initialise row 0 */
                                {-1,  0, 3} };          /* initialise row 1 */
```

Any elements not explicitly initialised will be initialised to 0. If an array is not initialised the element values are *undefined* if the array is internal or zero if it is external or a static internal. The simplest way to initialise all the elements of an internal array to zero is:

```
enum {rows = 2, columns = 3};
float matrix[rows][columns] = {0}          /* a multi-dimensional array */
```

element matrix[0][0] is explicitly initialised to 0 and the remainder zeroed automatically.

The elements of a multi-dimensional array are accessed using integer subscripts, e.g. to set successive elements of an array to the values 0, 1, 2, 3, 4 and 5:

```
enum {rows = 2, columns = 3};
float matrix[rows][columns] ;          /* a multi-dimensional array */
int row_index, column_index;

for (row_index = 0; row_index < 2 ; row_index++)
    for (column_index = 0; column_index < 3 ; column_index++)
        matrix[row_index][column_index] = row_index * 3 + column_index;
```

Take care not to inadvertently use the comma operator when specifying array subscripts:

```
matrix[0,1] = 0.0f;                     /* invalid */
```

This looks fine to a Pascal programmer and the expression matrix[0,1] is valid C code, i.e. the subscript [0,1] contains the comma operator and is evaluated as [1] which will access the array element matrix[1], the second row of matrix. In this case the assignment statement is invalid and would produce an error message, e.g. Microsoft C Version 6.00:

```
  25      matrix[0,1] = 0.0f;
***** X.C(25) : error C2106: '=' : left operand must be lvalue
```

Some compilers produce warnings when the comma operator is used in an array subscript, others just carry on and produce erroneous results, the cause of which can be very difficult to track down.

C stores multi-dimensional arrays such that the rightmost subscript varies fastest as elements are accessed in storage order, e.g.:

```
matrix[0][0], matrix[0][1], matrix[0][2], matrix[1][0], matrix[1][1], matrix[1][2]
```

For example, to access element matrix[i][j] the subscript calculation is (i * columns) + j (where columns is the number of columns in the declaration matrix[rows][columns]).

20.2 Multi-dimensional arrays as function parameters

When multi-dimensional arrays are passed as function parameters the number of elements in the right-most indices must be specified in the function header, i.e. to access element matrix[i][j] the number of columns in the declaration matrix[rows][columns] must be known to perform the subscript calculation (i * columns) + j (the value of rows is not needed in this case).

For example, if the above matrix is to be passes into a function the header could appear:

```
void matrix_print(float array[2][3])
```

or just:

```
void matrix_print(float array[][3])
```

with the number of elements in the left-most index not specified. When the function is called the actual argument is just the array name, e.g.:

```
matrix_print(matrix);
```

20.3 Functions to read, write and multiply a two-dimensional matrix

In order to multiply two matrices, c = a * b, the number of columns in the first matrix a must equal the number of rows in the second matrix b. The product matrix c will have the number of rows of a and the number of columns of b, i.e. if a is a_rows by a_columns and b is b_rows by b_columns the size of c will be a_rows by b_columns. The individual elements of c are given by:

$$c_{ij} = \sum_{k=1}^{n} a_{ik} * b_{kj} \qquad \text{where n = number of columns in matrix a (and rows in b)}$$

For example:

$$\begin{bmatrix} 2 & -1 & 0 \\ -1 & 0 & 3 \end{bmatrix} * \begin{bmatrix} 4 & 1 \\ 2 & 0 \\ -3 & 2 \end{bmatrix} = \begin{bmatrix} 6 & 2 \\ -13 & 5 \end{bmatrix}$$

Matrix multiplication is not commutative, i.e. a * b ≠ b * a. For example

$$\begin{bmatrix} 4 & 1 \\ 2 & 0 \\ -3 & 2 \end{bmatrix} * \begin{bmatrix} 2 & -1 & 0 \\ -1 & 0 & 3 \end{bmatrix} = \begin{bmatrix} 7 & -4 & 3 \\ 4 & -2 & 0 \\ -8 & 3 & 6 \end{bmatrix}$$

Even the product of square matrices is generally not commutative, e.g.:

$$\begin{bmatrix} 1 & 0 \\ -1 & 2 \end{bmatrix} * \begin{bmatrix} -1 & 0 \\ 0 & 2 \end{bmatrix} = \begin{bmatrix} -1 & 0 \\ 1 & 4 \end{bmatrix}$$

$$\begin{bmatrix} -1 & 0 \\ 0 & 2 \end{bmatrix} * \begin{bmatrix} 1 & 0 \\ -1 & 2 \end{bmatrix} = \begin{bmatrix} -1 & 0 \\ -2 & 4 \end{bmatrix}$$

Program 20.1 contains functions to read, write and multiply two-dimensional matrices:

main	lines 10 to 50, test program for the other functions
read_matrix	lines 53 to 74, reads the size of the matrix and then the matrix values
integer_read	lines 78 to 100, reads an integer number in the range 1 to maximum
float_read	lines 104 to 115, reads a float value from the keyboard
matrix_multiply	lines 120 to 143, multiplies matrices a and b and returns the result in c:
matrix_print	lines 147-156, prints the name, size and values of a matrix.

The functions which read values from the keyboard check for invalid characters and EOF (program terminates).

A run of the program was:

```
Matrix a[2,3] values are:
    a[0,0] =    2.00   a[0,1] =  -1.00   a[0,2] =   0.00
    a[1,0] =  -1.00    a[1,1] =   0.00   a[1,2] =   3.00

Matrix b[3,2] values are:
    b[0,0] =    4.00   b[0,1] =   1.00
    b[1,0] =    2.00   b[1,1] =   0.00
    b[2,0] =   -3.00   b[2,1] =   2.00

Multiply a * b
Matrix c[2,2] values are:
    c[0,0] =    6.00   c[0,1] =   2.00
    c[1,0] =  -13.00   c[1,1] =   5.00

Multiply b * a
Matrix c[3,3] values are:
    c[0,0] =    7.00   c[0,1] =  -4.00   c[0,2] =   3.00
    c[1,0] =    4.00   c[1,1] =  -2.00   c[1,2] =   0.00
    c[2,0] =   -8.00   c[2,1] =   3.00   c[2,2] =   6.00

Matrix a
 Enter number of rows in a ? ^Z
```

```
 1 /* Program 20.1 - matrix read, write and multiply */
 2
 3 #include <stdlib.h>
 4 #include <stdio.h>
 5
 6 /* define matrix size and type to hold a square matrix */
 7 enum {max_columns = 10, max_rows = 10};
 8 typedef float matrix_t[max_rows][max_columns];
 9
10 int main(void)
11 {
12     void matrix_read(const char name,
13         matrix_t matrix, int *const rows, int *const columns);
14     void matrix_print(const char name,
15         const matrix_t matrix, const int rows, const int columns);
16     int matrix_multiply(const matrix_t a, const int a_rows, const int a_columns,
17                         const matrix_t b, const int b_rows, const int b_columns,
18                         matrix_t c, int *const c_rows, int *const c_columns);
19
20     int a_rows = 2, a_columns = 3;                    /* matrix a size */
21     matrix_t a = { { 2, -1, 0} , {-1, 0, 3} };       /* and initial values */
22
23     int b_rows = 3, b_columns = 2;                    /* matrix b size */
24     matrix_t b = { { 4, 1} , { 2, 0} , {-3 , 2} };   /* and initial values */
25     int c_rows, c_columns;
26     matrix_t c;
27
28     for (;;)                                /* loop forever processing matrices */
29       {
30       matrix_print('a', a, a_rows, a_columns);        /* print a and b */
31       matrix_print('b', b, b_rows, b_columns);
32
33       printf("\nMultiply a * b");                     /* multiply a * b */
34       if (matrix_multiply(
35           a, a_rows, a_columns, b, b_rows, b_columns, c, &c_rows, &c_columns))
36         matrix_print('c', c, c_rows, c_columns);
37       else
38           printf("\nMatrix multiply failed a_rows <> b_columns\a\n");
39
40       printf("\nMultiply b * a");                     /* multiply b * a */
41       if (matrix_multiply(
42           b, b_rows, b_columns, a, a_rows, a_columns, c, &c_rows, &c_columns))
43           matrix_print('c', c, c_rows, c_columns);
44       else
45           printf("\nMatrix multiply failed a_rows <> b_columns\a\n");
46
47       matrix_read('a', a, &a_rows, &a_columns);       /* read new a and b */
48       matrix_read('b', b, &b_rows, &b_columns);
49       }
50 }
```

Program 20.1 Two-dimensional matrix read, write and multiply (continued on next page)

```
52 /*--------------------------------------------------------------------*
53  * function to read matrix (name is single character name of matrix)   *
54  *    read the number of rows and columns and then the matrix values   */
55 void matrix_read
56   (const char name, matrix_t matrix, int *const rows, int *const columns)
57 {
58     int integer_read(const int maximum);              /* function prototype */
59     float float_read(void);
60     int row, column;
61
62     printf("\nMatrix %c\n Enter number of rows in %c ? ", name, name);
63     *rows = integer_read(max_rows);                        /* read row size */
64     printf("\n Enter number of columns in %c ? ", name);
65     *columns = integer_read(max_columns);               /* read column size */
66
67     /* now read matrix values */
68     for (row = 0 ; row < *rows ; row++)
69         {
70         printf("\nEnter row %d (%d values) ? ", row, *columns);
71         for (column = 0 ; column < *columns ; column++)
72             matrix[row][column] = float_read();
73         }
74 }
75
76 /*--------------------------------------------------------------------*
77  * function to read an integer number in range 1 to maximum           */
78 int integer_read(const int maximum)
79 {
80     int value = maximum + 1, ch;
81
82     do                              /* read integer in range 1 to maximum */
83        {
84       if (scanf("%d", &value) != 1)
85          {                                            /* read error ! */
86         if ((ch = getchar()) == EOF) exit(0);         /* if EOF exit */
87         printf(" invalid character %c, try again ? ", ch);
88          }
89       else
90         if (value > maximum)                          /* range check */
91            printf(" value %1d > maximum size %1d, try again ? ",
92                    value, maximum);
93           else
94             if (value < 1)                            /* range check */
95            printf(" value %1d < minimum size 1, try again ? ",
96                    value);
97        }
98     while ((value < 1) || (value > maximum));
99     return value;
100 }
```

Program 20.1 Two-dimensional matrix read, write and multiply (continued on next page)

```
101
102 /*--------------------------------------------------------------------------*
103  * function to read a real number                                          */
104 float float_read(void)
105 {
106     float value;
107     int ch;
108
109     while (scanf("%f", &value) != 1)
110         {                                              /* read error ! */
111         if ((ch = getchar()) == EOF) exit(0);          /* if EOF exit */
112         printf(" invalid character %c, try again ? ", ch);
113         }
114     return value;
115 }
116
117 /*--------------------------------------------------------------------------*
118  * function to multiply matrix a by matrix b and return result in matrix c  *
119  *  sizes of matrices are a[a_rows][a_columns] & b[b_rows][b_columns]        */
120 int matrix_multiply(const matrix_t a, const int a_rows, const int a_columns,
121                     const matrix_t b, const int b_rows, const int b_columns,
122                     matrix_t c, int *const c_rows, int *const c_columns)
123 {
124     int i, j, k;                                       /* matrix indices */
125
126     /* the number of rows in a must equal the number of columns in b */
127     if (a_columns == b_rows)
128         {
129         /* evaluate c as a matrix size c[a_rows][b_columns] */
130         *c_rows = a_rows;
131         *c_columns = b_columns;
132         for (i = 0 ; i < *c_rows ; i++)
133             for (j = 0 ; j < *c_columns ; j++)
134                 {
135                 c[i][j] = 0.0f;                        /* evaluate element c[i][j] */
136                 for (k = 0 ; k < a_columns ; k++)
137                     c[i][j] = c[i][j] + a[i][k] * b[k][j];
138                 }
139         return 1;                                      /* return true for OK */
140         }
141     else
142         return 0;                                      /* return false for error */
143 }
144
```

Program 20.1 Two-dimensional matrix read, write and multiply (continued on next page)

```
145 /*-----------------------------------------------------------------------*
146  * function to print name and the contents of a matrix[rows,columns]     */
147 void matrix_print
148   (const char name, const matrix_t matrix, const int rows, const int columns)
149 {
150     int row, column;
151     printf("\nMatrix %c[%1d,%1d] values are:\n", name, rows, columns);
152     for (row = 0 ; row < rows ; printf("\n") , row++)
153         for (column = 0 ; column < columns ; column++)
154             printf("   %c[%1d,%1d] = %6.2f",
155                 name, row, column, matrix[row][column]);
156 }
```

Program 20.1 Two-dimensional matrix read, write and multiply

Program 20.1 contains functions to read, write and multiply two-dimensional matrices. The sequence of statements is:

lines

7	use enum to define int constants which specify matrix size
8	use typedef to define a new type, i.e. a float matrix size max_rows by max_columns this will be used to declare variables and formal parameters in function headers
10	start of function main
12-18	declar function prototypes
20	declare int variables to hold size of matrix a and initialise to 2 by 3
21	declare matrix a and initialise a 2 by 3 matrix
23	declare int variables to hold size of matrix b and initialise to 3 by 2
24	declare matrix b and initialise a 3 by 2 matrix
25	declare int variables to hold the size of matrix c
26	declare matrix c
28-49	is a for statement which loops forever
30-31	print current values of a and b (as initialised in lines 20 to 24)
34-35	multiply a by b to give matrix c
36	if multiply was OK print c
38	else print error message
41-42	multiply b by a to give matrix c
43	if multiply was OK print c
45	else print error message
47-48	read new values into a and b

In Line 7 the constants max_columns and max_rows specify the maximum size of the matrices. The actual size used to hold data can be less than this with the size being passed between functions by integer variables, e.g. a_rows, a_columns, etc.

In the following functions all formal parameters which should not be altered within the functions are const qualified.

Function `matrix_read`, lines 55 to 74, reads the size of the matrix from the keyboard and then the matrix values:

55-56   `void matrix_read`
           `(const char name, matrix_t matrix, int *const rows, int *const columns)`
      is the function header, the formal parameters are:
      `name`   (a const qualified `char`) holds the matrix name to be printed on the screen
      `matrix` (an array of type `matrix_t`) returns the matrix values read
      `rows`   (a const qualified pointer to an `int`) returns the number of rows read
      `columns` (a const qualified pointer to an `int`) returns the number of columns read
      (the pointers are used to achieve *passing by reference*, further discussion below)

58-60   declare function prototypes and internal variables
62   prompt user to enter the number of rows in the matrix
63   call `integer_read` to read the number of rows (the maximum is a parameter)
64   prompt user to enter the number of columns in the matrix
65   call `integer_read` to read the number of columns (the maximum is a parameter)
68-73   a `for` statement to read the rows of the matrix
      70   prompt user to enter a row of the matrix
      71-72   a `for` statement which calls `float_read` to read the matrix values

Because the size of the matrix (read in lines 63 and 65) needs to be returned to the calling function, the formal parameters `rows` and `columns` are pointers and the corresponding actual parameters are *passed by reference*, i.e. using the & operator in lines 47 and 48 in `main` (see Chapter 15.7).

    Function `integer_read`, lines 78 to 100, reads an integer number from the keyboard with a value in the range 1 to `maximum` (passed as a formal parameter). The function checks for invalid characters and EOF (the program terminates). The sequence of statements is:

82-98   a `do` statement looping until a value in the range 1 to `maximum` is entered
84   call `scanf` to read one integer number
86-87   if `scanf` failed to convert one number
      if EOF was entered terminate program using library function `exit`
      else print invalid character
90-96   check value is in the range 1 to `maximum`

Function `float_read`, lines 104 to 115, reads a `float` checking for invalid characters and EOF (the program terminates).

    Function `matrix_print`, lines 147-156, prints the name, size and values of a matrix. The sequence of statements is:

147-48   `void matrix_print`
           `(const char name, const matrix_t matrix, const int rows, const int columns)`
      is the function header, the formal parameters are:
      `name`   (a const qualified `char`) holds the matrix name to be printed on the screen
      `matrix` (a const qualified array of type `matrix_t`) holds the matrix to be printed
      `rows`   (a const qualified `int`) holds the number of rows in `matrix`
      `columns` (a const qualified `int`) holds the number of columns in `matrix`
151   print the name and size of the matrix
152-55 prints the values of the matrix
      Note the use of the comma operator in line 152 to print a newline after every row

Function matrix_multiply, lines 120 to 143, multiplies two matrices a and b and returns the result in matrix c:

120-22   int matrix_multiply(const matrix_t a, const int a_rows, const int a_columns,
                        const matrix_t b, const int b_rows, const int b_columns,
                        matrix_t c, int *const c_rows, int *const c_columns)

is the function header, the formal parameters are:

a   (a const qualified array of type matrix_t) holds the first matrix
a_rows and a_columns   (const qualified int) the size of matrix a
b   (a const qualified array of type matrix_t) holds the second matrix
b_rows and b_columns   (const qualified int) the size of matrix c
c   (an array of type matrix_t) returns the result of a * b
c_rows and c_columns   (const qualified pointers to int) returns size of matrix c
       (the pointers are used to achieve *passing by reference*, as in matrix_read)

127   check if matrices can be multiplied, i.e. a_columns == b_rows
129-40   multiply matrices
       130-31   sets up size of matrix c
       132-38   multiply a and b to give c
       139   return TRUE (non zero) to indicate multiply worked OK
141-42   else return FALSE (zero) to indicate matrices cannot be multiplied

On return the function result of matrix_multiply can be checked for success or failure.

20.4 Using arrays to index into other arrays

Program 20.2 contains an array names, each element of which is an array of char containing a person's name. The aim of the program is to sort the names into alphabetical order and then print them (Exercise 18.1 and the Problem for Chapter 18 described some simple sorting techniques). The array names itself could be sorted but the copying of the array elements which are themselves arrays imposes a very high overhead. The approach taken in Program 20.2 is to use an array indices, the elements of which are indices into the array names. Initially indices contains the values 0, 1, 2, 3, etc. which index the corresponding elements names [0], names [1], names [2], names [3], etc. The array indices is then sorted such that the elements index array names in alphabetical order (Chapter 25.3 will describe using an array of pointers to achieve the same effect). The sequence of statements in Program 20.2 is:

10   define number = 15, the number of elements in the array names
11   define type name_t, an array of char which will hold the names
13-16   define array names and initialise it with strings
18   define an array indices and initialise it with the values 0 to 14
         these values will be used to index names [0] to names [14]
19   define some array index variables for use in the program
22-23   print the contents of the array names as 'normal' (five names per line)
27-28   print the contents of the array names using array indices to index the elements
31-38   sort array indices such that it indexes the elements of names in alphabetical order
         this linear sort is similar to Exercise 18.1
42-44   print the contents of the array names using array indices to index the elements
         the names should now be printed in alphabetical order

```
 1 /* Program 20.2, Sort an array of array indices to an array of names.      *
 2  *    Rather than sort the array of names itself into alphabetical order,    *
 3  *    sort the array of indices so it indexes the names in alphabetical order */
 4
 5 #include <stdio.h>
 6 #include <string.h>
 7
 8 int main(void)
 9 {
10     enum {number = 15};                        /* number of names to be sorted */
11     typedef char name_t[8];                    /* define type to hold a name */
12     /* define and initialise an array of names */
13     name_t names[number] =
14                       {{"Bertie"},{"Alison"},{"Betty"},{"Bart"},{"Alex"},
15                        {"Aleson"},{"Bert"},{"Daisy"},{"Walter"},{"Mary"},
16                        {"Alan"},{"Sally"},{"Bert"},{"Bernie"},{"Mandy"}};
17     /* define and initialise an array of indices to names */
18     int indices[number] = { 0,1,2,3,4,5,6,7,8,9,10,11,12,13,14};
19     int index, index_1, index_2, name_index;              /* array indices */
20
21     printf("\nPrint original array of names");
22     for (index = 0 ; index < number ; index++)            /* print names */
23         printf("%c %-8s", index % 5 ? ' ' : '\n', names[index]);
24
25     /* use the array of indices to print the names */
26     printf("\n\nPrint names via the array of indices");
27     for (index = 0 ; index < number ; index++)
28         printf("%c %-8s", index % 5 ? ' ' : '\n', names[indices[index]]);
29
30     /* sort the array of indices (on first letter) using a linear sort */
31     for (index_1 = 0 ; index_1 < number - 1; index_1++)
32         for (index_2 = index_1 + 1 ; index_2 < number ; index_2++)
33             if (names[indices[index_2]][0] < names[indices[index_1]][0])
34             /*if (strcmp(names[indices[index_2]],names[indices[index_1]]) < 0)*/
35                 {
36                 name_index = indices[index_1];          /* swap indices */
37                 indices[index_1] = indices[index_2];
38                 indices[index_2] = name_index;
39                 }
40
41     /* print the names via the sorted array of indices */
42     printf("\n\nPrint names via sorted array of indices");
43     for (index = 0 ; index < number ; index++)
44         printf("%c %-8s", index % 5 ? ' ' : '\n', names[indices[index]]);
45     return 0;
46 }
```

Program 20.2 Sort an array of array indices to an array of person names

A run of Program 20.2 was:

```
Print original array of names
  Bertie    Alison    Betty    Bart      Alex
  Aleson    Bert      Daisy    Walter    Mary
  Alan      Sally     Bert     Bernie    Mandy

Print names via the array of indices
  Bertie    Alison    Betty    Bart      Alex
  Aleson    Bert      Daisy    Walter    Mary
  Alan      Sally     Bert     Bernie    Mandy

Print names via sorted array of indices
  Alison    Alex      Aleson   Alan      Bertie
  Betty     Bert      Bart     Bert      Bernie
  Daisy     Mary      Mandy    Sally     Walter
```

In Program 20.2 the names were only sorted on the first character. Replacing line 33 with line 34, which calls the function strcmp, would sort using all characters of the names, i.e.:

```
    if (strcmp(names[indices[index_2]],names[indices[index_1]]) < 0)
```

The function prototype of strcmp is:

```
    int strcmp(const char string_1[], const char string_2[]);
```

the contents of string_1 is compared with string_2 and the following result returned:

<0 if   string_1 comes before string_2 in the sorting sequence
0 if string_1 equals string_2
>0 if string_1 comes after string_2 in the sorting sequence

If the program is modified to use strcmp the results of the sort are then:

```
Print names via sorted array of indices
  Alan      Aleson    Alex     Alison    Bart
  Bernie    Bert      Bert     Bertie    Betty
  Daisy     Mandy     Mary     Sally     Walter
```

Problem for Chapter 20

Extend Program 20.1 to evaluate the transpose of a matrix:

$$c_{ji} = a_{ij}$$

interchanging the rows and columns of a matrix, e.g.:

$$X = \begin{bmatrix} 1 & 0 \\ -6 & 5 \\ 3 & 2 \end{bmatrix} \qquad X^T = \begin{bmatrix} 1 & -6 & 3 \\ 0 & 5 & 2 \end{bmatrix}$$

A function prototype could be:

```
void matrix_transpose (const matrix_t a, const int a_rows, const int a_columns,
                       matrix_t a_t, int *const a_t_rows, int *const a_t_columns);
```

Additional functions could be implemented to evaluate the determinant of a square matrix, inverse of a square matrix, etc.

21

Multi-file programs

Chapter 17 considered the problems of managing data storage and the flow of information between functions in programs implemented as a single source code file. This chapter will describe the techniques used to split up a program into several separate source code files, discuss the management of functions and data storage within the files and the flow of information between functions in different files.

21.1 Modular programming and multi-file programs

During the program specification and design stages logical tasks or sequences of tasks, which will become modules, are identified and specified. Once a specification of the logical steps performed by each module has been drawn up (modules can contain other modules and call other modules as required) the individual modules, which become *functions*, can then be designed, coded and tested. Modules are kept as independent as possible by controlling the passing of information between modules and only allowing an individual module access to data that it actually uses. Errors then tend to be localised to a module (Steward 1987) or a group of modules making them much easier to find than if all modules had access to all the data (Chapter 17 discussed *data hiding* when implementing large C programs). Once working satisfactorily, modules can be integrated to build up to the complete package. As modules are integrated with others, errors can occur due to faulty interaction of modules. Modular programming tends to limit such errors and isolate them to particular sets of modules within the package. In addition, if errors are found whilst the package is being used in its application environment, or when upgrades are required, it is easy to identify the relevant modules and modify just these.

In practice many modules provide common facilities which are required by programs in a given application area. Such modules tend to form logical groups which are implemented as libraries of functions, e.g. the standard maths library of C or a graphics library to support CAD packages. The program source code of such a library would be maintained in a separate file or files and as each module is completed it is added to the library. The library is then compiled into object code to be linked into the application programs as required.

In addition to aiding in the implementation and maintenance of libraries there are a number of other very good reasons for splitting a program up into separate files:

1   The code within each file is more manageable in terms of finding and editing particular sections of text.
2   If modules which are already implemented and tested are in separate files there is no likelihood of the programmer inadvertently corrupting them in an editing session.
3   It is easier to constrain the access of individual modules or groups of modules to the data sets required, i.e. the concept of *data hiding*.
4   The shorter the source code file the faster it will compile.

21.2 Declarations and definitions

A variable may need to be accessed by program code in a number of separate source code files. There then arises the problem of how and where storage for the variable is allocated and how code in other files can then access that storage, i.e. one could attempt to allocate storage to several variables of the same name which would cause errors at link time. This leads to the separate concepts of *declaration* and *definition* of a variable:

declaration   a specification of the name and nature of the variable
definition   a declaration which also reserves storage for the variable

The declarations in all the sample programs so far in this book have been *definitions* in that the variable types and identifiers were specified and storage allocated by the compiler, e.g.:

```
float x, y;                  /* declaration and definition of external variables */
int main(void)
{
      int i, j;              /* declaration and definition of internal variables */
      ....
}
```

If an external variable (not internal) defined in one file is to be accessed from another file it may be declared (but not defined) in that file by using the keyword extern. For example, if functions in another file are to access the above **external** variables:

```
extern float x, y;                       /* declaration of external variables */
```

This declares the variables x and y to be of type float but does not reserve storage.

In fact we have already (unknowingly) come across the concept of *declarations* and *definitions* when dealing with functions:

function prototype declaration   a specification of the name and use of the function
function definition   a function header followed by the function code

21.3 External identifiers

External identifiers are function names and the names of objects defined outside functions (see Chapter 17.3). Their scope is from the point of definition to the end of the file in which they are defined. In addition, an external identifier may be referenced by code either in the same file (prior to definition) or code in another file:

functions   by declaring a *function prototype* and then calling the function as normal
variables   by declaring the variable name prefixed with extern

Thus the *scope* of external identifiers may be extended beyond (or within) the file which contains its definition. This clashes with the concept of *data hiding* in that modules should only have access to the data sets which they require. Although C lacks the more rigorous techniques available in modern languages such as Modula 2 it is possible to restrict the scope of external identifiers to the file in which they are defined (using the *static* keyword, see next section). It is also up to the programmer to ensure that the information in declarations and definitions correspond, i.e. it is possible to define a variable as a float in one file and declare it (using extern) as an int in another.

21.4 Static variables and functions

Unfortunately the keyword *static* means two different things depending upon its context:

static internal variables   (see Chapter 17.5) are allocated permanent storage (and initialised) prior to program execution and maintained until the program terminates. The scope of static internal variables is the same as automatic internal variables, i.e. from the point of definition up to the end of the compound statement in which they are defined.

static external identifiers are external variables or functions with their scope restricted to the file in which they are defined, i.e. 'hiding' them from code in other files.

21.5 A program split into two source code files

Programs 21.1a and 21.1b (next page) are a modification of Program 17.1 split up into two files p21_1a.c and p21_1b.c respectively. They contain a mixture of external variables, functions and internal variables. The files are separately compiled and linked, e.g. using Turbo C:

```
tcc -w -c p21_1b.c              compile p21_1b.c
tcc -w p21_1a.c p21_1b.obj      compile p21_1a.c and link with p21_1b object code
```

Consider the statements in Program 21.1a:

5	declare *prototype* of function test (which is in file p21_1b.c)
7	declare external variable pi (const qualified)
8	declare external variables a and b (defined in file p21_1b.c)
9	define static external variables c and d
10	define external array e
12-21	definition of function main
	14 define internal (to main) variables i and x
	17-19 a for statement printing various data (see Program 17.1 for description)

In this file the identifiers main (function), pi, a, b, c, d, e and test (function) are all external but the scope of c and d is restricted to the file. Now consider Program 21.1b:

3	declare prototype of function test2
5	define external variable pi (const qualified) with its value
6	define external variables a and b with initial values
7	define static external variables c, e and i
9-15	definition of function test with formal parameters b and j
	the declaration of b 'hides' the b defined in line 6
17-21	definition of static function test2

In this file:

1   The identifiers test (function), test2 (function), pi, a, b, c, e and i are external.
2   The scope of identifiers test2 (function), c, e and i is restricted to the file.
3   The external identifier e is static and will therefore not clash with the external identifier e defined in line 10 of Program 21.1a.

Thus it is possible to have different external identifiers using the same name *defined* in different files so long as the keyword static is used to restrict the scope. If the static was missed off line 7 of Program 21.1b the linker would get multiply defined symbols, e.g. using Turbo C:

```
Error: _e defined in module p21_1a.c is duplicated in module p21_1b.c
```

```
1  /* Program 21.1a - Main program file of a multi-file program */
2
3  #include <stdio.h>
4
5  int test(float, int);                        /* declare function prototype */
6
7  extern const float pi;       /* declare external const qualified variable */
8  extern float a, b;                /* declare external variables a and b */
9  static int c, d;             /* define external variables local to file */
10 float e[10];                          /* define external array e */
11
12 int main(void)
13 {
14     int i, x = 5;                   /* variables internal to main */
15     /* can use external pi, a, b, c, d and e and internal i and x */
16
17     for (i = 1 ; i < b ; i++)
18         printf("\ni = %d, a = %4.1f, b = %f, pi = %f, x = %d, test = %d ",
19                 i, a, b, pi, x, test(a, x));
20     return 0;
21 }
```

Program 21.1a Main program file of a multi-file program (file p21_1a.c)

```
1  /* Program 21.1b - other file of a multi-file program */
2
3  static void test2(void);                     /* declare function prototype */
4
5  const float pi = 3.14159f;     /* define external const qualified variable */
6  float a = 2, b = 10;                /* define external variables a and b */
7  static int c, e, i = 2;        /* define external variables local to file */
8
9  int test(float b, int j)                      /* formal parameters b and j */
10 {
11     /* can use external a, pi, c, e and i and formal parameters b and j */
12     a = a + j;                   /* altering value of external variable */
13     test2();                               /* call function test2 */
14     return (b * i);                        /* function result */
15 }
16
17 static void test2(void)
18 {
19     /* can use external a, b, pi, c, e and i */
20     i = 10 * b;
21 }
```

Program 21.1b Other file of a multi-file program (file p21_1b.c)

21.6 Rules for the construction of identifiers

21.6.1 Identifiers used within the same source file

The rules for the construction of *identifiers* (of functions, variables, enums, etc.) are:

1   *Identifiers* are constructed from upper and lower case alphabetic letters, digits and the _ (underscore) character, with the proviso that the first letter must be alphabetic.
2   *Identifiers* may be of any length but must be unique within the first 31 characters , i.e. the names can be any length but C only takes account of the first 31 characters.

21.6.2 External identifiers used between different source files

External identifiers defined in one source file and declared (using extern) in others must be unique within the first six characters and upper and lower case letters may be treated the same. The reason for this restriction is that many C systems use the standard linker provided by the operating system and these tend to have very tight rules on the construction of module names. In such cases the linker, when linking the object code modules together to form the executable program, truncates the names to six characters and often converts all alphabetical characters to upper case. It is possible for a particular system to have a linker which allows external identifiers to be longer than six characters but if portable code is to be implemented it is wise to keep the first six characters of external identifiers unique. For example, all the C standard library functions are unique within the first six characters.

21.7 Using and constructing header files

Before a program can use functions and external variables defined in another file it must declare them. Although such declarations can be within the program source code (as in Program 21.1a) this becomes tedious and a source of typing errors if there are a large number of identifiers. A simpler alternative is to construct a header file which is included in the program using the preprocessor #include directive, e.g.:

```
#include <filename>                    /* include file from 'standard' place */
#include "filename"    /* include file from current directory else 'standard' place */
```

Both the directives include the contents of filename at that point in the source program (filename can contain any valid C code). In the first form (filename enclosed in <>) the file is assumed to be in a 'standard' directory in the file system which the C compiler automatically searches, e.g. the header files for Microsoft C Version 6.00 are usually stored in directory \c600\include. The second form of #include (filename enclosed in "") searches the current directory for filename and then, if it is not found, the 'standard' directory. For example:

```
#include <math.h>                    /* include standard header file math.h */
#include "my_own.h"                   /* include header file my_own.h */
#include "my_func.c"             /* include C function from file my_func.c */
```

Header files are constructed by extracting function headers and the definitions of external variables from a file (using the editor) and amending as required. Many compilers have an option which will generate a header file of *function prototypes* from a C source code file without compiling, e.g. the /Zg option to the Microsoft C compiler. For example, if a programmer is implementing libraries of functions which will then be used by other members of the team such a facility for automatic generation of header files would save having to do the operation 'by hand'.

```
/* Header file p21_1b.h for program file p21_1b.c */

extern float a, b;                      /* declare external variables a and b */
extern const float pi;           /* declare external const qualified variable */
int test(float, int);                       /* declare function prototype */
```

Header file p21_1b.h Header file of external identifiers defined in Program 21.1b

Header file p21_1b.h is the header file for the external identifiers of Program 21.1b. In Program 21.1a lines 5, 7 and 8 would be removed and the following inserted after line 3:

```
#include "p21_1b.h"                   /* include header file for Program 21.1b */
```

Care must be taken not to include the same file twice otherwise identifiers will be defined more than once which will generate compile time errors (more on this in Chapter 26.3).

21.8 Storage allocation and initialisation

When storage is allocated for a variable (a simple variable or a structured type such as an array or structure) depends upon its storage class:

automatic internal variable	defined within a compound statement
static internal variable	defined within a compound statement
formal parameter to a function	declared as a parameter in a function header
external variable	defined outside function bodies

21.8.1 Automatic internal variables

This is the default storage class for variables defined within compound statements (see also the *static* and *register* storage classes below). The scope of automatic internal variables is from the point of definition up to the end of the compound statement in which they are defined. They are allocated storage (and optionally initialised) on entry to a compound statement and deallocated on exit from the compound statement (any contents are then lost). Automatic internal variables may be initialised with any meaningful expression; with the exception of arrays and structures which may only be initialised with constants (every time the statement is reentered the automatic variables are recreated and reinitialised). The contents of automatic internal variables not explicitly initialised will be *undefined*. These are the 'normal' working variables of the program.

21.8.2 Static internal variables

If the definition of an internal variable is prefixed with the keyword static it is allocated permanent storage (and initialised) prior to program execution and maintained until the program terminates. The scope of static internal variables is the same as automatic internal variables, i.e. from the point of definition up to the end of the compound statement in which they are defined. Static internal variables may only be initialised with constant values. Any static internal variable not explicitly initialised will be initialised to 0.

21.8.3 Formal parameters to a function

Storage is allocated on entry to the function and initialised with the values of the actual parameters (see also the *register* storage class below). Their scope is from the point of declaration up to the end of the function.

21.8.4 External variables

Permanent storage is allocated and initialised prior to program execution and maintained until the program terminates. External variables may only be initialised with constant values. Any external variable not explicitly initialised will be initialised to 0. The scope is from the point of definition up to the end of the file. This may be extended (within the file and to other files) by declaring the variable with the keyword extern. The scope of external variables of the *static* storage class is limited to the file in which they are defined.

21.8.5 The stack and the heap

In general the data area used to store external and static internal variables is called the heap (allocated and initialised on program startup and maintained until the program terminates) and the data area used to store *automatics* and the formal parameters of functions is called the stack.

21.8.6 The storage class *register*

The storage class *register* only applies to *automatic* internal variables and the formal parameters of a function. It is used to advise the compiler that the associated variables are heavily used and should, if possible, be stored in high-speed processor registers. For example, the execution of a loop may be significantly improved if critical variables are stored in processor registers, e.g.:

```
int test(int a, register int b)
{
    register int i;
    for (i = 1 ; i < 10000 ; i++)
        {
        register int x, y;
        register const float pi = 3.14159f;
        ....
        }
}
```

The keyword *register* is purely advisory and the compiler does not have to take any notice of it (in the main, modern optimising compilers have removed the necessity for it). Register variables do not have an address (the & operator cannot be used with them) even if the compiler stores the variables in normal memory.

In practice, *register* variables should be used sparingly within time critical routines, keeping in mind that processor only has a few processor registers (ten to a hundred) and over use can slow a program down if the compiler has to save a large number of registers when entering a function. In the main, the normal optimisation processes of a modern compiler should be left to generate efficient code. If it is found that a particular section of code is executing too slowly (e.g. in a real-time system) various approaches can be taken:

1   The algorithm should be examined to see if it can be made more efficient.
2   Small critical functions can be implemented in assembly language (see Chapter 31).
3   A faster computer should be purchased (this is often cheaper than paying a programmer to make the code more efficient).

21.9 The type qualifier *const*

Applying the keyword *const* in a definition or declaration indicates to the compiler that the object is to be treated as a constant and may not be altered. What happens if an attempt is made to alter a const qualified object is implementation dependent. Some compilers issue a warning and then treat the object like any other variable. Again it is up to the programmer to ensure that an object qualified as const in a definition is similarly qualified in any declarations, e.g. pi defined in line 5 of Program 21.1b and declared in line 7 of Program 21.1a. In an embedded system objects defined as const qualified may be burnt into ROM (read only memory) and if a function in another file attempts to alter it (because it was not declared as const qualified) the program will crash. Collecting all the declarations in a header file, such as Header file p21_1b.h, helps to prevent this type of error.

21.10 The type qualifier *volatile*

Applying the keyword *volatile* in a definition or declaration indicates to the compiler that the contents of the object is subject to unpredictable alterations and references it must not be optimised. For example, it may be a variable which will be changed by an interrupt service routine, or an I/O register which will be changed by the action of the corresponding I/O device (see Chapter 33 on I/O programming). A typical situation is where a program is in a loop waiting for an I/O device to become ready, i.e. the loop continuously tests a bit in a memory mapped I/O register. The problem is that a modern optimising compiler will notice that the loop tests the same address again and again and, on entry to the loop, makes a copy of it in a high speed CPU register. It then tests the contents of the CPU register within the loop ! Using volatile tells the compiler that object is changed by external means and prevents the compiler optimising references to it. If a volatile I/O register should not be changed by the program it can also be type qualified with const, e.g.:

```
const volatile unsigned char io_register          /* a byte sized I/O register */
```

This declares a byte sized object io_register which may not be altered by the program but is subject to changes from outside the program.

21.11 Side effects and sequence points

It is recommended that a single program statement or a function (composed of a number of statements) should perform a single cohesive operation. For example, consider:

```
i = 2;
x[i] = 10 + i++;
```

The latter statement assigns a value to the array element x[i] with the side effect of the increment operation i++. The problem with this statement is that the ANSI standard does not specify where the increment takes place (this being compiler dependent). The value of i may be incremented after the evaluation of the sub expression 10 + i++, assigning 12 to x[3], or not until the complete expression x[i] = 10 + i++ has been evaluated, assigning 12 to x[2]. The standard does, however, specify that all expressions of a program statement, including possible side effects, will have been evaluated before execution of the next statement starts (the terminating ; being a *sequence point*, see below). Program 10.2 showed some examples of side effects of ++ and -- when used as parameters in calls to the function printf. Again, the standard specifies that function parameters will have been fully evaluated, including possible side effects, before the function is called.

The ANSI C standard specifies a number of *sequence points* where expressions, including possible side effects, will have been evaluated. These are:

1   When a function is called, after all the parameters have been evaluated.
2   The end of the first (left hand) operand of the &&, || and ?: operators.
3   The end of each operand of the comma operator (see Chapter 13.4)
4   Completion of the evaluation of a full expression, i.e.:
    (a) evaluation of a program statement (terminated by a semicolon)
    (b) the initialisation of an automatic variable (on entry to a compound statement)
    (c) evaluation of the controlling expressions of do, while, for and switch statements
    (d) evaluation of the expression of a return statement

Use the knowledge of sequence points to implement code that is not dependent upon the order of evaluation of an expression or expressions. Break suspect code down into separate statements so that the order of evaluation will be as required by the specification.

A possible source of *side effects* in procedural languages such as C, Pascal, Fortran, etc. occurs when functions (or procedures or subroutines) access and alter non-local variables. For example, in C a function could alter variables which had been passed by reference (see Chapter 15.7) or external (global) variables in scope (see Chapter 17.2 and section 21.3). Problems may arise from side effects:

1   It can be difficult to understand the overall program semantics unless the code is well designed and commented.
2   External variables may be inadvertently altered, e.g. if an internal variable name is misspelt and an external variable name in scope corresponds to the incorrect name.

In the majority of functions presented in sample programs in this book any alterations made to parameters passed by reference (e.g. swap_int in Program 15.2 swaps the contents of two parameters) and external variables (e.g. random_initialise and random_number in Program 17.2 alter the external variable random_seed) are required for the overall operation of the function (access to random_seed should be controlled so other functions cannot alter it). Consider, however, Program 17.1 where the external variable a is an actual parameter to the call of function test (in line 19) and is also altered within function test (in line 29). This is a dangerous side effect and such practices can lead to very obscure errors. Care must therefore been taken when passing parameters by reference and access to external variables should be restricted (section 21.4 discussed static external variables). If parameters which should not be altered are passed by reference (e.g. arrays which are always passed by reference) they should be const qualified.

Problem for Chapter 21

Implement the calculator program designed in outline in Chapter 2. Place the main and calculation functions in one file and the input/output functions in another.

22

Structures

Whereas arrays provide a means to group elements of the same type, structures provide a means to group objects of different types. For example, consider a program used to store student records in a college or university where the data could include:

1. students name, a character string
2. students age, an integer
3. course code, an integer
4. year of course, an integer
5. identification number for library card, etc., a large integer

The course code would probably provide an index into an array of course data which would provide the course name, length (in years), level (undergraduate, postgraduate), fees, etc.

22.1 Declaring and initialising structures

The members of a structure can be any simple data type, pointer, array or even another structure. For example, a structure to hold student data could be:

```
struct student_t {
                  char name[20];                  /* student name */
                  int age;                         /* student age */
                  int course_code;         /* institutions course code */
                  int course_year;              /* year of course */
                  long int student_identifier;  /* library card identifier */
                  };
struct student_t  student_1, student_2;            /* declare variables */
```

defines a type `struct student_t` (where `student_t` is called the structure *tag*) and then declares two variables `student_1` and `student_2` of that type. The type `struct student_t` is a structure with members `name`, `age`, `course_code`, `course_year` and `student_identifier`. Note that the same names can be used for members of different structures. An alternative and possibly more elegant way to define a structure is to use *typedef*, e.g.:

```
typedef struct {
                  char name[20];                  /* student name */
                  int age;                         /* student age */
                  int course_code;         /* institutions course code */
                  int course_year;              /* year of course */
                  long int student_identifier;  /* library card identifier */
                  }
                  student_t;                     /* structure type name */
student_t  student_1, student_2, students[100];    /* declare variables */
```

defines a type `student_t` and then declares two variables `student_1` and `student_2`, and an array `students` of 100 elements of that type.

22.1.1 Initialisation of structures

A structure may be initialised with constants in a similar way to an array, e.g.:

```
student_t   student_1 = { "Smith, Sam", 19, 405, 2 },
            students[5] = { { "Doe, John", 18, 201, 1 },
                            { "Smith, Sally", 18, 65, 1 },
                            { "Jones, Daisy", 21, 345, 3} };
```

Any members not explicitly initialised will be initialised to 0, i.e. the member student_identifier in the above statements would be initialised to 0 as would students[4] and students[5]. If a structure is not initialised the member values are *undefined* if the structure is internal, or zero if it is external or a static internal.

22.2 Accessing the members of a structure

To access a particular member of a structure the . (dot) structure member operator is used:

```
        student_t   student_1, student_2, students[100];          /* declare variables */

        strcpy(student_1.name, "Smith, Bert");                    /* set up name */
        student_1.age = 17;                                       /* set up age */
        printf("student name %s, age %d ",
                student_1.name, student_1.age);                   /* print student data */
        students[2].name[0] = 'x';                    /* change first character of name */
        student_2 = student_1;                        /* copy one structure to another */
```

Consider the assignment statement:

```
        students[2].name[0] = 'x';                    /* change first character of name */
```

This sets up the first character of member name of the third element of the array students. The . (dot), [and] operators associate from left to right, therefore:

students[2] accesses the third element of array students
students[2].name accesses the member name (which is an array) within the element
students[2].name[0] accesses the first element of the member name

There is a major difference in the way that C treats arrays and structures in that the name of an array refers to the address of its first element and the name of a structure refers to the whole structure. This has a number of implications:

1   A structure can be assigned to another of the same type (even if it contains arrays),
2   Structures are passed to functions using *call by value* (unlike arrays).
3   A function can return a structure as a function result (new in ANSI C).

Chapter 18 stated that an array cannot be assigned to another, arrays are passed using *call by reference* and arrays cannot be returned as a function result. The above rules for structures apply even if the structure contains an array. Thus, although it is not possible to assign the structure member name (an array) using a single statement:

```
        student_2.name = student_1.name;                  /* copy name, not allowed !! */
```

it is possible to assign the whole structure:

```
        student_2 = student_1;                         /* copy one structure to another */
```

Note that assignment is the only operation that may be carried out on the whole structure, i.e. structures (as a whole) cannot be added, multiplied or even compared.

Arrays of structures (such as students in the above example) obey the normal rules for an array (although the individual elements would obey the rules for structures).

22.3 Structures within structures

A structure may contain another structure, etc. For example, the course details in the above example could be expanded and placed in a separate structure

```
/* define structure to hold course information */
typedef struct {
                char course_name[20];                      /* name of course */
                int course_year;                           /* year of course */
                }
                course_t;

/* define structure type to hold student information */
typedef struct {
                char name[20];                             /* student name */
                int age;                                   /* student age */
                course_t course;                        /* details of course */
                long int student_identifier;        /* library card identifier */
                }
                student_t;                           /* structure type name */
student_t  student_1, student_2, students[100];       /* declare variables */
```

The above:

    (a) defines a type course_t which will hold course information,
    (b) defines a type student_t which will hold student information (including course_t),
and (c) declares variables and an array of type student_t.

The members of course_t can be accessed using the . (dot) operator:

```
strcpy(student_1.course.course_name, "B.Sc Elec. Eng.");
student_1.course.course_year = 2;
printf("course name %s ", student_1.course.course_name);
```

22.4 Structures as function parameters

Unlike arrays, structures are passed using *call by value* (they can be passed using *call by reference* by using pointers, see Chapters 15.7 and 23.6). In addition a function may return a structure as a function result. For example, if a structure of type student_t is to be passed as a parameter to a function the function header could be:

```
void stu_print(const student_t student)
```

The formal parameter student is a const qualified structure of type student_t.

    Care must be taken when passing large structures as function parameters. It is possible to run out of storage space on the stack (the data structure used to hold temporary information) and the time taken to copy a large structure will adversely effect program execution speed. Large structures should be passed using pointers to achieve *call by reference* (see Chapters 15.7 and 23.6). If, when passing a structure by reference, the contents should not be changed the formal parameter should be const qualified.

22.5 Program using structures to store student records

This section describes, in outline, a program to store student records using the structure student_t described above. The overall program consists of four files:

stu_lib.h a header file which contains the definition of the structures course_t and student_t and prototypes of functions from the library files stu_lib.c and stu_lib1.c.

p22_1.c (Program 22.1) which contains the main function which makes calls to functions in the library files stu_lib.c and stu_lib1.c.

stu_lib.c contains functions to manipulate individual student records (calls stu_lib1.c).

stu_lib1.c contains functions to maintain the overall student records data structure.

The files and functions were designed to promote *data hiding* in which particular functions only have access to functions and data which they actually need. For example, functions in file stu_lib.c only have access to individual student records, not to the underlying data structure which holds all the records (thus the underlying data structure can be changed without effecting the functions in p22_1.c and stu_lib.c, see Chapter 28.2 on linked lists).

```
/* Header file stu_lib.h - header file for student record functions */

enum {name_length = 20};              /* length of student name, course name, etc. */

/* define structure to hold course information */
typedef struct {
            char course_name[name_length];           /* name of course */
            int course_code;                  /* institutions course code */
            int course_year;                       /* year of course */
            }
            course_t;

/* define structure type to hold student information */
typedef struct {
            char name[name_length];                       /* student name */
            int age;                                  /* student age */
            int start_year;                    /* year of starting course */
            course_t course;                      /* details of course */
            long int identifier;              /* student identifier number */
            }
            student_t;                          /* structure type name */

/* prototypes for student record processing functions in stu_lib.c & stu_lib1.c */
int stu_read_data(student_t *student);                        /* read record */
int stu_store(const student_t student);                       /* store record */
void stu_print(const student_t student);                      /* print record */
void stu_all_print(void);                                /* print all records */
int stu_name(const student_t student, const char name[]);     /* compare names */
int stu_find(student_t *student, char student_name[]);         /* find record */
/* read string and integer read functions */
int str_read(const char prompt[], char string[], const int max_length);
int integer_read(const char prompt[], const int maximum);
```

Header file stu_lib.h For student record functions in library files stu_lib.c and stu_lib1.c

```
 1 /* Library stu_lib1.c - support for the student records system data structure */
 2
 3 #include "stu_lib.h"                    /* include student records header file */
 4
 5 enum {max_students = 4};                        /* maximum number of students  */
 6
 7 static student_t students[max_students];        /* array of student records */
 8 static int number_of_students = 0;        /* indicates number of records used */
 9
10 /*--------------------------------------------------------------------------*
11  * Store student record into data structure, return TRUE if stored OK       */
12 int stu_store(const student_t student)
13 {
14     if (number_of_students == max_students) return 0;   /* array full, error */
15     students[number_of_students++] = student;           /* store record */
16     return 1;                                           /* return TRUE */
17 }
18
19 /*--------------------------------------------------------------------------*
20  * return record for next student in the data structure                     *
21  *    if first is TRUE reset to first student                               *
22  *    if past end of records return record with student name set to ""      */
23 student_t stu_next(const int first)
24 {
25     static int stu_index = 0;            /* working index into array students */
26     student_t student = {""};            /* initialise student name to "" */
27
28     if (first) stu_index = 0;            /* if TRUE reset to first student */
29     if (stu_index < number_of_students)             /* if valid record */
30         student = students[stu_index++];            /* copy record */
31     return student;                                 /* return record */
32 }
```

Library stu_lib1.c Functions to support the student records system data structure

The library file stu_lib1.c defines the following:

students (line 7) an array of type student_t which will hold the student records

number_of_students (line 8) a variable which:

(a) indicates the number of student records stored in students

and (b) indexes to the next element of array students to be used (see line 15)

stu_store (function) which is called to store a student record into the array students

if successful it returns *true* else *false*, e.g. if the array students is full

stu_next (function) which returns a record (as a function result) from the array students

if the parameter first is *true* the first record is returned else the next in sequence

if unsuccessful (attempt to access outside records) the record name is set to "" (empty)

The array and variables are *static external*. Thus they will be allocated permanent storage but may not be accessed by functions in other files, i.e. the concept of *data hiding*, in that functions in other files have no knowledge of the underlying data structure and must call the functions stu_store and stu_next to access the records. The sequence of statements is:

3 include the header file "stu_lib.h" which defines the structure student_t, etc.

5 define max_students, the size of the array students (this is small for test purposes)

7 define the static array students type student_t to hold student records

8 define number_of_students which indicates the number of records in use and is also used as an index to the next element of array students (see line 15)

12-17 define stu_store which stores a record into array students, return *true* if OK

14 if number_of_students == max_students array is full, return *false* indicating failure

15 copy new record into the array students, postincrement number_of_students

16 return *true* for success

23-32 define stu_next, returns either the first record or the next (indexed by stu_index)
   if first is *true* stu_index is reset to index the first record
   if beyond the end of the records a record with an empty name ("") is returned

25 define static internal stu_index which will index the record to be returned (initialised to 0). It will be allocated permanent storage and retain its value from call to call of the function (but not be accessible by any other functions).

26 define internal variable student with name initialised to ""

28 if first is *true* reset stu_index to index first record

29-30 if stu_index < number_of_students it is a valid record
   30 copy record into student, postincrement stu_index to index next record

31 return student (either with empty name or with the value assigned in line 30)

The library stu_lib.c (next page but one) contains functions to manipulate individual student records. Lines 3 to 5 include standard library header files and line 6 includes the header file "stu_lib.h" which defines the structure student_t, etc. Line 8 is a prototype of the function stu_next (from file stu_lib1.c). This prototype is not in the header file "stu_lib.h" because the only functions which should use it are in the library stu_lib.c.

  Function stu_name, lines 12 to 15, compares a student name with the name stored in a student record and returns *true* if they are identical. It can be used as a general utility function to search for a record on a particular student (see function stu_find below).

  Function stu_read_data, lines 20 to 30, reads a student record from the keyboard. The function result (type int) indicates success (*true*) or failure (*false*). If successful the record is returned via the formal parameter student which is a pointer to type student_t. Thus the parameter in the calling function is *passed by reference* (see Chapter 15.7).

20 function header for stu_read_data
  (a) one parameter student, pointer to type student_t
  (b) returns an int function result: *true* if data read OK else *false*
23 prompt user to enter the student data
24 call str_read to read the students name, if successful
   25 call integer_read to read the students age, if successful
     26 call str_read to read the course name, if successful
       28 success, return *true*
29 failed ! return *false*

The formal parameter student is a pointer to an object of type student_t. Thus to access the storage allocated to the original object the name of the formal parameter is prefixed with the indirection operator *, e.g. line 24:

```
if (str_read("  student name ? ",(*student).name, name_length))
```

This calls the function str_read (string read) to read a string into the array (*student).name. Because the dot . operator has a higher precedence than the indirection operator * the parentheses are required to force the correct association (more discussion in Chapter 23.6).

Function stu_find, lines 35 to 44, searches the data structure for a record for a named student (name passed as a parameter):

35	function header for stu_find
	(a) two parameters student, pointer to type student_t, and the student_name
	(b) returns an int function result; *true* if found else *false*
37	call stu_next with parameter *true* to get the *first* student record into *student
38-42	a while statement, terminating when an empty name is found
	40 if the name is the one required return *true*
	41 call stu_next to get the *next* record in the data structure
43	failed ! return *false*

The function stu_print, lines 48 to 52, prints the contents of a single student record (passed as a parameter) to the display screen. The output is printed in columns (see sample run) the width of which is determined by the value of name_length. If the program is modified and name_length is altered the printed output should change accordingly. Consider the call to printf in lines 50 and 51:

```
printf("\n  %-*s  %2d  %-*s ", name_length, student.name,
                  student.age, name_length, student.course.course_name);
```

This prints the strings student.name and student.course.course_name left justified in a field of width name_length. The conversion specification %-*s (see Appendix C.12.6 for details):

-     indicates that the string is to be printed left justified in the field (default is right)
*   indicates that the field width is specified by the next parameter (must be an int)
s   indicates that the object to be printed is a string

The function stu_all_print, lines 56 to 69, prints all the student records to the screen:

60-61	print a heading (see discussion of the %-*s conversion specification above)
63	call stu_next with parameter *true* to get the *first* student record
64-68	a while statement, terminating when an empty name is found
	66 call stu_print to print the student record
	67 call stu_next to get the *next* record in the data structure

The function str_read, lines 101 to 111, reads a string of maximum length max_length (it is similar to str_read in Program 19.1 except that the characters are read individually using getchar rather than as a string using fgets). The function discards excess characters on the line and returns, as a function result, the number of characters read into the string:

103	define index (which will index string) and ch (the character read)
105	prompt the user with the string prompt
106-8	a while reading a character, terminating when newline or EOF is entered
	107 if the character printable and there is room in the string
	108 copy character into string, postincrement index
	note the cast converting the int (ch) to a char to be assigned to string
109	place terminating null '\0' on end of string
110	return index, the number of characters in string (not counting '\0')

Function integer_read, lines 73 to 93, reads an integer number in the range 1 to maximum. It is similar to function integer_read in Program 20.1 except that function str_read is used to read a string and sscanf is used to convert a decimal integer from the string. The function sscanf conversions are similar to scanf except that the characters are read from a string (passed as a parameter), see Chapter 27.6 and Appendix C.12.7.

```
 1 /* Library stu_lib.c - maintain and manipulate individual student records */
 2
 3 #include <stdio.h>                            /* standard function headers */
 4 #include <ctype.h>
 5 #include <string.h>
 6 #include "stu_lib.h"                      /* include student records header file */
 7
 8 student_t stu_next(const int first);      /* prototype for function stu_next */
 9
10 /*-----------------------------------------------------------------------*
11  * Check student name in record, return TRUE if identical              */
12 int stu_name(const student_t student, const char name[])
13 {
14     return (! strcmp(student.name, name));        /* compare the names */
15 }
16
17 /*-----------------------------------------------------------------------*
18  * read data into record pointed at by 'student' (name, age, course, etc.)  *
19  *  if all OK return function result TRUE else FALSE if data entry fails   */
20 int stu_read_data(student_t *student)
21 {
22     /* prompt for student data, read name, age, etc. */
23     printf("\n\nEnter data on next student \n");
24     if (str_read(" student name ? ",(*student).name, name_length))   /* name */
25         if (((*student).age = integer_read(" age ? ", 100)) != 0)      /* age */
26             if(str_read(" course ? ", (*student).course.course_name, name_length))
27                 /* extension required to read further course details, etc. */
28                 return 1;                              /* return success */
29     return 0;                                          /* return fail */
30 }
31
32 /*-----------------------------------------------------------------------*
33  * Find record for student_name, return into record pointed at by 'student'  *
34  *  if found return function result TRUE else FALSE                        */
35 int stu_find(student_t *student, char student_name[])
36 {
37     *student = stu_next(1);                    /* get first student record */
38     while (! stu_name(*student, ""))               /* if record OK */
39         {
40         if (stu_name(*student, student_name)) return 1;       /* found ? */
41         *student = stu_next(0);                    /* get next student record */
42         }
43     return 0;                              /* failed, return FALSE */
44 }
```

Library stu_lib.c Functions to maintain and manipulate individual student records

```
45
46 /*-------------------------------------------------------------------*
47  * print student record to screen                                  */
48 void stu_print(const student_t student)
49 {
50     printf("\n  %-*s  %2d  %-*s ", name_length, student.name,
51               student.age, name_length, student.course.course_name);
52 }
53
54 /*-------------------------------------------------------------------*
55  * print records for all students to screen                        */
56 void stu_all_print(void)
57 {
58     student_t student;
59
60     printf("\n\nPrint of all student records\n  %-*s age  %-*s",   /* heading */
61           name_length, "student name", name_length, "course");
62
63     student = stu_next(1);                          /* get first student record */
64     while (! stu_name(student, ""))                        /* if record OK */
65         {
66         stu_print(student);                        /* print the student record */
67         student = stu_next(0);                      /* get next student record */
68         }
69 }
70
71 /*-------------------------------------------------------------------*
72  * function: read an integer number in range 1 to maximum (return 0 on EOF)   */
73 int integer_read(const char prompt[], const int maximum)
74 {
75     int value = maximum + 1;
76     char string[name_length];
77
78     do                                  /* read integer in range 1 to maximum */
79         {
80         /* read a string and call sscanf to convert it into a decimal number */
81         if (! str_read(prompt, string, name_length)) return 0;
82         if (sscanf(string, "%d", &value) != 1)
83             printf("  non numeric character in input string, try again ? \n");
84         else
85           if (value > maximum)                                 /* range check */
86             printf("  value %1d > maximum %1d, try again ? ", value, maximum);
87           else
88             if (value < 1)                                     /* range check */
89                 printf("  value %1d < minimum 1, try again ? ", value);
90         }
91     while ((value < 1) || (value > maximum));
92     return value;
93 }
94
```

Library stu_lib.c Functions to maintain and manipulate individual student records

```
95   /*----------------------------------------------------------------------*
96    * read string up to \n, printable characters only !                    *
97    * on entry prompt[]      contains prompt string to print               *
98    *          max_length    contains maximum length of string             *
99    * return string read in array string[]                                 *
100   * return function result: number of characters in string               */
101  int str_read(const char prompt[], char string[], const int max_length)
102  {
103      int index = 0, ch;                          /* initialise index to 0 */
104
105      printf("%s", prompt);                              /* print prompt */
106      while (((ch = getchar()) != '\n') && (ch != EOF))  /* read to \n or EOF */
107          if (isprint(ch) && (index < max_length - 1))       /* if OK */
108              string[index++] = (char) ch;            /* put ch in string */
109      string[index] = '\0';                       /* terminate string */
110      return index;                                /* all OK return true */
111  }
```

Library stu_lib.c Functions to maintain and manipulate individual student records

Program 22.1 (next page) contains the main function of the students records program:

3	include standard I/O header <stdio.h>
4	include the header file "stu_lib.h" which defines the structure student_t, etc.
8	define student which will hold a student record
9	define student_name which will hold the name of a student to search for
12-16	a while statement which terminates when stu_read_data returns *false*
	12 call stu_read_data to read a record from the keyboard into student, if OK
	13 call stu_store to store the student record in the data structure
	14-16 print message indicating if record was stored successfully
19-23	a while which reads a student name and searches the data structure for the record
	19 call str_read to read the name, terminate while when the string is empty
	20 call stu_find to search for the record on the student
	21-23 print message indicating if record was found
25	call stu_print_all to print the records of all the students

In lines 12 and 20 the formal parameter student is prefixed with the address operator & to achieve *call by reference*. The address of student is passed to the functions which can then use it to return the record read (stu_read_data) or found (stu_find). Thus the overall program has shown a number of ways of passing structures in and out of functions:

1	parameters *passed by value*, e.g. stu_store, stu_name and stu_print
2	parameters *passed by reference*, e.g. stu_read_data and stu_find
3	returned as a function result, e.g. stu_next

The program will only be able to store data on four students (the size of array students defined in file stu_lib1.c). Attempts to store more records results in an error message and the alarm sounding. After testing the array size would be increased to that required. Chapter 28 presents two versions of the program the first using dynamic array allocation and the second a linked list. The problem for Chapter 34 is to implement a C++ version using the aggregate type *class* (an extension of the idea of *struct*).

```
 1 /* Program 22.1, student records using library stu_lib.c and stu_lib1.c */
 2
 3 #include <stdio.h>                                 /* standard I/O header */
 4 #include "stu_lib.h"                   /* include student records header file */
 5
 6 int main(void)
 7 {
 8     student_t student;                            /* 'working' record */
 9     char student_name[name_length];        /* holds student name to find */
10
11     /* read data on students and store in data structure */
12     while (stu_read_data(&student))                    /* read record */
13         if (stu_store(student))                        /* store it */
14             printf("\n  Data on '%s' stored ", student.name);         /* OK */
15         else
16             printf("\n\a  Failed to store '%s'", student.name);     /* fail */
17
18     /* search data structure for student names */
19     while (str_read("\n\nFind student name ? ", student_name, name_length))
20         if (stu_find(&student, student_name))                    /* search */
21             printf("\n    '%s' data found", student_name);
22         else
23             printf("\n\a    '%s' data not found ", student_name);
24
25     stu_all_print();                          /* print data on all students */
26     return  0;
27 }
28
```

Program 22.1 Student records system main program

Because of the primitive data structuring techniques available in C only limited success in *data hiding* can achieved without fragmenting and over complicating the overall program. C++ contains further data structuring facilities which facilitate *data hiding*, see Chapter 34.   For example, C++ can restrict access to members of a data structure, such as student_t, to particular functions. It would be possible to allow a function such as main in Program 22.1 to define objects of type student_t but not access the members (e.g. the access of student.name in line 16 would not be allowed). At the same time the functions in a libraries stu_lib.c and stu_lib1.c would have full access to members. Hence if the data structure student_t is modified only functions which have access to its members (may) need to be modified. Functions which cannot access the members (but only define objects of that type) need only be recompiled.

A sample run of Program 22.1 was:

```
Enter data on next student
  student name ? Jones, Sam ↓
  age ? 18 ↓
  course ? B.Sc Computer Science ↓
Data on 'Jones, Sam' stored

Enter data on next student
  student name ? Smith, Daisy ↓
  age ? 19 ↓
  course ? B.Sc Elec. Eng. ↓
Data on 'Smith, Daisy' stored

Enter data on next student
  student name ? Doe, John ↓
  age ? 19 ↓
  course ? B.Sc Mechanical Engineering ↓
Data on 'Doe, John' stored

Enter data on next student
  student name ?  ↓

Find student name ? Jones, Sam ↓
   data on student 'Jones, Sam' found

Find student name ? Smith, George ↓
   data on student 'Smith, George' not found

Find student name ? Doe, John ↓
   data on student 'Doe, John' found

Find student name ?  ↓

Print of all student records
  student name        age  course
  Jones, Sam           18  B.Sc Computer Scien
  Smith, Daisy         19  B.Sc Elec. Eng.
  Doe, John            19  B.Sc Mechanical Eng
```

The function str_read is correctly truncating the input at the array bounds name_length and then stripping the surplus characters off the line (including the terminating '\n'). The final table is in columns of the correct width. Changing the value of name_length to 30 and recompiling and executing the program gave the following final result:

```
Print of all student records
  student name                age  course
  Jones, Sam                   18  B.Sc Computer Science
  Smith, Daisy                 19  B.Sc Elec. Eng.
  Doe, John                    19  B.Sc Mechanical Engineering
```

22.6 Evaluation of complex numbers using structures

Unlike Fortran, C has no built in type which can directly represent and operate upon complex numbers (which are required in many mathematical, scientific and engineering applications). A complex number z has two components, e.g.:

```
z = a + ib
```

where a is the real part and b is the imaginary part (i being the square root of -1). Complex numbers may be added, multiplied and divided using the following equations:

addition $(a + ib) + (c + id) = (a + c) + i(b + d)$

multiplication $(a + ib) * (c + id) = (ac - bd) + i(bc + ad)$

division $\dfrac{(a + ib)}{(c + id)} = \dfrac{(ac + bd) - i(ad - bc)}{c^2 + d^2}$

absolute value $(a + ib) = (a^2 + b^2)^{\frac{1}{2}}$

There may also be functions of complex numbers, e.g. e^x:

```
e(a + ib) = ea ( sin(b) + icos(b) )
```

In C a complex number may be represented by two variables, an array of two elements or a structure of two members. Because a structure can be returned as a function result the use of a structure appears to be a good choice, e.g.:

```
typedef  struct {
                float real;                    /* real component */
                float imag;                    /* imaginary component */
                }
                complex;                       /* complex number type */
complex  x, y, z;                    /* declare variables of type complex */
```

This defines a type complex which has two float members (used to represent the real and imaginary components of a complex number) and then declares variables of that type. Two complex numbers stored in variables x and y could be added:

```
z.real = x.real + y.real;
z.imag = x.imag + y.imag;
```

This could easily be implemented as a function which is called with two variables of type complex, the result of which is returned as a function result of complex, e.g.

```
/*------------------------------------------------------------------*
 * Function to add a pair of complex numbers, result = x + y        */
complex c_add(complex x, const complex y)
{
    x.real = x.real + y.real;                    /* setup real part */
    x.imag = x.imag + y.imag;                    /* setup imaginary part */
    return x;                                    /* return function result */
}
```

Note that formal parameter x is used as a working variable within the function (structures are passed using *call by value* so the actual parameter will not be affected). The function could be called as follows:

```
z = c_add(x, y);
```

Library complex.c (below) contains a number of functions to manipulate complex numbers (add, subtract, multiply, print, etc.). The code within the functions is fairly simple and the comments should provide adequate explanation. The only exception is possibly lines 68 and 69 which print the real and imaginary components of a complex number:

```
printf("%s%2.2f %c i%2.2f", text, x.real,
          (x.imag >= 0) ? '+' : '-' , fabs(x.imag));
```

1   prints text, e.g. name of the variable, heading, etc.
2   prints the real component x.real,
3   prints a character + or - (the sign of the imaginary component),
4   prints an i (indicating the imaginary component follows)
5   prints the absolute value of the imaginary component x.imag.

```
 1 /* Library complex.c, implementing complex numbers using structures under C   */
 2
 3 #include <stdio.h>                                  /* include required headers */
 4 #include <math.h>
 5
 6 /* a structure type to hold the real and imaginary parts of a complex number */
 7 typedef   struct {
 8                  float real;                         /* real component */
 9                  float imag;                         /* imaginary component */
10                  }
11                  complex;                            /* complex number type */
12
13 /*-------------------------------------------------------------------------*
14  * Function to form a complex number (type complex) from two reals         *
15  * returns a function result of type complex                               */
16 complex c_numb(const float real, const float imag)
17 {
18     complex x;
19
20     x.real = real;                                  /* setup real part */
21     x.imag = imag;                                  /* setup imaginary part */
22     return x;                                       /* return function result */
23 }
24
25 /*-------------------------------------------------------------------------*
26  * Function to add a pair of complex numbers, result = x + y               */
27 complex c_add(const complex x, const complex y)
28 {
29     return c_numb(x.real + y.real, x.imag + y.imag);        /* function result */
30 }
31
32 /*-------------------------------------------------------------------------*
33  * Function to subtract a pair of complex numbers, result = x - y          */
34 complex c_sub(const complex x, const complex y)
35 {
36     return c_numb(x.real - y.real, x.imag - y.imag);        /* function result */
37 }
```

Library file complex.c Implements complex number functions (continued on next page)

```
38
39  /*-------------------------------------------------------------------*
40   * Function to multiply a pair of complex numbers, result = x * y           */
41  complex c_mult(const complex x, const complex y)
42  {
43      return c_numb(x.real * y.real - x.imag * y.imag,          /* real part */
44                  x.real * y.imag + x.imag * y.real);       /* imaginary part */
45  }
46
47  /*-------------------------------------------------------------------*
48   * Function to divide a pair of complex numbers, result = x / y             */
49  complex c_div(const complex x, const complex y)
50  {
51      float y_squared = y.real * y.real + y.imag * y.imag;
52
53      return c_numb((x.real * y.real + x.imag * y.imag) / y_squared,    /* real */
54                  (x.imag * y.real - x.real * y.imag) / y_squared);  /* imag */
55  }
56
57  /*-------------------------------------------------------------------*
58   * Function evaluate the absolute value of a complex number, returns a float  */
59  float c_abs(const complex x)
60  {
61      return ((float) sqrt(x.real * x.real + x.imag * x.imag));
62  }
63
64  /*-------------------------------------------------------------------*
65   * Function to print the value of a complex number with associated text      */
66  void c_print(const char text[], const complex x)
67  {
68      printf("%s%2.2f %c i%2.2f", text, x.real,
69              (x.imag >= 0) ? '+' : '-' , fabs(x.imag));
70  }
71
72  /*-------------------------------------------------------------------*
73   * Function evaluate exp(x), where x and result are complex numbers         *
74   *     c_exp = exp(x.real) * (sin(x.imag) + i cos(x.imag))                  */
75  complex c_exp(const complex x)
76  {
77      float exp_real = (float) exp(x.real);
78
79      return c_numb(exp_real * cos(x.imag),                     /* real part */
80                  exp_real * sin(x.imag));                  /* imaginary part */
81  }
```

Library file complex.c Implements complex number functions (continued from last page)

```
1  /* Program 22.2, test complex number functions under C                      */
2
3  #include <stdio.h>                        /* include standard I/O header file */
4  #include "complex.h"                       /* include complex number header file */
5
6  int main(void)
7  {
8      complex a = {{1.0f} , {2.0f}}, b, d, g;        /* declare complex numbers */
9      float c;
10
11     c_print("\nComplex number operations\na = ", a);            /* print a */
12     b = c_numb(4.0f, 5.0f);                                    /* set up b */
13     c_print(", b = ", b);                                      /* print b */
14     printf(", c_abs(a) = %2.2f", c_abs(a));              /* print abs(a) */
15     c_print("\na + b = ", c_add(a, b));                     /* a + b */
16     c_print("\na - b = ", c_sub(a, b));                     /* a - b */
17     c_print("\na * b = ", c_mult(a, b));                    /* a * b */
18     c_print("\na / b = ", c_div(a, b));                     /* a / b */
19     c_print("\n(a / b) * b = ",  c_mult(c_div(a, b), b));     /* (a / b) * b */
20
21     /* do a sample calculation */
22     c = 2.1f;
23     d = c_numb(-1.7f, 1.2f);
24     g = c_numb(0.2f, -0.7f);
25     a = c_mult(c_numb(c,0.0f), c_mult(d, c_exp(c_numb(0.0f, c))));
26     a = c_sub(c_div(a, g),g);
27     c_print("\n\nSample calculation = ", a);
28     return 0;
29 }
```

Program 22.2 Evaluation of complex numbers using structures

```
/* Header complex.h, implementing complex numbers using structures under C    */

#include <stdio.h>                          /* include required headers */
#include <math.h>

typedef  struct {                            /* complex number type */
                float real;                  /* real component */
                float imag;                  /* imaginary component */
             } complex;

complex c_numb(const float real, const float imag);     /* form a complex number */
complex c_add(const complex x, const complex y);        /* add, result = x + y */
complex c_sub(const complex x, const complex y);        /* subtract, result = x - y */
complex c_mult(const complex x, const complex y);       /* multiply, result = x * y */
complex c_div(const complex x, const complex y);        /* divide, result = x / y */
float c_abs(const complex x);                           /* absolute value */
void c_print(const char text[], const complex x);       /* print value with text */
complex c_exp(const complex x);                         /* exp(x) complex exponent */
```

Header file complex.h Declare complex and prototypes of the complex number functions

Program 22.2 performs some simple tests on the complex number functions. The header file complex.h (which declares the type complex and prototypes of the complex number functions) is included in line 4. Complex variables a = 1 + i2 and b = 4 + i5 are declared and initialised in lines 8 and 12 and printed in lines 11 and 13. Lines 15 to 19 perform some simple tests of the functions, e.g. line 19:

```
c_print("\n(a / b) * b = ",  c_mult(c_div(a, b), b));      /* (a / b) * b */
```

divides a by b and then multiplies the result by b, which should give the original value of a. Because c_div returns a / b as a function result it can be used as an argument to c_mult. For example, lines 22 to 26 evaluate the following expression:

$$\frac{c * d * e^{ic}}{g} - g$$

where: c = real number value 2.1
        d = complex number value -1.7 + i1.2
        g = complex number 0.2 - i0.7

Lines 22 to 24 set up the values of c, d and g and lines 25 and 26 evaluate the expression (the result of which should be 5.41 - i1.436).

It is worth noting that complex numbers are implemented in C++ in a much more elegant way. The aggregate type *class* (an extension of the idea of *struct* in C) enables the definition of a type with associated functions and operators. Using operator *overloading* a number of meanings may be given to an operator or a function, e.g. the operator + may be *overloaded* so that it can directly operate upon complex numbers (rather than having to call a function such as c_add in Program 22.2).

22.7 Unions

A union is similar to a structure in the way that it is declared and how its members are accessed, but there is a fundamental difference in the way storage is allocated:

structures   each member has its own area of storage.
unions   the members use the same area of storage, i.e. overlay each other.

For example, one of the problems at the end of this chapter is to implement a set of functions to support a structured display file on a raster scan display. The display file is built up from drawing elements each of which contains information on a particular drawing primitive such as a line (type line_t), circle (type circle_t) and box (type box_t), etc. For example:

```
typedef short int g_t;                      /* type used for graphics data */

/* line: its type and start and end coordinates */
typedef struct { g_t l_type; g_t x1; g_t y1; g_t x2; g_t y2; } line_t;

/* box: if filled and top left hand and bottom right hand coordinates */
typedef struct { g_t fill; g_t x_lh; g_t y_lh; g_t x_rh; g_t y_rh; } box_t;

/* circle: if filled and coordinates of centre and radius */
typedef struct { g_t fill; g_t x; g_t y; g_t radius; } circle_t;
```

Because a particular element would only store information on one primitive at any time a union is a suitable structure to hold such elements, e.g.:

```
/* define a union to hold drawing primitives */
typedef union {
            line_t line;                                    /* lines */
            box_t box;                                       /* boxes */
            circle_t circle;                              /* circles */
            }
            primitive_t;

primitive_t primitive, drawing[100];
```

This defines a type `primitive_t` and a variable and an array of that type. It is important to remember that the members `primitive.line`, `primitive.circle` and `primitive.box` all occupy the same area of memory. A simple variable (such as `primitive`) is not much use but an array (such as `drawing`) could be used to store a drawing built up from lines, circles and boxes. C performs no consistency checking on what is stored in a union and it is up to the programmer to keep track of which member is in use at any instant, i.e. if information is written into `primitive.line` and then read as `primitive.circle` the resultant circle information would be incorrect. The members of a union start at the same address and the overall size of the union is the size of its longest member.

Structures can contain unions and vice versa and one can have arrays of such structures. It is because structures can contain a union that structures cannot be compared, i.e. the compiler does not know which member of a union is in use and although a comparison at the bit level may yield identical structures it could be pure chance that the data stored in different union members had the same bit pattern.

A common practice is to have a union as a member of a structure where another member of the structure is a variable which keeps track of what is stored in the union, e.g.:

```
/* define drawing primitive indicators and size of display file */
typedef enum { a_line, a_box, a_circle, Df_size = 200 };

/* define a type to hold all the data on a drawing primitive */
typedef struct {
            g_t element_number;                   /* element number */
            g_t color;                             /* primitive colour */
            g_t indicator;                    /* indicates primitive type */
            primitive_t primitive;                 /* primitive type */
            }
            element_t;

element_t drawing[Df_size];               /* array of drawing elements */
```

When information is stored in `drawing[index].primitive` the corresponding value `a_line`, `a_circle` or `a_box` is assigned to member `drawing[index].indicator`. Functions processing the elements of the array `drawing` would then check the contents of member `indicator` to see what type of information was stored in the corresponding `primitive`.

22.8 Bitfields

Consider a process control program which contains a number of variables whose values indicate the state of control valves in the system:

```
/* variables holding information on the state of valves in a control system */
unsigned char valve_1;                              /* valve 1 open/closed */
unsigned char valve_2;                              /* valve 2 open/closed */
unsigned char valve_3;                             /* valve 3 - 8 positions */
unsigned char valve_4;                            /* valve 4 - 16 positions */
unsigned char valve_5;                            /* valve 5 - 256 positions */

valve_1 = 0;                                        /* valve 1 is closed */
valve_2 = 1;                                          /* valve 2 is open */
valve_3 = 2;                            /* valve 3 is approximately 30% open */
valve_4 = 9;                            /* valve 4 is approximately 60% open */
valve_5 = 191;                          /* valve 5 is approximately 75% open */
```

In the above example, valves 1 and 2 are either open or closed with 0 indicating closed and 1 indicating open. Valves 3, 4 and 5 have variable settings, e.g. the state of valve 4 varies between 0, closed, and 15, fully open. The variables are of type unsigned char, which is the smallest simple data type which can be defined (a char is always a byte, 8-bits). Storing a simple open/closed (binary 1/0) value in an unsigned char is very wasteful in terms of storage space, i.e. 7 bits of variable valve_1 are not used. The alternative is to store a number of such values within a byte; this may be achieved by:

1   using *bitfields* within a structure;
2   using the *bitwise* operators to access particular bits within a byte or a sequence of bytes (*bitwise* operators were covered in Chapter 9.4).

Bitfields, which may only be declared inside a structure or a union, allow the specification of very small objects of a given length in bits. For example, the information on the valves could be stored as follows:

```
/* structure to hold information on the state of valves in a control system */
typedef struct {
                unsigned int valve_1: 1;            /* valve 1 open/closed */
                unsigned int valve_2: 1;            /* valve 2 open/closed */
                unsigned int valve_3: 3;           /* valve 3 - 8 positions */
                unsigned int valve_4: 4;          /* valve 4 - 16 positions */
                unsigned char valve_5;            /* valve 5 - 256 positions */
                }
                valve_t;

valve_t valves;                            /* variable holding data on valves */

valves.valve_1 = 0;                                 /* valve 1 is closed */
valves.valve_2 = 1;                                   /* valve 2 is open */
valves.valve_3 = 2;                     /* valve 3 is approximately 30% open */
valves.valve_4 = 9;                     /* valve 4 is approximately 60% open */
valves.valve_5 = 191;                   /* valve 5 is approximately 75% open */
printf("\nvalve_1 %d ", valves.valve_1);
printf("\nvalve_2 %d ", valves.valve_2);
printf("\nvalve_3 %d ", valves.valve_3);
printf("\nvalve_4 %d ", valves.valve_4);
printf("\nvalve_5 %d ", valves.valve_5);
```

If a member of a structure or union is to be a bitfield the numbers of bits is specified following the identifier, i.e. valve_1 and valve_2 are one bit in length and valve_3 and valve_4 are three and four bits in length respectively (valve_5 is a byte). The bitfields are accessed and manipulated as are other members of a structure. The above example shows the assignment and printing of the values of the variables.

Bitfields behave like small integers, and when used in an expression (such as a parameter in the above calls to printf) undergo integral promotion (see Chapter 9.1.1). The unit of storage used to store bitfields, the order of the bitfields within the storage unit and whether or not bitfields may cross a unit boundary are all implementation dependent (to force alignment to a storage unit boundary a zero width field is specified).

Take care in using bitfields. Although the amount of storage used to store the data may be reduced, the overhead in terms of run-time code required to pack and unpack the fields can be considerable.

An alternative approach is to use the *bitwise* operators (see Chapter 9.4) explicitly to pack and unpack data by accessing and manipulating particular bits or groups of bits within a variable. For example:

```
/* define bit mask for valves within an 8-bit unsigned char */
enum { valve_1 = 0x80, valve_2 = 0x40, valve_3 = 0x30, valve_4 = 0x0f };

unsigned char valves = 0, valve_5;        /* define variable to store valve positions */

valves = valves & ~valve_1;                              /* valve 1 is closed */
valves = valves | valve_2;                               /* valve 2 is open */
valves = (valves & ~valve_3) | (2 << 4);     /* valve 3 is approximately 30% open */
valves = (valves & ~valve_4) | 9;            /* valve 4 is approximately 60% open */
valve_5 = 191;                               /* valve 5 is approximately 75% open */

printf("valves %#x ", valves);                           /* print values */
printf("\nvalve_1 %d ", (valves & valve_1) >> 7);
printf("\nvalve_2 %d ", (valves & valve_2) >> 6);
printf("\nvalve_3 %d ", (valves & valve_3) >> 4);
printf("\nvalve_4 %d ", (valves & valve_4));
printf("\nvalve_5 %d ", valve_5);
```

Within variable valves the value of valve_1 is stored in bit 8, valve_2 in bit 7, valve_3 in bits 5 and 6 and valve_4 in bits 0 to 4. The particular bits are accessed using the bit masks defined using enum (#define could be used) together with & (and) to clear bits, | (or) to set bits and shifts to position the fields within the variable. For example, valve 3 is represented by two bits (bits 4 and 5 of valves) giving a range from 0 (closed) to 7 (open):

```
valves = (valves & ~valve_3) | (2 << 4);      /* valve 3 is approximately 30% open */
```

(a) the value of valves is ANDed with the complement of valve_3 (clearing bits 4 and 5)
(b) the value 2 (approximately 30% of 7) is shifted 4 bits left (into bits 4 and 5)
(c) the results of (a) and (b) are ORed and the result assigned to valves

Using *bitwise* operators may or may not be more efficient than using bitfields but it at least makes the programmer aware of the overheads in terms of the code required to do the bit manipulation. This forces careful design of the data structures to achieve the most efficient methods of accessing and manipulating the bits. In practice, a small change in the position or order of fields can make orders of magnitude changes in program execution times. Another alternative is to implement assembly language functions (see Chapter 31) to carry out packing and unpacking operations on groups or blocks of fields at a time.

Problem for Chapter 22

Problem 22.1 Extend function `stu_store` to check for an identical student name before adding a new record to the data structure. Add functions to Library `stu_lib1.c` to delete and replace records (identified by `name`). Add functions to Library `stu_lib.c` to amend records, e.g. to correct student names, course names, etc.

Problem 22.2 Extend Program 22.2 to evaluate the following functions:

The log of a complex number: $\log(a + ib) = \frac{1}{2}\log(a^2 + b^2) + i\tan^{-1}(b/a)$

The sine of a complex number: $\sin(a + ib) = \sin(a)\cosh(b) + i\cos(a)\sinh(b)$

The cosine of a complex number: $\cos(a + ib) = \cos(a)\cosh(b) - i\sin(a)\sinh(b)$

To read a complex number, e.g. `complex c_read(const char prompt[])`

Extend the `main` to read a complex number from the keyboard (using `c_read`) and then call the various functions. The following relationships should be true:

$x = e^{\log(x)}$

$\sin^2(x) + \cos^2(x) = 1$ (no imaginary component)

Problem 22.3 Use the complex number functions from Program 22.2 to evaluate the impedance of a circuit at frequency f consisting of resistors R, inductors L and capacitors C:

$$\text{impedance} = R + i(2\pi fL - 1/(2\pi fC))$$

Apply a voltage to the circuit and determine the magnitude and phase of the current.

Problem 22.4 A raster scan graphics system (used on PCs and the majority of modern workstations) organises the display screen as a two-dimensional matrix of addressable points called pixels. For example, the VGA graphics system on IBM PC compatible microcomputers consists of 480 lines each of which has 640 pixels. Associated with each pixel on the screen is one or more bits in a RAM memory; usually called the bitmap. In a single plane system (one bit/pixel) if a particular bit is set the associated pixel on the screen is illuminated, if it is zero the pixel is blank. Additional memory planes can be used to represent various levels of intensity or colour. The bitmap is scanned 50 or 60 times per second (ignoring non-interlaced displays) with the corresponding pixels on the screen illuminated in the appropriate colour.

A vector or character can be represented by setting a pattern of bits in the bitmap to 1 and, thus, illuminating the associated pixels on the display screen. For example, the following shows the character X stored in bitmap memory and the resultant display.

```
        bitmap contents
      0000000000000000000
      0000001000000100000
      0000000100001000000
      0000000010010000000
      0000000001010000000
      0000000000100000000
      0000000010100000000
      0000000100010000000
      0000001000001000000
      0000010000000100000
      0000000000000000000
```

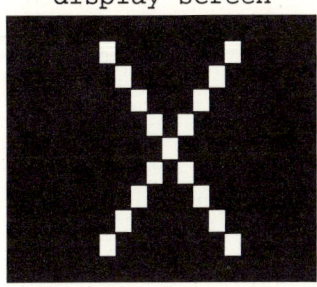

display screen

So long as the character is built up from sufficient pixels and the adjacent pixels (vertical and horizontal) on the display screen are sufficiently close together the eye will perceive a continuous shape rather than a number of separate points. The more pixels the finer the quality of the resultant image (assuming that the quality of the display screen is sufficient in terms of dot size, etc). For example, professional workstations, used for advanced CAD design work, typically have a 19 or 21 inch screen with a minimum of 1000 * 1000 pixels and 256 to 16 million colours.

When using a raster scan display system it is possible for the programmer to manipulate individual pixels and groups of pixels either directly by addressing the appropriate memory locations or by calling functions in a graphics library. Applications such as image processing, television picture manipulation, etc., would use pixel based 'bitmapped' graphics. In other application areas, however, the pictorial information is not naturally in a bitmapped pixel based form. For example, engineers may wish to draw pictures of resistors, capacitors, ICs, bridges, engines, jumbo jets, etc. Although these tend to be application specific they can all be built using simple drawing primitives such as lines, polygons, circles, arcs, etc. There are many graphics packages which enable the user to write a program in terms of such drawing primitives by calling functions which convert the primitive into the equivalent bitmapped form, i.e. a line would be converted into a series of illuminated pixels on the screen (Program 13.5 and Exercise 13.1 used the Turbo C and Microsoft C graphics libraries respectively; other compilers offer libraries with similar facilities).

A major problem for a programmer working in terms of drawing primitives is that once the object has been 'drawn' into the bitmap it is no longer recognisable to the program as a line, circle, arc, etc., it is just a series of pixels in a bitmap. If the program needs to delete a particular line or change the colour of a particular circle other information than that in the bitmap is required (it may be possible using image processing techniques to extract lines and circles from the bitmap but this is not easy !). Another data structure, in addition to the bitmap, is therefore required to hold information on the primitives which make up the drawing (Bramer & Sutcliffe 1981).

Implement a set of functions to support a structured display file of primitives which have been drawn to the screen. The functions will sit 'on top' of the normal raster graphics library functions (such as the Turbo C graphics library (graphics.h) and maintain a graphical display file of the information on the screen. The display file could be an array of drawing elements such as element_t described in section 22.7) where each element contains data on a primitive together with support information:

1   The element number: an integer number given so that a particular element may be identified at a later time, e.g. if it is to be deleted.
2   The element colour: the colour in which the primitive will be drawn.
3   The primitive indicator: indicates if the primitive is a line, circle, etc.
4   The data on the primitive, e.g. screen coordinates, line type and thickness, etc.

The functions implemented should included basic drawing functions (to draw primitives on the screen and update the display file) and file maintenance functions, e.g. to delete an element (redraw element on the screen in black and then delete from display file) and redraw all elements (deleting can result in 'holes' being left in the drawing).

23

Pointers

Although it is possible to implement programs in C with minimal use of pointers it is wise to have an understanding of pointers and where they may be used to advantage. In addition many library functions use pointer parameters and return pointers as function results.

23.1 Variables and addresses

Consider the following definitions of variables:

```
int i = 10, j = 20, k[10] = {0};          /* define variables of type int */
float x = 2.0f, z[20] = {0}, y = 5.0f;     /* define variables of type float */
```

Where i, j, k, x, y, and z are external variables. When program execution starts the C run-time system will allocate space to store the variables in RAM memory (such external variables are usually stored in a data area called the heap, see Chapter 21.8):

1   Each variable will be assigned storage in memory starting at a particular address.
2   The amount of storage depends upon the size of the variable (the program can use the sizeof operator to determine the size of an object in bytes) .

Assume that:

      (a) int variables are two bytes in size,
      (b) float variables are four bytes in size,
and   (c) storage is allocated starting at address 1000 hexadecimal.

The above variables could be stored at the following addresses:

variable name	address hexadecimal	size decimal bytes	comment
i	1000	2	int stored in locations 1000 and 1001
j	1002	2	int stored in locations 1002 and 1003
k	1004	20	array stored in locations 1004 to 1017
x	1018	4	float stored in locations 1018 to 101B
z	101C	80	array stored in locations 101C to 106B
y	106C	4	float stored in locations 106C to 106F
	1070		next 'free' location

When a variable name is used in an expression the contents of the object are accessed (except arrays where the array name refers to the address of the first element), e.g:

```
x = y;          /* assign the value of variable y to variable x  */
```

which, using the above addresses, copies the contents of y (locations 106C to 106F) into x (locations 1018 to 101B). Variables, therefore are areas in memory used to store information of a particular type (int, float, etc.) where the variables may be simple types (a single int) or a structured type such as an array or a structure.

A pointer is just another type of variable which is used to store the address of an object (it is said to 'point to' the object). For example, a pointer having a value 1018 would be a pointer to variable x in the above table (assuming that there is a simple one to one relationship between pointers and physical memory addresses). By using the address contained in the pointer it would be possible to access the contents of variable x. During program execution the contents of the pointer can be changed to 'point to' other objects of the same type.

23.2 Defining and using pointers in C

In C a pointer is defined as follows:

```
type *p_type;                                   /* define a pointer to type */
```

Prefixing an identifier with an * defines a variable of type type *, which is a 'pointer to type', i.e. p_type can hold the address of an object of type. For example:

```
int *p_int;                                   /* define a pointer to an int */
```

This defines p_int to be of type int * which is a 'pointer to int'.

The address operator &, which returns the *address of* an operand, is used to set up a pointer, e.g.:

```
int *p_int;                                   /* define a pointer to an int */
int number;                                     /* define an int variable */
p_int = &number;                         /* point p_int to variable number */
```

The statement p_int = &number; assigns the *value of the address* of variable number to pointer p_int, i.e. if number was at address 1010 hexadecimal in memory this address would be assigned to p_int (assuming a simple one to one relationship between pointers and physical addresses). Once set up p_int *points to* number. It is possible to define variables and arrays and pointers (to the same type) in a single definition (and also initialise the variables and pointers):

```
int number = 20,                /* define and initialise an int variable */
    *p_int = &number;        /* define a pointer and 'point it' to number */
```

This defines number (type int, an int variable) initialised to 20 and p_int (type int *, a 'pointer to int') initialised to point to number. Clearly the compiler must know about the variable before it can assign the address. For example, changing the order in the definition produced the following error message with Microsoft C version 6.00:

```
    1 int *p_int = &number, number;
***** X.C(1) : error C2065: 'number' : undefined
***** X.C(1) : error C2086: 'number' : redefinition
```

To access the object which a pointer points to (holds the address of), the pointer is prefixed by the indirection operator *, e.g.:

```
int *p_int;                                   /* define a pointer to an int */
int number;                                     /* define an int variable */
p_int = &number;                         /* point p_int to variable number */
*p_int = 10;                 /* assign the int pointed to by p_int the value 10 */
```

The last statement assigns the value 10 to the variable number, i.e. *p_int = 10; assigns 10 to the variable pointed to by p_int, which in this case 'points to' variable number, therefore 10 is assigned to number. A pointer may be used in an arithmetic expression, e.g.:

```
int *p_int;                          /* define a pointer to an int */
int i, number = 20;                        /* define int variables */

p_int = &number;                   /* point p_int to variable number */
i = *p_int * 10;        /* multiply object pointed to by 10, assign result to i */
```

This will multiply the value of the int pointed to by p_int by 10 and assign the result, 200, to i (this could be written i = 10 * *p_int; the indirection operator having a higher precedence than the multiplier operator). Consider the following:

```
i = 10/*p_int;           /* divide 10 by object pointed to, assign result to i */
```

Although this looks fine the characters /* in the middle of the expression 10/*p_int will be taken as the start of a comment to be terminated by the next */. In practice the next */ may be several lines further on and a large amount of code would be commented out. This type of error can be difficult to find as the error messages often refer to lines much later in the code (following the */). Note that the following two statements have the same effect:

```
j = i;                               /* assign value of i to j */
j = *&i;                             /* assign value of i to j */
```

It is important to note that different objects have different pointer types. For example, a pointer to an int is not the same type as a pointer to a float (in particular pointer arithmetic depends upon the type of object pointed to, see section 23.5.1), e.g.:

```
int i, *p_int = &i;                     /* an int and a 'pointer to an int' */
float x, *p_float;                    /* a float and a 'pointer to a float' */

/* assign the value of a 'pointer to an int' to a 'pointer to a float' */
p_float = p_int;                               /* not allowed !!! */
```

Microsoft C Version 6.00 generated the following error message for the latter statement:

```
     5     p_float = p_int;
***** X.C(5) : warning C4049: '=' : indirection to different types
```

This warns that assigning the value of a 'pointer to an int' to a 'pointer to a float' is a very doubtful operation. Assignment using the pointers is legal:

```
int i = 10, *p_int = &i;                /* an int and a 'pointer to an int' */
float x, *p_float = &x;               /* a float and a 'pointer to a float' */

/* assign value of int 'pointed to' by p_int to float 'pointed to' by p_float */
*p_float = *p_int;
printf("float value %f ", x);
```

The value of the int pointed to by p_int (i in this case) is converted to a float and assigned to the float pointed to by p_float (x in this case). The function printf would print the number 10.0.

It is very important to set up a pointer to 'point to' something before it is used. If a pointer is not explicitly initialised its value is undefined if it is an automatic internal or zero (NULL, see next section) if it is external or a static internal. To differentiate pointers from other types it is wise to use some naming convention, e.g. use p_ to start pointer names.

23.3 The constant pointer NULL

It is sometimes necessary to assign a value to a pointer without pointing it to some object, e.g. if some error condition occurs. This is achieved by using the symbolic constant NULL which is defined in <stddef.h> as the value 0. This value is guaranteed to be different from all legal pointer values and may be assigned to any pointer type. For example:

```
char *strchr(const char *string, const char ch);          /* search string for ch */
```

This searches the string pointed to by string for the character ch returning either a pointer to the first occurrence of ch or NULL if not found. The function result may be compared with NULL to determine if the character was found, e.g. string is an array of char:

```
if (strchr(string, 'x') == NULL) printf(" x is not in string ");
```

In ANSI C NULL or 0 is the only valid integer that may be assigned to or compared with a pointer. When doing low-level system programming it is sometimes necessary to assign other integer values to pointers (e.g. to access specific physical memory locations) but the code is highly machine dependent (see Chapter 32 for some sample applications).

23.4 The generic pointer type *void* *

Many library functions can operate on a range of data types, e.g. function memcpy (memory copy, from <string.h>) copies number bytes from array source to array destination:

```
void *memcpy(void *destination, const void *source, size_t number);
```

The parameters source and destination are of type void *, which is the generic pointer type 'pointer to void':

1 any pointer type can be assigned to a variable of type void *
2 a 'pointer to void' cannot itself be used to access or manipulate information; it must be cast to another pointer type first.

It is therefore possible to call memcpy with pointers to different types:

```
int i[10] ={0}, j[10];                            /* define int arrays */
double x[] = {1.0, 2.0, 3.0, 4.0 ,5.0}, y[5];     /* define double arrays */

memcpy(y, x, sizeof(x));            /* copy contents of double array x to y */
memcpy(j, i, sizeof(i));            /* copy contents of int array i to j */
```

Library <string.h> contains a number of very useful general purpose memory manipulation functions in addition to functions which process strings (null terminated arrays of char).

23.5 Arrays and pointers

The sample programs presented so far in this book have used an integer index or subscript to access the element of an array, e.g. to zero the contents of an array:

```
int array_index, x[100];                    /* define an int and an array of int */

for (array_index = 0 ; array_index < 100 ; array_index++)
    x[array_index] = 0;                     /* zero an array element */
```

In C, arrays and pointers have a very close relationship and it is possible, and sometimes more efficient, to use pointers to manipulate the elements of arrays. Also remember that library <string.h> contains functions to manipulate memory, e.g. to zero an array:

```
memset(x, 0, sizeof(x));                    /* zero the contents of array x */
```

23.5.1 Introduction to pointer arithmetic

Remember that the name of an array refers to the address of its first element and can be treated as a constant pointer to the first element. Consider:

```
int *p_array, x[100];              /* define pointer to int and array of int */

p_array = x;                       /* point to first element of array */
p_array = &x[0];                   /* point to first element of array */
```

This defines a pointer to int and an array of int and then shows two ways of assigning the value of the address of the first element of x to pointer p_array. Once the pointer is set up it can be used instead of the array name. For example, the following statements are alternative forms of accessing the first element of x and assigning 0 to it:

```
x[0] = 0;               /* zero first element of array */
*x = 0;                 /* zero first element of array */
*p_array = 0;           /* zero first element of array */
p_array[0] = 0;         /* zero first element of array */
```

Arithmetic may be performed with pointers in that integral values may be added to or subtracted from pointers and pointers of the same type can be compared and subtracted. As the name of an array is a pointer to the first element, successive elements can be accessed by adding an integer to the pointer, e.g. consider the array int x[100];:

x	refers to the address of the first element, i.e. &x[0]
x + 1	refers to the address of the second element, i.e. &x[1]
....	
x + n	refers to the address of the n'th element, i.e. &x[n]
....	
x + 99	refers to the address of the last element, i.e. &x[99]
x + 100	refers to an address beyond the end of the array

Table 23.1 shows examples of accessing array elements using either integer subscripts or a pointer with an integer offset (it is up to the programmer to ensure that the pointer stays within the array bounds when accessing the array elements).

element	using the array name		using a pointer name	
accessed	indexed	as a pointer	indexed	as a pointer
first	x[0]	*x	p_array[0]	*p_array
second	x[2]	*(x + 2)	p_array[2]	*(p_array + 2)
third	x[3]	*(x + 3)	p_array[3]	*(p_array + 3)
n'th	x[n]	*(x + n)	p_array[n]	*(p_array + n)
last	x[99]	*(x + 99)	p_array[99]	*(p_array + 99)

Table 23.1 Accessing array elements using the array name or a pointer

The parentheses in an expression such as *(x + n) are required because without them the indirection operator * would take effect before the +, i.e. *x + n is equivalent to x[0] + n.

Table 23.1 shows that an array name can be used like a pointer and a pointer (to an array) can be used like an array name. A major difference, however, is that an array name is a constant and may not be changed whereas a pointer (unless const qualified) can be changed. In fact, the compiler translates expressions using subscripts into the equivalent pointer notation, i.e. x[5] becomes *(x + 5).

An important point to note is that arithmetic on an particular type of pointer automatically takes account of the length of the object concerned. Hence the programmer does not have to be concerned if an int is two or four bytes in length. This is one of the reasons why pointers to different objects are different types, i.e. a particular pointer type has to take account (in its internal machine representation) of the object size. In summary the following arithmetic operations are allowed with pointers:

```
pointer  +   integer  yields a pointer
integer  +   pointer  yields a pointer
pointer  -   integer  yields a pointer
pointer  -   pointer  yields an integer  (the 'distance' between the two pointers)
```

The latter must be pointers to the same array otherwise the result is undefined. The following operations are not allowed:

```
pointer  +   pointer
integer  -   pointer
pointer  *   pointer
pointer  /   pointer
       etc., etc.
```

23.5.2 Using increment and decrement operators with pointers

The increment and decrement operators may be used with pointers, e.g.:

```
p_array++                            /* point p_array to next array element */
p_array--                            /* point p_array to previous array element */
```

Program 23.1 (next page) shows several for statements loading values into an array using:

1   the array name with subscripts as 'normal';
2   a pointer to the array using (a) subscripts and (b) pointer arithmetic.

The sequence of statements in Program 23.1 is:

7   define array_index which will be used as a 'normal' array subscript
8   define the array x of type int of length 100 elements
9   define p_array a pointer to int
10   define i initialised to 0
13-14   a for statement loading the values 0 to 99 into x
        the array name x is used with array_index as a subscript
15-16   print the first ten values of x
19-20   a for statement loading the values 100 to 199 into x
        a pointer p_array is used with array_index as a subscript
21-22   print the first ten values of x
25-26   a for statement loading the values 200 to 299 into x
        a pointer p_array in incremented from x to x + 100
27-28   print the first ten values of x
31-32   a for statement loading the values 300 to 399 into x
        a pointer p_array in incremented from x to &x[100]
33-34   print the first ten values of x

```
 1 /* Program 23.1  Using array name and pointers to access array elements */
 2
 3 #include <stdio.h>
 4
 5 int main(void)
 6 {
 7     int array_index,                          /* define array index */
 8         x[100],                                /* define int array */
 9         *p_array,                        /* define pointer to int */
10         i = 0;                       /* define working variable */
11
12     printf("\nLoad 0 to 99 into array using array name and subscripts\n");
13     for (array_index = 0 ; array_index < 100 ; i++, array_index++)
14         x[array_index] = i;
15     for (array_index = 0 ; array_index < 10 ; array_index++)
16         printf(" %3d ", x[array_index]);
17
18     printf("\nLoad 100 to 199 into array using pointer with subscripts\n");
19     for (p_array = x, array_index = 0 ;array_index < 100 ; i++, array_index++)
20         p_array[array_index] = i;
21     for (p_array = x, array_index = 0 ;array_index < 10 ; array_index++)
22         printf(" %3d ", p_array[array_index]);
23
24     printf("\nLoad 200 to 299 into array using pointer arithmetic\n");
25     for (p_array = x ; p_array < x + 100 ; i++, p_array++)
26         *p_array = i;
27     for (p_array = x ; p_array < x + 10 ; p_array++)
28         printf(" %3d ", *p_array);
29
30     printf("\nLoad 300 to 399 into array using pointer arithmetic\n");
31     for (p_array = x ; p_array < &x[100] ; i++, p_array++)
32         *p_array = i;
33     for (p_array = x ; p_array < &x[10] ; p_array++)
34         printf(" %3d ", *p_array);
35
36     return 0;
37 }
```

Program 23.1 Using the array name and pointers to access array elements

```
Using array name and subscripts
     0   1   2   3   4   5   6   7   8   9
Using pointer (to array) with subscripts
   100 101  102 103 104 105 106 107 108 109
Using pointer (to array) with pointer arithmetic
   200 201  202 203 204 205 206 207 208 209
Using pointer (to array) with pointer arithmetic
   300 301  302 303 304 305 306 307 308 309
```

Run of Program 23.1 Using the array name and pointers to access array elements

Consider lines 25 and 26 of Program 23.1:

```
    for (p_array = x ; p_array < x + 100 ; i++, p_array++)
        *p_array = i;
```

p_array is initialised to 'point to' the first element of x and then incremented to x + 100 where the for terminates (the last element of x accessed is x[99]). Lines 31 and 32 are identical except for the specification of the terminating address, i.e.:

```
    for (p_array = x ; p_array < &x[100] ; i++, p_array++)
        *p_array = i;
```

p_array is initialised to 'point to ' the first element of x and then incremented to &x[100] where the for terminates (x + 100 and &x[100] are the same address). Although the array element x[100] does not exist the ANSI standard permits the use of the address &x[100] (this permission extends to one element beyond the end of the array and no further), i.e.:

(a) the addressable elements are from x[0] to x[99]

and (b) the valid addresses are from &x[0] to &x[100] (one beyond the end).

Addresses evaluated outside the limits of (b) are undefined and may crash the program.

It is therefore possible to manipulate arrays using subscripts or pointer arithmetic. Which is used in practice is a matter of programming style with the aim of producing efficient, readable and maintainable code. In general, however, the recommendation is that array subscripts should be used unless there are good reasons for using pointer notation (non C programmers will certainly find it easier to read). The exception is strings and Chapter 24.3 will present a version (Program 24.1) of Program 19.1 modified to manipulate strings using pointers.

23.5.3 Using the indirection operator with increment and decrement

The indirection operator * can be combined with increment and decrement. Consider:

```
    int x[] = { 10, 20, 30, 40, 50 },          /* define a five element int array */
        y, *p_array;                           /* define an int and a pointer to an int */

    p_array = &x[2];                           /* point to third element of x */
    y = *p_array;                              /* assign y value of object pointed to */
```

The pointer p_array is initialised to 'point to' the third element of x and the variable y would be assigned the value 30. Table 23.2 shows some examples of the result of the latter statement when *p_array is replaced by various expressions.

expression	value assigned to y	contents of array after evaluation of expression	element p_array then points to
*++p_array	40	10 20 30 40 50	4
++*p_array	31	10 20 31 40 50	3
*p_array++	30	10 20 30 40 50	4
(*p_array)++	30	10 20 31 40 50	3

Table 23.2 Pointer operations with increment operator

The operators * and ++ are of the same precedence and associate from right to left, e.g.:

y = *++p_array   i.e. with parentheses y = *(++p_array)
1   the ++ is applied to p_array incrementing it to point to the fourth element of x;
2   the * is applied accessing the object pointed to by the pointer p_array;
3   the value of the fourth element of the array x is assigned to y, i.e 40.

y = ++*p_array   i.e. with parentheses y = ++(*array)
1   the * is applied accessing the object pointed to by p_array (the third element of x);
2   the ++ is applied to the object pointed to by p_array incrementing its value;
3   the incremented value of the third element of x is assigned to y, i.e. 31.

y = *p_array++   i.e. with parentheses y = *(p_array++)
1   the ++ is applied to p_array but because it is postfix its effect is delayed until after the expression has been evaluated;
2   the * is applied accessing the object pointed to by the pointer p_array (the third element of x);
3   the value of the third element of x is assigned to y, i.e. 30;
4   p_array is then incremented, pointing it to the fourth element of x;

y = (*p_array)++   parentheses are required (operators associate from right to left)
1   the * is applied accessing the object pointed to by the pointer p_array (the third element of x);
2   the ++ is applied to the object pointed to by p_array but because it is postfix its effect is delayed until after the expression has been evaluated;
3   the value of the third element of x is assigned to y, i.e. 30;
4   the value of the third element of x is then incremented.

assignment expression	contents of array after assignment	element p_array then points to
*++p_array = 500	10 20 30 500 50	4
*p_array++ = 500	10 20 500 40 50	4

Table 23.3 Assignment operations using a pointer with increment operator

Table 23.3 shows examples of using the increment and indirection operators on the left hand side of an assignment expression, i.e. assuming p_array points to &x[2]:

*++p_array = 500
1   the pointer is incremented to point to the fourth element of array x;
2   the fourth element of x is assigned the value 500;
3   the overall result of the expression is 500.

*p_array++ = 500
1   the third element of x is assigned the value 500;
2   the pointer is incremented to point to the fourth element of array x;
3   the overall result of the expression is 500.

The assignment operations ++*p_array = 500 and (*p_array)++ = 500 are illegal, e.g. using Microsoft C Version 6.00:

```
    5 ++*p_array = 500;
***** XXXX.C(5) : error C2106: '=' : left operand must be lvalue
    6 (*p_array)++ = 500;
***** XXXX.C(6) : error C2106: '=' : left operand must be lvalue
```

It is therefore possible to zero the contents of an array using the increment operator:

```
    int *p_array, x[100];                /* define pointer to int and array of int */

    p_array = x;                             /* point to first element of array */
    while( p_array < x + 100 )                    /* loop until end of array */
        *p_array++ = 0;              /* zero array element and increment pointer */
```

Exercise 23.1 (see Appendix B for sample answer)

Implement and test a program to check that the expressions in Tables 23.2 and 23.3 are evaluated as shown.

23.6 Pointers to structures

Consider a simplified version of the structure student_t from Program 22.1:

```
/* define structure type to hold student information */
typedef struct {
                char name[20];                         /* student name */
                int age;                               /* student age */
                }
                student_t;                       /* structure type name */
student_t student,              /* define a variable to hold student data */
          *p_student = &student;         /* define a pointer to the structure */
```

This defines type student_t, variable student of type student_t and p_student a 'pointer to type student_t' initialised to point to student. The pointer can be used to access the members of the structure, e.g. to set up the age and name of the student:

```
    (*p_student).age = 20;
    strcpy((*p_student).name, "daisy");
```

Because the dot (.) operator has a higher precedence than the indirection operator (*) the parentheses are required to force the correct association using p_student as the pointer, i.e. the expression *p_student.age is using the structure member p_student.age as though it is a pointer to something. The use of pointers with structures is very common and an equivalent simpler notation using the -> structure pointer operator is generally used:

```
    p_student->age = 30;
    strcpy(p_student->name, "mary");
```

23.7 *const* qualified pointers

The const type qualifier may be applied to pointers:

```
    int x[] = { 10, 20, 30, 40, 50 };                /* five element array */
    int *const p_array = x;                   /* constant pointer to array x */
```

p_array is a constant pointer to the first element of array x and may not be altered (incremented or pointed to something else) although the object pointed to may be altered. In effect p_array becomes a synonym for the array name x (which is itself a constant pointer). Now consider:

```
const int a = 20 , b = 30;              /* two const qualified variables */
const int *p_int = &a;                  /* pointer to a constant int */
```

p_int is a pointer to a constant object and may be changed to point to another object of the same type (e.g. b in the above example) although the object pointed to may not be altered. Now consider:

```
const int a = 20 , b = 30;              /* two const qualified variables */
const int *const p_int = &a;            /* constant pointer to a constant int */
```

p_int is a constant pointer to a constant object. Neither the pointer nor the object pointed to may be altered. If an object is defined as const qualified any pointer to it must be similarly const qualified. For example, using Microsoft C version 6.00:

```
7       const int a = 20 , b = 30;
8       int *p_int2 = &a;
***** X.C(8) : warning C4090: different 'const/volatile' qualifiers
```

Warning that a is const qualified but the pointer p_int, which 'points to' a, is not and an attempt could be made to change the value of a, e.g.:

```
*p_int2 = 110;          /* error, attempt to change the value of a const object */
```

23.8 Pointers and the *sizeof* operator

If the sizeof operator is used with a pointer it returns the number of bytes used to store the pointer, **not** the number of bytes in the object pointed to, e.g.:

```
int x[] = { 10, 20, 30, 40, 50 },       /* five element array */
    *p_array = x;                        /* pointer to array */
printf(" %d ", (int) sizeof(p_array));
```

would return the number of bytes used to store p_array. Now consider:

```
printf(" %d ", (int) sizeof(*p_array));
```

This would return the size of an int, i.e. the type that p_array points to. To determine the size of an array the array name itself is required.

Note the use of the cast (int) to convert the return type of sizeof (which is type size_t) to an int to ensure that it is the correct type to be printed with the conversion specification %d. This may or may not be necessary depending upon what size_t is defined as (typically it is an unsigned int).

Problem for Chapter 23

The Problem 4 for Chapter 18 was to implement a bubble sort to sort the elements of an array into ascending order. Rewrite the program to use pointers to access and manipulate the array elements.

24

Functions and pointers

24.1 Pointers as function parameters

Pointers can be passed as parameters to functions just like any other type of variable. For example, Chapter 15.7 described using pointers to pass function parameters using *call by reference* (remember that arrays are always passed using call by reference, see Chapter 18.6). The critical thing to remember is that the value of the pointer (the address) is passed using *call by value* so any alterations made to the pointer (formal parameter) inside the function do not affect the value of the pointer (actual parameter) in the calling function (although the object pointed to can be altered).

Because an array name is a constant pointer to the first element, arrays which are formal parameters to functions can generally be declared using either array or pointer notation. For example, in Program 19.1 the function header of str_copy was:

```
int str_copy(char string_1[], const char string_2[]);
```

copies the contents of string_2 into string_1; the number of characters copied is returned as a function result. In general, an alternative way of writing the function header is:

```
int str_copy(char *string_1, const char *string_2);
```

The body of the function could remain as in Program 19.1 or be altered to use pointer arithmetic (see Program 24.1).

24.2 Functions that return a pointer as the function result

A function can return a pointer as a function result, e.g. a prototype from Program 24.1:

```
char *str_ch_find(char *string, const char character)
```

The * prefixing the function name indicates that the function returns a pointer to a char (the function searches string for a character and returns either a pointer to the character (if found) or NULL. The pointer returned may then be used to access the object either to read its value or assign a new value, e.g.:

```
char *p_char, string[] = " hello alan ";
if ((p_char = str_ch_find(string, 'a')) != NULL)
      *p_char = 'x';
printf(" %s ", string);
```

This would print hello xlan on the display screen. Now consider:

```
const char *str_ch_find(char *string, const char character)
```

This returns a const qualified pointer to char, i.e. the pointer returned may be used to read the value of the object pointed to but not to change its value.

Do not return a pointer to an internal automatic variable defined within the function. The variable will be deallocated on function exit and the pointer will effectively be undefined (pointing to a memory area which could be allocated to something else).

24.3 String processing functions using pointers

```
 1 /* Program 24.1 - String processing functions using pointer arithmetic */
 2
 3 #include <stdio.h>
 4 #include <string.h>
 5
 6 int main(void)
 7 {
 8      int str_length(const char *string);                      /* prototypes */
 9      int str_copy(char *string_1, const char *string_2);
10      void str_remove_spaces(char *string);
11      void str_reverse(char *string);
12      char *str_ch_find(char *string, const char character);
13      int str_read(const char *prompt, char *string, const int max_length);
14
15      char text_1[20], text_2[20], *p_char;          /* internal variables */
16      int index;
17
18      while (str_read("\n\nEnter string ? ", text_1, 20))      /* read string */
19          {
20          printf("read    string length %3d (%3d) |%s| \n",     /* print string */
21                      str_length(text_1), (int) strlen(text_1), text_1);
22
23          index = str_copy(text_2, text_1);                    /* copy string */
24          printf("copied string  length %3d (%3d) |%s| \n",
25                      index, (int) strlen(text_2), text_2);
26
27          str_reverse(text_2);                                /* reverse string */
28          printf("reverse string length %3d (%3d) |%s| \n",
29                      str_length(text_2), strlen(text_2), text_2);
30
31          str_remove_spaces(text_1);                          /* remove spaces */
32          printf("spaces removed length %3d (%3d) |%s| \n",
33                      str_length(text_1), (int) strlen(text_1), text_1);
34
35          printf("Character 'a' found: ");                    /* search for 'a' */
36          p_char = text_1;                              /* point to start of string */
37          while ((p_char = str_ch_find(p_char, 'a')) != NULL)
38              {
39              *p_char = 'x';                              /* replace 'a' with 'x' */
40              printf(" |%s|", p_char++);                     /* and print string */
41              }
42          }
43      return 0;
44 }
45
```

Program 24.1 String processing functions using pointers (continued on next page)

```
46 /*-----------------------------------------------------------------------*
47  * function to find length of string, not counting terminating null      */
48 int str_length(const char *string)
49 {
50     const char *p_str = string;                    /* point to start of string */
51
52     while ( *p_str != '\0')
53         p_str++;                                   /* look for null */
54     return p_str - string;                         /* return length of string */
55 }
56
57 /*-----------------------------------------------------------------------*
58  * function to copy a string to another, return number of characters copied    */
59 int str_copy(char *string_1, const char *string_2)
60 {
61     int number = 0;
62
63     while ((*string_1++ = *string_2++) != '\0')          /* copy to null */
64         number++;                                  /* if not null increment number */
65     return number;                                 /* return number of characters copied *
66 }
67
68
69 /*-----------------------------------------------------------------------*
70  * function to reverse the contents of a string                          */
71 void str_reverse(char *string)
72 {
73     char *p_up = string,                           /* points to start of string */
74          *p_down = string + strlen(string);        /* points to end of string + 1 */
75     char value;                                    /* temporary data store */
76
77     while ( p_up < p_down )
78         (value = *p_up, *p_up++ = *--p_down, *p_down = value);
79 }
80
81 /*-----------------------------------------------------------------------*
82  * function to find character in string, return pointer to character else NULL*/
83 char *str_ch_find(char *string, const char character)
84 {
85     while (*string != '\0')                        /* look for null character */
86         if (*string == character) return string;   /* found character ! */
87         else                        string++;      /* increment pointer */
88     return NULL;                                   /* return NULL for fail */
89 }
90
```

Program 24.1 String processing functions using pointers (continued on next page)

```
 91 /*-----------------------------------------------------------------------*
 92  * function to remove leading and trailing spaces from a string          */
 93 void str_remove_spaces(char *string)
 94 {
 95     char *p_str1,                        /* points to first non space character */
 96           *p_str2,                       /* points to next position to copy to */
 97           *p_str3;                 /* points to position to put terminating null */
 98
 99     /* point p_str1 to first non space character */
100     for (p_str1 = string ; *p_str1 == ' ' ; p_str1++)
101         /* null statement */;
102     /* p_str1 = string + strspn(string, " ");              alternative !! */
103
104     p_str2 = p_str3 = string;                    /* point to start of string */
105     /* loop copying characters until null character found */
106     while (*p_str1 != '\0')
107         if ((*p_str2++ = *p_str1++) != ' ')               /* copy character */
108             p_str3 = p_str2;              /* not space, note position in p_str3 */
109     *p_str3 = '\0';                               /* put in terminating null */
110 }
111
112 /*-----------------------------------------------------------------------*
113  * read string using fgets, remove terminating \n and any trailing characters *
114  * on entry *prompt   contains prompt string to print                   *
115  *           max_length contains maximum length of string               *
116  * return string read in array *string                                  *
117  * return function result true if all OK else false on EOF              */
118 int str_read(const char *prompt, char *string, const int max_length)
119 {
120     char *p_str;                              /* define pointer to char */
121
122     printf("%s", prompt);                                /* print prompt */
123     if (fgets(string, max_length, stdin) == NULL)        /* get string */
124         return 0;                                   /* if EOF return false */
125     if ((p_str = strchr(string, '\n')) != NULL)          /* look for \n */
126         *p_str = '\0';                          /* replace \n with \0 */
127     else
128         while (getchar() != '\n')               /* else discard characters to \n */
129             /* null statement */;
130     return 1;                                   /* all OK return true */
131 }
```

Program 24.1 String processing functions using pointers

Program 24.1 is a version of Program 19.1 modified to use pointers to manipulate strings within the various functions. The function main is similar to that in Program 19.1.

Function str_length, lines 48 to 55, returns the length of the string (not counting the terminating null). The sequence of statements is:

48   `int str_length(const char *string)` the function header
50   declare pointer p_str and point it to the start of `string`
52-53 a `while` statement searching `string` for a null character `'\0'`
      the `while` terminates when a null is found
    53 if the character was not null increment the pointer p_str
54   returns the number of characters in `string`

In line 54 the expression p_str - `string` evaluates the length of the string, i.e. `string` and p_str point to the start of the string and the terminating null respectively and subtracting therm yields an integer which is the distance between the two. Because C treats 0 as *false* lines 52 and 53 could be written (perhaps less legibly):

```
while ( *p_str )
    p_str++;                                    /* look for null */
```

When `'\0'` is found ((*false*) the `while` terminates and the number of characters in `string` evaluated. The result from this function is printed in `main` together with the result returned by the library function `strlen`.

Function str_copy, lines 59 to 66, copies the contents of one string (string_2) to another (string_1) overwriting any existing contents. It returns the number of characters copied. The sequence of statements is:

59   `int str_copy(char *string_1, const char *string_2)` the function header
61   declare number and initialise it to 0 (used to hold the character count)
63-64 a `while` statement copying characters from string_2 into string_1
      the `while` terminates when a null `'\0'` is copied
    64 if the character was not null increment number
65   return the number of characters copied

Line 63 copies a character from string_2 to string_1 and terminates the `while` if the character is a `'\0'`. The `!= '\0'` could be removed but a modern compiler will issue a warning, e.g. Microsoft C:

```
63      while (*string_1++ = *string_2++)                    /* copy to null */
***** P24_1.C(63) : warning C4206: assignment within conditional expression
```

warning that there is an assignment within a conditional statement; which is what is required in this case.

The function str_reverse, lines 71 to 79, reverses the characters in a string. The sequence of statements is:

71 `void str_reverse(char *string)` is the function header
73 define pointer p_up and point to the first element of the string
74 define pointer p_down and point it to the last element of the string plus 1, i.e. the `'\0'`
77 a `while` statement which:
  (a) increments pointer p_up up the string
  (b) decrements pointer p_down down the string
  (c) terminates when p_up = p_down (half way up the string)

78 (value = *p_up, *p_up++ = *--p_down, *p_down = value) swaps two characters

   (a) value = *p_up copies the character pointed to by p_up into value

   (b) *p_up++ = *--p_down

      (i) decrements p_down

      (ii) copies character pointed to by p_down to character pointed to by p_up

      (iii) increments p_up

   (c) copies value into the character pointed to by p_down

The function str_ch_find, lines 83 to 89, searches string for a character. If the character is found it returns a pointer to the character else NULL. The sequence of statements is:

83   int str_ch_find(const char *string, const char character) the function header

85-87   a while statement scanning string for a null, if found the while terminates

       86 if *string == character return string (a pointer to the character found)

       87 else increment the pointer string to point to next character

88   character not found, return NULL to indicated fail

The function is called from main, lines 35 to 41, searching for occurrences of the character 'a' and replacing them with 'x' characters:

```
printf("Character 'a' found: ");              /* search for 'a' */
p_char = text_1;                              /* point to start of string */
while ((p_char = str_ch_find(p_char, 'a')) != NULL)
    {
    *p_char = 'x';                            /* replace 'a' with 'x' */
    printf(" |%s|", p_char++);                /* and print string */
    }
}
```

On the first call pointer p_char points to the start of the string text_1. The function str_ch_find assigns p_char a pointer to the position where the character was found or else NULL (the loop terminates). The character pointed to by p_char is replaced and the remainder of the string is printed. The pointer p_char is incremented and str_ch_find called again. Thus str_ch_find works down the string finding each occurrence of the character 'a'.

    Function str_remove_spaces, lines 93 to 110, removes leading and trailing spaces from a string. The sequence of statements is:

lines

93   void str_remove_spaces(char *string) the function header

95-97   declare pointers to char used in the function

100-1   find first non-space character in the string, on exit p_str1 points to it

102   alternative to lines 99 and 100, discussed below

104   point p_str2 and p_str3 to start of array string

106-8   a while loop which copies characters until '\0' is found

       107   copies a character (overwriting any leading spaces)

       108   if character copied was not a space copy pointer p_str2 to p_str3

109   terminate string (p_str3 points to last non space character plus 1)

Notes:

1   After executing lines 100 and 101 (or line 102) p_str1 points to the position of the first non space character in string.

2   Line 104 points p_str2 to the start of string ready for copying characters.
3   Line 104 points p_str3 to the start of string in case the string is empty or full of spaces, i.e. line 108 would not be executed to assign a value to p_str3.
4   Line 107 overwrites any leading spaces by overwriting the character pointed to by p_str2 with the one pointed to by p_str1.
5   In line 108 p_str3 is pointed to the last non-space character plus 1 which is then overwritten with '\0' in line 109.

Note that lines 100 and 101, which point p_str1 to the first non-space character, can be replaced with the statement in line 102, i.e.:

```
p_str1 = string + strspn(string, " ");
```

The prototype of the library function strspn is:

```
size_t strspn(const char *string1 , const char *string2);
```

This returns the length of the initial sub string in string1 which consists entirely of the characters in string2, i.e.:

```
strspn(string, " ")
```

This returns the number of spaces at the start of string. Therefore:

```
p_str1 = string + strspn(string, " ");
```

This points p_str1 to the first non-space character in string.
The function str_read, lines 118 to 131, reads a string of maximum length max_length from stdin using function fgets. It returns *true* if the string read was successful otherwise *false* if EOF was entered. If the length of the string is less than max_length characters the terminating newline is replaced with '\0', otherwise the characters remaining on the line are removed, including the newline. The sequence of statements is:

lines
118   int str_read(const char *prompt, char *string, int max_length)
       the function header declaring three parameters:
       prompt   a pointer to a message to print on the screen
       string   a pointer to an array of char to accept the characters input
       max_length an int specifying the maximum length of string
120   define a pointer to char
122   display prompt on the screen
123-24 call fgets to read a string length max_length - 1 from stdin
       124 if EOF was entered terminate function with result *false* (i.e. fgets returns NULL)
125-29 an if searching string for a '\n' character
       126   '\n' found, replace with '\0'
       else
       128-29 remove characters from stdin up to and including newline

The library function strchr is similar in specification to str_ch_find, i.e.:

```
char *strchr(const char *string, int character)
```

This searches string for first occurrence of character; if found it returns a pointer to the character else NULL. Therefore line 125:

```
    if ((p_str = strchr(string, '\n')) != NULL)                /* look for \n */
```

This searches `string` for a newline character. Line 126 is executed if the input text contained less than `max_length` - 1 characters (i.e. `'\n'` is in the string) otherwise the input text contained too many characters and lines 128 and 129 remove them (so that they do not appear when `fgets` is called again).

Section 24.1 stated that when arrays are formal parameters they may be declared using either array notation or pointer notation. In Program 24.1 pointer notation is used throughout but array notation could be used. For example, `str_copy` could be written:

```
int str_copy(char string_1[], const char string_2[])
{
    int number = 0;
    while ((*string_1++ = *string_2++) != '\0')              /* copy to null */
        number++;                                  /* if not null increment number */
    return number;                          /* return number of characters copied *
}
```

Although `string_1` and `string_2` are declared as arrays they can be used as pointers and manipulated using pointer arithmetic (including `++`). When an array is defined its name is a constant pointer to the first address. However, when an array name is a formal parameter it is assigned the value of the actual parameter (the address of the array) and it can then be treated like a pointer variable (more discussion in next section).

A run of Program 24.1 was (↓ indicates newline)

```
Enter string ? hello abc abc ↓
read      string length  13 ( 13) |hello abc abc|
copied string  length  13 ( 13) |hello abc abc|
reverse string length  13 ( 13) |cba cba olleh|
spaces removed length  13 ( 13) |hello abc abc|
Character 'a' found:  |xbc abc| |xbc|

Enter string ?        test spaces     ↓
read      string length  19 ( 19) |    test spaces    |
copied string  length  19 ( 19) |    test spaces    |
reverse string length  19 ( 19) |  secaps tset    |
spaces removed length  11 ( 11) |test spaces|
Character 'a' found:  |xces|

Enter string ? abcdefghijklmnopqrstuvwxyz ↓
read      string length  19 ( 19) |abcdefghijklmnopqrs|
copied string  length  19 ( 19) |abcdefghijklmnopqrs|
reverse string length  19 ( 19) |srqponmlkjihgfedcba|
spaces removed length  19 ( 19) |abcdefghijklmnopqrs|
Character 'a' found:  |xbcdefghijklmnopqrs|

Enter string ? ↓
read      string length   0 (  0) ||
copied string  length   0 (  0) ||
reverse string length   0 (  0) ||
spaces removed length   0 (  0) ||
Character 'a' found:

Enter string ? ˉz ↓
```

Exercise 24.1 (see Appendix B for sample answer)

Implement and test a function which searches for a string within a string. The function prototype of a string search function could be:

```
char *str_search(char *string_1, const char *string_2);
```

Search the string pointed to by string_1 for the next occurrence of the string pointed to by string_2. If found return a pointer to the character else NULL. Write a main program which read two strings and then calls str_search to look for occurrences of one string within the other (similar to lines 36 to 41 in Program 24.1).

Implement and test a function str_compare which compares two strings (similar to strcmp in the standard library):

```
int str_compare(const char *string_1, const char *string_2);
```

the content of the string pointed to by string_1 is compared with the string pointed to by string_2 and the following result returned:

<0 if *string_1 comes before *string_2 in the sorting sequence
0   if *string_1 equals *string_2
>0 if *string_1 comes after *string_2 in the sorting sequence

24.4 Pointers should only contain valid addresses

It must be emphasised that when a pointer is being used it should only contain a valid address or the value NULL. Consider the array:

```
int x[100];                          /* define an array of 100 elements */
```

Chapter 23.5.2 explained:

     (a) the addressable elements are from x[0] to x[99]
and (b) the valid addresses are from &x[0] to &x[100] (one beyond the end of the array).

Although array element x[100] does not exist the ANSI standard permits the use of the address &x[100] (mainly for use in determining the terminating conditions of loops, see Program 23.1). This permission extends to one element beyond the end of the array and no further and addresses evaluated outside the limits of (b) above are undefined and may crash the program. Consider a modified version of function str_reverse:

```
void str_reverse(char *string)
{
    char *p_up = string,                    /* points to start of string */
         *p_down = string + strlen(string) - 1;    /* points to end of string */
    char value;                             /* temporary data store */

    while ( p_up < p_down )
        (value = *p_up, *p_up++ = *p_down, *p_down-- = value);
}
```

This is similar to str_reverse of Program 24.1 with the exception that the pointer p_down is initialised to point to the last character in the string (the version in Program 24.1 initialised p_down to point to the last element of the string plus 1, i.e. the terminating '\0'). The statement which swaps the characters is then slightly modified to take account of the change. The above version of str_reverse will work without problems so long as the string is not empty. If the string is empty the statement:

```
*p_down = string + strlen(string) - 1;    /* points to end of string */
```

initialises p_down to an address before the start of string, i.e. outside the limits for valid addresses. What happens depends upon the architecture of the machine concerned. On some machines the value formed may be a valid memory address and the comparison:

```
while ( p_up < p_down )
```

would work without problems. On other machines the value formed may be an invalid address and the program could either produce incorrect results or crash with a memory segmentation fault.

Incorrect addresses stored in pointers are very common programming faults and can be very difficult to track down. Careful design of the algorithms is required to avoid problems such as the one described above. For example, when a program has worked without problems (for months or even years) then crashes or produces faulty results with new program data, suspect array bounds overflow as a major culprit. A problem is that an array bounds overflow may not show up until much later in the program when data sets corrupted by the overflow are used. Slight modifications to the program data may select alternate paths through the program and the error appears and disappears.

24.5 When is an actual parameter an array or a simple variable ?

If an actual parameter of a function is to be an array the function header and prototype can be written in array notation:

```
int str_copy(char string_1[], const char string_2[]);
```

or pointer notation:

```
int str_copy(char *string_1, const char *string_2);
```

Now consider, the following function header:

```
void test(int *pointer);
```

How is it possible to determine from the function header if the function expects a pointer to a simple int variable or to the first element of an array of int? The answer is that it is not possible, in that pointer could be a pointer to either.

It is therefore recommended to use array notation in function headers and prototypes when a formal parameter is to be an array, or, if using pointer notation use a suitable name for the formal parameter, e.g. string_1, p_array, etc. Similarly, if a formal parameter is to be a pointer to a simple variable use a suitable name. For example, from Program 15.2:

```
void swap_int(int *const p_int1, int *const p_int2);
```

The parameters are const qualified pointers to simple int variables.

Problem for Chapter 24

The Problem for Chapter 19 was to implement and test the string processing functions:

```
void str_concat(char *string_1, const char *string_2);
char *str_r_ch_find(const char *string, const char character);
```

Rewrite the functions to use pointers.

25

Pointers to pointers and arrays of pointers

25.1 Pointers to pointers

A pointer is a variable which can hold the address of (or 'point to') another variable. It is therefore possible to have pointers which can 'point to' a pointer which 'points to' an object. Consider:

```
int a,                              /* define an int */
    *p_int,                     /* define pointer to int */
    **p_p_int;           /* define pointer to pointer to int */
```

This defines three variables:

a   is an int, i.e. it can hold an integer numeric value
p_int   is a 'pointer to an int', i.e. it can hold the address of a variable of type int
p_p_int   is a 'pointer to a pointer to an int', i.e. it can hold the address of a variable of type 'pointer to an int'

Once defined the variables can be assigned values:

```
    a = 10;                     /* assign value to int variable */
    p_int = &a;             /* point p_int to variable a */
    p_p_int = &p_int;   /* point p_p_int to pointer p_int */
```

The indirection operator * is used to access the objects pointed to:

p_p_int   references the contents of p_p_int, i.e. the address of p_int
*p_p_int   the indirection operator * references the contents of the object pointed to by p_p_int, i.e. the address of a
**p_p_int   the double indirection operator ** references the contents of the object pointed to by the pointer pointed to by p_p_int, i.e. the contents of a which is the value 10

In the latter case p_p_int points to p_int which points to a, thus **p_p_int accesses the contents of a. For example, the following statements all print the value of the variable a:

```
    printf("%d ", a);
    printf("%d ", *p_int);
    printf("%d ", **p_p_int);
```

The following statements print the contents of p_int (an address):

```
    printf("%p ", p_int);
    printf("%p ", *p_p_int);
```

Note that p_int and p_p_int are different types, the former being a 'pointer to int' and the latter a 'pointer to a pointer to int'.

Program 25.1 shows some more examples of the use of pointers to pointers printing the addresses of variables, changing pointers to point to different variables, etc. A run of the program is shown under Turbo C Version 1.01.

```
 1 /* Program 25.1 -  Example of pointers to pointers */
 2
 3 #include <stdio.h>
 4
 5 int a = 10, b = 20,                                 /* define two ints */
 6     *p_int1 = &a, *p_int2 =&b,                   /* define pointers to int */
 7     **p_p_int = &p_int1;                    /* define pointer to pointer to int */
 8
 9 int main(void)
10 {
11
12     printf("\nAddresses of variables in the programs"
13            "\n&a = %p, &b = %p, &p_int1 = %p, &p_int2 = %p, &p_p_int = %p",
14               &a, &b, &p_int1, &p_int2, &p_p_int);
15
16     printf("\n\np_p_int points to p_int1 which points to a = 10 "
17            "\n     p_p_int = %p, *p_p_int = %p, **p_p_int = %d",
18               p_p_int, *p_p_int, **p_p_int);
19
20     /* now point p_p_int to pointer p_int2 which points to b */
21     p_p_int = &p_int2;
22     printf("\n\np_p_int points to p_int2 which points to b = 20 "
23            "\n     p_p_int = %p, *p_p_int = %p, **p_p_int = %d",
24               p_p_int, *p_p_int, **p_p_int);
25
26     /* point p_int2 to a */
27     p_int2 = &a;
28     printf("\n\np_p_int points to p_int2 which points to a = 10 "
29            "\n     p_p_int = %p, *p_p_int = %p, **p_p_int = %d",
30               p_p_int, *p_p_int, **p_p_int);
31     return 0;
32 }
```

Program 25.1 Program using pointers to pointers

```
Addresses of variables in the programs
&a = 00A8, &b = 00AA, &p_int1 = 00AC, &p_int2 = 00AE, &p_p_int = 00B0

p_p_int points to p_int1 which points to a = 10
    p_p_int = 00AC, *p_p_int = 00A8, **p_p_int = 10

p_p_int points to p_int2 which points to b = 20
    p_p_int = 00AE, *p_p_int = 00AA, **p_p_int = 20

p_p_int points to p_int2 which points to a = 10
    p_p_int = 00AE, *p_p_int = 00A8, **p_p_int = 10
```

Run 25.1 Run of Program 25.1 under Turbo C

25.2 Passing parameters to function *main*

All the programs so far have defined the function main to be without parameters, e.g.:

```
int main(void)
```

This specifies that main has no parameters and returns an int result. Many C environments, however, allow parameters to be passed from the operating system command line. For example, the program of Exercise 27.1 copies the contents of one file to another changing the characters to upper or lower case as specified by an option. The filenames and options are specified as part of the command line when the program is invoked, e.g.:

c:> **ex27_1 file_1 file_2 -lower** ↲

The program is able to access the character strings "file_1", "file_2" and "-lower" and take appropriate action. In such a case the function header for main is:

```
int main(int argc, char *argv[])
```

specifies two parameters:

argc   an int which contains the number of command line arguments;
*argv[] is an array of pointers to char (character strings which contain the parameters).

In the command line "ex27_1 file_1 file_2 -lower" the value of argc would be 4 and argv would appear as follows:

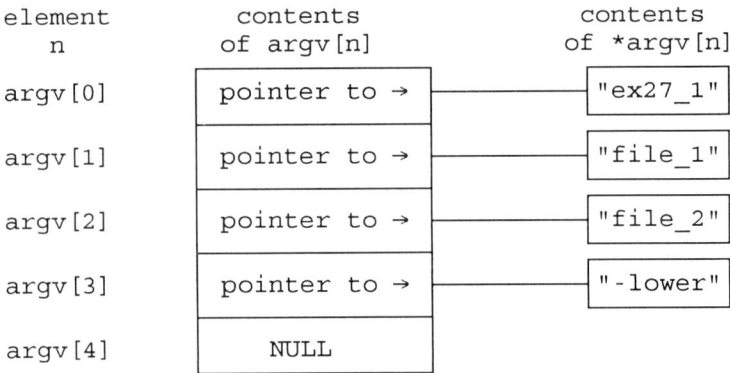

element n	contents of argv[n]	contents of *argv[n]
argv[0]	pointer to →	"ex27_1"
argv[1]	pointer to →	"file_1"
argv[2]	pointer to →	"file_2"
argv[3]	pointer to →	"-lower"
argv[4]	NULL	

Therefore the elements of argv are pointers to strings which contain the command line parameters (null terminated). By convention argv[0] points to a string which contains the name by which the program was invoked and element argv[argc] is a NULL pointer. The program can access the command line arguments and interpret them as it wishes. For example, the above command line could invoke the program ex27_1.exe which will copy file1 to file2 converting any upper case letters to lower case (option -lower). If insufficient or invalid parameters are specified the program displays an error message.

Program 25.2 (next page) reads the command line parameters and prints their values on the screen. The sequence of statements is:

10   define main with parameters argc and argv
14   print number of parameters, i.e. value of argc
15-22   a for statement incrementing index from 0 to argc

    17   print current parameter (%s expects a pointer to a string)

    18   if current parameter is string -lower

         19   print appropriate message

    20   if current parameter is string -upper

         21   print appropriate message

When executed using MS-DOS and Turbo C with the following command line:

```
p25_2 filename_1  filename_2  -lower
```

the following results were printed on the display screen:

```
Number of parameters in command line is 4
 parameter 0 is D:\C-BOOK\C-PROGS\P25_2.EXE
 parameter 1 is filename_1
 parameter 2 is filename_2
 parameter 3 is -lower     option -lower found !
```

The program name is expanded to include the full MS-DOS drive and path. Note line 17:

```
        printf("\n parameter %d is %s ", index, argv[index]);
```

The conversion specification %s expects that the corresponding parameter is the start address of an array of char (a string).

```
 1 /* Program 25.2 -  Print parameters passed from operating system to main */
 2
 3 #include <stdio.h>
 4 #include <string.h>
 5
 6 /*-----------------------------------------------------------------*
 7  * function main with parameters                                   *
 8  *    argc - number of elements in array argv                      *
 9  *    argv - an array of pointers to strings                       */
10 int main(int argc, char *argv[])
11 {
12     int index;
13
14     printf("\nNumber of parameters in command line is %d", argc);
15     for (index = 0; index < argc ; index++)
16        {
17        printf("\n parameter %d is %s ", index, argv[index]);
18        if (strcmp(argv[index],"-lower") == 0)
19            printf("   option -lower found ! ");
20        if (strcmp(argv[index],"-upper") == 0)
21            printf("   option -upper found ! ");
22        }
23     return 0;
24 }
```

Program 25.2 Print parameters passed from operating system to main

Exercise 25.1 *(see Appendix B for sample answer)*

Rewrite Program 25.2 to use a pointer to argv (rather than using an array index).

25.3 Arrays of pointers

```
 1 /* Program 25.3, Sort an array of pointers to an array of names.         *
 2  *    Rather than sort the array of names itself into alphabetical order,  *
 3  *    sort the array of pointers to the names in alphabetical order        */
 4
 5 #include <stdio.h>
 6 #include <string.h>
 7
 8 int main(void)
 9 {
10     enum {number = 15};                        /* number of names to be sorted */
11     typedef char name_t[8];                    /* define type to hold a name */
12     /* define and initialise an array of names */
13     name_t names[number] = {{"Bertie"},{"Alison"},{"Betty"},{"Bart"},{"Alex"},
14                             {"Aleson"},{"Bert"},{"Daisy"},{"Walter"},{"Mary"},
15                             {"Alan"},{"Sally"},{"Bert"},{"Bernie"},{"Mandy"}};
16     /* define an array of pointers to names */
17     name_t *p_name, *p_names[number];
18     int index, index_1, index_2;                  /* array indexes */
19
20     /* point the pointers to the names in the array and then print them */
21     printf("\n\nPrint names via array of pointers");
22     for (index = 0 ; index < number ; index++)
23         {
24         p_names[index] = &names[index];           /* set up pointer to names */
25         printf("%c %-8s", index % 5 ? ' ' : '\n', *p_names[index]);
26         }
27
28     /* sort the array of pointers (on first letter) using a linear sort */
29     for (index_1 = 0 ; index_1 < number - 1; index_1++)
30         for (index_2 = index_1 + 1 ; index_2 < number ; index_2++)
31             if (*p_names[index_2][0] < *p_names[index_1][0])
32             /*if (**p_names[index_2] < **p_names[index_1])*/
33             /*if (strcmp(*p_names[index_2],*p_names[index_1]) < 0)*/
34                 {
35                 p_name = p_names[index_1];              /* swap pointers */
36                 p_names[index_1] = p_names[index_2];
37                 p_names[index_2] = p_name;
38                 }
39
40     /* print the names via the sorted array of pointers */
41     printf("\n\nPrint names via sorted array of pointers");
42     for (index = 0 ; index < number ; index++)
43         printf("%c %-8s", index % 5 ? ' ' : '\n', *p_names[index]);
44     return 0;
45 }
```

Program 25.3 Sort an array of pointers to an array of person names

Program 20.2 contained an array names each element of which was an array of char which contained a name.   The program sorted the names into alphabetical order via an array indices the elements of which indexed into the array names. Initially indices contained the values 0, 1, 2, 3, etc. which indexed the corresponding elements names[0], names[1], names[2], names[3], etc. The array indices was then sorted such that the elements indexed array names in alphabetical order.

Program 25.3 is similar except that it uses an array of pointers p_names which point to the elements of names. Initially p_names contains pointers to elements names[0], names[1], names[2], names[3], etc. The array p_names is then sorted such that the elements point to the elements of array names in alphabetical order. The sequence of statements in Program 25.3 is:

10	define number, the number of elements in the array names
11	define type name_t, an array of char which will hold the name
13-15	define array names and initialise it with strings
17	define p_name and array p_names which are pointers to type names_t
	see discussion below on the initialisation of arrays of pointers
18	define some array index variables for use in the program
22-26	a for statement incrementing index from 0 to number - 1
	24 point element in p_names to the corresponding element of names
	25 print name pointed to by *p_names[index] (five names per line)
29-38	sort array p_names such that it points to the elements of names in alphabetical order using a linear sort as in Program 20.2 and Exercise 18.1
42-43	print the contents of the array names using array p_names to point to the elements the names should now be printed in alphabetical order

Note that line 31:

```
if (*p_names[index_2][0] < *p_names[index_1][0])
```

compares the first letter of the name pointed to by p_names[index_2] with the first letter of the name pointed to by p_names[index_1]. Because x[0] may be written *x line 31 could be written as line 32:

```
if (**p_names[index_2] < **p_names[index_1])
```

using two levels of indirection to access the first letter of each name. The above tests will only sort against the first letter of each name. Line 33 uses strcmp to sort against all letters of the name, i.e.:

```
if (strcmp(*p_names[index_2], *p_names[index_1]) < 0)
```

Note that it is not possible to initialise p_names in line 17 with the addresses of the elements of names, e.g.:

```
name_t *p_name, *p_names[number] = {{&names[0]},{&names[1]}};      /* invalid ! */
```

attempts to initialise the first two elements of p_names with the addresses of the first two elements of names. When attempted Microsoft C gave the following error message:

```
  17      name_t *p_name, *p_names[number] = {{&names[0]},{&names[1]}};
***** XX.C(17) : error C2097: illegal initialisation
***** XX.C(17) : error C2097: illegal initialisation
```

Arrays can only be initialised with constants that can be evaluated at compile time (see Chapter 18.1). Because names is an internal automatic variable it is created on entry to the function main and therefore its address is not a constant available to the compiler. If however, names and p_names are made external the compiler would allocate permanent storage and the addresses would be constants evaluated at compile/link time. The above initialisation statement would then work.

Although Program 25.3 accesses the array names using pointers it still accesses the array p_names using 'normal' array indices or subscripts. Program 25.4 is a modification of Program 25.3 which uses pointers throughout. The sequence of statements is:

10	define number, the number of elements in the array names
11	define type name_t, an array of char which will hold the person's names
13-14	define array names and initialise it with strings
16	define p_name and array p_names which are 'pointers to type names_t'
	define p_p_name1 and p_p_name2 which are 'pointers to type pointer to names_t'
20	initialise p_p_name1 to point to start of array p_names
21	initialise p_names to point to start of array names
22-26	a while statement incrementing p_p_name1 until it gets to the end of array p_names
	24 point element in p_names to the corresponding element of names
	i.e. p_p_name1 points to p_names and p_name points to names
	25 print name pointed to by **p_p_name1
	i.e. p_p_name1 points to p_names which points to names
29-41	sort array p_names such that it points to the elements of names in alphabetical order
45-46	print the contents of the array names using the pointer p_p_name1
	the names should now be printed in alphabetical order

Note that line 33:

```
if (**p_p_name2[0] < **p_p_name1[0])
```

compares the first letter of the name pointed to by *p_p_name2 with the first letter of the name pointed to by p_p_name1. It could be written as line 34:

```
if (***p_p_name2 < ***p_p_name1)          /* alternative ! */
```

using three levels of indirection to access the first letter of each name. The above tests will only sort against the first letter of each name. Line 35 uses strcmp to sort against all letters of the name, i.e.:

```
if (strcmp(**p_p_name2, **p_p_name1) < 0)
```

A run of Program 25.4 was:

```
Set up pointers and print names via array of pointers
 Bertie Alison Betty  Bart    Alex    Aleson Bert   Alan   Bert   Bernie

Print names via sorted array of pointers
 Alison Alex    Aleson Alan   Bertie Betty  Bert   Bart   Bert   Bernie
```

Note the use of while statements in Program 25.4 (lines 20 to 26 and 31 to 40) where Program 25.3 used for statements. Chapter 13.1 explained that the for statement is just a shorthand way of writing a while statement and recommended that once the for (expression1; expression2; expression3) statement is longer than a single line a while should be used. This would have been the case in Program 25.4 where the initialisation and termination expressions of equivalent for statements would have been very long.

```
 1 /* Program 25.4, Sort an array of pointers to an array of names.        *
 2  *    Rather than sort the array of names itself into alphabetical order, *
 3  *    sort the array of pointers to the names in alphabetical order       */
 4
 5 #include <stdio.h>
 6 #include <string.h>
 7
 8 int main(void)
 9 {
10     enum {number = 10};                      /* number of names to be sorted */
11     typedef char name_t[8];                  /* define type to hold a name */
12     /* define and initialise an array of names */
13     name_t names[number] = {{"Bertie"},{"Alison"},{"Betty"},{"Bart"},{"Alex"},
14                             {"Aleson"},{"Bert"},{"Alan"},{"Bert"},{"Bernie"}};
15     /* define an array of pointers to names */
16     name_t *p_name, *p_names[number], **p_p_name1, **p_p_name2;
17
18     /* point the pointers to the names in the array and print the names */
19     printf("\n\nSet up pointers and print names via array of pointers\n");
20     p_p_name1 = p_names;                     /* point to start of array p_names */
21     p_name = names;                          /* point to start of names */
22     while ( p_p_name1 < p_names + number )
23         {
24         *p_p_name1 = p_name++;               /* set up pointer to name */
25         printf(" %-6s",  **p_p_name1++);     /* print name pointed to */
26         }
27
28     /* sort the array of pointers (on first letter) using a linear sort */
29     for (p_p_name1 = p_names ; p_p_name1 < p_names + number - 1 ; p_p_name1++)
30         {
31         p_p_name2 = p_p_name1;
32         while (p_p_name2++ < p_names + number - 1)
33             if (**p_p_name2[0] < **p_p_name1[0])
34             /*if (***p_p_name2 < ***p_p_name1)*/        /* alternative ! */
35             /*if (strcmp(**p_p_name2,**p_p_name1) < 0)*/ /* alternative ! */
36                 {
37                 p_name = *p_p_name1;                     /* swap pointers */
38                 *p_p_name1 = *p_p_name2;
39                 *p_p_name2 = p_name;
40                 }
41         }
42
43     /* print the names via the sorted array of pointers */
44     printf("\n\nPrint names via sorted array of pointers\n");
45     for (p_p_name1 = p_names ; p_p_name1 < p_names + number ; p_p_name1++)
46         printf(" %-6s",  **p_p_name1);
47     return 0;
48 }
```

Program 25.4 Sort an array of pointers to an array of person names.

26

The Preprocessor

The preprocessor (introduced in Chapter 3) reads the program source file including header files, expanding macros, etc., and then passes the resultant intermediate file to the compiler for compilation. Previous chapters have introduced some of the preprocessor directives (#include and #define) which will now be described in more detail together with additional directives (a few specialised directives are not covered).

Remember that each preprocessor directive should be on a separate line and not terminated with a ;. A preprocessor directive may be continued onto the following line by terminating the line the sequence **backslash newline** (no spaces following the \) which becomes invisible to the C system (see Chapter 6.2.2 on program layout).

26.1 The *#define* and *#undef* directives

26.1.1 Defining symbolic constants

The preprocessor #define is used to create macros. Macros without parameters were introduced in Chapter 17.9 and are used to define symbolic constants:

```
#define IDENTIFIER   replacement_text
```

The preprocessor, when it reads the program source code file, replaces all occurrences of IDENTIFIER with the replacement_text. For example:

```
#define ARRAY_SIZE 100
#define MAX_TEMPERATURE 50.0
```

The identifiers ARRAY_SIZE and MAX_TEMPERATURE are called *symbolic constants* and by convention are in upper case. When the preprocessor reads the program file all occurrences of the symbolic constants are replaced with the corresponding replacement_text using literal substitution. For example, all occurrences of MAX_TEMPERATURE are replaced with 50.0:

```
#define MAX_TEMPERATURE 50.0f

    if (temperature > MAX_TEMPERATURE)
        ........
```

After preprocessing the compiler would get:

```
    if (temperature > 50.0f)
        ........
```

Hence the compiler knows nothing about symbolic constants. Remember that the preprocessor performs literal substitution and an error in a preprocessor directive will appear at compile time in a line of code that may look perfectly OK. For example, if a ; has been typed on the end of the #define by mistake:

```
#define MAX_TEMPERATURE 50.0f;

    if (temperature > MAX_TEMPERATURE)
        ........
```

After preprocessing the compiler would get:

```
if (temperature > 50.0;)
    ........
```

and generate an error due to the incorrect placing of the ;. For example, Microsoft C Version 6.00 generated the following error messages:

```
6       if (temperature > MAX_TEMPERATURE)
***** X.C(6) : error C2143: syntax error : missing ')' before ';'
***** X.C(6) : error C2143: syntax error : missing ';' before ')'
```

The problem is that the line of code where the error was found (line 6 in this case) looks correct; the error being in the #define directive. Because such errors can be quite difficult to find most compilers provide some means of examining the output of the preprocessor to track down such errors, e.g. the /P option of the Microsoft C version 6.00 compiler CL.EXE or the Turbo C version 1.01 program CPP.EXE (see section 26.5).

The #define directives are normally placed at the start of a file following the #include directives, and have file scope, i.e. from the #define to the end of the current file. However, the #undef directive (see section 26.1.4) may be used to 'undefine' an identifier.

One of the main uses of #define is in header files where it is used to define symbolic constants relevant to the library concerned, e.g. to define symbolic constants such as INT_MIN, INT_MAX, etc. in <limits.h>.

Symbolic constants can be used to improve program maintainability and readability by using relevant names for constants within the program. It must be emphasised, however, that the compiler knows nothing about symbolic constants and can perform no optimisation (unlike const qualified objects which the compiler knows about).

26.1.2 Macros with parameters

The #define directive can be used to define macros with parameters, e.g.:

```
#define IDENTIFIER(parm_1, parm_2, parm_3, ........) replacement_text
```

Note that there is no space between IDENTIFIER and the (otherwise the text (parm_1, parm_2, parm_3, ...) would be treated as part of replacement_text.

When the macro is called the preprocessor replaces each occurrence of the formal parameters parm_1, parm_2, etc. with the corresponding actual parameter. For example, consider a macro which evaluates the square of a number:

```
#define square(a) a * a
```

the macro could be used as follows:

```
int x = 10, z;
z = square(x);
```

after preprocessing the compiler would get:

```
int x = 10, z;
z = x * x;
```

which would assign the value 100 to z.

Because the macro call is replaced using literal substitution obscure errors can occur. Consider the following use of the macro square:

```
int x = 10, z;
z = square(x + 2);
```

the value assigned to z is 32 (not 144) because the macro call is expanded to:

```
z = x + 2 * x + 2;
```

the order of evaluation being x + (2 * x) + 2. Now consider:

```
int x = 10, y = 200, z;
z = y / square(x);
```

this would assign z the value 200 (not 2) because the macro call is expanded to:

```
z = y / x * x;
```

the order of evaluation being (y / x) * x.

To overcome these problems it is highly recommended that when the formal parameters are used in macros they are enclosed in parentheses and the whole replacement_text is enclosed in parentheses, e.g. square should have been written:

```
#define square(a) ((a) * (a))
```

and the above examples of its use would then work 'as expected'. Now consider:

```
int x = 10, z;
z = square(++x);
```

this would result in x being incremented twice and the value 144 assigned to z. Avoid operations which have side effects in macro calls, e.g. increment and decrement operators, input/output or calls to functions which return different values on successive calls (such as the fibonacci number function in Chapter 17.6).

The definition of a macro may contain a call to another macro (which has already been defined). For example, a macro to cube a value:

```
#define square(a) ((a) * (a))
#define cube(a)   (square(a) * (a))
```

Although macros appear to be similar to functions they are expanded in-line with the code and are therefore more efficient in terms of execution time. However, the complete macro code is generated on each call so long macros should be avoided (a function call becomes more efficient in terms of memory usage).

Because macros only deal with pure text replacement they have no knowledge of C types and the same macro can be used with any suitable type of data. For example, the above macro square could be used to square integers or floats. Consider:

```
#define swap(type, a, b) {type temp; temp = a; a = b; b = temp;};
```

This defines a macro which will swap two variables of type (the function swap of Program 15.2 could only swap integer values). Clearly care must be taken when calling the macro in that it may only be called where a statement may be used and the actual parameters must be simple variables. For example:

```
int x = 10, z = 25;
float a = 1, b = 2;

swap(int, z, x)
swap(float, a, b)
```

26.1.3 Macros with parameters within strings

If a macro contains a string constant (enclosed in " marks) this text will not be replaced by any parameter. Consider a macro which is to print the name and value of a `float` variable:

```
#define print_float(a) printf("variable a = %f ", a)
    float x_test = 10;
    print_float(x_test);
```

this would print on the screen:

```
variable a = 10.000000
```

The a characters within the `printf` control string `"variable a = %f "` in the macro have not been replaced by `x_test`, i.e. the following would be passed to the compiler:

```
    float x_test = 10;
    printf("variable a = %f ", x_test);
```

To overcome this problem a special technique is used in that when a macro is being expanded:

1   if a formal parameter is preceded by a # the actual parameter is enclosed in ""
2   consecutive string constants are concatenated, i.e "hel" "lo" becomes "hello".

Thus the above `print_float` macro and its call should be written:

```
#define print_float(a) printf("variable " #a " = %f ", a)
    float x_test = 10;
    print_float(x_test);
```

the macro would be expanded to:

```
    float x_test = 10;
    printf("variable x_test = %f ", x_test);
```

which would print the result required:

```
variable x_test = 10.000000
```

A more versatile print macro would be:

```
#define print(a, format) printf("variable " #a " = %" #format " ", a);
```

and it could be called as follows:

```
    float x_test = 10;
    int i = 5;
    print(x_test, f);
    print(i, d);
```

where the second parameter in the macro call specifies the conversion specification character.

26.1.4 The *#undef* directive

The #undef directive is used to undefine an identifier defined by #define, e.g.:

```
#undef print                              /* undefine print macro */
```

26.2 Condition selection

The conditional selection directives of the preprocessor enables the selection of sections of code which are to be passed (or not) to the compiler. The directives are:

```
#if expression         /* if expression is non-zero include the code following */
#ifdef identifier       /* if identifier is defined include the code following */
#ifndef identifier     /* if identifier is not defined include the code following */
```

If the condition is satisfied the code following (up to the next #else, #elif or #endif) is included otherwise it is skipped. The condition is terminated by:

```
#endif
```

The #else directive enables a choice of code selection, e.g.:

```
#ifdef identifier
    .....                              /* code included if identifier is defined */
#else
    .....                          /* code included if identifier is not defined */
#endif
```

The #elif directive is shorthand for else if, e.g.:

```
#ifdef identifier
    .....                              /* code included if identifier is defined */
#elif expression
    /* code included if identifier is not defined and expression is non-zero */
    .....
#endif
```

Conditional selection directives can be used as an aid to program portability. For example, a program may need to be executed on a range of target environments (host machine, operating system, etc.) and conditional selection directives can be used to include particular definitions and/or functions appropriate to the target.

26.3 The *#include* directive

The preprocessor #include directive was introduced in Chapter 21.7, e.g.:

```
#include <filename>                         /* include file from 'standard' place */
#include "filename"     /* include file from current directory else 'standard' place */
```

Both the directives include the contents of filename at that point in the source program (filename can contain any valid C code). In the first form (filename enclosed in <>) the file is assumed to be in a 'standard' directory in the file system which the C compiler automatically searches, e.g. the Microsoft C Version 6.00 header files are usually in directory \c600\include. The second form of #include (filename enclosed in "") searches the current directory for filename and then, if it is not found, the 'standard' directory, e.g.:

```
#include <math.h>                       /* include standard header file math.h */
#include "my_own.h"                     /* include header file my_own.h */
#include "my_func.c"                  /* include C function from file my_func.c */
```

The body of a particular header file should not be included more than once, it may lead to multiple definitions of identifiers which could cause problems. A header file may include other header files (which contain definitions it requires) therefore is it is possible to issue an #include for the same header file several times. The #ifndef directive can be used within a header file to check if it has already been included.

For example, if the header file "stu_lib.h" was included more than once in Program 22.1 multiple definitions of identifiers would occur. A version of the header file stu_lib.h modified to include a #ifndef directive is shown below. When the file is first included _stu_lib_h_ is not defined so the #ifndef directive includes the text which follows; the identifier _stu_lib_h_ is then defined followed by the remainder of the file. If the file was included again _stu_lib_h_ would be defined and the #ifndef would skip the remainder of the text up to #endif. The convention for the identifier name to be used in this way is to use the name of the header file prefixed and postfixed with _ and the . replaced with _.

```
/* Header file stu_lib.h - header file for student record functions */

#ifndef _stu_lib_h_                          /* if _stu_lib_h_ is not defined */
#define _stu_lib_h_                             /* define _stu_lib_h_ */

enum {name_length = 20};           /* length of student name, course name, etc. */

/* define structure to hold course information */
typedef struct {
            char course_name[name_length];            /* name of course */
            int course_code;                  /* institutions course code */
            int course_year;                      /* year of course */
            }
            course_t;

/* define structure type to hold student information */
typedef struct {
            char name[name_length];                      /* student name */
            int age;                                 /* student age */
            int start_year;                  /* year of starting course */
            course_t course;                      /* details of course */
            long int identifier;          /* student identifier number */
            }.
            student_t;                        /* structure type name */

/* prototypes for student record processing functions in stu_lib.c & stu_lib1.c */
int stu_read_data(student_t *student);                  /* read record */
int stu_store(const student_t student);                 /* store record */
void stu_print(const student_t student);                /* print record */
void stu_all_print(void);                            /* print all records */
int stu_name(const student_t student, const char name[]);   /* compare names */
int stu_find(student_t *student, char student_name[]);      /* find record */
int stu_write_file(const char filename[]);              /* write to file */
/* read string and integer read functions */
int str_read(const char prompt[], char string[], const int max_length);
int integer_read(const char prompt[], const int maximum);

#endif                                            /* end of condition */
```

Header file stu_lib.h Version using the #ifndef directive (see Chapter 22)

26.4 Macros in library header files

The ANSI standard allows library routines to be implemented using macros provided that there will be no problems with side effects (as described in section 26.1.1). For example, the functions getchar and putchar from <stdio.h> are often defined as macros to avoid the run-time overhead of a function call for every character read or printed. Consider:

```
#include <stdio.h>
int main(void)
{
    int ch;
    ch = getchar();
    putchar(ch);
}
```

With Microsoft C the preprocessor output was (edited to remove the text of <stdio.h>):

```
int main(void)
{
    int ch;
    ch = (--((&_iob[0]))->_cnt >= 0 ?
            0xff & *((&_iob[0]))->_ptr++ : _filbuf((&_iob[0])));
    (--((&_iob[1]))->_cnt >= 0 ? 0xff & (*((&_iob[1]))->_ptr++ =
            (char)((ch))) : _flsbuf(((ch)),((&_iob[1]))));
}
```

The standard does, however, guarantee that even if a library function is implemented as a macro there will also be a 'real' function. To invoke the 'real' function the macro can be undefined using #undef or the function name enclosed in parentheses. For example, the above program could be modified to call the 'real' functions getchar and putchar:

```
#include <stdio.h>
#undef getchar
main()
{
    int ch;
    ch = getchar();
    (putchar)(ch);
}
```

26.5 Examining the output of the preprocessor

The majority of compilers provide some means of examining the output of the preprocessor to track down errors in macro expansions (see discussion in section 26.1), e.g.:

```
cc -E filename.c          UNIX operating system using the cc compiler
cl /P filename.c          Microsoft C version 6.00 compiler cl.exe
cpp filename.c            Turbo C version 1.01 preprocessor cpp.exe
```

The C source is in file filename.c and preprocessor output is written to file filename.i.

Problem for Chapter 26

Enter the program from section 26.4. Preprocess the file and examine the resultant output. Modify the program to call the 'real' functions and repeat the process.

27

Input and output functions

In C all input and output operations are performed by library functions. The ANSI standard defines a number of basic functions (defined in <stdio.h>, see Appendix C.12) and most compilers provide additional non standard libraries to access facilities which are operating system dependent, e.g. Microsoft C and Turbo C provide <conio.h> which contains prototypes of functions to directly access the console keyboard and display screen.

In C input and output takes place via a *stream* which may be connected to a disk file, the keyboard, the display screen, a serial port, or any other suitable device. Before any input/output operations can take place the stream must be connected to something, e.g. a file on disk opened for input or output. Associated with each open stream is a structure of type FILE which is defined in <stdio.h>. The structure contains information which enables the program to control the flow of information, e.g. pointer to its I/O buffer, pointer to current position in buffer, error indicator, etc. When connected the stream name is a pointer to a structure of type FILE.

27.1 Standard input/output streams

When setting up the program run-time environment prior to the start of program execution the following three standard streams are automatically opened:

```
FILE  *stdin;                    /* input stream: usually connected to keyboard */
FILE  *stdout;          /* output stream: usually connected to display screen */
FILE  *stderr;           /* error output, usually connected to display screen */
```

The connection of the streams to physical devices is operating system dependent. When using interactive systems stdin is usually connected to the terminal keyboard and stdout and stderr to the terminal display screen (could be separate windows on a window managed system). The operating system usually provides some means of redirecting the streams to other devices, e.g. under UNIX or MS-DOS the redirection commands are:

```
program < data              execute program with stream stdin from file data
program > out_data          execute program with stream stdout to file out_data
program >> out_data         stream stdout is appended on the end of file out_data
```

27.2 Opening, closing, deleting and renaming files

Apart from the standard streams (stdin, stdout and stderr) a stream must be connected to a file or a device before it can be used (see Appendix C.12.1 for further discussion):

```
FILE  *fopen(const char *filename, const char *mode);        /* open a file for I/O */
```

fopen returns a pointer to a structure of type FILE (which is then used to identify the stream in future operations) or NULL if an error occurred (see next section). The parameters are:

filename: a pointer to a character string which contains the filename in a format acceptable to the operating system.

mode: a pointer to a character string specifying the mode of operation:

r   opens an existing file for reading

w   creates a new file for writing (if it already exists its contents are discarded)

a   opens an existing file for append, information written is appended onto existing
     data, otherwise a new file is created for writing

r+   opens an existing file for update (reading and writing)

w+   creates a new file for update (reading and writing)

a+   opens an existing file or creates a new file for update and append

The above modes are for opening *text* streams which are used to process character based data, i.e. lines of characters terminated by *newline*. C also supports *binary* streams which are used to process data transferred in machine dependent binary form. For *binary* streams the mode should include the letter b, e.g. rb, wb, wb+, etc. (see section 27.7).

Attempting to open a file which does not exist for reading or opening a file without the correct access rights will give an error (fopen returns a NULL). The library function perror can be used to display a relevant message to stderr (see next section). When input/output transfers are complete the file should be closed using the function fclose:

```
int  fclose(FILE *stream);
```

this closes the file pointed to by stream. If successful fclose returns 0 or, if an error occurred, EOF (see next section for reporting of error conditions).

If a temporary file is required function tmpfile creates a temporary file of mode wb+ which is automatically deleted when closed or on program termination:

```
FILE  *tmpfile(void);                          /* open temporary file */
```

Useful file maintenance functions are (both return 0 if successful):

```
int  remove(const char *filename);                        /* delete a file */
int  rename(const char *old_filename, const char *new_filename);   /* rename a file */
```

27.3 I/O status and error functions

If fopen fails it returns a NULL to the calling program and a message indicating open failure can be displayed on the screen. In addition C provides additional information regarding the failure which can assist in tracking down the cause of the problem.

Many of the input/output functions set up indicators in the FILE structure when an error or EOF (end of file) occurs which can be set and tested using the following functions:

```
void clearerr(FILE *stream);              /* clear EOF and error indicators */
int feof(FILE *stream);              /* returns non-zero if EOF indicator is set */
int ferror(FILE *stream);            /* returns non-zero if error indicator is set */
```

When an error occurs many of the functions set up an integer error number in errno which is declared in <errno.h> (errno is usually an external variable set up by the C run-time system and the name should not be used for anything else, see Appendix C.3). Although the value of errno can be accessed and printed the error values are operating system and compiler dependent and are meaningless without reference to manuals. The function perror prints a program specified string together with an implementation defined error message corresponding to errno to the stream stderr (see Appendix C.12.2):

```
void perror(const char *string);              /* print string then error message */
```

```
 1  /* Program 27.1  Open a file, write characters read from stdin, exit on EOF */
 2
 3  #include <stdio.h>
 4  #include <errno.h>
 5  #include <string.h>
 6
 7  int main(void)
 8  {
 9      FILE *out_file;                        /* define pointer to output file */
10      char *p_name, filename[20];
11      int ch;
12
13      printf("\nEnter name of output file ? ");
14      if((p_name = strchr(fgets(filename, 20, stdin), '\n')) != NULL)
15          *p_name = '\0';                    /* replace \n with \0 */
16
17      if ((out_file = fopen(filename, "w")) == NULL)      /* open output file */
18          {
19          printf("\nUnable to open file %s:  errno = %d", filename, errno);
20          perror(", message ");
21          return 1;                          /* open failed */
22          }
23
24      printf("\nFile opened OK; enter text terminate with EOF\n");
25      while ((ch = getchar()) != EOF)                /* read character */
26          putc(ch, out_file);                        /* write character */
27      fclose(out_file);                              /* close output file */
28      return 0;
29  }
```

Program 27.1 Open a file, write characters read from stdin and exit on EOF

Program 27.1 opens a file then loops reading characters from stdin (the keyboard) writing them to the file (closing the file and terminating on EOF). The sequence of statements is:

3-5   include header files (<errno.h> declares errno)

9   define out_file a pointer to type FILE (defined in <stdio.h>)

13   Prompt user to enter the name of a file

14-15   read filename into string filename and if it contains a *newline* replace it with '\0'
         (fgets will place the *newline* in the string if it is less than 20 characters in length)

17-22   call fopen to open file filename for writing (mode "w")
         19   failed: print message and value of errno (declared in <error.h>)
         20   call perror to print message corresponding to errno
         21   terminate program indicating failure

25-26   a while reading characters from stdin (terminates on EOF)
         26   call putc to write character to output stream out_file (see next section)

27   close the output file

The name of the file filename specified in the call to fopen in line 17 is the name which the file will have on disk. Filenames must therefore adhere to the conventions of the operating system, e.g. to separate subdirectory names MS-DOS and UNIX use \ and / respectively, e.g. `c_progs\test.c` or `c_progs/test.c`. A run of the program when an invalid filename was entered (run on an IBM PC compatible under Microsoft version 6.00) was:

```
Enter name of output file ? x\x

Unable to open file x\x:  errno = 2, message : No such file or directory
```

The value of errno means very little to the user and would normally not be printed.

27.4 Character and string input and output

Individual characters may be read by:

```
int  fgetc(FILE *stream);               /* read next character from stream */
int  getc(FILE *stream);          /* macro: read next character from stream */
int  getchar(void);                     /* read next character from stdin */
```

fgetc reads the next character from stream; it returns the character as an int, or EOF if end of file was found. getc is equivalent to fgetc but may be implemented as a macro (to save the overhead of a function call for every character transferred). getchar is a special version of getc which reads from the standard input stream stdin. The corresponding character output functions are:

```
int  fputc(int char, FILE *stream);       /* write character char to stream */
int  putc(int char, FILE *stream);  /* macro: write character char to stream */
int  putchar(int char);                   /* write character char to stdout */
```

fputc writes a character to stream, putc is equivalent but may be a macro and putchar is a version of putc which writes to stdout. The functions return the character written if successful or EOF if an error occurs.

The function ungetc is used to 'push' a character back into the input stream (normally a maximum of one character may be pushed and it is not possible push EOF):

```
int  ungetc(int char, FILE *stream);     /* push character back into input stream */
```

Exercise 15.1 shows the use of ungetc.

The functions getchar and putchar are often defined as macros to avoid the run-time overhead of a function call for every character read or printed. The standard does, however, guarantee that even if a library function is normally implemented as a macro there will also be a 'real' function. Chapter 26.4 discussed these points and the techniques used to invoke the 'real' function instead of the macro, e.g. by undefining the macro using #undef or enclosing the function name in parentheses.

Strings (arrays of char terminated by '\0') may be printed and read character by character using the individual character I/O functions (fgetc, getc, getchar, fputc, putc and putchar. Alternatively complete strings may be read and written using the string I/O functions (see Chapter 19.4 and Appendix C.12.5 for a full discussion):

```
char  *fgets(char *string, int n, FILE *stream);   /* read characters from stream */
char  *gets(char *string);                    /* read characters from stdin */
int  fputs(const char *string, FILE *stream);      /* write a string to stream */
int  puts(const char *string);           /* write a string plus '\n' to stdout */
```

Program 19.1 shows an example of the use of string I/O functions.

Exercise 27.1 (see Appendix B for sample answer)

Implement a program which copies the contents of one character based file to another. The filenames should be specified in the program command line, e.g. (program is ex27_1.exe):

```
ex27_1  file_1  file_2  -options
```

copies the contents of file_1 into file_2. The options specified by -options should be:

-upper   convert lower case characters to upper case
-lower   convert upper case characters to lower case

If neither option is specified copy the file without any conversion. Test the program, specifying invalid filenames, filenames which do not exist, etc.

27.5 The *fprintf, printf* and *sprintf* functions

The following output functions provide a means of converting the internal machine representation of information into sequences of characters in a specified format:

```
int fprintf(FILE *stream, const char *format, ...);      /* print to stream */
int printf(const char *format, ...);                     /* print to stdout */
int sprintf(char *string, const char *format, ...);      /* print to "string" */
```

the ... indicates a number of parameters which are processed under the control of the *control string* pointed to by format:

fprintf writes the converted output to the output stream
printf   writes the converted output to the output stream stdout
sprintf places the converted output in the character array pointed to by string

The parameter format points to an array of characters, the *control string*, which controls the format of the output. The *control string* contains ordinary characters witch are copied to the output and conversion specifications which control the conversion of the corresponding parameters to the output (see Appendix C.12.6 and Table C.1 for details).

   The function printf is used to print information to the display screen and fprintf performs a similar function to stream (e.g. a file on disk). The function sprintf is used for conversions within the program. For example, when displaying pictorial information using a graphics package it may be necessary to annotate parts of the image with numeric values (e.g. loads on a bridge). Under such circumstances it will be necessary to use the text output functions of the graphics package which are usually limited to string display (not conversion of numeric information). The function sprintf can be used to output the information required into a string which is then displayed on the screen.

   For example, the following code inserted following line 41 of Exercise 13.2 (see Appendix B) displays the x and y coordinates of the bouncing ball on the screen:

```
settextstyle(DEFAULT_FONT, HORIZ_DIR, 2);        /* set text style */
sprintf(text, "x = %3d, y = %3d ", x, y);        /* convert x and y */
text_x = (maxx / 2) - (textwidth(text) / 2);     /* get x position */
outtextxy(text_x, text_y, text);                 /* display text */
```

The program sequence (using Turbo C) is:

1   set the text style (in particular the text size is 2)
2   call sprintf to convert the x and y coordinates into a string
3   calculate x coordinate to print the text in the middle of the screen and display the text

As the ball bounces around the screen the updated x and y coordinates are shown centred horizontally towards the top of the screen. Note that the delay loop of Exercise 13.1 can be removed; the time taken to display the text slows the program down sufficiently to move the ball at a reasonable speed even on a 80486 machine.

27.6 The *fscanf, scanf* and *sscanf* functions

The standard input functions scanf, fscanf and sscanf provide a means of converting sequences of characters into the internal machine representation of integers, reals, etc.:

```
int fscanf(FILE *stream, const char *format, ...);          /* read from stream */
int scanf(const char *format, ...);                          /* read from stdout */
int sscanf(const char *string, const char *format, ...);    /* read from "string" */
```

The parameter format points to an array of characters, the *control string*, which controls the conversion of characters from the input into values to be assigned to parameters indicated by .... See Appendix C.12.7 for details of the *control string* and Table D.2 for details of the *conversion specifications*. The functions return an int function indicating the number of successful conversions:

1 If no conversions occurred 0 is returned.
2 If a matching failure occurs (a non-numeric character in a decimal number) conversion stops and the number of successful conversions returned (the faulty character is left in the input stream where the program can read it and take action, see Program 13.2).
3 If *end of file* occurs before any conversions the value EOF is returned.

Thus it is possible for all input to be verified and action taken in case of error, e.g. a message printed and the user prompted for more input (see Chapter 13 Program 13.2).

The function scanf is used to read information from the terminal keyboard and fscanf performs a similar function from stream (e.g. from a file on disk). The function sscanf is used for conversions within the program. For example, a text string may be read from an external device into an array of char and then sscanf used to extract numeric data from the string. For example, when using a graphics package based on the PHIGS (Programmer's Hierarchical Interactive Graphics System) ISO graphics standard it is usually not possible to access the keyboard using the standard input stream stdin. All interactive input has to be via the PHIGS input devices. If numeric values are to be read from the keyboard the PHIGS *request string* function can be used to read a string which can then be processed using sscanf, e.g. on an HP 700 workstation the prototype is (HP 1991):

```
void prqst(int wkid, int stdnr, int *stat, int *iostr, char str[lstr], short lstr);
```

where wkid specifies the workstation identifier, stdnr specifies the string device number, stat returns the status flag, iostr returns the number of characters read, str returns the string and lstr specifies the length of str.input devices). Assuming the string device has been initialised (wkid has been set up) a call could be:

```
prqst (wkid, 1, &status, &instring, string, strlen(string));
if (status == POK)
   {
   if ((scan = sscanf(string, "%d %d", &x, &y)) == 2)
       /* x and y read OK */
   .....
```

This calls prqst which returns the characters read in string. If status is POK (PHIGS OK) sscanf is called to obtain the values of x and y. The value of scan is then checked to ensure than the conversion of the two integer numbers worked correctly. If either if condition failed action would have to be taken to request input again (if possible). See function integer_read in file stu_lib.c, Chapter 22, for another example of sscanf.

27.7 Unformatted input and output

If the contents of a file are not to be directly examined by a human it is more efficient to use unformatted input and output (rather than fprintf, fscanf, etc.):

1 input/output is much faster because there is no overhead of converting between the internal machine format and the character based format;
2 there is no loss of information, e.g. converting a double value (with a minimum precision of 10 figures) using %f (with a default precision of 6 figures) will lose a significant amount of information.

Unformatted input/output is usually used with binary files (some systems make no distinction between binary and text files):

```
size_t  fread(void *p_data, size_t size, size_t number, FILE *stream);
size_t  fwrite(const void *p_data, size_t size, size_t number, FILE *stream);
```

where: p_data is a pointer to the data to be read or written
        size   specifies the size of the object(s) to be transferred
        number specifies the number of objects to be transferred
        stream is a pointer to a structure of type FILE

size_t is the unsigned integral type which the sizeof operator produces (defined in the header file <stddef.h>) and void * is the generic pointer (discussed in Chapter 23.4).

fread attempts to read number objects of size from stream returning the data in the array pointed to by p_data. It returns as an int function result the number of objects read (which may be less than the number requested). After calling fread the functions feof and ferror should be called to see if end of file was encountered or an error occurred.

fwrite attempts to write number objects of size from the array pointed to by p_data to stream. It returns as an int function result the number of objects written (which will be less than number if an error occurred).

For example, consider an array x of twenty int elements:

```
int x[20];
FILE *stream;

fread(x, sizeof(x), 1, stream);                /* read whole of array x */
fread(x, sizeof(int), 20, stream);             /* read whole of array x */
```

In both cases fread (if successful) reads data into all the elements of array x, i.e.:

1 The first call reads a single object of size sizeof(x); fread should return the value 1.
2 The second call reads twenty objects of size sizeof(int); fread should return 20.

The following calls read a single element of x:

```
fread(x, sizeof(int), 1, stream);              /* read first element of x */
fread(&x[5], sizeof(int), 1, stream);          /* read sixth element of x */
```

```
 1 /*---------------------------------------------------------------------*
 2  * write student data to file on disk, return TRUE if successful       */
 3 int stu_write_file(const char filename[])
 4 {
 5     FILE *out_file;                              /* pointer to output file */
 6     student_t student;
 7
 8     printf("\n\nWrite student records to file '%s' ", filename);
 9     if ((out_file = fopen(filename, "wb")) == NULL)       /* open output file */
10         {
11         perror("\a\nUnable to open student records output file");
12         return 0;                                /* open failed */
13         }
14
15     student = stu_next(1);                       /* get first student record */
16     while (! stu_name(student, ""))              /* if data OK */
17         {
18         fwrite(&student, sizeof(student_t), 1, out_file);   /* write record */
19         student = stu_next(0);                   /* get next student record */
20         }
21     fclose(out_file);
22     return 1;                                    /* indicate success */
23 }
```

Function stu_write_file Write student data to a disk file

The function stu_write_file (above) writes the student data of Program 22.1 to a file:

3   function header: parameter specifying the filename, returns *true* if successful
5-6   define stream out_file, a pointer to a structure of type FILE, and student record
9-13   call fopen to open filename for binary writing
         11-12   if open failed display error messages and return with *false*
15   call stu_next with parameter *true* to get the *first* student record
16-20   a while statement, terminating when an empty name is found
         18 call fwrite to write one record to disk
         19 call stu_next to get the *next* record in the data structure
21-22   close output file and return *true* for successful completion

The function performs no error checking on fwrite and should be extended to do this. Note that there is no point writing the whole array student; only a small part may be used.

Exercise 27.2 (see Appendix B for sample answer)

Modify the file copy program of Exercise 27.1 to use fread and fwrite, enabling any type of file to be copied (remove the -upper and -lower options).

Problem for Chapter 27

Implement and test a function to read the information written by stu_write_file, e.g. a prototype could be (returns number of records read):

```
    int stu_read_file(const char filename[]);
```

28

Dynamic storage allocation

Chapter 21.8 discussed the allocation and storage of variables:

automatic internal variable defined within a compound statement: allocated storage on entry to the compound statement and deallocated on exit from the compound statement.

static internal variable defined within a compound statement: allocated and initialised prior to program execution and maintained until program termination.

formal parameter to a function declared as a parameter in a function header: allocated on function entry and initialised with the values of the actual parameter.

external variable defined outside a function body: allocated and initialised prior to program execution and maintained until the program terminates.

The allocation and deallocation of the above variables is set up by the compiler and linker and, once defined, the size of such a variable may not be changed. In many applications, however, the actual size required to store a data set may not be known until run time. In Library stu_lib1.c in Chapter 22, for example, the array to store the student records was defined in line 7 (student_t students[max_students]; where max_students = 4) although the actual size was not known until run time. If the size required at run time was greater than max_students the program would fail (the source code would have to be edited and then compiled and linked). It would be possible to define a larger array but this would waste storage if student numbers were small and would still fail when the number of students became larger than the array size. It would be preferable if storage space of the required size could be acquired dynamically at run time and then released when no longer required.

28.1 Functions to allocate memory dynamically

The library <stdlib.h> contains functions which support dynamic memory allocation:

```
void *malloc(size_t size);                      /* allocate one object of 'size' */
void *calloc(size_t number, size_t size);     /* allocate 'number' objects of 'size' */
void *realloc(void *pointer, size_t size);     /* reallocate 'pointer' to 'size' */
void free(void *pointer);                       /* deallocate 'pointer' */
```

The type size_t is defined in <stdlib.h> and is typically an unsigned int (this is the type returned by the sizeof operator, see Chapter 9.6).

The function malloc allocates storage (from within the run-time system) for an object of size bytes and returns a pointer to the object, or NULL if the allocation failed. The pointer returned is type void * (see Chapter 23.4) which must be cast to the required data type before it can be used. The storage allocated is not initialised. For example, to allocate storage for one object of type student_t:

```
student_t *student;

student = (student_t *) malloc(sizeof(student_t));     /* allocate an student_t */
if (student == NULL)                                    /* allocation OK ? */
    printf("allocation failed ");                       /* no, failed */
```

Note the cast, (student_t *), which converts the pointer returned by malloc to a pointer to student_t. Once storage is allocated it can be accessed via the pointer student as normal.

The function calloc allocates storage for number objects of size bytes and returns a pointer to the objects, otherwise NULL. The storage allocated is initialised to zeros. For example, to allocate storage for one hundred objects of type student_t:

```
student_t *student;

if ((student = (student_t *) calloc(sizeof(student_t), 100)) == NULL)
    printf("allocation failed ");
```

The function malloc can be used to perform a similar function, i.e.:

```
student_t *student;

if ((student = (student_t *) malloc(100 * sizeof(student_t))) == NULL)
    printf("allocation failed ");
```

the difference is that calloc initialises the storage to zeros whereas malloc does not.

The function realloc changes the size of the storage area pointed to by pointer, to number bytes (which may be smaller or larger than already allocated). It returns a pointer to the reallocated storage, otherwise NULL if the reallocation failed. The current allocation may be extended (if possible) or new storage allocated; in any case the original contents are preserved and the extra storage is not initialised. For example, to reallocate the storage for two hundred objects of type student_t:

```
if ((student = (student_t *) realloc(student, 200 * sizeof(student_t))) == NULL)
    printf("reallocation failed ");
```

Once storage is finished with it can be deallocated using free, e.g.:

```
free(student);                                          /* deallocate storage */
```

Storage can be allocated and deallocated in any order but beware of fragmenting the memory. It is possible to end up in a situation where there is a large number of small 'free' areas in memory and allocation fails when storage is requested for something large.

Library stu_lib2.c (next page) is a version of library stu_lib1.c (from Chapter 22) modified to allocate the array to hold student records dynamically (note that Program 22.1 and Library stu_lib.c have not been changed). The sequence of statements is:

8	define students a pointer to type student_t
9	define number_of_students indicates number of records stored in the data structure
15	define max_students (static internal) size of array pointed to by pointer students
17-38	if number_of_students == max_students the current array is full
19	define new_students to use as a pointer to new array allocated
21	if max_students == 0 (on first call to stu_store)
23-24	call calloc to allocate storage for the student records
	else
27-28	call realloc to extend existing storage
29-33	if allocation failed display an error message and terminate
35	assign pointer to new storage area to students
36	assign max_students the size of the updated array
37	sound alarm to indicate success (this can be removed when fully tested)
39	copy record into array pointed to by students, postincrement number_of_students
40	return *true* for success

Once the storage for the array has been allocated the pointer students can be used with array indexes as in file stu_lib1.c. Thus lines 39 and 40 and the function stu_next (not shown in stu_lib2.c) have not been changed. Chapter 23.5 showed that array names can be used like pointers and pointers can be used with subscripts (like arrays).

In stu_lib2.c the array is initially allocated four elements (lines 23 and 24) and then extended by four elements (lines 27 and 28) as required; the alarm being sounded on each allocation to indicate success. When fully tested the size can be increased to a more reasonable size (e.g. 10 elements) and the sounding of the alarm removed.

```
1  /* Library stu_lib2.c, student data structure using dynamic memory allocation */
2  #include <stdio.h>                              /* standard headers */
3  #include <stdlib.h>
4  #include "stu_lib.h"                /* include student records header file */
5
6  enum {allocate_students = 4};    /* number of students to allocate storage for */
7
8  static student_t *students;              /* pointer to array of student records */
9  static int number_of_students = 0;       /* indicates number of records used */
10
11 /*-----------------------------------------------------------------*
12  * Store student record into data structure, return TRUE if stored OK        */
13 int stu_store(const student_t student)
14 {
15     static int max_students = 0;              /* size of array allocated */
16
17     if (number_of_students == max_students)        /* array full, allocate */
18         {
19         student_t *new_students;              /* pointer to new storage */
20
21         if (max_students == 0)                      /* first call ? */
22             /* yes, call calloc to allocate initial storage for student data */
23             new_students = (student_t *)
24                 calloc(allocate_students, sizeof(student_t));
25         else
26             /* no, call realloc to extend storage for student data */
27             new_students = (student_t *) realloc(students,
28                 (max_students + allocate_students) * sizeof(student_t));
29         if (new_students == NULL)            /* calloc/realloc OK ? */
30             {
31             printf("\n\afailed to allocated storage for student data ! ");
32             return 0;
33             };
34         /* OK set up pointer to storage and set up new size of array */
35         students = new_students;                          /* pointer */
36         max_students = max_students + allocate_students;   /* new size */
37         putchar('\a');                                    /* ring alarm */
38         }
39     students[number_of_students++] = student;        /* store record */
40     return 1;                                /* return TRUE */
41 }
```

Library stu_lib2.c Student records system using dynamic memory allocation

28.2 Linked lists

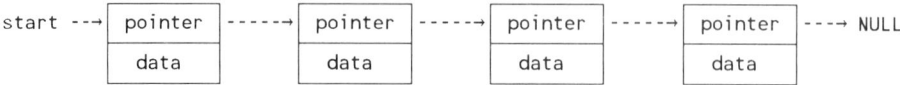

A linked list is data structure each element of which contains, in addition to any data, a pointer to the next element in the list. A pointer, start in the above diagram, points to the first element and the pointer of the final element points to NULL (which indicates the end of the list). Linked lists can be single linked (as above) or double linked with each element containing a link to the previous as well as the following element. Operations which can be carried out on linked lists include:

Create first element create an element (using malloc or calloc)
point start to the element, point pointer of the element to NULL

Add an element create new element (using malloc or calloc)
point pointer of last element in existing list to a new element
point pointer of new element to NULL

Delete element if first element copy pointer of element being deleted to start else copy
pointer of element being deleted to pointer of previous element
delete element using free

Library stu_lib3.c (below) is an implementation of the student records system of Chapter 22 using a linked list to store the records. Lines 8 to 12 define a type, link_t, which is a structure one of whose members is a pointer to the same type, i.e. a pointer to the next record in the linked list. This is achieved by using the tag s for the structure and then using it in the declaration of the first member, pointer p_next. The second member of the structure is of type student_t (defined in "stu_lib.h") which holds the student record. Once defined the type link_t is used to:

line 14 define students_start which will point to the first record in the linked list
line 15 define students_last which will point to the last record in the linked list

```
 1 /* Library stu_lib3.c, student record system using a linked list */
 2
 3 #include <stdio.h>                            /* standard headers */
 4 #include <stdlib.h>
 5 #include "stu_lib.h"              /* include student records header file */
 6
 7 /* define a type to hold the student records in a linked list */
 8 typedef struct S {
 9                 struct S *p_next;             /* pointer to next record */
10                 student_t student;           /* current student record */
11                 }
12                 link_t;
13
14 static link_t *students_start = NULL,    /* pointer to first record in list */
15                 *students_last = NULL;    /* pointer to last record in list */
```

Library stu_lib3.c, student record system using a linked list

```
16
17 /*--------------------------------------------------------------------*
18  * Store student record into data structure, return TRUE if stored OK       */
19 int stu_store(const student_t student)
20 {
21     link_t *p_new_record;              /* will point to new record created */
22
23     if ((p_new_record =                            /* create record */
24          (link_t *) calloc(sizeof(link_t), 1)) != NULL)
25        {                                          /* created OK */
26        if (students_start == NULL)            /* first record ? */
27            students_start = p_new_record;       /* yes, set it up */
28        else
29            students_last->p_next = p_new_record;   /* no, set up pointer */
30        students_last = p_new_record;            /* last to new record */
31        p_new_record->p_next = NULL;             /* point new to NULL */
32        }
33     else
34        {                                        /* create failed */
35        printf("\n\aCreation of new student record failed \n");
36        return 0;                                /* return fail */
37        };
38     p_new_record->student = student;            /* store record */
39     return 1;                                   /* return success */
40 }
41
42 /*--------------------------------------------------------------------*
43  * return record for next student in the data structure                *
44  *    if first is TRUE reset to first student                          *
45  *    if past end of records return record with student name set to ""    */
46 student_t stu_next(const int first)
47 {
48     static link_t *students = NULL;    /* pointer to current record in list */
49     student_t student = {""};            /* initialise student name to "" */
50
51     if (first) students = students_start;   /* if TRUE reset to first student */
52     if (students != NULL)                    /* if valid record */
53        {
54        student = students->student;            /* copy record */
55        students = students->p_next;        /* point to next record */
56        }
57     return student;                           /* return record */
58 }
```

Library stu_lib3.c, student record system using a linked list

The function stu_store, lines 19 to 40, attempts to create a new record and append it onto the end of the linked list. If successful it returns *true*. The sequence of statements is:

19   the function header with one parameter, student the record to be stored
21   define p_new_record a pointer which will point to the new record
23-37   call calloc to allocate one record (calloc zeros the storage)
      25-32   allocation successful, set up pointers to the new record
          26 if new record is first in linked list
              27 point students_start to it
             else 29 point pointer of last record in linked list to new record
          30 point students_last (pointer to last record) to new record
          31 set pointer to new record to NULL (this is the last record in the list)
      35-36   allocation failed, display error message and return indicating failure
38   copy student record into new record
39   return *true* for success

Chapter 23.6 stated that a pointer may be used to access a structure thus (line 38):

```
p_new_record->student = student;                    /* store record */
```

which is equivalent to:

```
(*p_new_record).student = student;                  /* store record */
```

the () are required because . has a higher precedence than *.

Function stu_next (lines 46 to 58) returns either the first record or the next in sequence (pointed to by pointer students):

46   function header with one parameter first, returns a record of type student_t
      if first is *true* students is reset to point to the first record in the linked list
      if beyond the end of records the function returns a record with an empty name
48   define students which will point to the record to be returned (initialised to NULL)
49   define internal variable student with name initialised to ""
51   if first is *true* reset students to point to first record
52-56   if students is not equal to NULL it points to a valid record
      54 copy record into student
      55 point students to next record in the linked list
57   return student (either with empty name or with the value assigned in line 54)

Program 22.1 and library stu_lib.c need no modifications to use library stu_lib3.c. This illustrates the importance of having a clearly defined loosely coupled interface between a library and the programs which use it. Thus the underlying library may be changed extensively without effecting the code of functions which use it, so long as the interface, in terms of function names, parameters passed, results returned, etc., remains unchanged.

Problem for Chapter 28

Extend function stu_store of Library stu_lib3.c to check for an identical student name before adding a new record to the data structure. Add functions to Library stu_lib3.c to delete and replace records (identified by name). Note that special care must be taken when deleting the first or last record in the linked list, i.e. student_start and students_last point to the first and last records respectively and care must be taken to update them correctly.

29

Advanced use of functions

29.1 Recursive functions

In C a function may be used recursively in that it may call itself either directly (from within itself) or indirectly (from a function which it has called). For example, the factorial of a number may be evaluated using the series (see Program 13.2):

N! = N * (N -1) * (N - 2) * (N - 3) 1   N > 0

or using the recursive relationship:

N! = N * (N - 1)!   for N > 1
   = 1   for N = 1

The function factorial in Program 29.1 is recursive. Consider lines:

22 if (n == 1) return 1; if n is 1 the recursion is terminated
23 else   return (n * factorial(n - 1)); the function calls itself to evaluate (n-1)!

```
 1 /* Program 29.1  Evaluate factorial using a recursive function            *
 2  *     N! = N * (N -1)! down to !1  = 1                                    */
 3
 4 #include <stdio.h>
 5
 6 int main(void)
 7 {
 8     long int factorial(long int n);                    /* function prototype */
 9
10     int n;                                             /* holds number */
11
12     /* read an integer number, terminate on EOF */
13     while(printf("\nNumber > 0 ? ") , (scanf(" %d", &n)) == 1)
14         printf(" number = %d,  factorial = %ld \n", n, factorial(n));
15     return 0;
16 }
17
18 /*-------------------------------------------------------------------*
19  * Factorial of an integer number:  n! = n * (n -1)! down to !1  = 1       */
20 long int factorial(long int n)
21 {
22     if (n == 1)  return 1;                             /* return 1! */
23     else         return (n * factorial(n - 1));        /* return n! */
24 }
```

Program 29.1 Evaluate factorial using a recursive function

Recursive functions should only be used when alternative non-recursive algorithms are not available or are more complex , e.g. evaluating factorial by recursion is very inefficient and a simple loop should be used as in Program 13.2. Recursion entails a high overhead in terms of parameter passing, creation of internal automatic variables (a new set of auto variables is created on each call), etc. The overhead is not only in terms of execution time but if the function has a large number of internal variables or the recursion is very deep the program can run out of stack space.

Exercise 29.1 (see Appendix B for sample answer)

A good example of where recursion can be used very effectively is the quicksort algorithm. In a given array an element x is selected and the other elements are partitioned into two subsets; one containing elements with a value less than x and the other with values greater than x. The partitioning process is then applied to the two subsets. An algorithm is:

1   Select an element in the array and assign its value to x. Although the element may be selected randomly the usual technique is to select the middle element.
2   Scan up the array until element array[up] >= x.
3   Scan down the array until element array[down] <= x.
4   Exchange elements array[up] and array[down]
5   return to step 2 to continue the process of scanning up and down until up > down.

When the scan is complete the array will be partitioned into two sets; a lower set with values less than or equal to x and an upper set with values greater than or equal to x. The upper and lower sets are then sorted using the algorithm. The algorithm lends itself to a recursive solution (the recursion terminates when arrays of two elements have been sorted).

29.2 Pointers to functions

Although functions are not variables they do have an address (associated with the function name) and it is possible to define pointers to functions. Consider:

```
double *function(double);                        /* declare function prototype */
```

this is a prototype for a function with one double parameter and which returns a pointer to a double as a function result. Now consider:

```
double (*p_function)(double);                        /* define a pointer */
```

this defines a variable p_function which is a 'pointer to a function with one double parameter and which returns a double function result'. Because unary * has a lower precedence than () the parentheses are required around (*p_function) to force the proper association, i.e. 'pointer to function'. Consider:

```
double (*p_function)(double);        /* define a pointer to a function */
double result;                       /* define a double */

p_function = sin;                    /* point to sin function */
result = p_function(0.5);            /* evaluate sin(0.5) */
```

this defines p_function (a pointer to a function) which is assigned to 'point to' the maths function sin. The function is then called via the pointer, i.e. the last two statements are equivalent to:

```
result = sin(0.5);                        /* evaluate sin(0.5) */
```

The pointer p_function can be set up to point to any function of the correct type, i.e. 'a function with one double parameter and which returns a double function result'. Thus it would be able to 'point to' many of the mathematical functions in the standard library, e.g. cos, sqrt, tan, etc. An alternative way to declare the pointer p_function is:

```
/* define a pointer to a function: double parameter returning a double */
typedef double (*p_func_t)(double);          /* define type p_func_t */

p_func_t p_function;                          /* define pointer p_function */
```

this defines p_func_t which is type 'pointer to a function with one double parameter and which returns a double function result'. It is then be used to define a pointer p_function.

29.3 Passing pointers to functions as function parameters

A pointer to a function may be passed as a function parameter just like any other pointer. Program 29.2 (next page) contains a general purpose function newton which uses the Newton-Raphson method of successive approximation to determine the root of a function $f(x) = 0$ (Chapter 16.4 described the technique in outline). Pointers to $f(x)$ and $f'(x)$ are passed to newton which can then call them as required. The function main calls newton twice to find the roots of $f(x) = \cosh(x) + \cos(x) - 3 = 0$ and $f(x) = x^2 - 25 = 0$:

9	prototype of function func_1 which evaluates $f(x) = \cosh(x) + \cos(x) - 3$
10	prototype of function fdiv_1 which evaluates the first derivative of func_1
11	prototype of function func_2 which evaluates $f(x) = x^2 - 25$
12	prototype of function fdiv_2 which evaluates the first derivative of func_2
14-15	prototype of function newton (further discussion below)
20	initial 'guess' of root of $f(x) = \cosh(x) + \cos(x) - 3 = 0$
21	call newton to find root of $f(x) = \cosh(x) + \cos(x) - 3$
22-23	print root found or error message
26	initial 'guess' of root of $f(x) = x^2 - 25 = 0$
27	call newton to find root of $f(x) = x^2 - 25$
28-29	print root found or error message

The sequence of statements in function newton, lines 61 to 76, is:

61-62
```
int newton(double *p_x, double (*p_f)(double), double (*p_fdiv)(double),
                int max_loop, const double accuracy, const int print)
```
a function header specifying the following parameters:

double *p_x	on entry *p_x contains 'guess' and on exit returns root found
(*p_f)(double)	pointer to the function $f(x)$
(*p_fdiv)(double)	pointer to the function $f'(x)$
int max_loop	specifies the maximum number of iterations
const double accuracy	specifies the required accuracy
const int print	if *true* information is printed during the iterations

The function returns a *true* if the root is found within max_loop iterations

66-73 a do evaluating successive approximations of the root x_n

69 evaluate $f(x_n) / f'(x_n)$ and assign the result to variable term

70 evaluate next approximation of x_n

73 terminate do when $|\text{term} / x_n|$ <= accuracy or --max_loop becomes 0

75 return max_loop: if > 0 root has been found thus returning *true*

```
 1 /* Program 29.2 - Passing pointers to functions as function parameters      *
 2  *  Function newton uses the Newton-Raphson method of finding roots          *
 3  *   parameters passed includes the functions f(x) and f'(x)                 */
 4 #include <stdio.h>
 5 #include <math.h>
 6
 7 int main()
 8 {
 9     double func_1(double);                    /* f(x) = cosh(x) + cos(x) - 3 = 0 */
10     double fdiv_1(double);                    /* f'(x) = sinh(x) - sin(x)        */
11     double func_2(double);                         /* f(x) = x*x -25 = 0 */
12     double fdiv_2(double);                         /* f'(x) = 2x         */
13     /* prototype for the function newton */
14     int newton
15        (double *, double (*)(double), double (*)(double), int, double, int);
16
17     double x;                                 /* holds value of root of f(x) */
18
19     printf("\nFind root of f(x) = cosh(x) + cos(x) - 3 = 0");
20     x = 1.0;                                  /* initial 'guess' at root */
21     if (newton( &x, func_1, fdiv_1, 100, 1.0e-8, 0))
22          printf("\n    root x = %g, test of f(x) = %g ", x, func_1(x));
23     else  printf("\n   failed to find root ");
24
25     printf("\n\nFind root of f(x) = x * x - 25 = 0");
26     x = 1.0;                                  /* initial 'guess' at root */
27     if ( newton( &x, func_2, fdiv_2, 100, 1.0e-8, 1))
28          printf("\n    root x = %g, test of f(x) = %g ", x, func_2(x));
29     else  printf("\n   failed to find root ");
30     return 0;
31 }
32
33 /*----------------------------------------------------------------------------*/
34 /* function f(x) = cosh(x) + cos(x) - 3 = 0     */
35 double func_1(double x)
36 {    return (cosh(x) + cos(x) - 3.0); }
37
38 /* first derivative f'(x) = sinh(x) - sin(x) */
39 double fdiv_1(double x)
40 {    return (sinh(x) - sin(x));  }
41
42 /*----------------------------------------------------------------------------*/
43 /* function f(x) = x*x -25 = 0 */
44 double func_2(double x)
45 {    return (x*x - 25.0);  }
46
47 /* f'(x) = 2x */
48 double fdiv_2(double x)
49 {    return (2.0 * x);  }
50
```

Program 29.2 Passing pointers to functions as function parameters

```
51 /*------------------------------------------------------------------*
52  * Using Newton-Raphson method find a root of the equation f(x)      *
53  * Parameters in:  *p_x           pointer to first approximation of root  *
54  *                 (*p_f)(x)      pointer to function f(x)           *
55  *                 (*p_fdiv)(x)   pointer to function f'(x)          *
56  *                 max_loop       maximum number of iterations       *
57  *                 accuracy       required accuracy                  *
58  *                 print          if TRUE print information to screen *
59  *            out: *p_x           return root found                  *
60  * function result: >0 (true) if root found, 0 (false) if max_loop exceeded */
61 int newton(double *p_x, double (*p_f)(double), double (*p_fdiv)(double),
62                  int max_loop, const double accuracy, const int print)
63 {
64      double term;
65
66      do
67          {
68          /* calculate next term f(x) / f'(x) then subtract from current root   */
69          term = (*p_f)(*p_x) / (*p_fdiv)(*p_x);
70          *p_x = *p_x - term;                              /* new root */
71          if (print) printf("\n    x = %20g term = %20g", *p_x , term);
72          }
73      while ((fabs(term / *p_x) > accuracy) && (--max_loop));
74      if (print) printf("\n root = %g, f(x) = %g ", *p_x , (*p_f)(*p_x));
75      return max_loop;
76 }
```

Program 29.2 Passing pointers to functions as function parameters

Consider the prototype of function newton in lines 15 and 16 of Program 29.2:

```
int newton(double *, double (*)(double), double (*)(double), int, double, int);
```

The second and third parameters, double (*)(double), are declared to be 'pointers to a function with a double parameter and which returns a double'. The parentheses around (*) are required to force the proper association, i.e. unary * has a lower precedence than ().

The function newton would be used as a general purpose function to test if the Newton-Raphson method was suitable for finding the root of a particular function. Specifying max_loops prevents the technique looping forever (and returns *false* if it fails) and using the print facility would show how well the technique converged. A run was:

```
Find root of f(x) = cosh(x) + cos(x) - 3 = 0
    root x = 1.85792, test of f(x) = 7.64363e-16
Find root of f(x) = x * x - 25 = 0
    x =                   13 term =                  -12
    x =              7.46154 term =              5.53846
    x =              5.40603 term =              2.05551
    x =              5.01525 term =             0.390779
    x =              5.00002 term =            0.0152244
    x =                    5 term =          2.31782e-05
    x =                    5 term =          5.37232e-11
 root = 5, f(x) = 0
    root x = 5, test of f(x) = 0
```

29.4 Returning pointers to functions as a function result

Consider the following (rather complicated) function prototype:

```
double (*get_func(int i))(double);              /* complicated function prototype */
```

This prototype declares a function get_func which has a single int parameter and returns, as a function result, a pointer to a function which has a single double parameter and returns a double function result. The use of typedef can simplify the declaration:

```
typedef double (*p_function)(double);       /* define a 'pointer to a function' */
p_function get_func(int i);              /* function prototype returning above type */
```

A common programming requirement is the selection, by the user, of a command from a menu of commands followed by the execution of associated statements or functions. For example, in Program 15.1, a character entered from the keyboard was used, via a switch statement, to select statements to execute. Program 29.3 (next page) is more sophisticated in that a menu array is used to hold commands to be displayed on the screen with associated functions. The function get_command displays the menu on the screen and prompts the user for a keyboard hit. A menu command is selected on the first character of the command string (toupper makes the character read upper case). The function returns either a pointer to the function associated with the command or NULL if a control character was entered:

8   define p_func_t 'pointer to a function with no parameters and no function result'

11-14   define menu_t a structure to hold the commands and associated function pointers

          command a 20 character string which indicates the command to be executed

          p_command a pointer to a function to be executed when the command is selected

16   define external data, holds the value to be processed by the functions selected

20   prototype for function get_command

21-23   prototypes to the functions to be executed via a command from the menu

26-29   define array menu with commands and pointers to functions

          each element of menu is a 20 character command string and an associated pointer

30   define p_function a pointer to a function

34-37   a do statement calling get_function to obtain a 'pointer to a function'

          if the pointer returned is NULL the do terminates otherwise the function is called

44-62   definitions of functions to read, print and square the value of the variable data

69   header for get_command; returns a 'pointer to a function' (line 70 is an alternative)

76-77   increment index from 0 until a NULL pointer is found (menu terminator)

       77   print menu command string on the screen

80-82   print "Enter command character:" followed by the first character of each command

86-93   a 'forever' loop reading characters until a command character is entered

       88   read character ch and if it is a control character return NULL

       89-91   search menu for a command beginning with character ch

            91   found command, return associated pointer to function

       92   character not in commands, ring bell

The Turbo C function getch (line 88) reads a character directly from the keyboard. Thus commands are entered character by character rather than on a line terminated by *newline*.

Note that some compilers generate errors when attempting to initialise menu (lines 26 to 29) with the addresses of functions. Making menu external by moving lines 21 to 29 before main (line 18) will generally overcome the problem.

```
 1 /* Program 29.3 - menu selection returning a pointer to a function */
 2
 3 #include <stdio.h>                                    /* standard headers */
 4 #include <ctype.h>
 5 #include <conio.h>                         /* Turbo C console I/O header */
 6
 7 /* define: a pointer to a function with no parameters and no function result */
 8 typedef void (*p_func_t)(void);
 9
10 /* define structure which holds command string and pointer to a function */
11 typedef struct {
12                 char command[20];               /* menu command to print */
13                 p_func_t p_command;      /* pointer to corresponding function */
14                 } menu_t;
15
16 float data;                          /* used to hold data value read and printed */
17
18 int main(void)
19 {
20     p_func_t get_command(menu_t menu[]);            /* function prototypes */
21     void read_data(void);
22     void print_data(void);
23     void square_data(void);
24
25     /* define menu: initialise with command strings and function pointers */
26     menu_t menu[4] = {{"Read value" , read_data} ,          /* menu data */
27                       {"Print value", print_data},
28                       {"Square value", square_data},
29                       {"", NULL}                  };       /* terminator */
30     p_func_t p_function;
31
32     clrscr();
33     /* loop reading and executing a command until a control character is read */
34     do
35         if ((p_function = get_command(menu)) != NULL)
36             p_function();                              /* call function */
37     while (p_function != NULL);
38     return 0;
39 }
40
41 /*-------------------------------------------------------------------*
42  * functions to perform the commands entered                        */
43
44 void read_data(void)                                /* read value */
45 {
46     clrscr();
47     printf("\n\nPlease enter data value (float) ? ");
48     scanf("%f", &data);
49 }
50
```

Program 29.3 Menu selection returning a pointer to a function (using Turbo C)

```
51 void print_data(void)                                           /* print value */
52 {
53     clrscr();
54     printf("\n\nValue of data = %f ", data);
55 }
56
57 void square_data(void)                                          /* square value */
58 {
59     clrscr();
60     data = data * data;
61     printf("\n\nData value squared ");
62 }
63
64 /*-----------------------------------------------------------------------*
65  * Function which displays a menu and returns a command selected        *
66  * The array menu contains command strings and function pointers        *
67  * Selection is on first character of command string                    *
68  * return a pointer to appropriate function else NULL (control character) */
69 p_func_t get_command(menu_t menu[])
70 /*void (*get_command(menu_t menu[]))(void)*/                    /* alternative header */
71 {
72     int ch, index;
73
74     /* print menu command strings on the screen */
75     printf("\n\nCommand menu is:");
76     for (index = 0 ; menu[index].p_command != NULL ; index++)
77         printf("\n     %s", menu[index].command);
78
79     /* print user prompt and first characters of command strings */
80     printf("\nPlease enter command character: ");
81     for (index = 0 ; menu[index].p_command != NULL ; index++)
82         printf("%c ", menu[index].command[0]);
83     putchar('?');
84
85     /* read characters until a command or a control character is entered */
86     for (;;)
87     {
88         if (iscntrl(ch = toupper(getch()))) return NULL;
89         for (index = 0 ; menu[index].p_command != NULL ; index++)
90             if (ch == menu[index].command[0])
91                 return menu[index].p_command;              /* return command */
92         putchar('\a');                                      /* illegal character ! */
93     }
94 }
```

Program 29.3 Menu selection returning a pointer to a function (using Turbo C)

It is very important that a function which returns a pointer to a function should return something indicating failure if a selection fails. Either returning NULL (which can be checked by the calling program) or a pointer to a error function which will print an error message and take appropriate action. If a valid pointer is not returned the program will crash when the pointer is used for a function call (this includes NULL).

29.5 Functions with a variable number of parameters

Although the vast majority of functions implemented will have a fixed number of parameters it is sometimes necessary to write a function which will be passed a different number of parameters on different calls.   Consider, for example, the library function printf:

```
printf("%d %f %c ", int_value, float_value, char_value);
```

The function printf can be called with a varying number of parameters and uses the conversion specifications in the control string to determine the number of parameters following the control string. The function header of printf is:

```
int printf(const char *format, ...);
```

where format is a pointer to the control string and ... indicates a variable number of parameters.

When implementing a function with a variable number of parameters there must be at least one named parameter in the function header (which is used as a starting point to access the unnamed parameters specified by ...).   For example, consider the following function header:

```
void my_func(int v, ...);
```

The standard header <stdarg.h> contains a set of macro definitions (see Chapter 27.1) which specifies how a program can access a sequence of parameters in a variable length parameter list. The implementation of the header is system dependent but typically looks something like:

```
typedef void *va_list;
#define va_start(ap, v)    ((void) (ap = (va_list) &v + sizeof(v)))
#define va_arg(ap, type)   (*((type *) (ap++)))
#define va_end(ap)         ((void) (ap = NULL))
```

Where v is the name of the parameter to the left of the variable parameter list , ...) and:

va_list	is a type which is used to define a pointer ap; the pointer will be used to access each parameter in turn
va_start	initialises pointer ap to point to the parameter following v
va_arg	returns a pointer to the next parameter and increments ap
	type specifies the type of parameter expected, va_arg uses this to:
	(a) return the correct type of pointer (note the (cast) in va_arg)
	and (b) to be able to increment ap to point to the next parameter
va_end	terminates the process and performs any cleanup operations necessary

In addition to being used by the above macros the parameter v would provide the called function with the number (and possibly type) of the variable number of unnamed parameters, i.e. in a similar way to printf using the number of conversion specifications in the control string.

Program 29.4 (at the end of the chapter) contains a function str_concat which will concatenate a variable number of strings. The function header in line 26 is:

```
char *str_concat(int number, ...)
```

The parameter number specifies the number of strings to be concatenated. The parameter number would be followed by number strings which are to be appended (concatenated) onto the end of the first string (which must not be a constant). On termination str_concat returns a pointer to the first string. For example, str_concat is called twice in main in lines 13 and 16, i.e.:

```
str_concat(6, string_1, " add 1 ", "add_2 ", "add 3 ", "add 4 ", "add 5");
p_str = str_concat(5, string_2, "alan ", "simon ", "george ", "henry ");
```

The sequence of statements in function str_concat is:

26	char *str_concat(int number, ...) the function header
28	va_list ap; define the pointer ap which will point to the unnamed parameters
29-30	define two pointers to char
32	va_start(ap, number); initialise ap to point to the parameter following number
33	p_str = va_arg(ap, char *); point p_str to the next parameter (the first string) char * specifies the type of parameter expected, i.e. 'pointer to char'
34	print the first string
37-42	a while statement concatenating number - 1 string onto the first
	39 p_str2 = va_arg(ap, char *); point p_str2 to start of next string (the type parameter is char * - 'pointer to char')
	40 print the string
	41 concatenate the string onto the end of the existing string (pointed to by p_str)
43	va_end(ap); perform any cleanup operations necessary
44	terminate the function and return pointer to the start of the first string

The named actual parameters (preceding the ...) are checked and converted to the type expected by the corresponding formal parameters (see Chapter 16.4). The unnamed parameters, however, specified by ... cannot be checked (the compiler has no idea what the function is expecting). The unnamed parameters are therefore treated as if a function prototype is not available, i.e. integral parameters undergo integral promotion and float parameters are converted to double. Clearly great care is required in accessing the parameters, i.e. an incorrect type specified in va_arg would not only return rubbish but could corrupt the stack and crash the system.

A run of the program was:

```
Parameters are "string_1" " add 1 " "add_2 " "add 3 " "add 4 " "add 5"
Result is: "string_1 add 1 add_2 add 3 add 4 add 5"
Parameters are "" "alan " "simon " "george " "henry "
Names are :"alan simon george henry "
```

Once tested and operational the printf statements in lines 34 and 40 would be removed.

Problem for Chapter 29

Implement a simple equivalent of function printf, e.g.:

```
int simple_printf(const char *format, ...);
```

Use conversion specifications in format to determinate the number and type of parameters (like printf). Implement the function to print integer decimal (%d), integer hexadecimal (%x), float (%f), character (%c) and strings (%s).

```
 1 /* Program 29.4  Function with a variable number of parameters */
 2
 3 #include <stdio.h>
 4 #include <stdarg.h>
 5 #include <string.h>
 6
 7 int main(void)
 8 {
 9     char *str_concat(int number, ...);                    /* function prototype */
10
11     char *p_str, string_1[100] = "string_1", string_2[100] = "";
12
13     str_concat(6, string_1, " add 1 ", "add_2 ", "add 3 ", "add 4 ", "add 5");
14     printf("\nResult is: \"%s\" ", string_1);
15
16     p_str = str_concat(5, string_2, "alan ", "simon ", "george ", "henry ");
17     printf("\nNames are :\"%s\"", p_str);
18     return 0;
19 }
20
21 /*-------------------------------------------------------------------*
22  * Function to concatenate a variable number of strings              *
23  *  on entry number (first parameter) specifies number of strings    *
24  *  followed by number strings                                       *
25  * Return pointer to first string                                    */
26 char *str_concat(int number, ...)
27 {
28     va_list ap;                                  /* pointer to the parameters */
29     char *p_str,                                 /* will point to first string */
30         *p_str2;                              /* will point to following strings */
31
32     va_start(ap, number);                        /* point ap to first string */
33     p_str = va_arg(ap, char *);                  /* get pointer to first string */
34     printf("\n\nParameters are \"%s\"", p_str);           /* and print it */
35
36     /* concatenate number -1 strings on the end of *p_str */
37     while( --number)
38         {
39         p_str2 = va_arg(ap, char *);             /* get pointer to next string */
40         printf(" \"%s\"", p_str2);                        /* and print it */
41         strcat(p_str, p_str2);                            /* concatenate */
42         }
43     va_end(ap);                                           /* cleanup */
44     return p_str;                                /* return pointer to first string */
45 }
```

Program 29.4 Function with a variable number of parameters

30

Accessing operating system facilities

The C standard library contains an extensive set of functions which provide a general programming environment to aid program portability. There are occasions when operations specific to a target operating system or hardware need to be performed:

1 To provide faster and more efficient access to system and I/O facilities than is possible via standard library functions, i.e. by making calls directly to the operating system or even driving the hardware directly (see Chapters 32 and 33 for further discussion).
2 To access facilities which are specific to a particular system, e.g. graphics facilities such as those used in Chapter 13.6 to draw a sine wave on the display screen.

Many compilers provide extra libraries to support different operating systems or target computers, e.g. the Turbo C graphics library <graphics.h> to drive IBM PC compatible graphics cards. In particular, the UNIX programming environment comes with extensive support libraries which provide user programs with access to system facilities. In addition, assuming the correct calling conventions are used, C programs may call modules written in other languages, e.g. the version of PHIGS (Programmer's Hierarchical Interactive Graphics System) ISO graphics standard for the HP 700 workstation (HP 1991) is implemented in Fortran but may be called from other languages including C and Pascal. If a library function is not available the host operating system must be called directly.

30.1 Hardware and software interrupts

An interrupt stops the execution of the current program and transfers control to an operating system function (usually called an interrupt service routine) which processes the interrupt and then returns control to the interrupted program.

Hardware interrupts are generated by a hardware device (memory management unit, timer, I/O device, etc.) to request service, e.g. a fault has occurred or an I/O operation is complete.

Software interrupts are generated by programs (user or system) to request a service provided by the operating system kernel (the base level functions of the system).

30.1.1 Interrupt instructions

In a sophisticated multiprogramming environment a user program is only allowed to access memory allocated to its own instructions and data and any access outside this generates a memory segmentation fault. Interrupt instructions provide a mechanism by which a program can stop execution, transfer control to the operating system to carry out some function, and then resume. For example, the Intel 8086 family has the INT instruction:

```
INT      operand
```

and the Motorola MC68000 family has the TRAP instruction:

```
TRAP     operand
```

In both cases the value of operand specifies the interrupt number and the particular operating system function to be invoked. Additional information is passed to the operating system via processor registers (which may contain pointers to further data areas in the user program). When the operating system has completed the required operation it places information in the CPU registers and resumes the user program by executing a *return from interrupt* instruction, e.g. IRET on the Intel 8086 and RTE on the Motorola MC68000.

30.2 Accessing MS-DOS operating system facilities

The MS-DOS operating system, used on IBM PC compatible microcomputers, is accessed via the INT instruction. It is possible to write an assembly language function which loads relevant values into the processor registers, executes INT and then returns register values to the calling function. The majority of C compilers which run under MS-DOS provide such a function, e.g. both Turbo C and Microsoft C have the function int86. When int86 is called information is passed to MS-DOS via the 16-bit processor registers, ax, bx, cx, dx, si and di or their byte equivalents (the 16-bit register ax can be addressed as two 8-bit registers ah (the high byte) and al (the low byte)). In Turbo C and Microsoft C the function prototype of int86 is declared in header file <dos.h> thus:

```
int int86(int int_number, union REGS *in_registers, union REGS *out_registers);
```

where:

int_number	is the interrupt number to invoke the required MS-DOS function
in_registers	is the value of the processor registers to be passed to MS-DOS
out_registers	is the value of the processor registers as returned by MS-DOS

The declaration of union REGS is of the form:

```
/* Intel 8086 family word registers (16-bit), cflag is the carry flag */
struct WORD_REGS { unsigned int ax, bx, cx, dx, si, di, cflag; };

/* Intel 8086 family byte registers (8-bit) */
struct BYTE_REGS { unsigned char al, ah, bl, bh, cl, ch, dl, dh; };

/* Intel 8086 general purpose registers: union overlays word and byte registers */
union REGS {
          struct WORD_REGS x;                    /* word registers
          struct BYTE_REGS h;                    /* byte registers */
        };
```

This declares the types struct WORD_REGS (a structure of seven unsigned int 16-bit members) and struct BYTE REGS (a structure of eight unsigned char 8-bit members). The union REGS overlays struct WORD_REGS and struct BYTE REGS. Using a variable of type union REGS a CPU register may be accessed as a 16-bit value or a pair of 8-bit values, e.g.:

```
union REGS cpu_registers;                 /* define variable to hold cpu registers */

cpu_registers.x.ax = 2;                        /* set cpu register ax to 2 */
cpu_registers.h.al = 1;                        /* set low byte al to 1 */
cpu_registers.h.ah = 0;                        /* set high byte ah to 0 */
printf("bx = %d ", cpu_registers.x.bx);            /* print value of bx */
```

Program 30.1 (next page but one) contains two screen control functions, scroll_text which scrolls a section of the text screen and cursor_text_to which positions the screen cursor.

The standard IBM PC compatible display default text mode is 80 characters per line and 25 lines high with sixteen colours (video mode 3, for full details consult a specialist text on IBM PC compatibles and MS-DOS). Various screen control functions are available (invoked via interrupt 10 hexadecimal) including:

Scrolling a window on the display screen. The following are specified and int86 called:

ah   equals 6 for scroll up and 7 for scroll down

al   equals the number of lines to scroll (0 means the window is cleared)

bh   attribute byte to put into the blanked characters, i.e. sets the screen colours:

      bits 0 to 3 specify the blue, green and red values of the foreground text colour

      bit 4 specifies the foreground intensity (0 normal, 1 intense)

      bits 5 to 7 specify the blue, green and red values of the background colour

      bit 7 specifies blink off (0) or on (1)

ch and cl   row and column position of top left hand corner of text window

dh and dl   row and column position of lower right hand corner of text window

Setting the cursor position. The following are specified and int86 called:

ah   equals 2 for set cursor position

bh   equals the page number (several text pages are supported, 0 is default page)

dh   equals the row or line on the page (the top line is row 0)

dl   equals the column or character position (the first character is column 0)

The sequence of statements in Program 30.1 is:

3   include <dos.h> which contains the prototype of int86 and the declaration of union REGS

8-9 function prototypes for scroll_text and cursor_text_to

11   call scroll_text to clear the whole screen to green background and black foreground
       text will now be displayed in black on a green background

12   call scroll_text to clear a window in the centre of the screen to blue background

13   call cursor_text_to to position the cursor at the centre of the text screen

14   print character 'x' in the middle of the screen

Function scroll_text, lines 24 to 37, scrolls a section of the screen as specified by:

up_down is 0 for scroll up and 1 for scroll down (line 29 adds 6 to this value to set up ah)

x_left and y_top specifies the top left hand column and row of the area to scroll

x_right and y_bottom specifies the lower left hand column and row of the area to scroll

attribute specifies the attribute byte to be loaded into the scrolled characters

Function cursor_text_to, lines 41 to 50, positions the cursor at screen coordinate x_column, y_row. The program comments together with the above explanations of the MS-DOS calls, should be sufficient to understand how the functions work. See Chapter 31.1.1 for an assembly language version of this function and Chapter 32.3 for a similar function which accesses the video RAM memory directly using pointers.

    The functions use the standard coordinates of the screen (top left hand corner is (0, 0) and bottom right hand corner is (79, 24)). MS-DOS screen handling functions supplied with compilers may use a different coordinate system, e.g. the Turbo C cursor position function gotoxy (in <conio.h>) assumes that the top left hand corner is coordinate (1, 1).

    The register values returned by the third parameter of int86 (lines 36 and 49) are not used in this program. Other MS-DOS functions use them to return status information and data (see section 30.3.4 which describes the use of PC serial ports under MS-DOS).

```
 1 /* Program 30.1 MS-DOS functions to scroll the screen and position the cursor */
 2
 3 #include <dos.h>                               /* MS-DOS specific header file */
 4 #include <stdio.h>                             /* standard I/O header file */
 5
 6 int main(void)
 7 {
 8     void scroll_text(int, int, int, int, int, int, int);        /* prototypes */
 9     void cursor_text_to(const int x_column, const int y_row);
10
11     scroll_text(1, 0, 0,  79, 25, 0, 0x20);           /* clear screen to green */
12     scroll_text(1, 20, 5, 59, 18, 0, 0x10);           /* scroll block to blue */
13     cursor_text_to(39 , 12);                   /* cursor to middle of screen */
14     putchar('x');                               /* print a character */
15     return 0;
16 }
17
18 /*------------------------------------------------------------------------*
19  * scroll text screen up or down setting attribute byte as specified      *
20  * on entry:  up_down   0 is scroll up, 1 is scroll down                   *
21  *            x_left, y_top & x_right & y_bottom specify window coordinates *
22  *            lines     number of lines to scroll                          *
23  *            attribute set IBM PC compatible attribute byte              */
24 void scroll_text(int up_down, int x_left, int y_top,
25                  int x_right, int y_bottom, int lines, int attribute)
26 {
27     union REGS registers;                      /* variable to hold 8086 registers */
28
29     registers.h.ah = (unsigned char) ( 6 + up_down);   /* scroll up 6, down 7 */
30     registers.h.al = (unsigned char) lines;            /* scroll whole window */
31     registers.h.bh = (unsigned char) attribute;        /* attribute byte */
32     registers.h.cl = (unsigned char) x_left;   /* start column, x position */
33     registers.h.ch = (unsigned char) y_top;      /* start row, y position */
34     registers.h.dl = (unsigned char) x_right;    /* end column, x position */
35     registers.h.dh = (unsigned char) y_bottom;     /* end row, y position */
36     int86(0x10, &registers, &registers);       /* interrupt 10 hexadecimal */
37 }
38
39 /*------------------------------------------------------------------------*
40  * position text cursor, note that top left hand corner is column 0 row 0  */
41 void cursor_text_to(const int x_column, const int y_row)
42 {
43     union REGS registers;                      /* variable to hold 8086 registers */
44
45     registers.h.ah = 2;                        /* command, set text cursor position */
46     registers.h.bh = 0;                                /* set page 0 */
47     registers.h.dl = (unsigned char) x_column;     /* column, x position */
48     registers.h.dh = (unsigned char) y_row;          /* row, y position */
49     int86(0x10, &registers, &registers);       /* interrupt 10 hexadecimal */
50 }
```

Program 30.1 MS-DOS functions to scroll the screen and position the cursor

30.3 Using the RS232 serial port via MS-DOS

30.3.1 Asynchronous serial communications

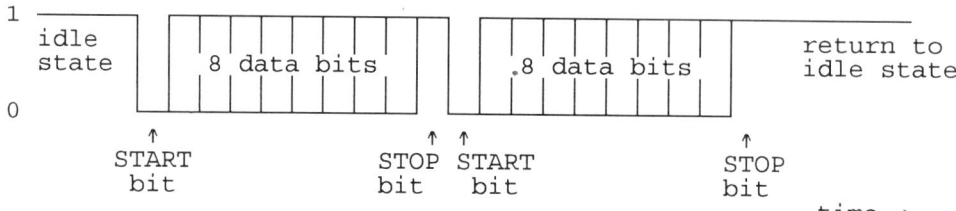

Fig. 30.1 Format of data on an asynchronous serial line

In a serial communications system a byte of data is transferred between the transmitter and receiver bit by bit over a single communications line. Bit 0 is transmitted, then bit 1, etc., through to bit 7. When the first byte is finished, the next byte, if any, can be sent. The data is transferred at an agreed rate of a number of bits per second, which is called the baud rate. To separate the data bytes a **START bit** is transmitted before the first data bit and one or two **STOP bits** are transmitted after the last data bit.

Fig. 30.1 shows the format of the data on a serial line when two 8-bit (byte) characters are transmitted (plus one START bit and one STOP bit in each case). When no data is being transmitted the line is in the idle state at logical 1, which corresponds to a nominal voltage level of -6 volt. When the serial interface is ready to transmit a data byte, it first transmits a START bit of logical 0 (nominal level +6 volt). The START bit serves to separate the idle state from the first data bit which could be a 0 or a 1. The data bits are then transmitted, bit 0 first, one after the other. After the data bits, one or two STOP bits, at logical 1, are transmitted. If, after the STOP bit(s), more data is available, the next START bit is transmitted, otherwise the line returns to the idle state. Thus if another data byte is to be immediately transmitted (as in Fig. 30.1), the STOP bit(s) serve to separate the last data bit of a data byte, from the START bit of the next data byte.

To check for errors when transmitting characters over a noisy communications channel, a parity check bit can be generated which can replace bit 7 of the character or be appended on the end of it to form a 9-bit code. Thus for each data byte transmitted, 10, 11 or 12 bits are actually transmitted (START + data bits + parity bit + STOP bit(s)). Typical baud rates are from 50 to 38.4K baud (bits/second). If, for example, the baud rate is 1200, each bit takes 0.8333 milliseconds to transmit with 120 bytes per second transferred if one STOP bit is used.

30.3.2 The EIA RS232C standard

The EIA RS232C standard was originally developed to foster data communications via public telephone networks. It defines the interface between a DTE (Data Terminal Equipment, i.e. a user terminal), and a DCE (Data Communications Equipment, i.e. a modem), using serial binary data interchange. The nominal signal levels are -6 volt for logical 1 (sometimes called MARK), but any level between -3 and -12 volt is accepted, and +6 volt for logical 0 (sometimes called SPACE), but any level between +3 and +12 volt is accepted. Signal levels between -3 and +3 volt are not valid and data would probably be corrupt.

The facilities of particular serial I/O ports vary with the computer concerned and the following refers to IBM PC and compatible microcomputers (using the standard RS232 25 way D type connector):

TXD (pin 2) and RXD (pin 3) are the serial transmit and receive data lines.

$\overline{\text{RTS}}$ **(Request To Send - output on pin 4)** is typically used as the **receive handshaking output** which the PC asserts to indicate that it can accept data.

$\overline{\text{CTS}}$ **(Clear To Send - input on pin 5)** is typically the hardware handshaking input to the PC. The external device asserts $\overline{\text{CTS}}$ to indicate that it is ready to accept data.

$\overline{\text{DSR}}$ **(Data Set Ready - input on pin 6)** indicates that the remote device (e.g. printer) is switched on and ready.

Signal ground (pin 7) is the common signal level reference (often ground).

$\overline{\text{DCD}}$ **(Data Carrier Detect - input on pin 8).** Can be used when the external device is able to send characters (e.g. a modem would negate $\overline{\text{DCD}}$ if the data carrier was lost due to a telephone line fault).

$\overline{\text{DTR}}$ **(Data Terminal Ready - output on pin 20)** indicates that the PC is switched on.

The $\overline{\text{RTS}}$, $\overline{\text{CTS}}$, $\overline{\text{DSR}}$, $\overline{\text{DCD}}$ and $\overline{\text{DTR}}$ are all **active low.** In such a case, if the signal is negated the line is at logical 1 (a -6 volt level), and if it is asserted or active the value is logical 0 (a +6 volt level). For example, if a printer attached to the PC is not ready to accept data the $\overline{\text{CTS}}$ line will be logical 1, otherwise, if it is ready $\overline{\text{CTS}}$ will be at logical 0.

An additional problem occurs with IBM PC compatibles in that the connectors used are often 9 way D type connectors instead of the standard RS232 25 way D type. For example, Fig. 30.2 shows how to connect two IBM PC compatible microcomputer 'back to back' using a *null* modem with either 9 way or 25 way D type connectors (the signals emulate the handshaking of a modem). Programs used to transfer files between PCs typically use the connections shown in Fig 30.2.

RS232C Signal name	25 pin	9 pin	cable connections	9 pin	25 pin	RS232C Signal name
data common	7	5		5	7	data common
RxD data	3	2		2	3	RxD data
TxD data	2	3		3	2	TxD data
$\overline{\text{RTS}}$ output	4	7		7	4	$\overline{\text{RTS}}$ output
$\overline{\text{CTS}}$ input	5	8		8	5	$\overline{\text{CTS}}$ input
$\overline{\text{DSR}}$ input	6	6		6	6	$\overline{\text{DSR}}$ input
$\overline{\text{DCD}}$ input	8	1		1	8	$\overline{\text{DCD}}$ input
$\overline{\text{DTR}}$ output	20	4		4	20	$\overline{\text{DTR}}$ output

Fig. 30.2 Serial port connection of two IBM PC compatible computers via a *null* modem

30.3.3 Handshaking with serial communications systems

When data is being transferred via a communications system it is possible for the transmitter to send information faster than the receiver can process it with the result that data can become lost. To prevent this a *handshaking protocol* is used in which the receiver signals the transmitter that it is *ready for data*.

Hardware handshaking makes use of the $\overline{\text{RTS}}$, $\overline{\text{CTS}}$, $\overline{\text{DCD}}$ and/or $\overline{\text{DTR}}$ lines of the serial interface. A common technique is to connect the $\overline{\text{RTS}}$ output of one computer to the $\overline{\text{CTS}}$ input of another (as in Fig. 30.2). When the receiver is ready for data it asserts $\overline{\text{RTS}}$ and the transmitter checks $\overline{\text{CTS}}$ before attempting to transmit.

Software handshaking is usually the XON/XOFF protocol in which the receiver transmits the XOFF character (transmit off, ASCII DC3 or CTRL/S) to stop the transmitter and the XON (transmit on, ASCII character DC1 or CTRL/Q) to restart transmission.

30.3.4 Accessing the serial ports via MS-DOS

The BIOS provides four functions via interrupt 14 hexadecimal for controlling the serial ports (MS-DOS devices COM1: to COM4:). In all cases ah contains the function number (0 to 4) and dx the serial port (note that COM1: is port 0, COM2: port 1, etc.). A brief description of each function is presented below (consult an MS-DOS text for full details).

Initialise serial port (function 0). The data word format is specified in al:

bits 1, 0	data word length: 10 is 7 bits and 11 is 8 bits
bit 2	number of stop bits: 0 is one stop bit, 1 is two stop bits
bits 4, 3	parity: 00 none, 01 odd, 10 none, 11 even
bits 7,6,5	baud rate: from 000 for 110 baud to 111 for 9600 baud

Transmit character (function 1). Character to transmit is in al. On return, bit 7 of ah will be set if an error occurred and the remainder of ah contains the status (see function 3).

Receive a character (function 2). When called this function waits for a character to be received. The character is returned in al and bit 7 of ah indicates if an error occurred (bits 1, 2, 3 and 4 indicate the status, see function 3).

Read serial port status (function 3). Returns the values of the line status register and modem status register of the serial port in al and ah:

ah bit	line status register
7	time out
6	TSRE transmitter shift register empty (all data transmitted)
5	THRE transmitter holding register empty (ready for next data to transmit)
4	BI break detected (a break signal received, line held at logical 0)
3	FE framing error (character not properly framed by start and stop bits)
2	PE parity error (parity bit of character received was not as expected)
1	OE overrun error (another character received before last character read)
0	DR received data ready (character received and may be read)

al bit	modem status register
7	DCD Data Carried Detect
6	RI ring indicator
5	DSR Data Set Ready (current level)
4	CTS Clear To Send (current level)
3	DDCD delta DCD (DCD changed since last checked)
2	TERI trailing edge ring indicator
1	DDSR delta DSR (DSR changed since last checked)
0	DCTS delta CTS (CTS changed since last checked)

Table 30.1 PC serial port line status and modem status registers

```
 1 /* Program 30.2  A terminal emulator using MS-DOS functions  */
 2 #include <stdio.h>                              /* standard I/O header */
 3 #include <conio.h>                   /* MS-DOS direct console I/O header */
 4 #include "rs_lib.h"              /* RS232 serial line functions header */
 5
 6 int main(void)
 7 {
 8     int io_port = 0, kb_char = 0, rs_char;       /* define various variables */
 9
10     printf("Simple terminal emulator, hit <ESC> to terminate \n\n");
11     rs_initialise(io_port);                      /* initialise io_port */
12     rs_putstring(io_port, "testing line \x0d\x0a");      /* send characters */
13
14     /* loop: transmit keyboard characters and display received characters */
15     while (kb_char != 27)                 /* terminate when <ESC> entered */
16        {
17        if (kbhit())     /* if keyboard hit transmit character to serial port */
18           {
19           kb_char = getch();                     /* read keyboard character */
20           if (kb_char == 0x0d)                   /* if <CR> send <CR> <LF> */
21               rs_putstring(io_port, "\x0d\x0a");
22           if (kb_char >= ' ')                     /* if printable ASCII */
23               rs_putch(io_port, kb_char);          /* transmit it */
24           }
25
26        /* if character received from serial port display it */
27        if (rs_received(io_port))                 /* if character received */
28           {
29           rs_char = rs_getch(io_port);             /* read it */
30           if (rs_char == 0x0d)                   /* if carriage return */
31               {putch(10); putch(13);}              /* do newline */
32           else
33               if (rs_char >= ' ') putch(rs_char);   /* printable ASCII */
34           }
35        }
36     rs_terminate(io_port);                       /* close io_port */
37     return 0;
38 }
```

Program 30.2 A serial line terminal emulator using MS-DOS functions

```
/* Header file rs_lib.h - prototypes for PC RS232 serial line functions */

void rs_initialise(const int io_port);                    /* initialise */
void rs_terminate(const int io_port);                      /* terminate */
void rs_putch(const int port, const int character);         /* put char */
void rs_putstring(const int io_port, const char *string);  /* put string */
int rs_received(int io_port);                              /* check char */
char rs_getch(const int io_port);                            /* get char */
int rs_status(const int io_port);                           /* get status */
```

Header file rs_lib.h Header file containing the PC RS232 serial line function prototypes

Program 30.2 is a serial line terminal emulator which calls functions in the library rs_lib1.c (prototypes in header file rs_lib.h, and the functions in library rs_lib1.c use the MS-DOS serial line functions described above). For example, if two IBM PC compatible microcomputers running the program are connected 'back to back' (as in Fig. 30.2) characters typed on the keyboard of one machine should appear on the screen of the other (and vice versa).

2-4   include header files including "rs_lib.h"

11   call rs_initialise to initialise io_port (the value of io_port is initialised to 0 in line 8 but could be read from the command line, see Program 25.2)

12   transmit a string to serial line io_port

15-35   a while loop which exits when <ESC> is hit on the keyboard

       17-24   if the keyboard has been hit

              19   read the character from the keyboard

              20   if the character is <CR> (carriage return)

                  21   transmit <cr> <lf> (carriage return, line feed)

              22   if the character code >= ' ' (printable ASCII)

                  23 transmit the character down the serial line

       27-34   if a character has been received from the serial line

              29   read the character into rs_char

              30   if the character is <CR> (carriage return)

                  31   call putch to print a newline (CR, LF)

              else

                  33   if the character code >= ' ' print the character

36   call rs_terminate to close the serial line

In Library rs_lib1.c (next page) the serial line functions specify the serial port as parameter io_port (port 0 is com1:, etc). Thus a program can drive a number of serial ports simultaneously (the library will work with both Turbo C and Microsoft C).

Function rs_initialise, lines 8 to 17, initialises the serial port to 9600 baud, 8 data bits, no parity and one stop bit. Function rs_status, lines 22 to 30, returns the line status and modem status register values (modem status in bits 0 to 7 and line status in bits 8 to 15). Function rs_putch, lines 34 to 46, transmits a character then checks for any error (if the character should be echoed to the screen remove the comments in line 38). Function rs_putstring, lines 50 to 54, calls rs_putch to transmit a string of characters. Function rs_received, lines 58 to 67, checks to see if a character has been received from the serial line (line 63 checks for a receive error and line 66 checks the DR bit in the line status register returning non zero (*true*) if a character has been received. Function rs_getch, lines 71 to 81, reads a character from a serial line; lines 75 and 76 wait for a character to be received and lines 77 to 80 read and return the character. Function rs_terminate, lines 85 to 88, does nothing but is added for completeness (required for libraries rs_lib2.c and rs_lib3.c which directly control the serial port).

In practice, depending upon the particular BIOS being used, there may be problems with hardware handshaking. Initialisation, function 0, normally asserts the output handshaking lines $\overline{RTS}$ and $\overline{DTR}$. Transmit character, function 1, normally checks the input handshaking line $\overline{CTS}$ (which is connected to the $\overline{RTS}$ line of the other machine). Check the documentation on the BIOS for details. An alternative technique is to address the hardware serial ports and control the handshaking lines directly (see Chapter 33.3).

```
 1 /* Library rs_lib1.c -  PC serial line functions calling MS-DOS functions */
 2
 3 #include <dos.h>                            /* MS-DOS specific header file */
 4 #include <stdio.h>                          /* standard I/O header file */
 5
 6 /*-------------------------------------------------------------------------*
 7  * Serial port: initialise io_port                                        */
 8 void rs_initialise(const int io_port)
 9 {
10     union REGS registers;               /* variable to hold 8086 registers */
11
12     registers.h.ah = 0;                           /* command, initialise */
13     /* set baud rate to 9600, 8 data bits, no parity and 1 stop bit */
14     registers.h.al = 0xe3;                       /* baud rate to 9600  */
15     registers.x.dx = io_port;                           /* for port */
16     int86(0x14, &registers, &registers);      /* interrupt 14 hexadecimal */
17 }
18
19 /*-------------------------------------------------------------------------*
20  * Serial port: return status of io_port                                  *
21  *    line status in top byte (ah), modem status in lower byte (al)       */
22 int rs_status(const int io_port)
23 {
24     union REGS registers;               /* variable to hold 8086 registers */
25
26     registers.h.ah = 3;                          /* command, read status */
27     registers.x.dx = io_port;                           /* from port */
28     int86(0x14, &registers, &registers);      /* interrupt 14 hexadecimal */
29     return registers.x.ax;                            /* return status */
30 }
31
32 /*-------------------------------------------------------------------------*
33  * Serial port: transmit character to io_port                             */
34 void rs_putch(const int io_port, const int character)
35 {
36     union REGS registers;               /* variable to hold 8086 registers */
37
38     /*putch(character);*/                    /* echo character if required */
39     registers.h.ah = 1;                       /* command, send character */
40     registers.h.al = (unsigned char) character;            /* character */
41     registers.x.dx = io_port;                              /* to port */
42     int86(0x14, &registers, &registers);      /* interrupt 14 hexadecimal */
43     if (registers.h.ah & 0x80)
44         printf("\nTransmit error on serial port %d, status %#x ",
45                     io_port, registers.h.ah);
46 }
47
```

Library rs_lib1.c   PC serial line functions calling MS-DOS functions

```
48 /*----------------------------------------------------------------*
49  * Serial port: transmit a string of characters to io_port        */
50 void rs_putstring(const int io_port, const char *string)
51 {
52     while (*string != '\0')
53         rs_putch(io_port, *string++);
54 }
55
56 /*----------------------------------------------------------------*
57  * Serial port: return TRUE if character available from serial line */
58 int rs_received(int io_port)
59 {
60     int status;
61
62     status = rs_status(io_port);                    /* get status */
63     if (status & 0xe00)                         /* receive error ?? */
64         printf("\n\aRead error on serial line %d, status = %#x\n",
65                         io_port, status & 0xe00);
66     return (status & 0x100);        /* test DR bit in line status register */
67 }
68
69 /*----------------------------------------------------------------*
70  * Serial port: read character from io_port                        */
71 char rs_getch(const int io_port)
72 {
73     union REGS registers;          /* variable to hold 8086 registers */
74
75     while (! rs_received(io_port))
76         /* wait for character received */ ;
77     registers.h.ah = 2;                    /* command, read character */
78     registers.x.dx = io_port;                       /* from port */
79     int86(0x14, &registers, &registers);    /* interrupt 14 hexadecimal */
80     return registers.h.al;                      /* return character */
81 }
82
83 /*----------------------------------------------------------------*
84  * Serial port: terminate io_port executing any close down operations */
85 void rs_terminate(const int io_port)
86 {
87     /* no code in this case */
88 }
```

Library rs_lib1.c PC serial line functions calling MS-DOS functions

30.4 Using a Microsoft compatible mouse under MS-DOS

The majority of IBM PC compatible microcomputers come equipped with a Microsoft compatible mouse which can be used to point to objects on the display screen. A program can read the position of the mouse and determine which, if any, of its buttons are pressed.

Before the mouse can be used a *device driver* must be installed. The driver interfaces with the mouse hardware and provides facilities, via interrupt 33 hexadecimal, to enable programs to control the mouse and read its position. The driver may be loaded from within the MS-DOS system configuration file CONFIG.SYS:

```
device = mouse.sys
```

When the mouse is being used a cursor, which tracks mouse movement, may be displayed on the screen (this is in addition to the text cursor which indicates where the next character will be displayed). The mouse software uses a coordinate system which is related to the display coordinates of the screen. For example, when the display is in the default text mode the mouse uses a coordinate system of 640 points horizontal by 200 points vertical (refer to a mouse manual for full details). Dividing the mouse coordinates by eight maps to the default text coordinates of 80 characters across the screen by 25 lines high.

The mouse driver provides a number of functions for controlling the mouse and reading its status. A function is selected by setting ax to the function number and executing an int86 with 33 hexadecimal specified as the interrupt number. The functions include:

Reset mouse and determine status (function 0). Setting ax to 0 and calling int86 will reset the mouse software (if installed) and position the mouse cursor in the centre of the display screen. On return ax will be 0 if the mouse is not available otherwise it will be -1 and bx will contain the number of mouse buttons.

Display mouse cursor (function 1). By default the mouse cursor is not displayed. Setting ax to 1 and calling int86 will display the mouse cursor on the screen at its current position (in a text mode two cursors are displayed; the 'normal' text cursor and the mouse cursor which will move when the mouse is moved).

Remove mouse cursor (function 2). Setting ax to 2 and calling int86 will remove the mouse cursor from the screen. Note that the mouse cursor should be removed before attempting to draw to the screen. If this is not done and the cursor is physically displayed on the screen part of the displayed image will disappear the next time the cursor is blinked off.

Read mouse cursor position and button status (function 3). Setting ax to 3 and calling int86 will return the mouse cursor position in cx (horizontal) and dx (vertical) and the button values in bx (the left hand button is bit 0 and the right hand button is bit 1; a bit being set indicates that the corresponding button is pressed).

Set cursor position (function 4). Setting ax to 3, cx to the horizontal coordinate, dx to the vertical coordinate and calling int86 will set the mouse cursor position (the coordinates must be valid values).

Determine mouse motion (function 11). Setting ax to 3 and calling int86 will return an indication of mouse movement since the last call (to this function). A horizontal count (positive is move right and negative is move left) is returned in cx and a vertical count (positive is move down and negative is move up) in dx. A 0 in both counts indicates the mouse has not moved.

For example, prototypes of functions to interface to the mouse could be (see the problems at the end of the chapter):

```
/* Initialise mouse, if OK return number of mouse buttons else 0 for failure */
int msm_init_mouse(void);
/* switch mouse cursor off (on_off = 0) or on (on_off = 1)  */
void msm_onoff_cursor(const int on_off);
/* Read mouse cursor position into x_pos & y_pos and button values */
void msm_read_cursor(int *x_pos, int *y_pos, int *lh_button, int *rh_button);
```

30.5 Invoking processes

A common requirement in advanced programs is to be able to execute one program (the child) from within another (the parent). The facilities available vary with the operating system and compiler. This section will present a **brief** review of common facilities (see Kernighan and Pike 1984 for more discussion of UNIX facilities).

The function system (available under UNIX and many other systems) has a single parameter, a command line exactly as typed at the keyboard (without the newline), e.g. using Turbo C or Microsoft C under MS-DOS (include the header file <process.h>):

```
system("print test.c");                    /* print a file under MS-DOS */
```

The parent process is suspended and the command line print test.c is passed to the MS-DOS command interpreter which, assuming all is well, executes the print facility to print the file test.c. When the command interpreter terminates, the parent process is resumed with system returning the return code from the command processor.

The function system only returns the return code from the command interpreter and gives no idea if the command invoked by the command interpreter worked or not.

The function execlp (and variations, see compiler manuals) overlays the current process with the named program, e.g. to invoke the Microsoft C compiler under MS-DOS:

```
/* execute Microsoft C compiler (and terminate program) */
if(execlp("cl", "cl", "test.c", NULL))
    printf("\nexeclp 'cl test.c' failed");
```

The first parameter is the filename of the command (i.e. CL.EXE in the above example) and the second and subsequent parameters are the command and command line parameters to be passed to the child process (as in the array argv, see Chapter 25.2). If successful the parent process is terminated and the child process loaded and executed otherwise execlp returns to the parent process, e..g. if the file does not exist. Under UNIX the command to invoke the C compiler would be:

```
/* execute UNIX C compiler (and terminate program) */
if(execlp("cc", "cc", "test.c", NULL))
    printf("\nexeclp 'cc test.c' failed");
```

execlp (and similar) is used when the parent process is to be terminated. There are many occasions when the parent process either wishes to resume execution when the child terminates or to run concurrently with the child (assuming a multiprocessing environment such as UNIX). MS-DOS C compilers usually have a function spawnlp (plus variations, see compiler manuals), e.g. to use the MS-DOS command xdel to delete files:

```
/* spawn a process to delete files */
error = spawnlp(P_WAIT, "xdel", "xdel", "*.old", "/N", NULL);
if (error == 0) printf("spawnlp 'xdel *.old/N' successful");
else            perror("spawnlp 'xdel *.old/N' failed ");
```

The first parameter is mode, which indicates the state the parent process should take when the child is invoked and the remainder are as for execpl. In the above example the mode is P_WAIT which suspends the parent process until the child terminates (the modes available depend upon the compiler and operating system, see compiler manuals). When the child terminates the parent process resumes and spawnlp returns, as a function result, the exit status of the child process (in this case indicating if xdel was successful).

Under UNIX the function fork makes a copy of the process and executes it concurrently with the parent. The only difference between the two processes is that fork returns the child process ID to the parent and zero to the child (if fork fails -1 is returned and errno set). The child can then call execlp to carry out the required task. For example,

```
if ((pid = fork()) == 0)                              /* fork process */
    {
    if(execlp("rm", "rm", "test1.c", NULL))     /* child process: delete files */
        printf("\nexeclp 'rm test1.c' failed");
    exit(1);                                       /* set exit status to fail */
    }
else
    if (pid == -1) printf("fork() failed ");          /* fork failed */
```

This calls fork to create a child process. The child process (a 0 function result from fork) then calls execlp to invoke the UNIX command rm to delete the file test1.c.

After a fork the parent continues to run concurrently with the child. Inter process communication can be achieved using the function pipe to create an inter process input/output mechanism and then the low-level I/O functions read and write to pass information (see UNIX systems manuals for details). If required the parent can wait for a child to terminate:

```
wait(&status);
```

Wait returns the process ID of the terminating child process (this can be checked against the value returned by fork) and status is assigned the low-order eight bits of the child exit status (from return or a call to exit, 0 for normal termination and non-zero for some error condition).

Problem for Chapter 30

Problem 30.1 Connect two IBM PC compatible computers 'back to back' (as in Fig. 30.2). Using the functions from Program 30.2 implement a file transfer program, e.g.:
(a) read characters from the serial port saving them to a named file on disk (on the other machine use a command such as copy file com1: to transmit a file).
(b) Extend the program so that one machine acts as a host and the other a slave (under the command of the host). The user should be able to enter commands on the host to read and write file from/to corresponding files on the slave. The same program should be able to act as either host or slave.
(c) extend the program to check for errors on the serial line. Parity can be used to check characters and a checksum or CRC check performed on block transfers.

Problem 30.2 Implement and test functions to interface to a Microsoft compatible mouse (see Section 30.4). Test using the default text screen mode reading the cursor position and printing a character at that position when the left hand button is pressed. Terminate the program when the right hand button is pressed.

Problem 30.3 Using the mouse functions and a suitable graphics library implement a painting system. A section of the screen should be reserved as a command area with facilities to select a drawing colour, different brushes, lines, etc.

31

Using assembly language from C

On occasion there may be a requirement to use assembly language from a C program:

1   to speed up time critical functions (however, it is often cheaper to buy a faster computer than rewriting the code in assembly language);
2   to access machine specific hardware facilities for which library functions do not already exist.

In practice 99% of a program will be implemented in C with assembly language limited to critical areas (Bramer 1988, Hintz 1992). Assembly language code may be implemented:

1   As independent assembly language source code files which have to be assembled and then linked to the calling program by the linker.
2   As in-line code, where assembly language statements are included within the C program (the C compiler calls a suitable assembler when it comes across such statements). Not all C compilers support this facility.

This chapter introduces the techniques used to interface assembly language functions to C; it assumes a knowledge of the target assembly language and an understanding of parameter passing on the system stack.

31.1 Separate assembly language functions

When implementing a function in assembly language it is important to obey the rules imposed by the C compiler which will be used to compile the calling functions:

1   Memory allocation: where code and data is placed.
2   Parameter passing: the order in which parameters are passed and their size in bytes.
3   Register usage: which processor registers must **not** be changed, which may be used but must be restored to their original values and which may be freely used.

Refer to the appropriate compiler manuals for full details.

31.1.1 Microsoft C compiler under the MS-DOS operating system

The rules for interfacing assembly language functions when using the Microsoft C compiler version 6.00 (Microsoft 1990b) under MS-DOS include the following:

1   Program code is placed in the segment _TEXT and variables in the segment _DATA.
2   Actual parameters are passed on the stack from right to left, i.e. the last parameter is pushed first (the _fastcall calling convention should not be used, Microsoft 1990b).
3   The AX, BX, CX, DX, ES and flags registers can be freely used (all others should be saved and restored).
4   A 16-bit function result (char, int or near pointer) is returned in AX.
    A 32-bit function result is returned in DX (high-order) and AX (low-order).
    If the return value is longer than 32-bits store it in memory and return a pointer to it.

```
 1  ; position text cursor, note that top left hand corner is column 0 row 0
 2  ; The C prototype should be:
 3  ;    void _cdecl _far cursor_text_to(const int x_column, const int y_row);
 4  ; i.e.: _cdecl to use the C calling convention and _far to use a 32-bit CALL
 5  ;
 6          PUBLIC  _cursor_text_to         ;declare symbol to use in other modules
 7  _TEXT   SEGMENT WORD PUBLIC 'CODE'      ;place code in _TEXT segment
 8          ASSUME  CS: _TEXT               ;use CS to access the following code
 9  ;
10  _cursor_text_to PROC FAR
11          push    bp                      ;save bp
12          mov     bp,sp                   ;move sp into bp
13          mov     ah,2                    ;command, set text cursor position
14          mov     bh,0                    ;set page 0
15          mov     dl, [bp + 6]            ;column, x position
16          mov     dh, [bp + 8]            ;row, y position
17          int     10h                     ;interrupt 10 hexadecimal
18          pop     bp                      ;restore bp
19          ret                             ;return to calling function
20  _cursor_text_to ENDP                    ;end of _cursor_text_to
21  _TEXT   ENDS
22          END
```

Fig. 31.1 Microsoft Macro Assembler 5.1 version of function _cursor_text_to

Fig. 31.1 shows an assembly language version (Microsoft Macro Assembler 5.1) of the function cursor_text_to described in Program 30.2. The sequence of statements is:

6   the name _cursor_text_to is declared to be PUBLIC so that it can be accessed from other modules (note that C compilers place a _ before function names)
7   the following code is within the segment _TEXT
8   the segment register CS will be used to access the code
10 start of the function _cursor_text_to (PROC defines the start of a procedure/function) PROC FAR indicates that the function will be called with a 32-bit CALL instruction
11 save register BP (it must be preserved)
12 copy the stack pointer SP into BP
13 set up AH for function 2 (see Chapter 30.2)
14 set up BH to page 0
15 load the parameter x_column into DL
16 load the parameter y_row into DH
17 call MS-DOS via interrupt number 10 hexadecimal (see Chapter 30.2)
18 restore BP
19 return to calling function (the type of return corresponds to PROC FAR in line 10)
20 end of function

The function may be assembled using the majority of PC assemblers including the Microsoft Macro Assembler MASM or the Turbo Assembler TSAM, e.g. assuming the text of Fig 31.1 is in the file text_to.asm:

```
MASM /MX text_to.asm text_to.obj     using the Microsoft assembler
TASM /mx text_to.asm                 using the Turbo assembler
```

The /MX and /mx options specify that symbols are case sensitive (otherwise the assembler converts symbols such as _cursor_text_to to upper case). The resultant object file text_to.obj must be linked to the object files of the calling C program.

When using Microsoft C the function prototype of the code in Fig. 31.1 should be specified as follows:

```
void _cdecl _far cursor_text_to(const int x_column, const int y_row);
```

The Microsoft C keywords _cdecl and _far instruct the compiler:

_cdecl: to use the C calling convention (in case _fastcall, _pascal, etc. is the default).
_far: to use a CALL instruction with a 32-bit address (to match the PROC FAR). Hence whatever memory model is the default, the function will be called correctly.

Fig. 31.1 will also work with Turbo C where the function prototype should be:

```
void far cursor_text_to(const int x_column, const int y_row);
```

31.1.2 Whitesmiths C cross compiler for a MC68000 target microcomputer

The rules defining the Whitesmiths C interface to 68000 assembly language are complex (Whitesmiths 1986, Bramer & Bramer 1991) and include (only integral data is considered):

1 Executable code is generated into the **.text** segment.
2 Literal and global data is generated into the **.data** segment.
3 Short integers are 16-bit words, integers and long integers are 32-bit long words.
4 Function calls are performed thus:
   (a) in a function call parameters are moved onto the stack **right to left**, i.e. the last argument is moved onto the stack first;
   (b) when used as function arguments character and short data is sign extended to a long word (integer and long integer data is already long word);
   (c) the function is called via jsr _func (_ prefixes the function name);
   (d) the function may use registers D0, D1, D2, D6, D7, A0, A1 and A2 without problems, if any others are used they must be **preserved** (by using MOVEM);
   (e) the function result (if any) is returned in D7.

Fig. 31.2 (next page) contains two functions which enable a C program to access the Motorola MC68000 MOVEP (Move Peripheral Data) instruction which transfers two or four bytes of data between a specified processor **data register** and **alternate byte locations in memory** (see Chapter 33 for further discussion). In a C program the function movep_l_to_memory would be declared using the prototype (see Program 33.1):

```
int movep_l_to_memory(int value, iobyte *address);
```

This function moves value (a 32-bit int) to alternate locations starting at the specified address. The type iobyte is used to access byte sized memory mapped I/O registers:

```
typedef volatile unsigned char iobyte;    /* I/O device register is a volatile byte */
```

The function movep_l_to_memory could be called as follows:

```
movep_l_to_memory(250000, (iobyte *) 0x680025);
```

The value 250000 is loaded into alternate bytes starting at address 0x680025. Note the cast (iobyte *) which converts the integer to a 'pointer to iobyte', this is highly machine dependent (see Chapter 32.1).   Before movep_l_to_memory is called the value 0x680025 is pushed onto the stack followed by the value 250000.   When movep_l_to_memory is called the 32-bit return address is pushed onto the stack and the first instruction of movep_l_to_memory executed.   The sequence of statements is (referring to line numbers alongside Fig. 31.2):

9   move the address value 0x680025 off the stack into register A0
10   move the value 250000 off the stack into D0
11   move the 32-bit value in D0 to alternate memory locations starting at address 0x680025
12   copy the value in D0 to D7 (the function result is returned in D7)
13   execute RTS (return from subroutine) to return to calling function

The calling function would then remove the parameters from the stack.

```
 1 * MOVEP.S  Assembly language functions to support Whitesmiths C cross compiler
 2 *    Using Whitesmiths AS68K cross assembler to MC68000 target computer
 3            .text                    * start code section
 4            .even                    * align to even address
 5 *
 6 * Function to perform a long word sized MOVEP to memory, C prototype is:
 7 *     int movep_l_to_memory(int value, iobyte *address);
 8 _movep_l_to_memory:
 9            movea.l   8(a7),a0        * get address into A0
10            move.l    4(a7),d0        * get value into D0
11            movep.l   d0,0(a0)        * move value from D0 to address (A0)
12            move.l    d0,d7           * return value written
13            rts                       * return with function result in D7
14 *
15 * Function to perform a long word sized MOVEP from memory, C prototype is:
16 *     int movep_l_from_memory(iobyte *address);
17 _movep_l_from_memory:
18            movea.l   4(a7),a0        * get address into A0
19            movep.l   0(a0),d7        * move value from (A0) into D7
20            rts                       * return with function result in D7
21 *
22 * declare global identifiers (external identifiers for C programs)
23            .globl    _movep_l_to_memory
24            .globl    _movep_l_from_memory
```

Fig. 31.2 Assembly language functions to support Whitesmiths C cross compiler

31.2 In-line assembly language statements

Some compilers allow assembly language statements to be placed in-line with C statements. For example, Microsoft C uses the _asm keyword which invokes an in-line assembler.   An _asm statement may appear wherever a C statement may be used, e.g.:

```
_asm    mov    ah,2                    /* command, set text cursor position */
_asm    mov    bh,0                    /* set page 0 */
```

Alternatively an _asm block may be enclosed in braces {}.   An _asm statement can freely use the AX, BX, CX and DX registers (save and restore any others) and can refer to any C symbols which are in scope (C symbols are variable and function names and labels; not symbolic constants).   Thus it is possible to write a function letting C handle the parameter passing (which is quite complex) and then drop into assembly language.

Fig. 31.3 shows the function _cursor_text_to with the parameter passing handled by C and the internals of the function in assembly language (as in Fig. 31.1). In lines 8 and 9 the C formal parameters x_column and y_row are accessed by name (BYTE PTR lets the assembler know that values are byte sized; otherwise warnings are generated).

```
 1 /* position text cursor, note that top left hand corner is column 0 row 0      */
 2 void cursor_text_to(const int x_column, const int y_row)
 3 {
 4     _asm {
 5             mov     ah,2                          /* command, set text cursor position */
 6             mov     bh,0                                         /* set page 0 */
 7             mov     dl, BYTE PTR x_column                /* column, x position */
 8             mov     dh, BYTE PTR y_row                     /* row, y position */
 9             int     0x10                          /* interrupt 10 hexadecimal */
10         }
11 }
```

Fig. 31.3 C function _cursor_text_to using in-line assembly language (Microsoft C)

Turbo C allows in-line code by use of the asm directive, see Fig. 31.4. The Turbo assembler TASM.EXE must be on the current path or another assembler specified:

tcc -Emasm.exe filename.c   invoke Turbo C compiler specifying assembler masm.exe

```
 1 /* position text cursor, note that top left hand corner is column 0 row 0      */
 2 void cursor_text_to(const int x_column, const int y_row)
 3 {
 4     asm { mov     ah,2                          /* command, set text cursor position */
 5           mov     bh,0                                         /* set page 0 */
 6           mov     dl, BYTE PTR x_column                /* column, x position */
 7           mov     dh, BYTE PTR y_row                     /* row, y position */
 8           int     0x10                          /* interrupt 10 hexadecimal */
 9         }
10 }
```

Fig. 31.4 C function _cursor_text_to using in-line assembly language (Turbo C)

31.3 Interfacing other high-level languages with C

The interfacing of other high-level languages to C is dependent upon the operating system, compiler and linker being used. Of particular importance is:

1   How memory is allocated to store to code and data, and the types and sizes of the data objects, e.g. a language may have data types which do not exist in other languages.

2   How function parameters are passed and the function result returned. C pushes parameters on to the stack from right to left (so that a variable number of parameters can be accessed). Fortran and Pascal generally push the parameters from left to right.

For example, a Microsoft C function can be called from Microsoft Pascal and Fortran (and vice versa). The use of the keywords _Cdecl, _pascal and _fortran indicates which calling convention is to be used (see compiler manuals for full details).

32

Accessing physical memory

It is sometimes necessary to access specified locations in the physical memory map of a computer system directly, e.g.:

1   to perform RAM memory tests, e.g. at power up (see section 32.2);
2   to directly manipulate the video memory of a graphics display (see section 32.3);
3   to access memory mapped I/O registers (see Chapter 33 for more details);

Accessing physical memory is dependent upon:

The computer architecture: e.g. using linear addressing (as in the Motorola MC68000 family) or using segment addressing (as on the Intel 8086 family).

The operating system:
    (a) A simple operating system, such as MS-DOS, allows any program unlimited access to physical memory. A more sophisticated multi-tasking operating system, such as UNIX or OS/2, restricts the program to its own address space.
    (b) In a multi-tasking environment the memory addresses used by the program are logical addresses within the program memory map, not actual physical addresses.

The compiler: which provides library facilities to suit the host operating system.

32.1 Setting up pointers to 'point to' locations in physical memory
Consider:

```
int *mem_pointer;                          /* define a 'pointer to int' */

mem_pointer = 0x1000;                       /* assign an integer to the pointer */
```

A 'pointer to an int' is defined and then assigned the integer value 0x1000. This is a highly machine dependent assignment and a modern compiler will issue a warning, e.g. using Turbo C on an IBM PC compatible:

```
mem_pointer = 0x1000;                       /* assign an integer to the pointer */
Warning x.c 5: Nonportable pointer conversion in function main
```

To assure the compiler that you know what you are doing the integer should be cast to the correct pointer type and the warning will disappear, e.g.:

```
mem_pointer = (int *) 0x1000;               /* assign an integer to the pointer */
```

The compiler converts the integer value 0x1000 into the equivalent value for a 'pointer to int'.

When using pointers to physical memory locations it is very important to have an understanding of the architecture of the machine concerned, the internal format of the pointers (the addressing mode used for the pointer) and a knowledge of exactly what one is trying to achieve. Compilers often have library functions to manipulate addresses to suit the host operating system and machine architecture.

32.2 Memory test for a Motorola MC68000 based system

```
1  /* Program 32.1 -  MC68000 single board microcomputer memory test program */
2
3  #include <stdio.h>                            /* include standard I/O header */
4
5  typedef unsigned char byte;    /* define an MC68000 memory location as a byte */
6
7  int main()
8  {
9      byte test_data = 0xff,                           /* test data value */
10         *mem_address,                        /* pointer to byte being tested */
11         *start_address = (byte *) 0x10000,     /* address to start test */
12         *end_address   = (byte *) 0x11000,     /* address + 1 to end test */
13         *fault_address = (byte *) 0x10010;     /* address to generate fault */
14
15     /* write test pattern into memory area */
16     printf("\nfilling memory from %p to %p with test pattern %x",
17             start_address, end_address, test_data);
18     for (mem_address = start_address; mem_address < end_address; mem_address++)
19         if (mem_address == fault_address)              /* if at fault address */
20             *mem_address = 0xaf;                       /* write rubbish */
21         else                                           /* else */
22             *mem_address = test_data;                  /* write test data */
23
24     /* read memory area and check value written */
25     printf("\n\ntesting memory from %p to %p against test pattern %x",
26             start_address, end_address, test_data);
27     for (mem_address = start_address; mem_address < end_address; mem_address++)
28         if (*mem_address != test_data)
29             printf("\n error at address %p, value read %x, value expected %x",
30                     mem_address, *mem_address, test_data);
31 }
```

Program 32.1   MC68000 single board microcomputer memory test program

When implementing an embedded control system using a single board microcomputer one of the initial tasks to be carried out on power-up or when the system is boot strapped is a RAM memory integrity check. This involves writing test values into the RAM memory of the machine and reading them back.

Program 32.1 shows a simple memory test which was implemented on a Bytronic MC68000 single board microcomputer (see Chapter 33.4 for further details) using Whitesmiths C (Whitesmiths 1987a, 1987b). The physical memory of the Bytronic board is mapped from address 0 up to some maximum determined by the amount of RAM fitted. Addresses below 0x1000 are used for the exception vector table (see Bramer and Bramer 1991 for full details), the operating system data area and the stack. The user program code starts at address 0x1000 followed by data areas as specified by the user. Program 32.1 writes the test value 0xff into memory locations 0x10000 to 0x10fff and then reads them back. To ensure that the code works a deliberate error is introduced at address 0x10010. The sequence of statements is:

5   define the type byte which is used to access a byte sized memory location
9   define test_data and initialise it to the value 0xff
10   define mem_address which will point to the location being tested
11   define start_address, the address to start the RAM test
12   define end_address, the address plus 1 to terminate the RAM test
13   define fault_address, the address to generate a memory 'fault'
18-22   a loop writing data into memory from start_address to end_address - 1
            19 if mem_address is the fault_address
                20 write a faulty value into the location (to generate an error when tested)
            else
                22 write the test_data into the location
27-30   a loop comparing the value in memory with test_data
            28 if the value in the location is not test_data
                29 print the address of the location, the value read and the value expected

The Motorola MC68000 uses a linear memory map so the integer values map directly into addresses and the physical memory locations 0x10000 to 0x10fff are tested. A run of the program was:

```
filling memory from 10000 to 11000 with test pattern ff
testing memory from 10000 to 11000 against test pattern ff
  error at address 10010, value read af, value expected ff
```

The memory test works correctly detecting the 'fault' a location 0x10010. When the program was fully tested the deliberate fault would be removed.

In practice such a power up test would more complex (see the problem at the end of the chapter) and be implemented as an assembly language function (which could be called from a C program) to achieve the best possible execution speed.

32.3 Directly accessing video RAM of an IBM PC compatible computer

Chapter 30.2 introduced functions to manipulate information on the screen of an IBM PC compatible microcomputer by means of ROM BIOS functions accessed via MS-DOS calls. A faster, but more difficult and potentially dangerous, method of manipulating such information is to directly access the RAM memory which holds the video information. An IBM PC compatible computer with an EGA or VGA video card generally operates in a default text mode of 80 characters per line and 25 lines high with sixteen colours (video mode 3, for full details consult a specialist text on IBM PC compatibles). In this case the video RAM used to store the text starts at address B800:0000 (where B800 is the segment register value and 0000 is the offset value). When using Turbo C a pointer to this address may be defined:

```
typedef unsigned char far byte;              /* define a memory location as a byte */
byte *video_start = (byte *) 0xB8000000L;         /* define start of PC video RAM */
```

This defines the type byte and the pointer video_start (a 'pointer to byte') initialised to the address of the start of the video RAM. The far indicates that a 32-bit pointer should be used (use _far with Microsoft C otherwise consult compiler manuals to see how pointers such as this are defined and initialised). Once initialised the pointer can be used to read and write the contents of the video RAM directly. It should be noted that each character position on the screen consists of two bytes in video RAM; the character to be displayed and the attribute byte which specifies the colours (see Chapter 30.2 for details). Thus to access a character at screen position x_column, y_row the address is:

```
character address = video_start + y_row * 160 + x_column * 2
```

Program 32.2 contains a number of functions which access the video RAM directly to clear the screen and write characters. The program starts by defining two pointers:

line
3   define the type byte
5   define video_start which holds the start address of the video RAM
6   define video_text which holds the address to write the next character to
         (initialised to the start of the video RAM)

The function main, lines 8 to 21, tests the screen functions:

10-13   prototypes of the screen manipulation functions
15   •   call clear_screen to clear the text screen to a green background (attribute 0x20)
16-17   set character position to 39, 12 and write an 'x' (white on blue)
18-19   set character position to 33, 14 ånd write a string (red on cyan)

Note that the character position referred to above has nothing to do with the MS-DOS screen cursor (which will not move) and is just used to position the characters to be written (for details of how to move the actual screen cursor consult a technical manual or call the MS-DOS cursor move function).

Function clear_screen, lines 25 to 35, clears the whole of the text screen to spaces setting up the attribute byte as specified by a parameter:

27   define pointer video_mem initialised to the start address of the video RAM
30-34   a while loop clearing the screen
      32   set the character to space, incrementing video_mem
      33   set up the attribute byte, incrementing video_mem

The pointer video_mem accesses RAM from address video_start (the start of the video RAM) to video_start + (160 * 25) - 1 (the address of last character on the screen); remember the screen is 80 characters wide by 25 lines high and each character position consists of two bytes.

The function write_char, lines 38 to 43, writes a character to the address specified by video_text (which is incremented to point to the next character position). Function write_string writes a string of characters. Function position_text sets up the address corresponding to the screen position x_column, y_row in pointer video_text.

Note that the above functions take no account of the end of a line on the screen (wrapping around to the start of the next line) and, more importantly, no account of the end of the screen (thus it is possible to overwrite RAM following). In practice the functions should check for valid addresses before writing data.

In practice such screen manipulation functions would probably be implemented in assembly language (to be called from C programs) to achieve the best possible execution speed (which is essential for such interactive operations).

```
 1 /* Program 32.2 - accessing IBM PC compatible video RAM directly          */
 2
 3 typedef unsigned char far byte;        /* define a memory location as a byte */
 4
 5 byte *video_start = (byte *) 0xB8000000L;      /* define start of PC video RAM */
 6 byte *video_text  = (byte *) 0xB8000000L;      /* address to display character */
 7
 8 int main()
 9 {
10     void clear_screen(int attribute);                      /* prototypes */
11     void position_text(const int x_column, const int y_row);
12     void write_char(const char ch, const int attribute);
13     void write_string(const char *string, const int attribute);
14
15     clear_screen(0x20);            /* clear the screen to green background */
16     position_text(39, 12);          /* position cursor in middle of screen */
17     write_char('x', 0x17);                    /* write x, white on blue */
18     position_text(33, 14);               /* and display a string below it */
19     write_string("hello john doe", 0x34);            /* red on cyan */
20     return 0;
21 }
22
23 /*------------------------------------------------------------------*
24  * clear the screen to spaces setting attribute bytes to specified value    */
25 void clear_screen(int attribute)
26 {
27     byte *video_mem = video_start;       /* pointer initialised to video RAM */
28
29     /* clear 25 lines of 80 characters (character plus attribute byte) */
30     while (video_mem < video_start + 160 * 25)
31         {
32         *video_mem++ = ' ';                      /* set character to space */
33         *video_mem++ = (byte) attribute;              /* set attribute */
34         }
35 }
36
37 /*------------------------------------------------------------------*
38  * write character ch with attribute at current cursor position             */
39 void write_char(const char ch, const int attribute)
40 {
41     *video_text++ = ch;                           /* write character */
42     *video_text++ = (byte) attribute;                   /* set attribute */
43 }
44
```

Program 32.2   Accessing IBM PC compatible video RAM directly

```
45 /*----------------------------------------------------------------*
46  * write string with attribute at current cursor position        */
47 void write_string(const char *string, const int attribute)
48 {
49     while (*string != '\0')
50         {
51             *video_text++ = *string++;              /* write character */
52             *video_text++ = (byte) attribute;        /* set attribute */
53         }
54 }
55
56 /*----------------------------------------------------------------*
57  * position text on screen, note that top left hand corner is column 0 row 0  */
58 void position_text(const int x_column, const int y_row)
59 {
60     /* set up address to write next character to,                  *
61      * i.e. each character is two bytes (character plus attribute)  *
62      *  and there are 80 character on at line (in y direction)     */
63     video_text = video_start + y_row * 160 + x_column * 2;
64 }
```

Program 32.2   Accessing IBM PC compatible video RAM directly

Problem for Chapter 32

The memory test described in section 32.2 only performs a single test with the pattern
0xff. Extend the program to test with the following test patterns which should show up
errors due to shorts to 0 or 1, shorts between pins, crossed pins, etc.

```
    0000        $FFFF       $5555       $AAAA
    rotating 1 pattern -
        0001 0002 0004 0008 0010 0020 to 2000 4000 8000
    marching 1's pattern -
        0001 0003 0007 000F 001F 003F 007F 00FF 01FF 03FF
            to 1FFF 3FFF 7FFF FFFF FFFE FFFC FFF8 FFF0
            to FC00 F800 F000 E000 C000 8000
```

For details of a much more exhaustive test see the Problem for Chapter 17 of Bramer and
Bramer 1991.

33

Direct control of input/output devices

33.1 Accessing input/output device registers

Each I/O device interface contains a number of registers which pass data and status/control information between a program running in the processor and the I/O device circuits. There are two techniques for accessing I/O device registers:

(a) by means of special I/O instructions;

or (b) by having the I/O registers appear as part of the primary memory map.

In both cases, before any I/O programming can be carried out, the I/O addresses and the format of the information within them must be known (from hardware manuals).

Special I/O instructions Some processors have a set of special instructions for accessing I/O device registers. Each register is assigned an I/O port number (built into the hardware of the interface) and this is used as an operand in I/O instructions. For example, the Intel 8086 family of microprocessors uses the I/O instructions IN and OUT, thus:

```
IN    AL,n        read contents of I/O port n to register AL
OUT   n,AL        output contents of register AL to port n
```

Memory mapped I/O registers appear as part of the primary memory map of the computer. In general, any instructions which are used to read and write memory can be used to access the I/O registers. Although the registers are mapped as part of the memory address space of the computer, they are **not** normal memory for program and data storage.

33.2 Polled and interrupt I/O programming

Before a program can transfer data to an I/O device it must ensure that the device is not busy (e.g. a printer may be in the process of printing a character). The simplest I/O programming technique is to use a polling loop, in which the program polls or examines the interface status register to determine if the device is ready for a data transfer. If the device is busy the program loops back to check the status register again. If the status register indicates that the device is ready for more data the next data transfer is performed.

In the case of interrupt I/O normal program execution runs in parallel with an I/O data transfer. When the I/O device interface is ready for the next data transfer it sends a signal to the processor which interrupts the program being executed, and transfers control to an **interrupt service routine** (which is similar in format to a normal C function). The interrupt service routine code performs the data transfer to the I/O device and terminates with an instruction which resumes execution of the program that had been interrupted. The drawbacks with interrupt driven I/O systems is that the interface is more complex and it is more difficult to write and test the I/O driver programs than when using polled I/O techniques. See Chapter 18 of Bramer & Bramer 1991 for a more detailed discussion.

33.3 Directly accessing the serial ports of an IBM PC compatible

The serial ports of IBM PC compatible computers are generally based on the Intel 8250 ACE (Asynchronous Communications Element) interface chip or equivalent. Up to four serial ports may be attached (ports 0 to 3 which are called COM1: to COM4: at MS-DOS command level, see Chapter 30.3) and are accessed via IN and OUT instructions. Each port consists of a number of registers which are accessed at sequential port I/O addresses from the following base address:

port number	0 (COM1:)	1 (COM2:)	2 (Com3:)	3 (COM4:)
base address	0x3F8	0x2F8	0x3E8	0x2E8

The main registers of the 8250 are (to simplify the description the divisor latch is omitted):

register name	offset from base	register function
DataReg	0 write	transmitter buffer: holds next character to transmit
	0 read	receiver buffer: holds character received
IntEna	1	Interrupt enable: bits enable various interrupts
IntIdent	2	Interrupt identification: bits identify interrupt cause
LineCtrl	3	Line control: bits set parity, word length, etc.
ModCtrl	4	Modem control: bits set RTS, DTR, etc. see below
LineStatus	5	Line status: state of DR, THRE, etc. see Table 30.1
ModStatus	6	Modem status: state of CTS, DSR, etc. see Table 30.1

Thus the line control register of serial port 1 is at I/O port address 0x2FB (0x2F8 + 3). When using Microsoft C the I/O ports can be accessed either from _asm assembly language statements (see Chapter 31.2) or via the functions (declared in header file <conio.h>):

```
int _far_ _cdecl inp(unsigned int io_port);          /* read a byte from io_port */
int _far_ _cdecl outp(unsigned int io_port, int data);   /* write a byte to io_port */
```

inp returns the byte read from the specified port and outp writes a byte to the specified port (it returns as a function result the byte written to the port), e.g. using serial port 0:

```
char ch;                                 /* define a character */
ch = inp(0x3f8);                  /* read a byte from serial port 0 receiver buffer */
outp(0x3f8, 'x');     /* write character 'x' to serial port 0 transmitter buffer */
```

Note before:

1   A byte is read from the receiver buffer the DR bit in the line status register (see Table 30.1) should be tested to ensure that a character has been received.

2   A byte is written to the transmitter buffer (called the holding register) the THRE bit in the line status register (see Table 30.1) should be tested to ensure that it is empty. In addition it is normal to check the hardware handshaking line $\overline{CTS}$ to ensure that the receiver is ready for data (see Chapter 30.3.3 on hardware handshaking).

Bits in the modem control register are used to control the status of the hardware handshaking output lines $\overline{RTS}$ and $\overline{DTR}$ (see Fig. 30.2) and the interrupt enable to the 8259 PIC:

bit	modem control register (reset all other bits to 0)
3	OUT2 interrupt enable (set to pass 8250 interrupt signals to 8259 PIC)
1	RTS Request to Send output line (set to 1 to assert the output)
0	DTR Data Terminal Ready output line (set to 1 to assert the output)

```
1  /* Library rs_lib2.c -  PC serial line functions controlling the 8250 ACE */
2
3  #include <dos.h>                          /* MS-DOS specific header file */
4  #include <conio.h>                       /* direct console I/O functions */
5  #include <stdio.h>                          /* standard I/O header file */
6
7  /* define 8250 port base addresses for RS232 ports 0 to 3 (com1: to com4:) */
8  static const short int rs_ports[] = {0x3f8, 0x2f8, 0x3e8, 0x2e8 };
9
10 /* 8250 register offsets from base address */
11 enum {DataReg, IntEna, IntIdent, LineCtrl, ModCtrl, LineStatus, ModStatus};
12
13 /* 8250 bits in line status, modem status and modem control registers */
14 enum {DR = 0x100, THRE = 0x2000, CTS = 0x10, DTR = 0x1, RTS = 0x2};
15
16 /*-------------------------------------------------------------------*
17  * Serial port: initialise io_port, sets DTR and RTS to high         */
18 void rs_initialise(const int io_port)
19 {
20     union REGS registers;                 /* variable to hold 8086 registers */
21
22     registers.h.ah = 0;                              /* command, initialise */
23     /* set baud rate to 9600, 8 data bits, no parity and 1 stop bit */
24     registers.h.al = 0xe3;                           /* baud rate to 9600  */
25     registers.x.dx = io_port;                             /* for port */
26     int86(0x14, &registers, &registers);         /* interrupt 14 hexadecimal */
27     /* set DTR and RTS in modem control reg */
28     outp(rs_ports[io_port] + ModCtrl, DTR + RTS);
29 }
30
31 /*-------------------------------------------------------------------*
32  * Serial port: terminate io_port, sets DTR and RTS to low           */
33 void rs_terminate(const int io_port)
34 {
35     /* set all bits 0 in modem control register */
36     outp(rs_ports[io_port] + ModCtrl, 0);
37 }
38
39 /*-------------------------------------------------------------------*
```

Library rs_lib2.c PC serial line functions directly controlling the 8250 ACE

```
40    * Serial port: return status of io_port                                        *
41    *   line status in top byte (ah), modem status in lower byte (al)              */
42   int rs_status(const int io_port)
43   {
44       int status = 0;
45
46       status = inp(rs_ports[io_port] + LineStatus);           /* read line status */
47       /* shift line status to top byte and then read modem status */
48       status = (status << 8) + inp(rs_ports[io_port] + ModStatus);
49       return status;                                          /* and return value */
50   }
51
52   /*------------------------------------------------------------------------*
53    * Serial port: transmit character to io_port                            */
54   void rs_putch(const int io_port, const int character)
55   {
56       while (! ((rs_status(io_port) & THRE) && (rs_status(io_port) & CTS)))
57           /* wait for transmitter holding register empty and CTS */ ;
58       /*putch(character);*/                       /* echo character if required */
59       outp(rs_ports[io_port], character);         /* transmit character */
60   }
61
62   /*------------------------------------------------------------------------*
63    * Serial port: transmit a string of characters to io_port               */
64   void rs_putstring(const int io_port, const char *string)
65   {
66       while (*string != '\0')
67           rs_putch(io_port, *string++);
68   }
69
70   /*------------------------------------------------------------------------*
71    * Serial port: return TRUE if character available from serial line      */
72   int rs_received(int io_port)
73   {
74       int status;
75
76       status = rs_status(io_port);                            /* get status */
77       if (status & 0xe00)                                     /* receive error ?? */
78           printf("\n\aRead error on serial line, status = %#x\n", status & 0xe00);
79       return (status & DR);              /* test DR bit in line status register */
80   }
81
82   /*------------------------------------------------------------------------*
83    * Serial port: read character from io_port                              */
84   char rs_getch(const int io_port)
85   {
86       while (! rs_received(io_port))
87           /* wait for character received */ ;
88       return ((char) inp(rs_ports[io_port]));     /* read character */
89   }
```

Library rs_lib2.c PC serial line functions directly controlling the 8250 ACE

The interface to Library rs_lib2.c is identical to that of rs_lib1.c in Chapter 30 (thus the header file rs_lib.h and Program 30.2 need no modification).   Whereas rs_lib1.c controlled the RS232 serial ports via MS-DOS system calls the functions in rs_lib2.c control the 8250 ACE serial chip directly. The sequence of statements is:

8   define const qualified array rs_ports which holds the serial port base addresses
11   define the offsets of the 8250 registers from the base address
14   define bits within the 8250 registers

Function rs_initialise, lines 18 to 29, calls the MS-DOS serial port function 0 to initialise the baud rate, etc. of the specified port and then asserts the hardware handshaking output lines $\overline{RTS}$ and $\overline{DTR}$ (line 28), i.e.

```
outp(rs_ports[io_port] + ModCtrl, DTR + RTS);
```

This writes a byte value DTR + RTS to port rs_ports[io_port] + ModCtrl (base address specified by io_port). Asserting $\overline{RTS}$ (probably connected to $\overline{CTS}$ of the remote device) indicates that characters can now be received.

Function rs_terminate, lines 33 to 37, terminates communication by clearing all the bits in the modem control register. In particular $\overline{RTS}$ and $\overline{DTR}$ are negated indicating to the remote device that characters can no longer be received.

Function rs_status, lines 42 to 50, returns the line status (line 46) and modem status (line 48) register values (modem status in bits 0 to 7 and line status in bits 8 to 15).

Function, rs_putch, lines 54 to 60, waits for transmitter holding register empty (THRE bit set in line status register) and $\overline{CTS}$ asserted (in the modem status register), and then transmits a character (to echo the character to the screen remove the comments in line 58). Function rs_putstring, lines 64 to 68, calls rs_putch to transmit a string of characters.

Function rs_received, lines 72 to 80, checks to see if a character has been received from the serial line (line 77 checks for a receive error and line 79 checks the DR bit in the line status register returning non zero (*true*) if a character has been received.

Function rs_getch, lines 84 to 89, reads a character from a serial line; lines 86 and 87 wait for a character to be received and line 88 reads the receiver data buffer.

33.4 Controlling a MC68230 timer from a MC68000 processor

The Motorola MC68000 family is used in a wide range of computer systems from single board systems up to professional workstations. For example, the Bytronic 68000 trainer is a typical single board microcomputer with the following facilities (Bytronic 1991):

MC68000 or MC68010 processor with 8MHz clock
256K, 512K or 1Mbyte of static RAM
256K or 512Kbyte EPROM
MC68681 DUART (dual asynchronous receiver transmitter)
MC68230 PIT (Parallel Interface/Timer) via a 40 way connector
16/64word EEROM (electrically erasable ROM)

The MC68000 does not have any special I/O instructions (like the Intel 8086 family) but uses memory mapped I/O registers in which the I/O registers appear as part of the primary memory of the computer. In general, any instructions which are used to read and write memory can be used to access the I/O registers. To simplify address decoding, I/O registers for a particular device often use alternate (even or odd) memory addresses. In such cases the MOVEP (Move Peripheral Data) instruction can be used to transfer two or four bytes of data between a specified processor **data register** and **alternate byte locations in memory** (see Chapter 31.1.2 for an example of a function which enables a C program to use the MOVEP instruction).

Program 33.1, implemented using the Whitesmiths cross compiler (Whitesmiths 1986), displays an * on the screen every second. The events are timed using the MC68230 PIT (Parallel Interface/Timer) (Motorola 1983, Bramer and Bramer 1991) which contains:

(a) three 8-bit bidirectional, parallel interface ports which can be used to control external devices such as motors, heaters, keyboards, etc. (Bytronic 1989)

and (b) a 24-bit timer which can be used for accurate timing of events.

In outline the MC68230 PIT timer is programmed as follows:

1   The Timer Control Register is loaded selecting the clock source (which can be the MC68000 clock or an external clock) , enabling interrupts (if required), etc. with the timer enable bit (bit 0) reset to 0. Thus the timer is halted.

2   The Counter Preload Register is loaded with the required 24-bit count value.

3   Timer Control Register bit 0 is set (to 1) to start the timer (bits 1-7 are not changed).

The timer is then running and on each pulse of the clock the counter is decremented. Once set up, the MC68230 is independent of the program in the processor, thus allowing real-time acquisition and processing of data (e.g. for reading data from an analogue to digital converter). This assumes that there is sufficient time between the interrupts to process the data. When the counter becomes zero the ZDS flag is set in the Timer Status Register (TSR). The program can detect when the ZDS flag is set:

(a) the ZDS flag bit in the Timer Status Register can be polled by the program;

or (b) if interrupts are enabled an interrupt request is sent to the processor and an interrupt service routine can service the event.

The sequence of events in Program 33.1 is:

6	define the type iobyte which is used to access I/O device registers
9	define the base address of the MC68230 in memory (Bytronic MC68000 trainer)
10-14	define const qualified pointers to the I/O registers of the timer; initialised with offsets from the base address (Bramer and Bramer 1991)
17-18	prototypes for functions to perform MOVEP instructions (see Chapter 31.1.2)
29	set up the Timer Control Register (see program comments for register settings)
33	load the Counter Preload Register with the count (an 8MHz clock is being used with a divide by 32 prescaler so a count of 250000 would time 1 second)
37	set bit 0 of the Timer Control Register to start the timer (other bits as in line 29)
39-45	a for statement which loops forever printing an * every second
	41-42 a while waits for the ZDS flag (bit 0) to set in the Timer Status Register
	43 clears the ZDS in the Timer Status Register (direct method of resetting)
	44 display an * on the screen

The *pointers* defined in lines 10 to 14 are const qualified to prevent the program altering them. The *bytes pointed to* are volatile qualified (they may be altered by factors external to the program and references to them must not be optimised), e.g. lines 42 and 43:

```
while ((*tsr & 1) == 0)
    /* wait for ZDS flag in status register to set */;
```

The byte pointed to by tsr (the Timer Status Register) is read and *bitwise* ANDed with 1 to obtain the value of the ZDS flag (ZDS is bit 0 and is set when the counter reaches zero).

```
1  /* Program 33.1 - MC68230 PIT timer polled I/O,  print an * every second */
2
3  #include <stdio.h>                            /* include standard I/O header */
4
5  /* define an MC68000 I/O device register as a volatile byte  */
6  typedef volatile unsigned char iobyte;
7
8  /* define MC68230 PIT timer registers for the Bytronic MC68000 board */
9  #define  PIT            0x680001               /* MC68230 PIT base address    */
10 iobyte *const tcr   = (iobyte *) PIT + 0x20;   /* timer control register      */
11 iobyte *const tivr  = (iobyte *) PIT + 0x22;   /* timer interrupt vector reg  */
12 iobyte *const tcpr  = (iobyte *) PIT + 0x24;   /* timer preload MOVEP address */
13 iobyte *const tcreg = (iobyte *) PIT + 0x2C;   /* timer count MOVEP address   */
14 iobyte *const tsr   = (iobyte *) PIT + 0x34;   /* timer status register       */
15
16 /* function prototypes for MC68000 specific functions */
17 int movep_l_to_memory(int value, iobyte *address);      /* MOVEP long word */
18 int movep_l_from_memory(iobyte *address);
19
20 int main()
21 {
22     printf("display an * every second \n");
23
24     /* set up Timer Control Register                                      *
25      * (a) TOUT/TIACK control to 000                                      *
26      * (b) counter is reloaded from preload register after zero detect    *
27      * (c) use 68000 clock (on CLK pin)                                   *
28      * (d) bit 0 is 0 to disable timer                                    */
29     *tcr = 0;                                 /* set Timer Control Register */
30
31     /* Set Counter Preload Register to time 1 second (with an 8MHz clock  *
32      *  & divide by 32 prescaler the counter decrements 250000 times/sec) */
33     printf("move to TCPR %d \n", movep_l_to_memory(250000, tcpr));
34     printf("read TCPR %d \n", movep_l_from_memory(tcpr));
35
36     /* set timer control register bit 0 to start timer (other bits unchanged) */
37     *tcr = *tcr | 1;                           /* timer enable (start counting) */
38
39     for (;;)                    /* loop forever displaying an * every second */
40         {
41         while ((*tsr & 1) == 0)
42             /* wait for ZDS flag in status register to set */;
43         *tsr = 1;                              /* clear the ZDS flag */
44         putchar('*');                          /* second elapsed, display * */
45         }
46 }
```

Program 33.1 MC68230 PIT timer polled I/O, print * every second

33.5 Interrupt control of the serial ports of an IBM PC compatible

Interrupt I/O enables normal program execution to continue in parallel with the I/O of one or more devices. When a particular I/O device interface is ready for a data transfer it sends a signal to the processor which interrupts the program being executed, and transfers control to an **interrupt service routine** (which is similar in format to a normal C function). The interrupt service routine code performs the data transfer to the I/O device and terminates with an instruction which resumes execution of the program that had been interrupted (e.g. IRET in the 8086 family and RTE in the MC68000 family).

When an interrupt occurs, some mechanism is required to transfer control to the corresponding interrupt service routine. The majority of modern processors use a vector table in primary memory which contains the addresses of the interrupt service routines. When an interrupt occurs, the corresponding entry (the routine address) is obtained from the vector table and placed in the processors Program Counter Register (PC). Program execution then continues with the first instruction of the interrupt service routine. The size of the vector table, its position in memory and precisely how it is used depends upon the processor concerned (see Bramer & Bramer 1991 for a description of the MC68000). The support provided by C compilers for interrupt I/O varies with the compiler and host operating system. For example, Turbo C under MS-DOS:

```
void setvect (int int_numb, void interrupt (far * int_function)());
```

This loads the vector table entry for interrupt number int_numb with the address of the interrupt service routine int_function. The interrupt service function would be defined:

```
void interrupt far int_function(void)
{
    /* function body to process data transfer */
}
```

The keyword interrupt tells the compiler that this is an interrupt service routine. The compiler will generate the appropriate entry and exit sequences including saving and restoring registers and terminating the function with an IRET (interrupt return) instruction (instead of RET). The keyword far indicates that it will be 'called' (when an interrupt occurs) using a full 32-bit address. Using Microsoft C under MS-DOS the function to set up the interrupt vector is:

```
void _dos_setvect(unsigned int_numb, void (_interrupt _far * int_function)());
```

The following points are important when writing interrupt service routines (refer to manuals for more details):

1   The cause of the interrupt should be cleared within the service function (or it will interrupt again immediately on exit; if the system 'locks up' this is a likely cause).
2   Interrupts are disabled when the service function is called. If the function is long the cause of the interrupt should be cleared and _enable (under Microsoft C) called to enable interrupts.
3   Take care calling functions from within service routines; in particular functions which call the operating system (MS-DOS is not reentrant). Refer to manuals.
4   External variables (in the host C program) can be accessed from within the service routine (it is wise to declare them with the Turbo C far or Microsoft C _far attribute to ensure 32-bit addressing).

In an IBM PC compatible computer there are a number of possible interrupt sources which are assigned various levels of priority (this is set within the hardware). For example, RS232 serial ports 0 and 2 (COM1: and COM3:) are at level 4 and ports 1 and 3 are at level 3. A 8259 PIC (programmable Interrupt Controller) controls which interrupt levels are enabled at any time and arbitrates between the different priorities (see a manual on the 8259 PIC for full details). In outline, the steps which must be taken to set up interrupts for the serial port receiver are:

1   The address of the existing interrupt service routine is saved (to be restored on exit).
2   The address of the new interrupt service routine is loaded into the correct vector (interrupt level 4 is vector 12 and interrupt level 3 is vector 11).
3   Receiver interrupts are enabled in the 8250 Interrupt Enable Register (setting bit 0 enables receiver interrupts).
4   The correct interrupt level must be enabled in the Operations Control Word 1 (OCW1) of the 8259 PIC (Programmable Interrupt Controller) which controls system wide interrupts for PC. For level 4 interrupts bit 4 is cleared and for level 3 bit 3 is cleared (the other bits should not be changed).
5   The OUT2 bit must be set in the 8250 Modem Control Register (this enables circuitry which passes the interrupt signal from the 8250 to the 8259 PIC).

Consult technical manuals on the PC, the 8250 ACE and the 8259 PIC for full details. When a receive interrupt occurs (a character has arrived from a remote device) the interrupt service routine is called:

1   The character is read from the 8250 Receiver Data Buffer (which clears the cause of the interrupt) and placed into a suitable data structure (e.g. a ring buffer). Functions waiting the data will be polling the data structure to see if any characters have arrived.
2   The interrupt must be acknowledged at the correct level in the Operations Control Word 2 (OCW2) of the 8259 PIC. The values written for level 4 and level 3 interrupts are 0x64 and 0x63 respectively (OCW2 bit EOI = 1, ST = 1, R = 0 and L0 to L2 is the interrupt level, see 8259 PIC manuals).

So long as the function is defined as an interrupt service routine (Turbo C keywords interrupt far or the Microsoft C keywords _interrupt _far) the C compiler will look after saving and restoring any registers and terminating the service routine correctly. When the program terminates the interrupts must be disabled:

1   Interrupts are disabled in the 8250 Interrupt Enable Register (writing 0 disables all interrupts).
2   The OUT2 bit is cleared in the 8250 Modem Control Register.
3   The correct interrupt level must be disabled in the Operations Control Word 1 (OCW1) of the 8259 PIC. For level 4 interrupts bit 4 is set and for level 3 bit 3 is set (the other bits should not be changed).
4   The address of the original interrupt service routine (saved when enabling interrupts) is restored.

Library rs_lib3.c is a version (for either Turbo C or Microsoft C) of the PC serial line function library with the receiver using interrupts. As written the code uses Turbo C keywords and function names but if the compiler being used is not Turbo C the keywords and function names are replaced with the Microsoft C equivalents. The Turbo C compiler defines the identifier __TURBOC__ which can be used in conditional compilation directives.

In line 21 of Library rs_lib3.c the preprocessor #ifndef (if not defined) directive checks to see if __TURBOC__ is defined, and if not, defines (using #define directives in lines 22 to 25) the Microsoft C equivalents to the Turbo C keywords and function names. The program sequence in Library rs_lib3.c is:

21 use ifndef to see if the identifier __TURBOC__ is not defined
　　22-25　if not, define Microsoft C equivalents to the Turbo C keywords and functions
　　26　　end of conditional compilation
30 define the I/O port addresses of the 8250 serial ports
34 define the I/O port addresses for the 8259 PIC (Programmable interrupt controller)
37 define the 8250 serial register offsets from the base addresses
40 define the bits within the 8250 registers of the serial ports to be used in the program
42 declare a function prototype for new_rs232 (the interrupt service routine)
43 define pointer old_rs232 which will hold the address of the old interrupt service routine
45 define rs_port which holds the serial port number
46 define rs_vect which holds the associated vector
48 define rs_data which holds the character received from the serial line
49 define rs_stat_data which holds the receiver status associated with the character
51 define rs_intenable which holds the interrupt enable value for OCW1 of the 8259 PIC
52 define rs_eoi which holds the 'end of interrupt' value for the OCW2 of the 8259 PIC

Function rs_initialise, lines 57 to 93, initialises the serial port and enables interrupts:

61-65 call MS-DOS function 0 to initialise the baud rate, word length, etc.
67-78 a switch which sets up the values of rs_vect, rs_intenable and rs_eoi for the port
81　　save existing interrupt service routine address for vector rs_vect in old_rs232
82　　set up interrupt service routine address for vector rs_vect to function new_rs232
85　　enable receiver interrupts in the 8250 Interrupt Enable Register (set bit 0)
88　　set up OCW1 in the 8259 PIC to enable interrupts at the required level
91　　set DTR, RTS and OUT2 in the 8250 Modem Control Register

Function rs_terminate, lines 97 to 107, disables interrupts:

100 set up OCW1 in the 8259 PIC to disable interrupts at the required level
103 clear the 8250 Interrupt Enable Register (disabling all interrupts)
104 clear the 8250 Modem Control Register (clears OUT2 and negates DTR and RTS)
106 restore the old interrupt service routine address for vector rs_vect (saved in line 81)

Function new_rs232, lines 113 to 121, is the interrupt service routine which processes serial line receiver interrupts (for only one port at a time):

113 function header with the Turbo C keywords interrupt far
115 read the 8250 line status register into rs_stat_data (note the cast (char))
116 if rs_data is non-zero (last character has not been read by host program
　　117 indicate data overrun in rs_stat_data
118 read the 8250 receiver buffer into rs_data (note the cast (char))
120 indicate 'end of interrupt' in the OCW2 (operations control word 2) of 8259 PIC

Function rs_received, lines 125 to 132, returns *true* if a character has been received:

127   test rs_stat_data for a receive error

       128   if error display status with message

130   clear the status indicator rs_stat_data

131   return *true* if a character has been received in rs_data (value is non zero)

Function rs_getch, lines 136 to 145, returns a character received:

140-41   a while which waits for a character to be received

142   copy the character received from rs_data into ch

143   clear rs_data (indicating that the character has been read)

144   return ch (the character received)

The functions rs_status, rs_putch and rs_putstring are unchanged from library rs_lib2.c and are not shown in the listing of library rs_lib3.c.

Note that rs_lib1.c and rs_lib2.c could be used to control several serial ports concurrently (as specified by the parameter io_port passed to every function). As written, library rs_lib3.c can only handle receive interrupts from one serial port at any time, i.e. the interrupt service routine can only process interrupts from the port specified by the external variable rs_port. To extend the library to handle more than one port concurrently the interrupt service routine would need to check which port caused the interrupt (by looking the Line Status Registers) and using separate data buffers for each port.

Problem for Chapter 33

The library rs_lib3.c only buffers one character at a time (in rs_data). Extend the program to use a ring buffer (e.g. of length 1024 bytes) with hardware handshaking (e.g. when the buffer is 70% full stop the transmitter and when 30% full restart it, see Chapter 30.3.3). Extend the program to control two serial ports concurrently.

Implement a data link protocol to provide error free transmission of data frames between two PCs. The protocol should cope with data transmission errors, lost data frames, lost acknowledgements, etc. (refer to a book on communications and networks for details of data link protocols).

Implement a program, using the above protocol, to transfer files between a pair of PCs (connected as Fig. 30.2). One machine acts as a slave, the other the host. A user of the host machine should be able to:

1   Transfer a file from slave to host: enter the name of a file on the slave, the program then transfers the file reporting any errors. Transfer ASCII text initially. Extend program to handle any type by encoding the file (read and write using unformatted I/O, see Chapter 27.7) into blocks of ASCII characters with suitable error checking.

2   Transfer a file from host to slave: as above.

3   Display a subdirectory on slave.

```
 1 /* Library rs_lib3.c -  Interrupt driven PC serial line functions, 8250 ACE  */
 2
 3 /*-----------------------------------------------------------------------*
 4  * Functions for the 8250 RS232 serial interface                         *
 5  * Receiver is interrupt driven                                          *
 6  *   (a)  single character buffer only; needs extending to a ring buffer *
 7  *          with RTS/CTS hardware handshaking when 70% full              *
 8  *   (b) the receiver functions will only work for one port at a time    *
 9  *        interrupt handler, etc. needs extending to cope with more      *
10  * The PC uses an 8259 PIC (programmable interrupt controller) see manuals */
11
12
13 #include <dos.h>                              /* MS-DOS specific header file */
14 #include <conio.h>                            /* direct console I/O functions */
15 #include <stdio.h>                            /* standard I/O header file */
16
17 /*-----------------------------------------------------------------------*
18  * The functions as written uses Turbo C keywords and function calls     *
19  * If Turbo C is no being used the following selects Microsoft C keywords, etc*/
20
21 #ifndef __TURBOC__                     /* if NOT Turbo C assume Microsoft C */
22 #define far _far                                      /* _far keyword */
23 #define interrupt _interrupt                     /* _interrupt keyword */
24 #define setvect _dos_setvect                     /* and function names */
25 #define getvect _dos_getvect
26 #endif
27
28 /*-----------------------------------------------------------------------*/
29 /* define 8250 port base addresses for RS232 ports 0 to 3 (com1: to com4:) */
30 static const short int rs_ports[] = {0x3f8, 0x2f8, 0x3e8, 0x2e8 };
31
32 /* I/O port addresses for 8259 PIC (Programmable interrupt controller)  *
33  *    OCW1 operation control word2 and OCW2 operation control word 2    */
34 enum {pic_ocw1 = 0x21, pic_ocw2 = 0x20};
35
36 /* 8250 register offsets from base address */
37 enum {DataReg, IntEna, IntIdent, LineCtrl, ModCtrl, LineStatus, ModStatus};
38
39 /* 8250 bits in line status, modem status and modem control registers */
40 enum {DR = 0x100, THRE = 0x2000, CTS = 0x10, DTR = 0x1, RTS = 0x2, OUT2 = 0x8};
41
42 void interrupt far new_rs232( void );                  /* function prototype */
43 void (interrupt far *old_rs232)( void );      /* define 'pointer to function' */
44
45 static short int far rs_port,                    /* holds serial port number */
46                      rs_vect;              /* holds interrupt vector for port */
47
```

Library rs_lib3.c Interrupt driven PC serial line functions, 8250 ACE
(functions rs_status, rs_putch and rs_putstring are as in library rs_lib2.c)

```
48  static volatile unsigned char far rs_data = 0,          /* character buffer */
49                                     rs_stat_data = 0;      /* and its status */
50
51  static unsigned char rs_intenable,        /* 8259 PIC 'interrupt enable' */
52                       rs_eoi;              /* 8259 PIC 'end of interrupt ' */
53
54  /*------------------------------------------------------------------*
55   * Serial port: initialise io_port, set 9600 baud, 8 data bits, one stop bit  *
56   *    enable interrupts and set DTR and RTS active                  */
57  void rs_initialise(const int io_port)
58  {
59      union REGS registers;              /* variable to hold 8086 registers */
60
61      registers.h.ah = 0;                        /* command, initialise */
62      /* set baud rate to 9600, 8 data bits, no parity and 1 stop bit */
63      registers.h.al = 0xe3;                     /* baud rate to 9600  */
64      registers.x.dx = io_port;                       /* for port */
65      int86(0x14, &registers, &registers);    /* interrupt 14 hexadecimal */
66
67      switch (io_port)
68          {
69          case 0: case 2:           /* com1: and com3: use interrupt level 4 */
70                      rs_vect = 12;                    /* interrupt vector */
71                      rs_intenable = 0xef;   /* 8259 PIC, interrupt enable */
72                      rs_eoi = 0x64;         /* 8259 PIC, end of interrupt */
73                      break;
74          case 1: case 3:           /* com2: and com4: use interrupt level 3 */
75                      rs_vect = 11;                    /* interrupt vector */
76                      rs_intenable = 0xf7;   /* 8259 PIC, interrupt enable */
77                      rs_eoi = 0x63;         /* 8259 PIC, end of interrupt */
78          }
79
80      /* set up vector to interrupt handler and enable interrupts */
81      old_rs232 = getvect(rs_vect);              /* get current vector */
82      setvect( rs_vect, new_rs232 );                /* set new vector */
83
84      rs_port = rs_ports[io_port];             /* get port base address */
85      outp(rs_port + IntEna, 1);     /* enable receiver interrupts (bit 0) */
86
87      /* enable interrupt level in 8259 PIC OCW1 (operation control word 1) */
88      outp(pic_ocw1, inp(pic_ocw1) & rs_intenable);
89
90      /* OUT2 must be set in modem control reg to send interrupt to 8259 PIC */
91      outp(rs_port + ModCtrl, DTR + RTS + OUT2);     /* set DTR, RTS and OUT2 */
92
93  }
94
95  /*------------------------------------------------------------------*
```

Library rs_lib3.c   Interrupt driven PC serial line functions, 8250 ACE

```
 96      * Serial port: terminate io_port, sets DTR and RTS to low                    *
 97     void rs_terminate(const int io_port)
 98     {
 99          /* disable interrupt level in 8259 PIC OCW1 (operation control word 1) */
100          outp(pic_ocw1, inp(pic_ocw1) | ~rs_intenable);
101
102          rs_port = rs_ports[io_port];                         /* get port base address */
103          outp(rs_port + IntEna, 0);               /* disable all serial interrupts */
104          outp(rs_port + ModCtrl, 0);              /* clear modem control register */
105
106          setvect( rs_vect, old_rs232 );                       /* reset old vector */
107     }
108
109     /*------------------------------------------------------------------------*
110      * Serial port: handler for receive interrupt on serial port rs_port      *
111      *  read receiver buffer to clear interrupt and send EOI (end of interrupt) *
112      *   to 8259 OCW2 (operation control word 2) to acknowledge the interrupt  */
113     void interrupt far new_rs232(void)
114     {
115          rs_stat_data = (char) inp(rs_port  + LineStatus);    /* read line status */
116          if (rs_data)                              /* if character already in buffer */
117              rs_stat_data = (char) (rs_stat_data | 0x2); /* indicate overrun error */
118          rs_data = (char) inp(rs_port);                       /* read character */
119          /* 8259 PIC end of interrupt: bit EOI = 1, SL = 1, R = 0, L0-L2 = level */
120          outp(pic_ocw2, rs_eoi);                      /* send EOI to 8259 OCW2 */
121     }
122
123     /*------------------------------------------------------------------------*
124      * Serial port: return TRUE is character available from serial line       */
125     int rs_received(int io_port)
126     {
127          if (rs_stat_data & 0xe)                              /* receive error ?? */
128              printf("\n\aRead error on serial line, status = %#x\n",
129                      rs_stat_data & 0xe);
130          rs_stat_data = 0;                                    /* clear status */
131          return rs_data;                          /* return > 0 if character ready */
132     }
133
134     /*------------------------------------------------------------------------*
135      * Serial port: read character from io_port (ignored in this version)     */
136     char rs_getch(const int io_port)
137     {
138          char ch;
139
140          while (! rs_received(io_port))
141              /* wait for character received */ ;
142          ch = rs_data;                            /* GET CHARACTER RECEIVED */
143          rs_data = 0;
144          return ch;    /* read character */
145     }
```

Library rs_lib3.c   Interrupt driven PC serial line functions, 8250 ACE

34

Introduction to C++

The C++ programming language is a superset of the original C language with enhancements to support object orientated programming techniques. In an object orientated environment an *object* is seen to be composed of two integrated components:

 (a) the data storage (such as variables, arrays, etc.),
and (b) the functions which operate upon the data.

Information (data and functions) within an object can be private or public:

private: accessible only to members of the object (the concept of *data hiding*).
public: accessed by other objects with access privileges specified by an interface.

In Software Engineering terminology such an object would be called an *abstract data type*.

In traditional programming languages the data and associated functions are distinct, in that the data is declared and then the functions are implemented. By using modular programming techniques data and associated functions can be grouped into modules. How successfully *data hiding* can be achieved depends upon the facilities of the language, e.g. in C the use of the *static* storage class specifier will 'hide' external objects and functions within a source file. Other modules can access data and functions by using the public interface between the module and the outside world. For example, in C a module would have an associated header file which defines types and declares objects and function prototypes which may be used by functions in other modules. Hierarchies of modules can be created with data objects being built up from types defined in other modules.

Objected orientated programming languages contain facilities which directly support the implementation of objects as integrated entities, i.e. the encapsulation of a set of data types and associated functions with an interface to the external world. In C++ this is achieved using the aggregate type *class* (an extension of the idea of *struct* in C) which enables the definition of an object with associated data types, functions and operators. To support *data hiding* a *class* can contain *private* and *public* members (data and/or functions). Object reuse is promoted by an *inheritance* mechanism in which a new class can be derived from an existing *base* class to achieve a hierarchy of related objects which can share code.

In addition to *class*, C++ extended the original C in a number of areas, in particular to aid the implementation and use of functions with facilities such as function prototypes, default parameters, reference parameters and inline functions. A technique called *overloading* enables several meanings to be given to a function or operator depending upon the context. For example, a number of versions of a function may exist which differ in the number and types of the formal parameters. When the function is called the compiler calls the appropriate version as determined by the number and types of the actual parameters.

Because C++ is a superset of the original C all the facilities of C are available (many compliers support both C and C++, e.g. Turbo C++, Microsoft C Version 7, etc. (Child 1992)). Many facilities of C++ were subsequently incorporated in ANSI C, e.g. function prototypes, the const qualifier, the ability to return a structure as a function result, etc.

34.1 The *cout* and *cin* standard I/O streams

In C++ the standard I/O streams cout and cin (declared in header file <iostream.h>) automatically apply the correct conversions for the object types passed as parameters. For example, if i and pi are int and float variables respectively:

```
i = 10;                                          // assign integer value
pi = 3.14159f;                                   // assign real value
cout << "integer = " << i << " float = " << pi;  // print values to screen
```

prints 'integer = 10 float = 3.14159' on the screen. The identifier cout is the name of the standard output stream and the output operator << (referred to as the *insertion* or *put to* operator) passes the parameters in turn to the output stream converting the type automatically (when using printf the programmer has to specify in the *control string* the the correct *conversion specification* for each parameter).

The fragment of code also shows the use of the C++ comment symbol //, in which the comment runs from // to the end of the current line. Comments enclosed in /* ... */ can still be used and are recommended in preprocessor directives (some preprocessors have problems with //).

Information is read from the input stream cin using the input operator >> (referred to as the *extraction* or *get from* operator) as follows:

```
cin >> i;                        // read next integer from the input stream
```

This reads an integer value from the input stream cin and assigns the value to i (note that the address operator &, used when specifying parameters to scanf, is not required).

The format of the information output or input can be controlled using *format state flags* and *manipulators*, e.g. to set the field width, precision, hexadecimal conversion, etc. This can be a longwinded process and many programmers still prefer to use functions from <stdio.h>.

34.2 Functions in C + +

C++ made a number of enhancements to the original C in the use of functions:

function prototypes: enable parameter checking (number and types) on a function call
reference parameters: enable function parameters to be passed *by reference*
inline functions: enable the *inline* generation of a function body instead of calling a function
overloading: enables several versions of a function to exist (with different parameter types)
default parameters: parameters can be given default values when the function is defined

Function prototypes were subsequently incorporated into ANSI C (see Chapter 15.3).

34.2.1 Inline functions

The inline specifier is used in the header of a function definition as follows:

```
inline result_type function_name(parameter_list)
{
    ....                                         // function body
}
```

The inline specifier requests the compiler to replace calls to the function with the compiled code of the function body (in a similar way to macro expansion) thus saving the overhead of a function call. The inline specifier is a request (similar to the register storage specifier) and may be ignored by the compiler. In any case it should be used sparingly and only with small functions. Before an inline function can be called it must be defined (the body of the function fully specified), not just the prototype declared.

34.2.2 Reference parameters

By default, function parameters in C++ are *passed by value* (as in C). Although parameter passing *by reference* may be achieved using pointers (as in C, see Chapter 15.7) an alternative and more elegant way is to use *reference parameters*.

In C++ a reference type (which is closely related to a pointer type) is an alias for an object of a specified type. The main use for reference types is to specify *reference parameters* in function headers and prototypes to achieve *call by reference*. To specify that a parameter is to be a reference parameter the & operator is used:

```
void func(int i, int &r_j)                          // function header
{
    r_j = r_j * i;                    // change value of actual parameter
}
```

The function header of func specifies two parameters:

i   type int, is *passed by value*
                 a copy of the actual parameter is passed to the function func
&r_j   type 'reference to int', is *passed by reference*
                 the function func has access to the actual parameter via the name r_j

Inside func the formal parameter name r_j becomes an alias for the actual parameter directly accessing the storage allocated to it (thus enabling its value to be changed), e.g.:

```
    func(10, int_variable);                             // call function
```

The value of int_variable would be assigned the value int_variable * 10. Note that the address operator does not prefix the second parameter (as when using a pointer to achieve call by reference). The compiler would know from the prototype that the second parameter was to be passed by reference.

Even if the value of an actual parameter is not to be changed it can be advantageous to use reference parameters in that it removes the overhead of creating and initialising the temporary object being *passed by value*. It is of particular use in passing large structures where the overhead in creating the temporary copy of the structure is not only wasteful of processor time but may cause stack overflow. If the actual parameter should not be changed the reference parameter should be const qualified, i.e.:

```
void func(int i, const int &r_j)                    // function header
```

The second parameter is passed by reference (and the function will have access to the storage allocated to the actual parameter) but, because it is const qualified, the actual parameter cannot be changed.

If, when a function is called, an actual parameter which corresponds to reference type is of a different type, the compiler creates a temporary object of the correct type, assigns a converted value to it and then passes a reference to the temporary object (the types have to be assignment compatible). Any modifications made to the reference parameter inside the function only effect the value of the temporary object, not the actual parameter (a compiler warning will normally be issued because in effect the parameter is being passed by value).

34.2.3 Overloading functions

In a C program only one copy of a function with a particular identifier can exist, otherwise the linker will generate 'multiple definitions' or similar error message. In C++ a function may be *overloaded* by which the same identifier is used to name a number of versions of a function which differ in the number and/or types of parameters. For example, consider the following prototypes of functions to swap the values of two variables:

```
void swap(int &int1, int &int2);             // prototype to swap two ints
void swap(float &float1, float &float2);     // prototype to swap two floats
```

If swap is called with two int variables the first version is called, if it is called with two float variables the second version is called. As many versions of swap can be created as required, e.g. to swap long int, double, structures, etc. Declarations and/or definitions of *overloaded* functions must have the same scope (i.e. a prototype of swap declared within a compound statement would 'hide' any prototypes declared outside the statement). *Overloaded* functions are used extensively in *class* objects, see section 34.3.

The different versions of an *overloaded* function may differ in the type of function result returned. It is not possible, however, to have versions which differ only in the type of the function result (the number and/or types of parameters must differ).

34.2.4 Functions to swap integer and real variables

Program 34.1 demonstrates the use of inline functions, *reference parameters* and *overloaded functions*:

lines
10-17   define the inline function swap with two 'reference to int' parameters
      14-16 swap the values of the *reference parameters* int1 and int2
             thus swapping the values of the actual parameters
19   declare prototype of function swap with two 'reference to float' parameters
22-39   definition of function main
24-38   a for loop which terminates (in line 31) when EOF is entered on the keyboard
      26-27 define two int and two float internal auto variables
      29   prompt user for input
      30   read four values (two int and two float) from cin
      31   call function cin.eof to check for EOF entered, terminate if so
      34   print values of variables on the screen
      35   call swap to swap the two int variables
      36   call swap to swap the two float variables
      37   print (swapped) values of variables on the screen
45-50   define the function swap with two 'reference to float' parameters
      49 a single statement using the , operator (alternative to lines 14 to 17)
            the choice is a matter of programming style

In line 35 the function swap defined in lines 10 to 17 would be generated inline or called (two 'reference to int' parameters). In line 36 the function swap defined in lines 45 to 50 (prototype in line 19) would be called (two 'reference to float' parameters). If the function prototype in line 19 was moved inside main (after line 23) the version of swap defined in lines 10 to 17 would be 'hidden'. The call to swap in line 35 would generate temporary float variables to be passed (and the compiler would display a warning).

```
 1  // Program 34_1 - C++ program to demonstrate the following:
 2  //  (a) inline functions (b) overloaded functions (c) calling by reference
 3
 4  #include <iostream.h>              /* include C++ standard I/O stream header */
 5
 6  //------------------------------------------------------------------------//
 7  // Inline Function to swap the values of two int parameters                //
 8  //  Parameters: int1 and int2 (both 'reference to int') to be swapped      //
 9  //------------------------------------------------------------------------//
10  inline void swap(int &int1, int &int2)
11  {
12      int temporary;                              // temporary storage
13
14      temporary = int1;              // copy first variable into temporary
15      int1 = int2;                   // copy second variable into first
16      int2 = temporary;              // copy temporary variable into first
17  }
18
19  void swap(float &float1, float &float2);        // prototype to swap two floats
20
21  // Function main, read pairs of int and float variables and swap the values
22  int main()
23      {
24      for (;;)
25          {
26          int x, y;                               // local int variable
27          float a, b;                             // local float variable
28
29          cout << "\n\nEnter two integers and two floats ? ";      // prompt user
30          cin  >> x >> y >> a >> b;                 // read variables
31          if (cin.eof()) return 0;                  // if EOF terminate
32
33          // print values, swap them and print them again
34          cout << "\n x = " << x << " y = " << y << " a = " << a << " b = " << b;
35          swap(x, y);                             // swap x and y
36          swap(a, b);                             // swap a and b
37          cout << "\n x = " << x << " y = " << y << " a = " << a << " b = " << b;
38          }
39      }
40
41  //------------------------------------------------------------------------//
42  // Function to swap the values of two float parameters                     //
43  //  Parameters: float1 and float2 (both 'reference to float') to be swapped //
44  //------------------------------------------------------------------------//
45  void swap(float &float1, float &float2)
46  {
47      float temporary;                            // temporary storage
48
49      temporary = float1, float1 = float2, float2 = temporary;   // copy variables
50  }
```

Program 34.1 C++ inline functions, overloaded functions and calling by reference

34.3 The aggregate type *class*

The aggregate type class enables the specification of an object with associated data types, functions and operators (such an object is called an *abstract data type*). The declaration of a class is similar to a struct but with the following additions:

1   In addition to data declaration members it can have members which are functions.
2   It can contain *private* (the default) and *public* members:

    private: accessible only by functions which are members or *friends* of the class.
    public: accessible by member and non-member functions.

The implementation details of the *private* members of the class are 'hidden', therefore promoting *data hiding* which is an important factor in object orientated programming. If the implementation details of a private member are changed, only the code of members of the class will need to be modified so long as the public interface is not affected.

    Program 34.2 (next page) declares the class string (lines 7 to 21) which contains a private array data which stores a string of characters (including white space) and public functions to process the string. By default class members are private therefore line:

9   data declaration of private member data (array of char)
11   the keyword public starts the declaration of the public members
13-14   define inline member function p_name, returns a const qualified pointer to data
15-16   define inline member function strlen, returns the length of the string in data
17   declare prototype of member function read which reads a string from cin
18   declare prototype of member function store which stores characters in data
20   declare prototype of *friend* function cmp_strings which compares two strings

Notes:
1   Public and private members may be data declarations or function definitions or function prototype declarations.
2   If a member function is defined (with a body) it will be treated as inline, otherwise a function may be declared inline in the prototype (with the definition elsewhere).
3   A *friend* of a class is a function or class that, although not a member of the class, has full access to private and public members.

The declaration of the class is followed by the definition of the member functions read (lines 24 to 29) and store (lines 32 to 36) and the *friend* function cmp_strings (lines 39 to 40). For example, consider the member functions read and store:

24 int string::read(void) function header, no parameters returns an int function result
      the :: operator indicates that read is a member of string (discussed below)
26 cin.get(data, 80); reads characters (including white space) into data (see manuals)
      get reads until *newline* is found or 79 characters have been read. The characters are null terminated and the *newline* is left in the input stream. Note that cin >> data; would not do what is required (reading would stop when white space was found).
27 cin.ignore(1000, '\n'); skips up to 1000 characters in cin up to '\n' (see manuals)
      this removes surplus characters in case more than 79 were on the line
28 return ::strlen(data); returns the number of characters in data (:: discussed below)
32 void string::store(const char *text) function header, one parameter (pointer to char)
34 strncpy(data, text, 79); copy up to 79 characters (pointed to by text) to data
35 data[79] = '\0'; terminate the string (in case text is longer than 79 characters)

The :: operator is the scope access or resolution modifier and indicates the scope of an identifier. In lines 24 and 32 string:: indicates that the identifiers read and store belong to the class string (otherwise they would be normal program functions). In lines 16 and 28 :: tells the compiler that the version of strlen to call is the one outside the current scope, i.e. the strlen prototyped in <string.h>, not the strlen defined in lines 15 and 16.

The *friend* function cmp_string is defined in lines 39 to 41. A *friend* function is a normal program function which has full access to the private members of a class, i.e. function cmp_strings needs to be able to access the member data (in line 40).

```
1  // Program 34.2   C++ using a class to create a string type with functions
2
3  #include <iostream.h>                              /* I/O stream header file */
4  #include <string.h>
5
6  // declare a string type, can contain white space
7  class string
8       { // private members
9            char data[80];                    //  array of char to hold the string
10
11       public:
12          // member functions
13            const char *p_name(void)          // return pointer to the string
14               { return data; }
15            int strlen(void)                        // return the string length
16               { return ::strlen(data); }           // call strlen in <string.h>
17            int read(void);                                   // read a string
18            void store(const char * text);                   // store a string
19          // friend function, returns TRUE if strings are identical
20            friend int cmp_strings(const string &string1, const string &string2);
21       };
22
23 // member function to read characters (including white space) from cin
24 int string::read(void)
25 {
26     cin.get(data, 80);                       // get upto 79 characters from cin
27     cin.ignore(1000, '\n');                  // discard rest of line up to '\n'
28     return ::strlen(data);                   // return number of characters read
29 }
30
31 // member function to store characters from parameter 'text' into data
32 void string::store(const char *text)
33 {
34     strncpy(data, text, 79);                          // copy up to 79 characters
35     data[79] = '\0';                                  // add null terminator
36 }
37
38 // friend function, returns TRUE if strings are identical
39 int cmp_strings(const string &string1, const string &string2)
40 {    return(! strcmp(string1.data, string2.data)); }          // compare string
41
```

Program 34.2 C++ using a class to create a string type with associated functions

```
42 int main(void)
43 {
44     string string1, string2;                    // define two string variables
45
46     string1.store("hello John Doe");                    // store in string1
47     cout << "\nstring1 " << string1.strlen() << ":" << string1.p_name();
48
49     cout << "\n\n Enter string2 ? ";
50     string2.read();                                     // read string2
51     cout << "\nstring2 " << string2.strlen() << ":" << string2.p_name();
52
53     // compare the strings, print message indicating if same
54     if (cmp_strings(string1, string2)) cout << "\n    string1 = string2";
55     else                                cout << "\n    string1 != string2";
56
57     string2 = string1;                          // assign string1 to string2
58     cout << "\n\nstring2 " << string2.strlen() << ":" << string2.p_name();
59 }
```

Program 34.2 C++ using a class to create a string type with associated functions

Once a class has been declared objects of that type may be defined in a similar way to variables (an object is more than a variable in that a variable contains only data, an object contains data and operators to operate upon it). For example, in function main of Program 34.2 the objects string1 and string2 are defined in line 44:

```
string string1, string2;                    // define two string objects
```

Once an object has been defined functions which are members of the class may be called to operate upon information stored within the object. The dot (.) operator is used to access the member of a class (as it is used to access members of structures), e.g. line 46:

```
string1.store("hello John Doe");                    // store in string1
```

The function string::store is called to store the string "hello John Doe" into the hidden data member string1.data. If the member data had been public or main was a *friend* of class string the characters could have been copied directly. In this case attempting to access data from main would generate an error, e.g. using Turbo C++:

```
strcpy(string1.data, "hello John Doe");             // store in string1
Error x2.cpp 47: 'string::data' is not accessible in function main()
```

The member function p_name, which returns a pointer to the private member data, is used in cout statements (lines 47, 51 and 58) to print the strings stored in the objects. The pointer returned is const qualified to prevent it being used to alter the contents of data. In practice returning pointers to private members should be avoided with direct access limited to member and friend functions only (section 34.5 will show how to *overload* << to print the string stored in an object, thus removing the requirement for p_name).

The name of a class object refers to the whole of the object (like the name of a structure), thus an object can be assigned to another of the same class, e.g. line 57:

```
string2 = string1;                          // assign string1 to string2
```

This copies the data components of string1 to string2 (beware, if the object contains pointers the pointer values are copied, not the data structures pointed to, see Section 34.5).

34.3.1 The pointer *this*

Consider the function call in line 46 of Program 34.2:

```
string1.store("hello John Doe");                         // store in string1
```

When the function `string::store` is called, a pointer to the object `string1` is passed as a hidden parameter. Inside the function the pointer is used to access the member data, e.g. lines 34 and 35 would access member `string1.data`:

```
strncpy(data, text, 79);                          // copy up to 79 characters
data[79] = '\0';                                  // add null terminator
```

The hidden pointer is called `this` and may be used explicitly, e.g. the compiled code of lines 34 and 35 actually looks like:

```
strncpy(this->data, text, 79);                    // copy up to 79 characters
this->data[79] = '\0';                            // add null terminator
```

Remember `this->data` is another way of writing `(*this).data`. In the above call to `store` the pointer `this` would point to the object `string1` and member `string1.data` would be accessed. It is sometimes necessary to use `this` explicitly to refer to the whole of an object from within a member function (see funtion `string::read` in Header file `strinhp.h` in Section 34.5).

34.3.2 Summary, *member* and *friend* functions

It is important to understand the difference between *member* and *friend* functions and the roles they fulfil. The *member* functions are fundamental components of an object (along with data declarations) and are called, using the dot operator, to operate upon a specified object. Consider the function call in line 50 of Program 34.2:

```
string2.read();                                       // read string2
```

This calls the member function `string::read` to operate upon the object `string2` (it reads a character string from the keyboard into `string2.data`). Inside the function `string::read` members can be accessed using the identifiers only, e.g. line 26 of Program 34.2:

```
cin.get(data, 80);                       // get upto 79 characters from cin
```

This statement accesses the member `string2.data` using the hidden parameter `this`.

A *friend* function is a normal program function which needs to access the *private* members (data declarations or functions) of a class. It is called like any other program function; not using the dot operator (hence it has no hidden parameter `this`). For example, function `cmp_strings` in Program 34.2 is not a member of `class string` but needs to be able to directly access the member `data` of string objects to compare the stored strings (in line 40). It could have been written as a member:

```
int string::cmp_strings(const string &string2)
   { return(! strcmp(data, string2.data)); }           // compare strings
```

Line 54 of Program 34.2 would then have to be written:

```
if (string1.cmp_strings(string2)) cout << "\n    string1 = string2";
```

In many cases a function may be implemented as a *member* or a *friend* depending upon the context of its use (which determines how it is to be called). In general if a function is to operate upon the internal components of a particular object it would be implemented as a *member* otherwise, a more general function, would be implemented as a *friend*.

34.4 Constructors and destructors

When an object is created storage is allocated to hold the data members, e.g. in line 44 of Program 34.2 storage would be allocated to hold string1.data and student2.data. In addition C++ enables *constructor* functions to be implemented which are called when an object is created to carry out any initialisation, e.g. line 44 of Program 34.2 could be:

```
    string string1("hello John Doe"), string2(string1);          // define objects
```

When created string1.data is initialised with the character string "hello John Doe" and string2.data is initialised with the value of string1.data.

34.4.1 Constructors for a complex number object

Chapter 22.6 described a structure to store the real and imaginary components of a complex number. In C++ a better alternative is to declare a class which will hold the components of a complex number, together with associated functions and *overloaded* operators (discussed in section 34.5). For example, an outline declaration could be:

```
class complex                                 // declare a complex number type
        { // private members
            double real, imag;               // real and imaginary components
        public:
          // public functions, etc.
        }
```

This could be used to define complex number objects as follows:

```
    complex a, b, c, d;                              // define complex objects
```

If the objects are external or static internal the data members will be initialised to zero, if automatic internal their values will be undefined. A *constructor* function which will ensure that the real and imaginary components are always zeroed would be:

```
// default constructor (without parameters) for complex number objects
complex()
        { real = imag = 0.0; }               // zero real and imaginary components
```

A constructor function has the same name as the *class* and no return type. In this case function complex initialises the real and imaginary components to zero. This constructor (without parameters) is the *default constructor* which is called when creating objects defined without parameters, arrays, temporary objects required during the evaluation of expressions, etc. There should be a default constructor if any at all are implemented.

A constructor can be overloaded just like any other function. Constructor functions may have parameters which can be used to initialise the data members of an object, e.g. to initialise the real and imaginary components of a complex number object:

```
// constructor with one (real) or two parameters (real and imag)
complex(double r_val, double i_val = 0.0)
        { real = r_val; imag =i_val; }              // initialise real and imaginary
```

Depending upon the form of object definition the correct constructor would be called, e.g.:

```
    complex a, b(1.0), c(4.0, 5.0), d = complex(6.0, 7.0);  // define complex objects
```

Object a is constructed using the default constructor and b, c and d using the constructor with parameters (the constructor can be called implicitly as in the case of b and c or explicitly as in the case of d). The constructor with parameters shows the use of default parameters in that if the second parameter is omitted (as in the definition of b) it will be assumed to be 0 (note that any function in C++ can use default parameters in this way). Because the name of a class object refers to the whole object complex number objects can be assigned in an assignment statement:

```
a = b;                                          // assign b to a
```

In addition the constructor with parameters can be used to assign values to complex number objects at run time in assignment statements:

```
a = complex(20.0, 0.0);                 // call constructor explicitly
a = 20.0;                               // call constructor implicitly
d = complex(5.0, -6.0);                 // call constructor explicitly
```

If a real value only is to be assigned the constructor may be called implicitly (as in the second assignment statement). Note that the following will not assign 9 + i8 to d:

```
d = (9.0, 8.0);                         // assign d = 9.0 + i8.0
```

In this case the , is the comma or sequence operator. The expression (9.0, 8.0) is evaluated and the result 8.0 assigned to d (value 8.0 + i0.0).

34.4.2 Constructors for a string object containing a pointer

The class string declared in Program 34.2 is very restricted in that the length of the array data is fixed at 80 characters. This would be wasteful if the strings being processed were short and restrictive if larger strings needed storing. In class string this could be overcome by declaring data to be pointer to an array of char:

```
class string
      { char *data;            // pointer to array of char to hold the string
```

When an object of this type is created storage will automatically be allocated for the pointer data. However, storage for the array pointed to has to be explicitly allocated using dynamic memory allocation functions, e.g. a default *constructor* to allocate an array of 80 char and initialise the array to "" would be:

```
string()                      // constructor without parameter, set to empty string
{
    data = new char[80];              // allocate an array of 80 char
    strcpy(data, "");                 // copy empty string into array
}
```

The C++ function new returns a pointer to the area allocated. It is similar to malloc but has the advantages:

1   It automatically takes account of the size of the data type.
2   If a class object is being allocated the constructor, if it exists, will be called, e.g. the expression new string[100] would call the default string constructor 100 times.

A constructor with a parameter specifying the array size could be:

```
string(int length)        // constructor with an int parameter specifying array length
{
    data = new char[length];          // allocate an array of length char
    strcpy(data,"");                  // copy empty string into array
}
```

String objects may now be defined:

```
string string1, string2(40), string3("hello user");        // define strings
```

The definition of `string1` would call the default constructor and the definition of `string2` would call the constructor with a single `int` parameter. The definition of `string3` would be rejected; the parameter is a string constant and neither constructor can cope with it. However, it is a simple matter to define one:

```
string(char *text)                              // constructor with a string parameter
{
    data = new char[::strlen(text) + 1];        // allocate an array of to hold string
    strcpy(data, text);                         // copy string into array
}
```

This constructor allocates an array of size `strlen(text) + 1` (the additional element is to hold the terminating null) and then copies the string pointed to by `text` into the array pointed to by `data`.

When an object is deallocated (e.g. when the compound statement in which it is defined terminates) any dynamic storage allocated by a constructor must be deallocated. This task is carried out by a *destructor* function, which in `class string` would be:

```
~string() { delete data; }                      // delete array
```

The name of the destructor (there may only be one) is the class name prefixed by `~`. The destructor is called and then the object itself deallocated. In this case the destructor calls the memory deallocation function `delete` to deallocate the array pointed to by `data`. The C++ `delete` function is similar to `free` but when deallocating class objects will call destructors, e.g. when `delete` is used with string objects the above destructor would automatically be called. Note that `class complex` described in 34.4.1 does not need a destructor (it contains no dynamic arrays).

34.5 Overloading operators

34.5.1 Overloading operators to process complex number objects

In Section 34.4.1 the `class complex` was described together with associated constructors. It would now be possible to implement member functions to carry out arithmetic operations upon complex number object similar to those described in Chapter 22.6 (e.g. `c_add`, `c_mult`, etc). In C++ a much more elegant way to implement such facilities is to *overload* operators (such as +, -, ==, >>, etc.) to give them additional meanings dependent upon the types of the operands. Consider the following expression where a, b and c are complex number objects:

```
c = a + b;
```

To be able to add complex number objects using the + operator a function called `operator+` is implemented (to *overload* +) which takes two parameters (both complex number objects) and returns a complex number object, e.g:

```
// overload +, add two complex numbers return a complex
 friend complex operator+(const complex &numb1, const complex &numb2)
{
    return complex (numb1.real + numb2.real, numb1.imag + numb2.imag);
}
```

This uses the constructor `complex` with parameters (described in Section 34.4.1) to create a temporary object which contains the result of the addition of complex number objects `numb1` and `numb2`. The `return` statement returns the value as a function result. The statement:

```
c = a + b;
```

is translated by the compiler into the following call to `operator+`:

```
c = operator+(a, b);
```

In this case there is no need to overload the = operator; the assignment operator will copy the contents of the temporary object returned by `operator+` into `c` without problem (the next subsection will show an example where it is necessary to overload =).

The above function `operator+` would be implemented within class `complex` and is a *friend* of the class (so that it can access the private members `real` and `imag`). Such functions can be implemented as *members* or *friends* depending upon the context in which they are called. For example, the above function could have been implemented as a member:

```
// overload +, add two complex numbers return a complex
complex operator+(const complex &numb2)
    {
    return complex (real + numb2.real, imag + numb2.imag);
    }
```

In this case the expression `c = a + b;` is translated to the call:

```
c = a.operator+(b);
```

In general, if an operator is to operate upon the internal components of one of the parameters it would be implemented as a *member* function , e.g. =, --, ++, +=, etc. A more general operator which takes parameters and returns a result to be used in expressions would be implemented as a friend, e.g. +, *, ==, etc.

Program 34.3 (next page) shows a simple program using class complex with overloaded operators + and <<:

line

9   declare the real and imaginary components

13   define default constructor to initialise the real and imaginary components to zero

16-17   define constructor with parameters (real and imaginary components)

20-24   define friend function to overload + to add two complex number objects, return a complex number object

27-28   define friend function to overload +, add a complex number to a double, return a complex number object

31-32   define friend function to overload +, add a double to a complex number, return a complex number object (note that this could not be implemented as a *member* because the first parameter is not a complex object)

35-41   define friend function to overload << operator, output a complex number object

         37   output real component to `stream`

         38-39   output +i or -i followed by absolute value of imaginary component

         40   return `stream`

46   define complex number objects (calling the appropriate constructor)

48   output value of a using overloaded << operator (should be 0)

49   assign the value 20.0 + i0.0 to a (implicitly calling constructor)
50-52   output values of a, b and c using overloaded << operator
53-54   assign the value -3.0 + i5.0 to d (explicitly calling constructor) and output value
55-56   perform arithmetic operations using the overload + operator and output result

```
1  // Program 34.3   C++ complex numbers using overloaded functions
2
3  #include <iostream.h>
4  #include <math.h>
5
6  // declare a complex number type with a real and imaginary components
7  class complex
8        { // private members
9            double real, imag;                        // real and imaginary components
10
11      public:
12         // default constructor (without parameters), zero components
13         complex() { real = imag = 0.0; }
14
15         // constructor with one (real) or two parameters (real and imag)
16         complex(double r_val, double i_val = 0.0)          // with parameter(s)
17                { real = r_val; imag =i_val; }
18
19         // overload +, add two complex numbers return a complex
20         friend complex operator+(const complex &numb1, const complex &numb2)
21              {
22                  return complex (numb1.real + numb2.real,
23                               numb1.imag + numb2.imag);
24              }
25
26         // overload +, add a complex number + a double
27         friend complex operator+(const complex &numb1, const double numb2)
28              { return complex (numb1.real + numb2, numb1.imag); }
29
30         // overload +, add a double + a complex number
31         friend complex operator+(const double numb1, const complex &numb2)
32              { return complex (numb2.real + numb1, numb2.imag); }
33
34         // overload <<, to put a complex number to stream
35         friend ostream& operator<<( ostream &stream, const complex &numb)
36              {
37                  stream << numb.real                        // print real part
38                         << ((numb.imag >= 0) ? '+' : '-')   // print + or -
39                         << "i" << abs(numb.imag);           // print imag part
40                  return stream;
41              }
42       };
```

Program 34.3 C++ complex numbers using overloaded functions

```
43
44 int main(void)
45 {
46     complex a, b(1.0), c(4.0, 5.0), d;                    // define complex objects
47
48     cout << "\na = " << a;                                // print a
49     a = 20.0;                                             // assign a
50     cout << "\na = " << a;                                // print a
51     cout << "\nb = " << b;                                // print b
52     cout << "\nc = " << c;                                // print c
53     d = complex(-3.0, 5.0);
54     cout << "\nd = " << d;                                // print d
55     c = 1.0 + a + complex(0.0, 6.0) + c + 5.0 + b + d;    // calculate
56     cout << "\nc = 1.0 + a + i6 + c + 5.0 + b + d = " << c;  // print c
57 }
```

Program 34.3 C++ complex numbers using overloaded functions

Consider the expression in line 55:

```
c = 1.0 + a + complex(0.0, 6.0) + c + 5.0 + b + d;        // calculate
```

During the evaluation of the expression the default constructor is implicitly called to create temporary objects and the second constructor is explicitly called to create the constant 0.0 + i6.0. The three overloaded operator+ functions are called to evaluate the various combinations of complex and double additions (note that the order of evaluation is not specified).

The second and third overloaded operator+ functions are not really necessary. If they were not available a constructor would be called to convert the constants 1.0 and 5.0 to the values 1.0 + i0.0 and 5.0 + i0.0 respectively and then a complex + complex addition carried out. The advantage of having the extra overloaded operator+ functions is that it saves the extra function call to the constructor at run time.

34.5.2 Overloading operators to process string objects

In Program 34.2 the member data of class string was an array of 80 char, i.e. line 9:

```
char data[80];                           //  array of char to hold the string
```

Because the name of a class object refers to the whole of the object it is possible to assign an object to another of the same class. For example, in line 57 of Program 34.2 the contents of array string1.data are copied to string2.data:

```
string2 = string1;                       // assign string1 to string2
```

Now consider the alternative, discussed in section 34.4.2, where the member data is a pointer to an array which is allocated using a constructor. The assignment would overwrite the pointer string2.data with the value of the pointer string1.data. This has two results:

1   string1.data and string2.data both end up pointing to the array allocated to string1.
2   The array set up when the constructor for string2 was called is left with nothing pointing to it (it is effectively 'lost' although still allocated memory).

What is required is to *overload* the assignment operator = so that an assignment expression will copy the contents of the array pointed to by data, not the value of data. The following function (which is a member of class string) would overload = to assign an object of class string to another object of the same type:

```
void operator=(const string &str)        // overload = to assign one object to another
{
    strcpy(data, str.data);                  // copy string from object
}
```

The parameter to operator= is a string object (passed by reference for efficiency and const qualified so that it cannot be altered). The assignment:

```
    string2 = string1;                       // assign string1 to string2
```

is translated by the compiler into the function call:

```
    string2.operator=(string1);              // assign string1 to string2
```

This copies the characters stored in the array pointed to by string1.data into the array pointed to by string2.data.

In line 46 of Program 34.2 the member function string::store was used to store a null terminated character string in a string object, i.e.:

```
    string1.store("hello John Doe");         // store in string1
```

The = operator could be overload (again) to carry out this operation, e.g.:

```
void operator=(const char *str)          // overload = to assign a string to an object
{
    strcpy(data, str);                       // copy string
}
```

In this case the parameter is a pointer to an array of char. The statement:

```
    string1 = "hello john doe";
```

is translated by the compiler into the function call:

```
    string1.operator=("hello john doe");
```

This copies the string "hello john doe" into the array pointed to by string1.data

The header file stringp.h (next page but one) contains a more sophisticated version of the class string used in Program 34.2. The class string is declared in lines 7 to 49 followed by definition of member and friend functions:

line

9   data declaration of private member data, a pointer to array of char

10   data declaration of size which holds the length of the array pointed to by data
          (this value is used by member functions to prevent array overflow)

12   start of public declarations

14   define default constructor (no parameter) which is called to allocate objects
          defined without a parameter, arrays, etc. Initially an array of one character is
          allocated (which may be extended later using the = operator).

16-17   define constructor, parameter specifies the array length

19-24   define constructor, parameter points to a string

26-31   define constructor, parameter is a string object to be copied into new object

33   define destructor, deletes data

36   define inline member function length, returns the length of the array allocated

37	define inline member function strlen, returns number of characters stored in array
38	declare prototype of *virtual* function read (*virtual* is discussed in section 34.7)
41	declare member function prototype to overload =, assign a string to a string object
42	define member function to overload =, assign a string object to a string object
	use overloaded function operator= declared in line 41 to assign a string
43	declare friend function prototype to overload +, to concatenate two string objects
44-45	define friend function to overload == operator, compare two string objects
	45 compare strings stored in member data, return non zero (true) if same
46-47	define friend function to overload << operator, output a string object
	47 output array to stream and return stream
48	prototype of friend function to overload >> operator, read a string object
52-58	define virtual member function read which reads a string from cin into array
	54 prompt user
	55 flush white space out of cin (see compiler manual for details)
	56 read a string object from cin using overload >> operator
	note the explicit use of pointer this (see section 34.3.1)
	57 return number of characters read into the array
61-67	overload = operator, assign a character string to a string object
	63 delete existing array pointed to by data
	64 calculate size of array to hold the string (using strlen from <string.h>
	65 allocate array to hold the string being assigned
	66 copy the string into the array pointed to by data
70-75	friend function to overload + operator, concatenate two string objects
	70 takes two string object parameters and returns a string object
	72 define a string object to receive the contents of the parameters
	a constructor will be called to allocate an array of the required size
	73 copy first parameter then concatenate second parameter
	74 return string object (destructor will be called to deallocate array)
78-83	friend function to overload the >> *get from* operator
	80 call stream.get to read at most str.size - 1 characters from stream
	81 discard any remaining characters up to newline
	82 return stream

A string of characters can be read into an object either using the member function read (which displays a prompt) or as part of a cin statement using the overloaded >> operator.

The internal representation of the string is hidden from any function which uses class string with all manipulation being carried out using public member or friend functions. This means that the data structure of class string could be totally altered without having to modify programs which use it, assuming that the public interface remains the same. For example, in class string the member data points to a char array which holds a null terminated string of characters. If the string of characters was read from a database it could be in some other format (e.g. an array of characters with an associated character count). So long as the public member functions maintained the existing interface (translating between the new internal form and that presented to the outside world) any functions which used the class would need no modification (only recompilation).

```
 1 // Header file stringp.h - a class to process strings containing white space
 2
 3 #include <iostream.h>                          /* I/O stream header file */
 4 #include <string.h>
 5
 6 // declare a string type, can contain white space
 7 class string
 8     { // private members
 9         char *data;              // pointer to array of char to hold the string
10         short int size;                              // length of array
11
12     public:
13       // constructor 1, (default) without parameter, set to empty string
14           string() {data = new char[1]; size = 1; data[0] = '\0'; }
15       // constructor 2, with an int parameter specifying length
16           string(int length)
17               {data = new char[length]; size = length; data[0] = '\0';  }
18       // constructor 3, with a string parameter
19           string(char *text)
20               {
21                 size = ::strlen(text) + 1;          // get size of string
22                 data = new char[size];                   // create array
23                 strcpy(data, text);                      // copy string
24               }
25       // constructor 4, with a string object parameter
26           string(const string &str)
27               {
28                 size = ::strlen(str.data) + 1;      // get size of array
29                 data = new char[size];                   // create array
30                 strcpy(data, str.data);                  // copy string
31               }
32       // destructor
33           ~string() { delete data; }                   // delete array
34
35       // member functions
36           int length(void) { return size; }        // return array length
37           int strlen(void) { return ::strlen(data); }  // return string length
38           virtual int read(void);                       // read string
39
40       // overloaded operators, = (string and object) + == << and >>
41           void operator=(const char *str);                  // assign
42           void operator=(const string &str) { *this = str.data; }
43           friend string operator+(const string &str1, const string &str2);
44           friend int operator==(const string &str1, const string &str2)
45                   { return(! strcmp(str1.data, str2.data)); }     // compare
46           friend ostream& operator<<( ostream &stream, const string &str)
47                   { stream << str.data; return stream; }          // output
48           friend istream& operator>>( istream &stream, string &str);
49     };
50
```

Header file stringp.h A class to process strings containing white space

```
51 // member function, read a string into object, use overloaded >> operator
52 int string::read(void)
53 {
54     cout << "\nEnter string (up to " << (size - 1) << " characters) ? ";
55     cin >> ws;                              // remove any white space
56     cin >> *this;                           // read the string
57     return ::strlen(data);                  // return length
58 }
59
60 // member function, overload =, assign a null terminal string to a string object
61 void string::operator=(const char *str)
62 {
63     delete data;                            // delete the old array
64     size = ::strlen(str) + 1;               // get size of new array
65     data = new char[size];                  // create array
66     strcpy(data, str);                      // copy string
67 }
68
69 // friend function, overload + add two string objects return a string object
70 string operator+(const string &str1, const string &str2)
71 {
72     string str(::strlen(str1.data) + ::strlen(str2.data) + 1);   // temp object
73     strcat(strcpy(str.data, str1.data), str2.data);              // build object
74     return str;                             // return object
75 }
76
77 // friend function, overload >> to read a string into a string object
78 istream& operator>>( istream &stream, string &str)
79 {
80     stream.get(str.data, str.size);         // read up to size - 1 characters
81     stream.ignore(1000, '\n');              // discard rest of line
82     return stream;                          // return stream
83 }
```

Header file stringp.h A class to process strings containing white space

Program 34.4 (next page) shows some examples of the use class string:

line
7   shows the definition of four string objects using the four different constructors.
9-14   shows the use of various functions to print the lengths of the arrays allocated, the
           number of characters stored in the arrays and the string
16   shows the assignment of a null terminated string to a string object
20   shows the use of the overloaded >> to read a string into string2
25   shows the use of the overloaded == operator to compare two string objects
28   shows the use of the overloaded + and = operators

Line 28 is of particular interest:

```
string1 = string1 + " sam " + string2 + string1 + string3 + " end";
```

When evaluating this expression a constructor is called to create temporary string objects to hold the strings "sam" and "end". The overloaded + operator then concatenates two string objects and returns a string object. Any temporary objects are destructed when the expression is evaluated and the result assigned to string (using the overloaded = operator).

```
1 // Program 34.4   C++ program using class string
2
3 #include "stringp.h"                                    // class string functions
4
5 int main(void)
6 {
7       string  string1, string2(40), string3(" string 3 "), string4(string3);
8
9       cout << "\nString1 " << string1.length() << " " << string1.strlen();
10      cout << "\nString2 " << string2.length() << " " << string2.strlen();
11      cout << "\nString3 " << string3.length() << " " << string3.strlen()
12           << " " << string3;
13      cout << "\nString4 " << string4.length() << " " << string4.strlen()
14           << " " << string4;
15
16      string1 = "string1";
17      cout << "\nString1 " << string1.length() << " " << string1.strlen()
18           << " " << string1;
19
20      cin >> string2;
21      cout << "\nString2 " << string2.length() << " " << string2.strlen()
22           << " " << string2;
23
24      // compare the strings, print message indicating if same
25      if (string1 == string2) cout << "\n\n    string1 = string2";
26      else                    cout << "\n\n    string1 != string2";
27
28      string1 = string1 + " sam " + string2 + string1 + string3 + " end";
29      cout << "\nString1 " << string1.length() << " " << string1.strlen()
30           << " " << string1;
31 }
```

Program 34.4 C++ program using class string

34.6 Derived classes

Another important concept in object orientated programming is the 'reuse' of code and data via *inheritance* by which a new object inherits the features of an existing object. At a simple level object 'reuse' can be achieved by declaring a class object as a member of another class (just like any other type of variable). Information may be stored in the object and manipulated using public functions. However, *inheritance* means much more in that a new object inherits data, function and operator members from an existing class thus saving implementation of facilities which are common to both.

In C++ inheritance is achieved by *deriving* a new class from an existing *base* class. Features of the base class can be added to or altered to form the new class thus facilitating the building of a hierarchy of classes. Consider, for example, the class string (described in previous sections) which provided storage for a character string (which includes white space) and functions to maintain and manipulate the string. A slight variation may be a requirement for a class to store and manipulate strings which do not contain white spaces, i.e. individual words which may be used to build up a sentence to be stored as a string. Many of the operations required to support such a type already exist in class string and the approach to take would be to derive the new type from class string. Program 34.5 (next page) shows a simple version of class word:

3   include "stringp.h" which contains the declaration of class string
6   class word: public string declares class word which is derived from class string
10-12   define constructors for class word which use the corresponding constructors from class string
14   prototype for member function read (which overloads read in class string)
16   prototype for friend function to overload >> *get from* operator
21-26   definition of member function read
           23   prompt user to enter a word
           24   use overloaded >> operator to read a word into *this
           25   call string::strlen to return length of string read
29-35   define function operator>> to overload the >> *get from* operator
           31   define an array of char to hold the characters read
           32   read characters framed by white space from stream into text
                when reading a character string (array of char) with >> any initial white space is skipped and then characters read up to the next white space
           33   use overloaded = operator to assign the character string to the word object
           34   return the stream identifier
39   define some string objects using the various string constructors
40   define some word objects using the various word constructors
42-44   read and print a string object (characters terminated by newline)
46-48   read and print a word object (characters framed by white space)

The class word *inherits* all the members of class string which it has access too, i.e.:

1   If a derived class has no constructors the default constructor of the base class will be used when defining objects without parameters (similarly the base class destructor).
2   The member functions length, strlen and read become members of class word (class word then overloads read with its own version)
3   The overloaded operators =, +, ==, << and >> (class word then overloads >> with its own version of operator>>).

Note that class word cannot access the private members of class string (unless it is declared as a *friend* in class string). Thus it has to call the function string::strlen in line 25 to determine the length of the string whereas the function ::strlen from <string.h> can be called directly from class string (line 57 if Header File stringp.h).

String and word objects may be mixed in an expression such as (using the operators overloaded in class string):

    word1 = "start " + word1 + string1 + " end";

In practice, the = and + operators would probably be overloaded in class word to take account of the special properties of word objects (which should contain no white space).

```
 1 // Program 34.5  C++ program, class word derived from class string
 2
 3 #include "stringp.h"
 4
 5 // declare a word type, i.e. a string containing no white space
 6 class word: public string                   // word is derived from class string
 7     {
 8       public:
 9          // constructors using equivalent ones from class string
10             word():string() {}
11             word(int length):string(length) {}
12             word(char *text): string(text) {}
13          // overload member function read (in class string)
14             virtual int read(void);
15          // overload >> operator, read a string up to white space
16             friend istream& operator>>( istream &stream, word &str);
17      };
18
19 // member function, read a word into object, use overloaded >> operator
20 //    overload virtual read function in class string
21 int word::read(void)
22 {
23     cout << "\nEnter word (up to " << (length() - 1) << " characters) ? ";
24     cin >> *this;                            // read string up to white space
25     return strlen();                                       // return length
26 }
27
28 // friend function, overload >> operator to read a word
29 istream& operator>>( istream &stream, word &str)
30 {
31     char text[80];                           // array to read string into
32     stream >> text;                          // read string framed by white space
33     str = text;                              // assign string to object
34     return stream;                           // return stream
35 }
36
37 int main(void)
38 {
39     string  string1, string2(80), string3("hello");   // define string objects
40     word  word1, word2(80), word3("hello");            // define word objects
41
42     cout << "\nenter string (terminated by newline) ? ";
43     cin >> string2;
44     cout << "\nstring2 " << string2.strlen() << " |" << string2 << "|";
45
46     cout << "\n\nenter word (framed by white space) ? ";
47     cin >> word2;
48     cout << "\nword2 "  << word2.strlen() << " |" << word2 << "|";
49     return 0;
50 }
```

Program 34.5 C + + program, class word derived from class string

A run of program 34.5 was:

```
enter string (terminated by newline) ?       hello john doe      ↲
string2 24 |      hello john doe       |

enter word (framed by white space) ?       hello john doe      ↲
word2 5 |hello|
```

34.7 Virtual functions

Consider the following statements involving string and word objects:

```
string string1(80), *p_string = &string1;      // define string object and pointer
word word1(80), *p_word = &word1;               // define word object and pointer

string1.read();                                 // read a string including white space
word1.read();                                   // read a string framed by white space
```

The expression string1.read() would call the function string::read (from class string) and the expression word1.read() would call word::read (overloaded in class word). The compiler determines which version of read to call from the type of the corresponding object. The call is set up at compile time and is said to be *statically bound* to the object.

Now consider using the pointers to the objects (p_string initialised to point to string1 and p_word initialised to point to word1):

```
p_string->read();                               // read a string including white space
p_word->read();                                 // read a string framed by white space
```

The first statement would call the function string::read (from class string) and the second statement would call word::read (overloaded in class word), as one would expect.

The problem which arises is that a pointer to a particular type of object may also point to objects derived from the class. Thus the pointer p_string is not only able to point to string objects, it may also point to word objects (because class word is derived from class string), e.g.:

```
p_string = &word1;                              // point p_string to word
p_string->read();                               // read, string or word ??
```

Which version of read would be called string::read or word::read ? If string::read had not been declared as a virtual function it would be called (non virtual function calls are statically bound at compile time). However, string::read is declared as virtual in stringp.h and the function called would be word::read.

With virtual functions the binding of the object to the function does not take place until run time (called *dynamic binding*). The run time system determines from the type of the object being processed which function should be called. Member functions which may be overloaded in derived classes should be declared to be virtual in the base class and the property then applies in any derived classes (they don't need to be declared virtual in derived classes but it is recommended for documentation purposes).

```
37 int main(void)
38 {
39     string  string1(80), *p_string = &string1;      // string object & pointer
40     word   word1(80), *p_word = &word1;             // word object & pointer
41
42     p_string->read();                               // read a string object
43     cout << "\np_string " << p_string->strlen() << " |" << *p_string << "|";
44
45     p_word->read();                                 // read a word object
46     cout << "\np_word "  << p_word->strlen() << " |" << *p_word << "|";
47
48     p_string = &word1;                              // point p_string to word1
49     p_string->read();                               // read, string or word ??
50     cout << "\np_string " << p_string->strlen() << " |" << *p_string << "|";
51 }
```

Program 34.6 C++ program, using pointers to objects (lines 1 to 35 as Program 34.5)

Program 34.6 demonstrates the use of pointers to string and word objects (as discussed above). A run of the program was:

```
Enter string (up to 79 characters) ?      hello john doe      ↲
p_string 19 |hello john doe     |
Enter word (up to 79 characters) ?      hello john doe      ↲
p_word 5 |hello|
Enter word (up to 5 characters) ?
p_string 4 |john|
```

It can be seen that:

1   line 42 calls string::read which skips initial white space (line 55 of Header file stringp.h) and then reads characters up to newline (line 56 of Header file stringp.h).
2   Lines 45 and 49 call word::read to read characters framed by white space.

Although line 49 is using the pointer p_string (defined as a 'pointer to string'), p_string actually points to word1 (assigned in line 48) and, because string::read is a virtual function, word::read is called.

C++ summary

This overview of C++ has necessarily been very brief. In summary the C++ aggregate type *class* provides support for important concepts in object orientated programming:

An object   The encapsulation of data declarations and the functions which operate upon the data into an integrated entity.

data hiding The private and public members of a class object promote data hiding:

    private: access is restricted to those functions which really need it;

    public: provides the interface between the object and the functions which use it.

inheritance A new object inherits the features of an existing object.

Problem for Chapter 34

Implement the student records system of Chapter 22.5 using class objects.

Appendix A

The ASCII character code

0	00	NUL		32	20	SP		64	40	@		96	60	`
1	01	SOH		33	21	!		65	41	A		97	61	a
2	02	STX		34	22	"		66	42	B		98	62	b
3	03	ETX		35	23	#		67	43	C		99	63	c
4	04	EOT		36	24	$		68	44	D		100	64	d
5	05	ENQ		37	25	%		69	45	E		101	65	e
6	06	ACK		38	26	&		70	46	F		102	66	f
7	07	BEL		39	27	'		71	47	G		103	67	g
8	08	BS		40	28	(		72	48	H		104	68	h
9	09	HT		41	29	)		73	49	I		105	69	i
10	0A	LF		42	2A	*		74	4A	J		106	6A	j
11	0B	VT		43	2B	+		75	4B	K		107	6B	k
12	0C	FF		44	2C	,		76	4C	L		108	6C	l
13	0D	CR		45	2D	-		77	4D	M		109	6D	m
14	0E	SO		46	2E	.		78	4E	N		110	6E	n
15	0F	SI		47	2F	/		79	4F	O		111	6F	o
16	10	DLE		48	30	0		80	50	P		112	70	p
17	11	DC1		49	31	1		81	51	Q		113	71	q
18	12	DC2		50	32	2		82	52	R		114	72	r
19	13	DC3		51	33	3		83	53	S		115	73	s
20	14	DC4		52	34	4		84	54	T		116	74	t
21	15	NAK		53	35	5		85	55	U		117	75	u
22	16	SYN		54	36	6		86	56	V		118	76	v
23	17	ETB		55	37	7		87	57	W		119	77	w
24	18	CAN		56	38	8		88	58	X		120	78	x
25	19	EM		57	39	9		89	59	Y		121	79	y
26	1A	SUB		58	3A	:		90	5A	Z		122	7A	z
27	1B	ESC		59	3B	;		91	5B	[		123	7B	{
28	1C	FS		60	3C	<		92	5C	\		124	7C		
29	1D	GS		61	3D	=		93	5D	]		125	7D	}
30	1E	RS		62	3E	>		94	5E	^		126	7E	~
31	1F	US		63	3F	?		95	5F	_		127	7F	DEL

In the above table the columns are decimal and hexadecimal numeric ASCII character code value followed by the character. The characters below 32 decimal (20 hexadecimal) are non-printing control characters, e.g.:

BEL   bell: rings the keyboard bell or buzzer
BS   backspace: move back one character width
HT   horizontal tabulate: move horizontally to next tabulate position
LF   line feed: move page vertically one character height
CR   carriage return: move to start of current line
ESC   escape: used in many systems as a program control character
SP   space: move horizontal by one character width

Appendix B

Answers to the Exercises

Exercise 5.1 (page 28)

1   The program when executed should give the following result:

        `radius = 2.000000, area = 12.566370, radius check = 2.000000`

2   If the `#include <math.h>` is missing the program will either crash on the call to `sqrt` or return incorrect results. For example, a run using Turbo C Version 1.01 printed the following:

        `radius = 2.000000, area = 12.566370, radius check = -32736.000000`

If the compiler failed to warn of missing math function prototypes when compiling the warnings are probably switched off. Switch them on !

3   Replace line 15 of Program 5.1 with the following:

        `printf(" converted %d \n", printf(", radius check = %f \n", radius_check));`

The `int` function result returned by the first call to `printf` is used as the parameter to another call to `printf` to display the number of characters printed (`%d` is the `int` conversion specification). This is an instance of a general rule of C that anywhere where it is permissible to use the value of a variable (of some type) an expression (of the same type) may be used. The modified program should then print:

        `radius = 2.000000, area = 12.566370, radius check = 2.000000`
        `converted 27`

Indicating that `printf(", radius check = %f \n", radius_check)` printed 27 characters.

Exercise 5.2 (page 32) Modify Program 5.3.

In the evaluation of lines 16 and 17 of Exercise 5.2 (next page) the results of previous calculations are used. This saves execution time but must be used with care, e.g. if an equation is altered it then affects all following calculations which use its result. In line 21 the maths function `pow(x, 1.0/3.0)` is used to evaluate the cube root.

    If the `&` is removed from before the variable name `radius` in the call to `scanf` in line 13 of Exercise 5.2 the value of `radius` will be passed instead of its address (which scanf needs to return the value read from the keyboard). What happens is implementation dependent. For example, a run using Microsoft C printed the following:

`Enter radius of circle (real number) ? 2.0`
`radius = 0.000000, area = 0.000000, radius check = 0.000000`
`run-time error R601`
` -null pointer assignment`

Microsoft C initialises variables to 0 and the error message indicates that `scanf` received a null or zero pointer (pointers are covered in Chapter 23).

```
 1 /* Exercise 5.2 - read radius of circle/sphere calculate circle area,     *
 2  *  sphere area & sphere volume and recalculate radius from sphere volume   */
 3
 4 #include <stdio.h>
 5 #include <math.h>
 6
 7 int main(void)
 8 {
 9     const float pi = 3.1415926f;
10     float radius, circle_area, sphere_area, sphere_volume, radius_check;
11
12     printf("Enter radius of circle (real number) ? ");
13     scanf("%f", &radius);                              /* read radius */
14     circle_area = pi * radius * radius;                /* circle area */
15     printf("radius = %f, \n    circle area   = %f", radius, circle_area);
16     sphere_area   = circle_area * 4.0f;                /* sphere area */
17     sphere_volume = sphere_area * radius / 3.0f;       /* sphere volume */
18     printf("\n    sphere area   = %f", sphere_area);
19     printf("\n    sphere volume = %f\n", sphere_volume);
20     /* recalculate radius from sphere volume */
21     radius_check = pow(3.0f * sphere_volume / (4.0f * pi), 1.0f / 3.0f);
22     printf("    radius check  = %f \n", radius_check);
23     return 0;
24 }
```

Exercise 5.2 Calculate circle area, sphere area and volume and recalculate radius

Exercise 6.1 (page 38)

MS-DOS batch file to execute a program and indicate success or failure.

```
rem Exercise 6.1 - execute program and indicate success or failure
%1
IF ERRORLEVEL 1 GOTO fail
   rem program successful
   goto exit
:fail
   rem program failed
:exit
```

The name of the program is passed as the first parameter %1 of the batch file. After program execution the ERRORLEVEL value is tested for being success, 0, or failure (the ERRORLEVEL value is returned to the operating system by the C statement return n;). The control statement IF ERRORLEVEL 1 GOTO fail branches to label fail if ERRORLEVEL is greater than or equal to 1.

Exercise 9.1 (page 54) A run of Program 9.1 should give:

```
i + j * k;   = 20
(i + j) * k; = 60
i + (j * k); = 20
i * j / k;   = 4
(i * j) / k; = 4
i * (j / k); = 0
```

Exercise 9.2 (page 55)

Program (below) to calculate the average of six numbers. Two runs were:

```
Enter up to six numbers terminate with a $ ? 1.0 2.0 3.0 4.0 5.0 6.0↵
  Average of 6 numbers = 3.500000
```

```
Enter up to six numbers terminate with a $ ? 1.0 2.0 3.0 $↵
  Average of 3 numbers = 2.000000
```

Consider line 15 of Exercise 9.2:

```
    number = scanf("%f%f%f%f%f%f", &x1, &x2, &x3, &x4, &x5, &x6);
```

scanf can read up to six float values the number of successful conversions being assigned to number. Note that line 11 initialises the six float variables to 0 to ensure that any values not converted are 0. Line 18 then calculates the average of the six numbers:

```
    average = (x1 + x2 + x3 + x4 + x5 + x6) / number;
```

```
 1 /* Exercise 9.2 - to calculate the average of a sequence of real numbers    *
 2 *      maximum six numbers, input terminated by an invalid character        */
 3
 4 #include <stdio.h>
 5
 6 int main(void)
 7 {
 8     float x1, x2, x3, x4, x5, x6, average;
 9     int number;
10
11     x1 = x2 = x3 = x4 = x5 = x6 = 0.0f;                 /* initialise to 0 */
12     printf("\nEnter up to six numbers terminate with a $ ? ");
13
14     /* read up to six numbers, getting number converted correctly */
15     number = scanf("%f%f%f%f%f%f", &x1, &x2, &x3, &x4, &x5, &x6);
16
17     /* calculate average (will crash if number = 0) */
18     average = (x1 + x2 + x3 + x4 + x5 + x6) / number;
19     printf("\n  Average of %d numbers = %f ", number, average);
20     return 0;
21 }
```

Exercise 9.2 Calculate the average of up to six numbers

Exercise 10.1 (page 63) Assembly listing of Program 10.1

The assembly listing file p10_1.asm (next page) was generated using the Turbo C compiler:

```
    tcc -A -S -f287 p10_1.c
```

The listing includes lines of the C program followed by the assembly language code (Intel 8086 family) generated.   The assembly listing file has been edited to show the assignment statements only and the comments to the right have been added to clarify the operations. Assembly language listings of C programs can be useful when looking for ways of making a program more efficient or when finding faults in low-level code. Clearly one has to understand the assembly language of the machine concerned.

```
;    char_2 = char_1;
;
mov         al,byte ptr DGROUP:_char_1              copy char_1 to char_2
mov         byte ptr DGROUP:_char_2,al             no integral promotion
;
;    char_3 = char_1 + 1;
;
mov         al,byte ptr DGROUP:_char_1              copy char_1 into al
cbw                                                 integral promotion to int
inc         ax                                      add 1 (int)
mov         byte ptr DGROUP:_char_3,al             copy al (byte) to char_3
;
;    int_i = long_i + int_i;
;
mov         ax,word ptr DGROUP:_int_i               copy int_1 to ax
cwd                                                 convert to long int
mov         bx,word ptr DGROUP:_long_i+2            copy long_i into bx & dx
mov         cx,word ptr DGROUP:_long_i
add         cx,ax                                   add least significant word
adc         bx,dx                                   add most significant word
mov         word ptr DGROUP:_int_i,cx               copy least significant word to int_i
;                                                     dropping most significant word
;    float_value = float_value + int_i;
;
mov         ax,word ptr DGROUP:_int_i               copy int_i
mov         word ptr [bp-2],ax
FILD        word ptr [bp-2]                         convert to float
FADD        dword ptr DGROUP:_float_value           add float_value
FSTP        dword ptr DGROUP:_float_value           result to float_value
;
;    double_value = double_value - float_value;
;
FLD         dword ptr DGROUP:_float_value           copy float_value
FSUBR       qword ptr DGROUP:_double_value          add double_value
FSTP        qword ptr DGROUP:_double_value          result to double_value
;
;    ldouble_value = ldouble_value + float_value;
;
FLD         dword ptr DGROUP:_float_value           copy float_value
FLD         tbyte ptr DGROUP:_ldouble_value         copy ldouble_value
FADD                                                add
FSTP        tbyte ptr DGROUP:_ldouble_value         result to ldouble_value
;
;    float_value = ldouble_value + float_value;
;
FLD         dword ptr DGROUP:_float_value           copy float_value
FLD         tbyte ptr DGROUP:_ldouble_value         copy ldouble_value
FADD                                                add
FSTP        dword ptr DGROUP:_float_value           result to float_value
```

Partial assembly listing of Program 10.1 using the Turbo C compiler

Exercise 11.1 (page 68) Modifications to Program 11.1.

Removing the ; on the end of line 12 gave the following error using Microsoft C:

```
    13    else
***** P11_1.C(13) : error C2143: syntax error : missing ';' before 'else'
```

Replacing the == operator in line 11 with = gives the following warning with Microsoft C:

```
    11    if (ch = EOF)
***** P11_1.C(11) : warning C4206: assignment within conditional expression
```

indicating that the conditional expression of the if contains an assignment; which might be correct or not (discussed in Chapter 11.3).

Exercise 11.2 (page 75) Modification of Program 11.4 to use functions from <ctype.h>.

The character test functions in <ctype.h> return *true* if the character is a member of the set. For example, to read a character and test if it is a digit:

```
printf("Please enter a character ? ");
ch = getchar();
if (isdigit(ch))
    printf("\n Character %c is a digit \n", ch);
.....
```

Exercise 11.2 is a sequence of such tests.

```
 1 /* Exercise 11.2 - read a character and check for           *
 2  *     EOF (end of file), digit, lower or upper case, etc.   */
 3
 4 #include <stdio.h>
 5 #include <ctype.h>
 6
 7 int main(void)
 8 {
 9     int ch;
10
11     printf("Please enter a character ? ");
12     ch = getchar();
13     if (ch == EOF)
14         printf("\n end of file found \n");
15     else
16         if (isdigit(ch))
17             printf("\n Character %c is a digit \n", ch);
18         else
19             if (isupper(ch))
20                 printf("\n Character %c is upper case \n", ch);
21             else
22                 if (islower(ch))
23                     printf("\n Character %c is lower case \n", ch);
24                 else
25                     printf("\n Character %c is other letter \n", ch);
26     return 0;
27 }
```

Exercise 11.2 Read a character and check for EOF, digit, lower or upper case, etc.

Exercise 12.1 (page 78)

```
 1 /* Exercise 12.1 - read a decimal number terminate on non digit character */
 2
 3 #include <stdio.h>
 4 #include <ctype.h>
 5
 6 int main(void)
 7 {
 8     int number = 0, ch;
 9
10     printf("Enter decimal integer (non digit character to terminate) ? ");
11     while (isdigit(ch = getchar()))
12         number = number * 10 + (ch - '0');
13     printf("\nNumber = %d\n", number);
14     return 0;
15 }
```

Exercise 12.1 Read a decimal number terminate on non digit character

Lines 11 and 12 are a while executed while the character read using getchar is a digit in the range '0' to '9'. If it is a digit the numerical value, calculated by subtracting the character code for '0' from the character, is added to the existing value times 10.

Exercise 12.2 (page 79)

In Exercise 12.2 (next page) lines 11 to 35 are a do statement which reads decimal numbers until EOF is entered. Consider lines:

13 declare and initialise variables local to the do (reallocated on every iteration)
15 prompt for user input
17-21 a for statement which checks for a preceding + or - sign
   19 if - was entered set negative *true*
   20 call getchar to replace the + or - character
24-30 a do statement executed until EOF or **white space** is entered
   26-27   if the character is a digit in the range '0' to '9' add to current number*10
   28   read another character
32 if the first character was a - make number negative
33 print the value of number

Consider line 17:

```
    if (((ch = getchar()) == '-') || (ch == '+'))
```

In an expression using a binary logical operator such as && or || C guarantees that the operands will be evaluated from **left to right** (after any precedence, see Chapter 11.5). In addition, if the final result of the expression can be determined from the value of the operand on the left, the operand on the right will not be evaluated. Thus:

	(a) ch = getchar() reads the next character assigning it to ch,
and	(b) if the character was '-' lines 18 to 21 are executed,
otherwise	(c) (ch == '+') is evaluated and if true lines 18 to 21 are executed,
otherwise	(d) execution continues at line 24.

Hence the character is read and then the tests carried out. If the order of evaluation was not specified for binary logical operations the expression (ch == '+') could be evaluated before ((ch = getchar()) == '-') and the program would not work correctly.

```
 1  /* Exercise 12.2 - read signed decimal numbers until EOF entered       *
 2   *       ignore invalid characters, terminate number on white space       */
 3
 4  #include <stdio.h>
 5  #include <ctype.h>
 6
 7  int main(void)
 8  {
 9      int ch;
10
11      do
12          {
13          int number = 0, negative = 0;                 /* declare and initialise */
14
15          printf("Enter signed decimal integer (space to terminate) ? ");
16          /* test for a preceding + or - character */
17          if (((ch = getchar()) == '-') || (ch == '+'))
18              {
19              if (ch == '-') negative = 1;              /* indicate negative */
20              ch = getchar();                            /* replace ch */
21              }
22
23          /* read characters until white space or EOF */
24          do
25              {
26              if (isdigit(ch))
27                  number = number * 10 + (ch - '0');    /* add digit */
28              ch = getchar();
29              }
30          while ((ch != EOF) && (! isspace(ch)));
31
32          if (negative) number = - number;              /* negative ? */
33          printf("\nNumber = %d\n", number);
34          }
35      while (ch != EOF);                                /* terminate on EOF */
36      return 0;
37  }
```

Exercise 12.2 Read signed decimal numbers until EOF entered

Note:

1   In line 13 the internal variables number and negative are declared and initialised (the
    variables are reallocated on every entry to the for loop and deallocated on exit)

2   The do statement in lines 24 to 30 is entered with ch containing a character read in
    line 17 or 20 (if the first character was - or +). On each iteration of the do a new
    value is read in line 28. Invalid characters are ignored in the input of the number.

Exercise 13.1 (page 92)

Exercise 13.1 (below and on next page) displays a bouncing ball using the Turbo C graphics package (Turbo C 1991). The program sequence is:

10	define integral constants for size of circle and size of ball movement.
11	declare variables used by initgraph
12-14	declare variables used in ball movement
15-16	declare variables used in time period calculations
19	call initgraph to initialise the graphics system (see below)
20-24	if the result of graphresult was not grOK (graphics OK) display error report
	22 grapherrormsg(graphdriver) returns a pointer to an error message string
27-29	count the number of loops a while performs in one second (see below)
33-34	read the maximum x and y coordinates
35-36	draw a white box around the edges of the screen
39-54	a do statement loops until the keyboard is hit
	kbhit is a Turbo C function which returns *true* when a key is hit
41-42	draw circle at current position in white
43-44	delay for a period of time (see below)
45-48	if the ball has hit the edge of the screen reverse its movement
49-50	redraw circle position in black (to erase the circle drawn in lines 41 and 42)
51-52	calculate next drawing position

When a key is hit the do terminates and line 55 closes the graphics system.

The purpose of the delay (lines 43 and 44, a for loop counting i from 0 to time_count/20), is to slow down the movement of the ball so that it moves at a reasonable pace. Because machines execute instruction at different speed time_count is evaluated (lines 27 to 29) by counting the number of while loops performed in one second (Program 12.3 describes the clock function). The magnitude of time_count is proportional to the speed of the processor concerned and when used in the delay loop gives a similar speed of ball movement on all machines (it is not exactly the same because the remainder of the do statement in lines 45 to 54 takes different times to execute on different machines).

In line 19 initgraph initialises the graphics system. The first parameter specifies the graphics driver to use and the second parameter the mode of the driver. In the above example graphdriver is set to DETECT (defined in <graphics.h>) which will automatically detect what sort of graphics card is fitted (graphmode is not used in this case). The third parameter is the pathname to the directory containing the Turbo C graphics driver files. The function initgraph returns information indicating any error condition or, if successful, what driver was found. In the case of an error graphresult() != grOk the function grapherrormsg(graphdriver) returns a pointer to a string containing an error message (which is printed by scanf using the %s conversion specification).

```
1  /* Exercise 13.1 - Bouncing ball program using Turbo C graphics */
2
3  #include <graphics.h>                    /* for graphics library functions */
4  #include <stdio.h>
5  #include <conio.h>
6  #include <time.h>
7
```

```
 8 int main(void)
 9 {
10     enum {Circle_size = 20, Move_size = 5 };                /* define constants */
11     int graphdriver = DETECT, graphmode, i;
12     int x = 150, y = 100,            /* current position of ball on the screen */
13         x_move = Move_size, y_move = Move_size,         /* x & Y movements */
14         maxx, maxy;                                      /* screen size */
15     long int time_count = 0;                   /* holds loop time counter */
16     clock_t  clock_start;                      /* holds clock start time */
17
18     /* Initialize graphics system */
19     initgraph(&graphdriver, &graphmode, "c:\tc\bgi");
20     if (graphresult() != grOk)
21         {
22         printf("initgraph failed: %s ", grapherrormsg(graphdriver) );
23         return 1;                                /* failed, return */
24         }
25
26     /* count loops for one second, used to time bouncing ball on the screen */
27     clock_start = clock();
28     while (((clock() - clock_start) / CLOCKS_PER_SEC) < 1)
29         time_count++;
30     printf("\ntime_count = %ld ", time_count);
31
32     /* get the size of the screen and draw a box around the edges */
33     maxx = getmaxx();
34     maxy = getmaxy();
35     setcolor(WHITE);                              /* set colour white */
36     rectangle(0, 0, maxx, maxy);                  /* draw box aound screen */
37
38     /* loop bouncing ball around the screen */
39     do
40         {
41         setcolor(WHITE);                          /* draw ball in white */
42         circle(x, y, Circle_size);
43         for (i = 0 ; i < time_count/20 ; i++)      /* show ball on screen */
44             /* null for delay */;
45         if (x > maxx - Circle_size) x_move = -Move_size;  /* change direction *
46         if (x < Circle_size) x_move = Move_size;
47         if (y > maxy - Circle_size) y_move = -Move_size;
48         if (y < Circle_size) y_move = Move_size;
49         setcolor(BLACK);                          /* delete old ball */
50         circle(x, y, Circle_size);
51         x = x + x_move;                           /* calculate new x & y */
52         y = y + y_move;
53         }
54     while (! kbhit());
55     closegraph();
56     return 0;
57 }
```

Exercise 13.1 Bouncing ball program using Turbo C graphics

Exercise 15.1 (page 104) Function to read a binary number.

```
 1 /* Exercise 15.1 - call a function to read binary numbers */
 2
 3 #include <stdio.h>
 4 #include <ctype.h>
 5
 6 main(void)
 7 {
 8     long int read_binary(void);                        /* function prototype */
 9     int ch;                                   /* holds last character read */
10     long int n;                                  /* holds number read */
11
12     do                                      /* read until EOF found */
13         {
14         printf("\n Enter binary number ? ");
15         n = read_binary();                           /* read number */
16         if (isspace(ch = getchar()))
17             printf("Value was %ld, %#lo, %#lx \n", n, n, n);     /* number OK */
18         else
19             printf("\nInvaid character %c %d ", ch, ch);          /* error ! */
20         }
21     while (ch != 0);                            /* if EOF terminate */
22     return 0;
23 }
24
25 /*----------------------------------------------------------------*
26  * Function to read a binary number from the keyboard              *
27  *    terminate input when character read was not 0 or 1           *
28  *    leave last character read in the input stream with EOF as 0  *
29  * Parameters none                                                 *
30  * Function result: value of number read as a long int            *
31  *----------------------------------------------------------------*/
32 long int read_binary(void)                           /* function header */
33 {
34     long int n = 0;                         /* holds number while reading */
35     int  ch;                                /* holds character read */
36
37     while (((ch = getchar()) == '0') || (ch == '1'))    /* read a 0 or 1 ? */
38         n = n * 2 + (ch - '0');                 /* if so add bit to value */
39     if (ch == EOF) ch = 0;                       /* replace EOF with 0 */
40     ungetc(ch, stdin);                        /* unget last character */
41     return n;                                  /* return number */
42 }
```

Exercise 15.1 Call a function to read a binary number

Exercise 15.1 is composed of function main plus function read_binary:

line

8   long int read_binary(void); a function prototype indicating that read_binary has no parameters and returns a long int function result

9-10   declare variables local to main

12-21   a do statement executed until EOF is entered on the keyboard (read_binary leaves the last character read in the input stream with EOF represented by 0)

        14 prompt the user to enter a binary value

        15 call read_binary assigning function result to variable n

        16 read last character (number terminator) from input stream and if it was:

            white space: line 17 print value of n

            otherwise: line 19 print error message with faulty character

32   long int read_binary(void) is the function header

34-35   declare variables local to read_binary (created on each call and lost on exit)

37-38   a while statement executed while the character read was '0' or '1'

        38 add value of bit to current n * 2

39   if last character was EOF replace it with 0 (ready for ungetc)

40   push last character read back into the input stream stdin (keyboard input)

41   return the value of n as a function result

The read_binary function terminates when the character entered is not a '0' or '1'. The character is then pushed back into the input stream in line 40 (EOF cannot be pushed back into the input stream using ungetc so it is replaced in line 39 with 0). The calling function can read the character to check if the number was terminated correctly with white space, or an invalid character or EOF was entered.

The use of getchar and the || in line 37 is similar that in line 17 of Exercise 12.2:

            (a) ch = getchar() reads the next character assigning it to ch

and   (b) if the character was '0' line 38 is executed, i.e. n = n * 2 + (ch - '0');

otherwise   (c) (ch == '1') is evaluated and if true line 38 is evaluated

otherwise   (d) the while terminates.

Hence the character is read and then the tests carried out. If the order of evaluation was not specified (ch == '1') could be evaluated before ((ch = getchar()) == '0') and the program would not work correctly.

Exercise 15.2 (page 108) Function to read a binary number.

The program of Exercise 15.2 (next page) is similar to that of Exercise 15.1. The variable number is passed to read_binary using *call by reference* in line 15 (the function result indicates success/failure in a similar way to scanf). The function read_binary uses the pointer number to return the number read:

31   int read_binary(long int *const number) is the function header

33-34   declare variables local to read_binary (created on each call and lost on exit)

36-37   a while statement executed while the character read was '0' or '1'

        37 add value of bit to current n * 2

39-43   if the last character entered was white space:

        41 return value entered using pointer number

        42 return function result (non zero) indicating success

44   if last character was EOF return EOF as a function result

45   push last character read back into the input stream stdin (keyboard input)

46   return function result (zero) indicating failure

Note that the value of the variable pointed to is not changed unless the terminator is white space.

```
 1 /* Exercise 15.2 - call function to read a binary value (call by reference) */
 2
 3 #include <stdio.h>
 4 #include <ctype.h>
 5
 6 main(void)
 7 {
 8     int read_binary(long int *const);                /* function prototype */
 9     int result;                              /* holds result of function */
10     long int n;                                  /* holds number read */
11
12     do                                       /* read until EOF found */
13         {
14         printf("\n Enter binary number ? ");
15         if ((result = read_binary(&n)) == 1)              /* read number */
16             printf("Value was %ld, %#lo, %#lx \n", n, n, n);    /* number OK */
17         else
18             if (result == 0)
19                 printf("\nInvaid character %c ", getchar());     /* error ! */
20         }
21     while (result != EOF);                           /* if EOF terminate */
22     return 0;
23 }
24
25 /*-------------------------------------------------------------------------*
26  * Function to read a binary number from the keyboard                      *
27  *   terminate input when character read was not 0 or 1                    *
28  *   if last character is invalid leave in input stream                    *
29  * Parameters out:  number (long int) number read                         *
30  * Function result: 1 if number OK, 0 for error, EOF on EOF               */
31 int read_binary(long int *const number)              /* function header */
32 {
33     long int n = 0;                          /* holds number while reading */
34     int  ch;                                 /* holds character read */
35
36     while (((ch = getchar()) == '0') || (ch == '1'))      /* read a 0 or 1 ? */
37         n = n * 2 + (ch - '0');                  /* if so add bit to value */
38
39     if (isspace(ch))                         /* now check last character entered */
40         {                                    /* it was white space */
41         *number = n;                             /* return number */
42         return 1;                                /* indicate success */
43         }
44     if (ch == EOF) return EOF;                       /* was it EOF ? */
45     ungetc(ch, stdin);                       /* invalid, unget last character */
46     return 0;                                    /* and return failure */
47 }
```

Exercise 15.2 Call a function to read a binary number using call by reference

Exercise 17.1 (page 126) Function to generate pseudo random numbers.

```
1 /* Exercise 17.1 - Pseudo random numbers using static internal variables     */
2
3 #include <stdio.h>
4 #include <time.h>
5
6 int main(void)
7 {
8     float random_number(void);                          /* function prototype */
9     int i;
10
11     for (i=0; i < 10 ; i++)
12         printf("\n %10f", random_number());             /* print next number */
13     return 0;
14 }
15
16 /*------------------------------------------------------------------*
17  * Return pseudo random number in the range 0 to 1.0                */
18 float random_number(void)
19 {
20     static short int initialised = 0;     /* indicates if seed is initialised */
21     static unsigned int random_seed;         /* holds random number seed */
22
23     if (! initialised)
24         {
25         /* Initialise pseudo random number generator:                */
26         /*  To start with a 'random' seed set seed to the current time  */
27         random_seed = (unsigned int) time(NULL);
28         initialised = 1;                      /* indicated initialised */
29         }
30
31     /* calculate next value of seed and return value */
32     random_seed = (unsigned int) ((25173UL * random_seed + 13849UL) % 65536UL);
33     return ((float) random_seed / 65535.0);
34 }
```

Exercise 17.1   Pseudo random numbers using static internal variables

The sequence of statements in function random_number in Exercise 17.1 is:

20   declare static internal variable initialised, giving it the initial value 0 (false)
21   declare static internal variable random_seed
23-29   if variable initialised is 0 (false) initialise the seed
         27 initialise the seed using the current time
         28 indicate that the seed has been initialised, i.e. set initialised to true
32   calculate the next value in the pseudo random sequence
33   return the number as a float in the range 0 to 1.0

Hence on the first call to random_number the seed variable random_seed is initialised from the current time. Note that there is really no need to initialise variable initialised to 0 in line 20, i.e. being static internal it will automatically be initialised to 0. Explicitly initialising it to 0, however, emphasises its function and clarifies the code.

Exercise 18.1 (page 140) Function to sort the contents of an array.

```
 1 /*-------------------------------------------------------------------*
 2  * function to sort the contents of an array                        */
 3 void array_sort(float array[], const int number)
 4 {
 5     int index_1, index_2;                          /* array index values */
 6
 7     /* look at each element of the array in turn */
 8     for (index_1 = 0 ; index_1 < number - 1; index_1++)
 9         {
10         float minimum = array[index_1];            /* holds minimum value */
11
12         /* scan remainder of array looking for minimum value */
13         for (index_2 = index_1 + 1 ; index_2 < number ; index_2++)
14             if (array[index_2] < minimum)
15                 {
16                 minimum = array[index_2];           /* found new minimum */
17                 array[index_2] = array[index_1];    /* swap values */
18                 array[index_1] = minimum;
19                 }
20         }
21 }
```

Exercise 18.2 Sort the contents of an array (main is similar to Program 18.2)

The sequence of statements in function array_sort is:

3   void array_sort(float array[], const int number) the function header
8-20   a for incrementing index_1 from 0 to number-2
        10   declare minimum and initialise it to the value of array[index_1]
        13-19   a for incrementing index_2 from index_1+1 to number-1
               14   if array[index_2] < current minimum
                    reset minimum and swap array[index_1] and array[index_2]

There is no need for the outer for loop, line 8, to look at the last element. It should already contain the maximum value when the for terminates. A run of the program which read an array of up to ten values, called function array_sort and then printed the result was:

```
Enter up to 10 numbers (<CR> to end)
    ? 12 6 7 3 15 10 18 5 ↲
    12.000      6.000      7.000      3.000     15.000
    10.000     18.000      5.000

     3.000      5.000      6.000      7.000     10.000
    12.000     15.000     18.000


Enter up to 10 numbers (<CR> to end)
    ? ↲
```

Exercise 19.1 (page 152) Functions to search and compare strings.

```
 1 /* Exercise 19.1 - string search and compare functions */
 2
 3 #include <stdio.h>
 4
 5 int main(void)
 6 {
 7       int str_search(const char string_1[], const char string_2[], int index);
 8       int str_compare(const char string_1[], const char string_2[]);
 9       char text_1[30], text_2[30];                    /* strings to search */
10
11       while (printf("\n\nEnter first string ? "), gets(text_1) != NULL)
12           {
13           printf("Enter second string ? ");
14           if (gets(text_2) != NULL)                   /* read string, exit if EOF */
15               {
16               int index = -1;                         /* search from index = 0 */
17
18               printf("Index positions of %s = ", text_2);
19               while ((index = str_search(text_1, text_2, ++index)) >= 0)
20                     printf("\n%d %s ", index, &text_1[index]);
21               if (str_compare(text_1, text_2) == 0)
22                     printf("\n\n%s and %s are identcal ", text_1, text_2);
23               else
24                   if (str_compare(text_1, text_2) < 0)
25                         printf("\n\n%s < %s  ", text_1, text_2);
26                   else
27                         printf("\n\n%s > %s  ", text_1, text_2);
28               }
29           }
30       return 0;
31 }
```

Exercise 19.1   String search and compare functions (continued on next page)

The sequence of statements in function main is:
11   call gets to read the first string text_1
14   call gets to read the second string text_2
16   initialise index to first element of array - 1
19-20   a while calling str_search to search for next occurrence of text_2 in text_1
            the while terminates when text_2 is not found (-1 returned)
        20 if text_2 is found print value of index and text_1 from index
            &text_1[index] passes the address of a particular element
21-27   a sequence of if statements calling str_compare
        22 print message if text_1 equals text_2
        25 print message if text_1 less than text_2
        27 print message if text_1 greater than text_2

Lines 11 and 14 are examples of the use of gets. Remember that gets performs no bound checking and in practice fgets should be used !

```
32
33  /*-----------------------------------------------------------------*
34   * search string for a string                                      *
35   * on entry string_1[]   contains string to search                 *
36   *          string_2[]   contains string to search for             *
37   *          index        index to position to start search         *
38   * return function result: index position if found -1 if not found */
39  int str_search(const char string_1[], const char string_2[], int index)
40  {
41      while(string_1[index] != '\0')                    /* look for '\0' */
42          {
43          if (string_1[index] == string_2[0])       /* first character found ? */
44              {
45              int i = 0;                            /* yes, check rest of string_2 */
46
47              do
48                  if (string_2[++i] == '\0') return index;   /* string_2 found */
49              while (string_1[index + i] == string_2[i]);
50              }
51          index++;                                  /* not found, try again */
52          }
53      return -1;                                    /* not found, return fail */
54  }
55
56  /*-----------------------------------------------------------------*
57   * Compare two strings (similar to library function strcmp)         *
58   *  return 0 if equal, >0 if string1 > string2 , <0 if string1 < string2  */
59  int str_compare(const char string_1[], const char string_2[])
60  {
61      int index = -1;
62
63      /* loop looking for terminating nulls */
64      do
65          {
66          index ++;                                 /* index to next character */
67          if (string_1[index] > string_2[index]) return 1;       /* return > 0  */
68          /* character in string_1 <= string_2, if not the same return < 0 */
69          if (string_1[index] != string_2[index]) return -1;     /* return < 0 */
70          /* strings identical so far, check next character */
71          }
72      while ((string_1[index] != '\0') && (string_2[index] != '\0'));
73      /*printf("\n %s %s", string_1, string_2);*/
74      return 0;                                      /* strings are identical return 0 */
75  }
```

Exercise 19.1   String search and compare functions (continued from previous page)

Discussion of program continued on next page

The sequence of statements in `string_search` is:

```
39      int str_search(const char string_1[], const char string_2[], int index)
            is the function header with the formal parameters:
            string_1 the character array to search
            string_2 the character array to search for
            index the index position to start search from
            The function returns the index if the string is found or -1 if not found
41-52   while which terminates when '\0' is found in string_1
    43      check if current character in string_1 is the first character in string_2
        44-50   characters the same, compare rest of string_2
            48  if terminator of string_2 has been found return result index
            49  continue do if characters in string_1 and string_2 are the same
    51      string_2 not found, test next character in string_1
53  string_2 not found, return with -1
```

The function `str_compare` compares two strings `string_1` and `string_2` and returns 0 if they are equal, >0 if `string1` > `string2` and <0 if `string1` < `string2`. The do statement, lines 64 to 72, tests in turn each character in `string_1` against the corresponding character in `string_2`:

1   line 67: if `string1[index]` > `string2[index]`, if the value of the character in `string1` > `string2` the function returns with value > 0

2   line 69: if `string1[index]` != `string2[index]`, if the value of `string1` < `string2` the function returns with value < 0

3   otherwise the characters are the same and the loop tests the next character after incrementing `index`

4   line 74 is executed if `string_1` and `string_2` are identical and 0 is returned

A run of the program was:

```
Enter first string ? abc abc abc abc ↓
Enter second string ?  ↓
Index positions of ab =
0 abc abc abc abc
4 abc abc abc
8 abc abc
12 abc

abc abc abc abc > ab

Enter first string ? alex ↓
Enter second string ? alan ↓
Index positions of alan =

alex > alan

Enter first string ? alan ↓
Enter second string ? alex ↓
Index positions of alex =

alan < alex

Enter first string ? alan ↓
Enter second string ? alan ↓
Index positions of alan =
0 alan

alan and alan are identcal

Enter first string ? ^Z ↓
```

Exercise 23.1 (page 204) Pointers and the increment operator.

```
 1 /* Exercise 23.1  Using pointers with the increment operator */
 2
 3 #include <stdio.h>
 4
 5 int main(void)
 6 {
 7     int i;                                        /* case select value */
 8
 9     for (i = 1 ; i < 7 ; i++ )
10        {
11        int x[] = { 10, 20, 30, 40, 50 },          /* five element array */
12            *p_array = &x[2],                     /* pointer to third element */
13            array_index;                           /* general index */
14
15        printf("\n *p = %d, ", *p_array);
16        switch (i)
17           {
18           case 1: printf("*++p    = %d, ", *++p_array); break;
19           case 2: printf("++*p    = %d, ", ++*p_array); break;
20           case 3: printf("*p++    = %d, ", *p_array++); break;
21           case 4: printf("(*p)++ = %d, ", (*p_array)++); break;
22           case 5: printf("*++p = 500, "); *++p_array = 500; break;
23           case 6: printf("*p++ = 500, "); *p_array++ = 500; break;
24           /*case 7: printf("++*p = 500, "); ++*p_array = 500; break;
25           case 8: printf("(*p)++ = 500, "); (*p_array)++ = 500; break;*/
26           }
27        printf("p - x = %d, array = ", p_array - x);
28        for (array_index = 0 ; array_index < 5 ; array_index++)
29            printf(" %3d", x[array_index]);
30        }
31     return 0;
32 }
```

Exercise 23.1 Using pointers with the increment operator

A for statement, lines 9 to 30, is executed six times with the various valid combinations of the indirection and increment operators operating upon the array x. On every iteration the array x is recreated and initialised (line 11) and the pointer p_array pointed at the third element.   The switch statement, lines 16 to 26, selects the operation to be performed; note that lines 24 and 25, which would generate errors, are commented out. The following is a print of a run under Turbo C:

```
*p = 30, *++p    = 40, p - x = 3, array =   10  20  30  40  50
*p = 30, ++*p    = 31, p - x = 2, array =   10  20  31  40  50
*p = 30, *p++    = 30, p - x = 3, array =   10  20  30  40  50
*p = 30, (*p)++ = 30, p - x = 2, array =   10  20  31  40  50
*p = 30, *++p = 500, p - x = 3, array =   10  20  30 500  50
*p = 30, *p++ = 500, p - x = 3, array =   10  20 500  40  50
```

1   *p = the value of the element p_array points to before the operation
2   *++p (etc.) the value of the element p_array points to after the operation
3   p - x the element of x that p_array points to after the operation
4   array = the values stored in the array after the operation

Exercise 24.1 (page 214) Functions to search and compare strings (using pointers).

```
 1 | /* Exercise 24.1 - string search and compare functions */
 2 |
 3 | #include <stdio.h>
 4 |
 5 | int main(void)
 6 | {
 7 |     char *str_search(char *string_1, char *string_2);
 8 |     int str_compare(const char *string_1, const char *string_2);
 9 |     char text_1[30], text_2[30];                    /* strings to search */
10 |
11 |     while (printf("\n\nEnter first string ? "), gets(text_1) != NULL)
12 |         {
13 |         printf("Enter second string ? ");
14 |         if (gets(text_2) != NULL)               /* read string, exit if EOF */
15 |             {
16 |             char *p_char = text_1;
17 |
18 |             printf("Index positions of %s = ", text_2);
19 |             while ((p_char = str_search(p_char, text_2)) != NULL)
20 |                 printf("\n %s ", p_char++);
21 |             if (str_compare(text_1, text_2) == 0)
22 |                 printf("\n\n%s and %s are identcal ", text_1, text_2);
23 |             else
24 |                 if (str_compare(text_1, text_2) < 0)
25 |                     printf("\n\n%s < %s  ", text_1, text_2);
26 |                 else
27 |                     printf("\n\n%s > %s  ", text_1, text_2);
28 |             }
29 |         }
30 |     return 0;
31 | }
```

Exercise 24.1   String search and compare functions (continued on next page)

The sequence of statements in string_search is:

38   char *str_search(char *string_1, char *string_2)
                is the function header with the formal parameters:
                string_1 points to the string to search
                string_2 points to the string to search for
            If string2 is found a pointer to its position in string_1 is returned else NULL
40-52   while which terminates when '\0' is found in string_1
            42   check if current character in string_1 is the first character in string_2
                43-50   characters the same, compare rest of string_2
                        48   if terminator of string_2 return pointer to position in string_1
                        49   continue do if characters in string_1 and string_2 are the same
            51   string_2 not found, increment pointer to test next character in string_1
53   string_2 not found, return NULL

The function str_compare compares two strings string_1 and string_2 and returns 0 if they are equal, >0 if string1 > string2 and <0 if string1 < string2. The do statement, lines 64 to 72, tests in turn each character in string_1 against the corresponding character in string_2:

1   line 67: if (*string_1 > *string_2)   (value of character pointed to by string1 is greater than that pointed to by string2, return with value > 0

2   line 69: if (*string_1 != *string_2) (characters are not equal) return with value < 0

3   otherwise the characters are the same and the loop tests the next character

4   line 73 is executed if string_1 and string_2 are identical and 0 is returned

```
32
33 /*-------------------------------------------------------------------*
34  * search string for a string                                       *
35  * on entry string_1     points to string to search                 *
36  *           string_2    pointer to string to search for            *
37  * return function result: pointer if found, NULL if not found       */
38 char *str_search(char *string_1, char *string_2)
39 {
40     while(*string_1 != '\0')                        /* look for '\0' */
41         {
42         if (*string_1 == *string_2)           /* first character found ? */
43             {
44             char *p_char1 = string_1,
45                   *p_char2 = string_2;        /* yes, check rest of string_2 */
46
47             do
48                 if (*++p_char2 == '\0') return string_1;   /* string_2 found */
49             while (*++p_char1 == *p_char2);
50             }
51         string_1++;                             /* not found, try again */
52         }
53     return NULL;                            /* not found, return fail */
54 }
55
56 /*-------------------------------------------------------------------*
57  * Compare two strings (similar to library function strcmp)          *
58  *   return 0 if equal, >0 if string1 > string2 , <0 if string1 < string2   */
59 int str_compare(const char *string_1, const char *string_2)
60 {
61     int index = -1;
62
63     /* loop looking for terminating nulls */
64     do
65         {
66         index ++;                               /* index to next character */
67         if (*string_1 > *string_2) return 1;           /* return > 0  */
68         /* character in string_1 <= string_2, if not the same return < 0 */
69         if (*string_1 != *string_2) return -1;         /* return < 0 */
70         /* strings identical so far, check next character */
71         }
72     while ((*string_1++ != '\0') && (*string_2++ != '\0'));
73     return 0;                               /* strings are identical return 0 */
74 }
```

Exercise 24.1   String search and compare functions (continued from previous page)

Exercise 25.1 (page 219) Passing parameters to a C program.

```
1 /* Exercise 25.1 -  Print parameters passed from operating system to main */
2
3 #include <stdio.h>
4 #include <string.h>
5
6 /*---------------------------------------------------------------------*
7  * function main with parameters                                       *
8  *   argc - number of elements in array argv                           *
9  *   argv - an array of pointers to strings                            */
10 int main(int argc, char *argv[])
11 {
12     char **p_to_argv;
13
14     printf("\nNumber of parameters in command line is %d", argc);
15     for (p_to_argv = argv ; *p_to_argv != NULL ; p_to_argv++)
16         {
17         printf("\n parameter is %s ", *p_to_argv);
18         if (strcmp(*p_to_argv,"-lower") == 0)
19             printf("  option -lower found ! ");
20         if (strcmp(*p_to_argv,"-upper") == 0)
21             printf("  option -upper found ! ");
22         }
23     return 0;
24 }
```

Exercise 25.1 Print parameters passed from operating system to main

The sequence of statements in Exercise 25.1 is:

10	define main with parameters argc and argv
12	define p_to_argv a pointer which points to a pointer to char
14	print number of parameters, i.e. value of argc
15-22	a for statement incrementing p_to_argv from argv until a NULL is found

       17 print current parameter (%s expects a pointer to a string)
       18 if current parameter is string -lower
          19 print appropriate message
       20 if current parameter is string -upper
          21 print appropriate message

Thus p_to_argv is a pointer to argv the elements of which point to the strings from the command line:

*p_to_argv   accesses a particular element of argv
**p_to_argv would access the character that the pointer argv points to

Thus the first character of the parameter may be printed:

```
    printf("\n first character of parameter is %c ", *p_to_argv[0]);
```

or:

```
    printf("\n first character of parameter is %c ", **p_to_argv);
```

Exercise 27.1 (page 235) Program to copy one text file to another.

```
 1 /* Exercise 27.1    Text file copy program, e.g. to copy file_1 to file_2:    *
 2  *    ex27_1  file_1 file_2 -options                                           *
 3  * options: -upper and -lower to convert characters to upper and lower case   */
 4
 5 #include <stdio.h>
 6 #include <string.h>
 7 #include <ctype.h>
 8
 9 int main(int argc, char *argv[])
10 {
11     FILE *in_file, *out_file;                /* input and output file pointers */
12     int ch,                                  /* holds character being transferred */
13         convert = 0;        /* if = 1 convert to upper case, = 2 to lower case */
14
15     if (argc < 3)                            /* check for filenames in command line */
16         {
17         printf("\nInsufficent parameters ");
18         return 1;
19         }
20
21     /* open input file, first parameter of command line */
22     printf("\nOpening input file '%s' ", argv[1]);
23     if ((in_file = fopen(argv[1], "r")) == NULL)
24         {
25         perror(" failed");                   /* open fail, print error message */
26         return 1;
27         }
28
29     /* open output file, second parameter of command line */
30     printf("\nOpening output file '%s' ", argv[2]);
31     if ((out_file = fopen(argv[2], "w")) == NULL)
32         {
33         perror(" failed");                   /* open fail, print error message */
34         fclose(in_file);                            /* close the input file */
35         return 1;
36         }
37
38     printf("\nFiles opened OK");
39     if (argc == 4)                                      /* check for options */
40         if(strcmp(argv[3], "-upper") == 0)
41             {
42             printf("\nConverting text to upper case ");
43             convert = 1;                          /* set upper case indicator */
44             }
45         else
46             if(strcmp(argv[3], "-lower") == 0)
47                 {
48                 printf("\nConverting text to lower case ");
49                 convert = 2;                      /* set lower case indicator */
50                 }
```

```
52     while ((ch = getc(in_file)) != EOF)                    /* read character */
53        {
54        if (convert)
55           ch = (convert == 1) ? toupper(ch) : tolower(ch);
56        putc(ch, out_file);                                 /* write character */
57        }
58
59     fclose(in_file);                                       /* close the input file */
60     fclose(out_file);                                      /* close output file */
61     printf("\nCopy complete");
62
63     return 0;
64 }
```

Exercise 27.1   Program to copy a text file

The sequence of statements in Exercise 27.1 is:

15-19   check that sufficient parameters were entered on command line, if not terminate
22-27   attempt to open input file, if fail print message and terminate
30-36   attempt to open output file, if fail print message, close input file and terminate
39   if command line contains four parameters
      40-44   check for option -upper
      46-50   check for option -lower
52-57   a while reading characters from in_file until EOF is found
      54 if converting to upper or lower case
          55 select toupper or tolower to convert the character
      56 write the character to the output file
59-63   close files and terminate

Exercise 27.2 (page 238) Program to copy one file to another (binary or text file).

The code for a binary file copy program is similar to Exercise 27.1 with the following modifications:

1   Lines 12 and 13 are remove and replaced with:

```
unsigned char size, data[100];          /* holds byte data being transferred */
```

2   The fopen calls (lines 23 and 31) open the files in binary mode (mode "rb" and "wb")

3   Lines 39 to 50 are removed.

4   Lines 52 to 57 (which copy the file contents) are replaced with:

```
while (! feof(in_file))                             /* copy data until EOF found */
   {
   size = fread(data, 1, 100, in_file);             /* read a block of data */
   if (ferror(in_file))                             /* read error ? */
      { perror("\nerror reading file"); break; }    /* yes, abort ! */
   fwrite(data, 1, size, out_file);                 /* write block out */
   if (ferror(out_file))                            /* write error ? */
      { perror("\nerror writing file"); break; }    /* yes, abort ! */
   }
```

This reads and writes 100 byte blocks of the file until EOF is found. Error checks are performed on read and write with break used to abort the while if an error occurs.

Exercise 29.1 (page 246)

Run of the quicksort program:

```
Enter up to 10 numbers (<CR> to end)
   ? 1  3  2   4  3  4  5  1  3  8↵
      1.000       3.000      2.000     4.000      3.000
      4.000       5.000      1.000     3.000      8.000
Partitioned array
      1.000       3.000      2.000     1.000      3.000
      4.000       5.000      4.000     3.000      8.000
Partitioned array
      1.000       1.000      2.000     3.000
Partitioned array
      1.000       1.000      2.000
Partitioned array
      1.000       2.000
Partitioned array
      3.000       4.000      5.000     4.000      8.000
Partitioned array
      3.000       4.000
Partitioned array
      4.000       5.000      8.000
Partitioned array
      5.000       8.000
Sorted array
      1.000       1.000      2.000     3.000      3.000
      3.000       4.000      4.000     5.000      8.000
```

```
 1  /* Exercise 29.1 -  sort an array using quicksort                    */
 2
 3  #include <stdio.h>
 4
 5  int main(void)
 6  {
 7      int array_read(float array[], const int max_index);        /* prototypes */
 8      void array_write(float *array, const int number);
 9      void array_qsort(
10            float array[], const int left_index, const int right_index);
11
12      float  data[20];
13      int index;
14
15      while ((index = array_read(data, 10)) >  0)            /* terminate on EOF */
16          {
17          array_write(data, index);
18          array_qsort(data, 0, index-1);                    /* sort the array */
19          printf("\nSorted array ");
20          array_write(data, index);                         /* and print it */
21          }
22      return 0;
23  }
```

Exercise 29.1   Sort an array using quicksort (continued on next page)

```
24
25 /*-----------------------------------------------------------------------*
26  * function (recursive) to sort the contents of an array - use quicksort    *
27  *  sort array contents from array[left] to array[right]                    */
28 void array_qsort(float array[], const int left, const int right)
29 {
30     void array_write(float *array, const int number);
31     int up, down;                                    /* array index values */
32     float x, temporary;                              /* working variables */
33
34     x = array[(left + right) / 2];          /* pick element half way between */
35     up = left;                                   /* scan up the array from left */
36     down = right;                             /* scan down the array from right */
37     /* scan up and down array */
38     do
39         {
40         while (array[up] < x) up++;                      /* find element >= x */
41         while (array[down] > x) down--;                  /* find element <= x */
42
43         if (up <= down)
44             {                              /* exchange array[up] and array[down] */
45             temporary = array[up];
46             array[up] = array[down];
47             array[down] = temporary;
48             up++;
49             down--;
50             }
51         }                          /* continue process of scanning up and down */
52     while (up <= down);
53     printf("\nPartitioned array ");                  /* print partitioned array */
54     array_write(&array[left], right - left + 1);
55
56     /* scan complete array partitioned into two sets: lower <= x & upper >= x */
57     if (left < down)  array_qsort(array, left, down);     /* sort lower set */
58     if (up < right) array_qsort(array, up, right);        /* sort upper set */
59 }
```

Exercise 29.1   Sort an array using quicksort (continued from previous page)

The print statements in lines 53 and 54 are used to show the progress of the sort. They would be removed when the program is fully tested.

Appendix C The standard library

The ANSI C standard defines a standard library which contains a range of functions and macros to support programs implemented in C.   A number of *standard header files* contain *type definitions* (see Chapter 17.8), *macro definitions* (see Chapter 26.1) and *function prototypes declarations* (see Chapter 15.3):

<assert.h>	<ctype.h>	<errno.h>	<float.h>	<limits.h>
<locale.h>	<math.h>	<setjmp.h>	<signal.h>	<stdarg.h>
<stddef.h>	<stdio.h>	<stdlib.h>	<string.h>	<time.h>

A *standard header file* is included in the program using the preprocessor directive:

```
#include <name.h>
```

This appendix briefly describes most of the functions (refer to system and compiler manuals for full details).   In addition many C compilers provide a range of extra facilities, e.g. low level system dependent I/O, graphics support, etc.

C.1 Diagnostics <assert.h>

The assert macro is used to aid diagnostics in a program:

```
void assert(int expression);
```

if expression is zero when assert is called a diagnostic message such as:

```
Assertion failed: expression, file filename, line number
```

will be printed on stderr and then abort() called to terminate program execution.

C.2 Character tests <ctype.h>

The header file <ctype.h> declares a set of functions for testing a character parameter:

```
int isalpha(int);           /* a letter of the alphabet 'a' to 'z' or 'A' to 'Z' */
int isupper(int);                      /* an upper case letter 'A' to 'Z'*/
int islower(int);                      /* a lower case letter 'a' to 'z' */
int isdigit(int);                             /* a digit '0' to '9' */
int isxdigit(int);      /* a hexadecimal digit '0' to '9', 'a' to 'f' or 'A' to 'F' */
int isspace(int);        /* white space: space, newline, carriage return and tabs */
int ispunct(int);            /* printing character except space, letter or digit */
int isalnum(int);            /* letter or digit, i.e. isalpha or isdigit is true */
int isprint(int);                 /* any printing character including space */
int isgraph(int);                 /* any printing character except space */
int iscntrl(int);                          /* a control character */
```

The character is passed to the function as an int (promoted as required) and the function returns *true* (non zero) if the condition is satisfied otherwise *false* (zero).   These functions are typically implemented as macros (examine the file ctype.h for details) but are also available as true functions (see Chapter 26.4).

In addition <ctype.h> contains the following functions which convert to upper or lower case:

```
int toupper(int);               /* if lower case letter convert to upper case */
int tolower(int);               /* if upper case letter convert to lower case */
```

If the character in not an upper or lower case letter it is returned intact.

C.3 Errors <errno.h>

The header file <errno.h> defines the identifier errno together with macros which are used to report error conditions. If an error condition occurs when executing a library function, the function sets up a system dependent integer error number in errno (errno is usually an external variable of type int). For example, two values commonly used by the mathematical functions in <math.h> are:

```
#define EDOM    33              /* Maths function domain error, see <math.h> */
#define ERANGE  34              /* Maths function range error, see <math.h> */
```

The numeric values defined by the macros are system dependent. The program can call the function perror (in <stdio.h>) and strerror in <string.h> to print a meaningful message associated with the value.

C.4 Implementation defined floating point limits <float.h>

<float.h> contains macros which define implementation dependent floating point constants. The following are the minimum magnitudes; larger may be used in practice:

```
#define FLT_RADIX      2                   /* radix of exponent representation */
#define FLT_ROUNDS                   /* floating point rounding mode for addition */
#define FLT_DIG        6                   /* float decimal digits of precision */
#define FLT_MANT_DIG   24              /* number of FLT_RADIX digits in mantissa */
#define FLT_EPSILON    1E-5       /* smallest number x such that 1.0 + x ≠ 1.0 */
#define FLT_MIN        1E-37         /* minimum normalised floating point number */
#define FLT_MAX        1E+37                  /* maximum floating point number */
#define FLT_MAX_EXP            /* maximum n such that FLT_RADIX$^n$ is representable */
#define FLT_MIN_EXP           /* minimum n such that 10$^n$ is a normalised number */
#define DBL_DIG        10                  /* double decimal digits of precision */
#define DBL_MANT_DIG              /* number of FLT_RADIX digits in mantissa */
#define DBL_EPSILON    1E-9       /* smallest number x such that 1.0 + x ≠ 1.0 */
#define DBL_MIN        1E-37         /* minimum normalised floating point number */
#define DBL_MAX        1E+37                  /* maximum floating point number */
#define DBL_MAX_EXP           /* maximum n such that FLT_RADIX$^n$ is representable */
#define DBL_MIN_EXP           /* minimum n such that 10$^n$ is a normalised number */
```

C.5 Implementation defined limits <limits.h>

<limits.h> contains macros which define implementation dependent integral limits. The following values are the minimum magnitudes; larger may be used in practice:

```
#define CHAR_BIT        8               /* number of bits in a character */
#define CHAR_MAX        127 or 255              /* maximum value of a char */
#define CHAR_MIN        (-128) or 0             /* minimum value of a char */
#define SCHAR_MAX       127              /* maximum value of signed char */
#define SCHAR_MIN       (-128)      /* minimum value of signed character */
#define UCHAR_MAX       255            /* maximum value of unsigned char */
#define SHRT_MAX        32767              /* maximum value of short int */
#define SHRT_MIN        -32767             /* minimum value of short int */
#define USHRT_MAX       65535     /* maximum value of unsigned short int */
#define INT_MAX         32767                    /* maximum value of int */
#define INT_MIN         -32767                   /* minimum value of int */
#define UINT_MAX        65535           /* maximum value of unsigned int */
#define LONG_MAX        2147483647          /* maximum value of long int */
#define LONG_MIN        -2147483647         /* minimum value of long int */
#define ULONG_MAX       4294967295 /* maximum value of unsigned long int */
```

C.6 Localisation `<locale.h>`

The header file `<locale.h>` contains program constructs which can be used to set or access properties suitable for the current locale, i.e. application or country specific. See compiler manuals for details.

C.7 Mathematical functions `<math.h>`

The `<math.h>` header file contains the following prototypes for the mathematical functions:

```
double  acos(double x);                  /* cos⁻¹(x) range 0 to π, x range -1 to 1 */
double  asin(double x);               /* sin⁻¹(x) range -π/2 to π/2, x range -1 to 1 */
double  atan(double x);                      /* tan⁻¹(x) range -π/2 to π/2 */
double  atan2(double y, double x);         /* tan⁻¹(y/x) range -π to π */
double  ceil(double x);               /* smallest integer greater than x */
double  cos(double x);                        /* cosine of x (radians) */
double  cosh(double x);                    /* hyperbolic cosine of x */
double  exp(double x);                   /* exponential function eˣ */
double  fabs(double x);                       /* absolute value |x| */
double  floor(double x);                  /* largest integer below x */
double  fmod(double x, double y);             /* remainder of x/y */
double  frexp(double x, int *exponent);   /* splits x into mantissa (range [½, 1]) */
                                        /* & exponent of 2: x = mantissa * 2ᵉˣᵖᵒⁿᵉⁿᵗ */
double  ldexp(double x, int exponent);        /* returns x * 2ᵉˣᵖᵒⁿᵉⁿᵗ */
double  log(double x);                    /* natural logarithm ln(x), x > 0 */
double  log10(double x);                  /* base 10 logarithm log₁₀(x), x > 0 */
double  modf(double x, double *ipart);    /* breaks x into integral and fractional */
                                        /* parts, i.e. x = ipart + fraction */
double  pow(double x, double y);          /* returns xʸ, a domain error occurs */
                                        /* if x < 0 and y is not an integer */
double  sin(double x);                        /* sine of x (radians) */
double  sinh(double x);                    /* hyperbolic sine of x */
double  sqrt(double x);                /* square root of x, √x where x ≥ 0 */
double  tan(double x);                        /* tangent of x (radians) */
double  tanh(double x);                    /* hyperbolic tangent of x */
```

The *domain* of a mathematical function is the set of parameter values for which it is defined. If a function is called with a parameter not within its *domain* a *domain error* occurs, errno (defined in `<errno.h>`) is assigned the value EDOM and the function returns with an implementation defined value.

A *range error* occurs when the result of a function cannot be defined as a double; errno is assigned the value ERANGE and the function returns the value HUGH_VAL (defined in `<math.h>`) with the correct sign. If *underflow* (value too small to be represented) occurs zero is returned and errno may be assigned the value ERANGE (system dependent).

C.8 Nonlocal jumps `<setjmp.h>`

The header file `<setjmp.h>` enables the program to make non local jumps, i.e. *goto* another function. See compiler manual for details.

C.9 Signal handling `<signal.h>`

The header `<signal.h>` contains constructs which enable the handling of errors and other exceptional conditions. Typically the following system dependent values are defined:

```
#define SIGINT   2                                        /* interrupt */
#define SIGILL   4                                /* Illegal instruction */
#define SIGFPE   8                     /* floating point trap, e.g. division by 0 */
#define SIGSEGV 11                              /* Memory access violation */
#define SIGTERM 15                            /* asynchronous termination */
#define SIGABRT 22                 /* abnormal termination, initiated by abort() */
```

When a signal occurs the system calls a signal handling function, which has one int parameter which is assigned the signal value (a handling function can process a number of signals). The function signal is used to specify the handling function for a signal:

```
void (*signal(int signal, void (*function)(int))) (int);
```

The prototype specifies that function signal has two parameters:

signal   an integer number specifying the signal number, e.g. SIGINT, SIGPE, etc.;
function   a pointer to the signal handling function

and it returns a pointer to the previous handling function for the signal.

    A number of handlers are usually supplied including SIG_DFL which takes implementation dependent default action and SIG_IGN which ignores the signal.

    In the following code the function call signal(SIGFPE, fp_err) instructs the system to call function fp_err with the parameter SIGFPE when a floating point error occurs, e.g.:

```
void fp_err(int signal)                    /* floating point error signal handler */
{
    printf("floating point error ! \a");
}

int main(void)
{
    float x = 1, y = 0;
    signal(SIGFPE, fp_err);                /* set up handler for floating point error */
    x = x / y;                             /* floating point divide by 0 */
    printf("%f", x);
    return 0;
}
```

When x / y is evaluated a division by 0 occurs and function fp_err is called (with the parameter SIGFPE) and a message displayed. When fp_err terminates execution is resumed following the instruction where the error occurred. To test a signal handling function the function raise sends the specified signal to the environment:

```
int raise(int signal);
```

If a handler is not specified by the program, implementation-defined default behaviour is taken when a signal occurs. By using signal a program may implement its own error processing, enabling orderly error recovery or program termination (the normal error processing may crash the program without orderly closing down files, etc.)

C.10 Variable number of parameters `<stdarg.h>`

The header file `<stdarg.h>` enables the programmer to write functions with a variable number of parameters (such as printf and scanf). See Chapter 25.2 for full details.

C.11 Common definitions <stddef.h>

The header file <stddef.h> contains a number of system dependent, commonly used definitions and macros. For example, the definition of size_t, NULL, etc.

C.12 Standard Input and output <stdio.h>

In C input and output takes place via a *stream* which may be connected to a disk file, the keyboard, the display screen, a serial port, or any other suitable device. Before any input/output operations can take place the stream must be connected to something, e.g. a file on disk opened for input or output. Associated with each open stream is a structure of type FILE (defined in <stdio.h>) which contains information which enables the program to control the flow of information, e.g. pointer to its I/O buffer, pointer to current position in buffer, error indicator, etc. A stream is connected to a device with an *open* operation and disconnected with a *close* operation. When connected the stream name is pointer to a structure of type FILE. When setting up the program run-time environment prior to the start of program execution the following three standard streams: stdin, stdout and stderr are automatically opened (see Chapter 27.1).

C.12.1 Operations on files

```
FILE *fopen(const char *filename, const char *mode);
```

opens a file returning a stream (pointer to FILE) or NULL if an error occurred:

filename: a pointer to a character string which contains the filename in a format acceptable to the operating system.

mode: a pointer to a character string specifying the mode of operation:
   r   opens an existing file for reading
   w   creates a new file for writing (if it already exists its contents are discarded)
   a   opens an existing file for append, information written is appended onto existing data, otherwise a new file is created for writing
   r+ opens an existing file for update (reading and writing)
   w+ creates a new file for update (reading and writing)
   a+ opens an existing file or creates a new file for update and append

The above modes are for opening *text* streams which are used to process character based data, i.e. lines of characters terminated by *newline*. The run time system may need to convert between the external representation of text files and the format acceptable to C, e.g. *newline* may be represented externally by the combination carriage return and line feed. C also supports *binary* streams which are used to process data transferred in machine dependent binary form. For *binary* streams the mode should include the letter b, e.g. rb, wb, wb+, etc.

```
FILE *freopen(const char *filename, const char *mode, FILE *stream);
```

freopen takes the existing stream and associates it with a new file (closing any currently open file), e.g. it is useful to reassign stdin, stdout and stderr.

```
int fclose(FILE *stream);
```

fclose flushes any unwritten data, discards any unread data and closes the file. If successful 0 is returned otherwise EOF if an error occurred.

```
int fflush(FILE *stream);
```

fflush writes any buffered on an output stream (it is ignored for an input stream). If successful 0 is returned or EOF is returned if a write error occurred. fflush(NULL) flushes all output streams.

```
int  remove(const char *filename);
```
removes filename from the file system, returns 0 if successful.

```
int  rename(const char *old_filename, const char *new_filename);
```
renames a file, returns 0 if successful.

```
FILE  *tmpfile(void);
```
creates a temporary file of mode wb+; removed when closed or on program termination.

```
int  setvbuf(FILE *stream, char *buffer, int mode, size_t size);
```
sets up a buffer of size for stream; mode indicates the form of the buffering,
>   _IONBF unbuffered: minimum internal storage is used in an attempt to send or receive
>   data as soon as possible.
>   _IOLBF line buffered: characters are processed on a line by line basis.
>   _IOFBF fully buffered: buffers are flushed when full.

setvbuf must be called before any reading or writing is carried out and fflush may be
called at any time to flush the buffers.

C.12.2 I/O status and error functions

Many of the input/output functions set up indicators in the FILE structure when an
error or EOF (end of file) occurs which can be set and tested using the following
functions:

```
void clearerr(FILE *stream);                /* clear EOF and error indicators */
int feof(FILE *stream);              /* returns non-zero if EOF indicator is set */
int ferror(FILE *stream);            /* returns non-zero if error indicator is set */
```

When an error occurs many of the functions set up an integer error number in errno
(declared in <errno.h>). The function perror prints a program specified string together
with an implementation defined error message corresponding to errno to the stream stderr:

```
void perror(const char *string);          /* print string then error message */
```

C.12.3 File positioning functions

Unless otherwise specified file I/O is sequential. For example, if the sequence read,
flush, write, flush, read, flush, write, flush, read is performed, each successive operation
operates upon the record following the one just processed, i.e. the last read reads data
following the end of the information just written (fflush must be called between each
read/write cycle). The file positioning functions allow the user explicitly to set the
position indicator in the file where the next read/write operation is to be performed.

```
long ftell(FILE *stream);
```
returns the current file position or -1L if an error occurs:
>   **binary stream**: the position is the number of bytes from the start of the file
>   **text stream**: the position is in some internal format and may only be used on a
>   subsequent call to fseek

```
void rewind(FILE *stream);
```
sets the file position indicator to 0

```
int fgetpos(FILE *stream, fpos_t *position);
```
stores the current file position for stream in the object (type fpos_t) pointed to by position
(the value can be used later by fsetpos). If successful it returns 0 else non zero.

```
int fsetpos(FILE *stream, const fpos_t *position);
```

sets the file position for stream to position. If successful it returns 0 else non zero.

```
int fseek(FILE *stream, long offset, int place);
```

sets the file position for stream to offset bytes from place, which may be:

> SEEK_SET beginning of file
> SEEK_CUR current position in file
> SEEK_END end of file

For a text stream offset must be 0 or a value returned by ftell (in which case place must be SEEK_SET). If successful it returns 0 else non zero.

C.12.4 Character input and output

Individual characters may be read and written by:

```
int  fgetc(FILE *stream);                    /* read next character from stream */
int  getc(FILE *stream);                /* macro: read next character from stream */
int  getchar(void);                          /* read next character from stdin */
int  fputc(int char, FILE *stream);          /* write character char to stream */
int  putc(int char, FILE *stream);      /* macro: write character char to stream */
int  putchar(int char);                      /* write character char to stdout */
```

The function ungetc is used to 'push' a character back into the input stream:

```
int  ungetc(int char, FILE *stream);     /* push character back into input stream */
```

Normally a maximum of one character may be pushed back into a stream and it is not possible to push EOF.

C.12.5 String input and output

Null terminated strings (arrays of char) may be printed and read using:

```
char  *fgets(char *string, int n, FILE *stream);   /* read characters from stream */
char  *gets(char *string);                         /* read characters from stdin */
```

string is a pointer to an array of characters:

fgets reads at most n - 1 characters from stream into the array of characters pointed to by string. Reading stops when the newline character is found ('\n' is placed in the string) or when n - 1 characters have been read. A terminating '\0' is appended.

gets reads characters from the standard input stream stdin into the character array pointed to by string until newline '\n' is entered. The newline is replaced by '\0'.

If successful both functions return a pointer to string or the null pointer NULL if EOF was entered. The function gets performs no array bound checking and it is recommended that fgets is used in practice. Note that fgets puts the newline character into the string whereas gets does not.

The string output functions are:

```
int  fputs(const char *string, FILE *stream);      /* write a string to stream */
int  puts(const char *string);          /* write a string plus '\n' to stdout */
```

string points to an array of characters which may be a string constant:

puts writes string (terminated by '\0') to stdout and appends a newline. It returns EOF if an error occurred otherwise some non-negative value.

fputs writes string (terminated by '\0') to stream (a newline is not appended).

See Program 19.1 for an example of the use of string I/O functions.

C.12.6 The *fprintf*, *printf* and *sprintf* function

The standard output functions printf, fprintf and sprintf provide a means of converting the internal machine representation of information into sequences of characters in a format as specified by the program.

```
int fprintf(FILE *stream, const char *format, ...);      /* print to stream */
int printf(const char *format, ...);                     /* print to stdout */
int sprintf(char *string, const char *format, ...);      /* print to "string" */
```

the ... indicates a number of parameters which are processed under the control of the *control string* pointed to by format:

fprintf writes the converted output to the output stream
printf writes the converted output to the output stream stdout
sprintf places the converted output in the character array pointed to by string

The function printf is used to print information to the display screen and fprintf performs a similar function to stream (e.g. a file on disk). The function sprintf is used for conversions within the program (see Chapter 27.5).

The parameter format points to an array of characters, the *control string*, which controls the format of the output. The *control string* contains ordinary characters which are copied to the output and conversion specifications which control the conversion of the corresponding parameters to the output. The *conversion specifications* start with a % and end with a conversion character (e.g. c, s, d, f, p, etc). Between the % and the conversion character there may be (in the following order):

Flags (in any order) which specify:

-	left justification in the field (default is right justify)
+	sign is printed (+ is suppressed by default)
space	if the first character is not a sign a space will be prefixed
0	numeric conversions are padded with leading zeros (leading zeros are suppressed by default)
#	specifies alternate output form:

o	(octal) the first digit will be a 0
x or X	(hexadecimal) a 0x or 0X will prefix a non-zero result
e, E, f, g or G	the output will always have a decimal point
g or G	trailing zeros will not be removed

A number specifying the minimum field width:
The converted parameter will be printed with a minimum field width as specified. If the converted parameter will not fit, the field will be extended as necessary. If the converted parameter has fewer characters than specified it will be padded on the left or right (left by default, right by specifying the - flag). The padding character is normally space unless the zero padding flag is specified.

A period (.) followed by a number specifying the precision:

s	string: specifies the maximum number of characters to be printed
d	the number of digits to be printed (prefixed with zeros as required)
e, E or f	the number of digits to be printed after the decimal point
or G	the number of significant digits

The *field width* or *precision* may be specified as * in which case the numeric value of the next parameter is used (must be an int).

The functions printf, fprintf and sprintf return, as an int function result, the number of characters converted, or a negative value if an error occurred.

Table C.1 shows the printf conversion specifications (if the character following the % is not a conversion specification undefined behaviour occurs).

conversion specification	parameter type	converted to
%c	int	single character (after conversion to unsigned char)
%s	char *	characters for a string terminated by '\0' or until the number of characters specified have been converted
%d or %i	int, short, char	signed decimal notation
%u	int, short, char	unsigned decimal notation
%o	int, short, char	unsigned octal notation (without leading 0)
%x or %X	int, short, char	unsigned hexadecimal notation (without leading 0x or 0X) using abcdef for x & ABCDEF for X
%ld %lu %lx %lo	long int	as above but for long int
%f	float, double	signed decimal real number in form [-]mmm.ddd number of d's specified by precision (default 6), a precision of 0 suppresses the decimal point
%e or %E	float, double	signed decimal real number in form [-]m.dddddе±xx or [-]m.dddddЕ±xx, the number the number of d's is specified by the precision (default 6), a 0 precision suppresses the decimal point
%g or %G	float, double	%e or %E is used if the exponent is less than -4 or greater than the precision otherwise %f is used
%Lf %Le %Lg	long double	as above but for long double real
%p	void *	a pointer in implementation dependent format
%n	int *	the number of characters converted so far are written into the parameter
%		printed as a %

Table C.1 *printf* conversion specifications for integral data types

The information printed by the %p conversion specification is a hexadecimal address, the representation of which is implementation dependent, e.g. depending upon factors such as the architecture of the computer (does it have composite address space like the Motorola 68000 or does it use memory segmentation like the Intel 8086 series), is a memory management unit being used (the addresses printed may be actual physical addresses or addresses within the logical address space of the program), etc. The interpretation of the address printed using %p requires care (see compiler manuals) but can sometimes be useful in tracking down problems with pointers. A linker map can be used to determine the addresses of external identifiers.

C.12.7 The *fscanf*, *scanf* and *sscanf* functions

The standard input functions scanf, fscanf and sscanf provide a means of converting sequences of characters into the internal machine representation of integers, reals, etc.:

```
int fscanf(FILE *stream, const char *format, ...);        /* read from stream */
int scanf(const char *format, ...);                       /* read from stdin */
int sscanf(const char *string, const char *format, ...);  /* read from "string" */
```

the ... indicates a number of parameters which are pointers to variables which will receive the converted values. The conversion process is under the control of the *control string* pointed to by format:

fscanf   read from input stream converting as specified by format
scanf   read from input stream stdin converting as specified by format
sscanf   read from string converting as specified by format

The function scanf is used to read information from the terminal keyboard and fscanf performs a similar function from stream (e.g. from a file on disk). The function sscanf is used for conversions within the program (see Chapter 27.6).

The parameter format points to an array of characters, the *control string*, which controls the conversion of characters from the input into values to be assigned to parameters indicated by .... The control string may contain:

1   Spaces which cause the input stream to be read up to the next non **white space** character (**white space** is the C term for spaces, tabs and newlines).
2   Characters other than **white space** and conversion specifications; the next character in the input stream must match this character.
3   Conversion specifications beginning with % and followed by:
     (a) an optional assignment suppression character *
     (b) an optional number specifying the maximum scan width
     (c) the conversion character(s), see Table C.2.

If converted successfully the value is returned in the variable which is pointed to by the corresponding parameter. If assignment suppression is indicated the corresponding field is skipped (e.g. %*d will skip an integer decimal number in the input stream).

conversion specification	parameter type	converted to
%c	char *	characters are read into the array of char up to the field width (default is 1) '\0' is not appended, white space is not skipped
%s	char *	characters are read into the array of char leading white space is skipped, characters are then read until white space is found, '\0' is then appended
%d	int *	optionally signed decimal integer
%i	int *	optionally signed decimal, octal (with leading 0) or hexadecimal (leading 0x or 0X) integer
%u	int *	unsigned decimal integer
%o	int *	optionally signed octal int (optional leading 0)
%x or %X	int *	optionally signed hexadecimal int (optional 0x)
%hd %hu %ho %hx	short int *	as above, but for data type short int
%ld %lu %lo %lx	long int *	as above, but for data type long int
%f %e %g	float *	signed decimal real number type float: optional sign, string of numbers possibly containing a decimal point, an optional exponent (e or E) followed by an (optionally signed) integer
%lf %le %lg	double *	signed decimal real number type double
%Lf %Le %Lg	long double *	signed decimal real number type long double
%p	void *	pointer in format as printed by printf
%n	int *	returns the number of characters read so far, no input read, conversion count not incremented
[...]	char *	characters matching those in the scanset ... are read into the array of char, reading stops when a character not in ... is read, '\0' is then appended. []...] includes] in the set
[^...]	char *	characters not matching those in the scanset ... are read into the array of char, reading stops when a character in ... is read, '\0' is then appended. [^]...] includes] in the set

Table C.2 *scanf* conversion specifications

The functions return an int function indicating the number of successful conversions:

1   If no conversions occurred 0 is returned.
2   If a matching failure occurs (e.g. a non-numeric character in a decimal number) conversion stops and the number of successful conversions returned (the faulty character is left in the input stream where the program can read it and take action, see Program 11.2).
3   If *end of file* occurs before any conversions the value EOF is returned.

Thus it is possible for all input to be verified and action taken in case of error, e.g. an error message printed and the user prompted for more input (see Chapter 13 Program 13.2).

C.12.8   Unformatted input and output

Unformatted input/output is usually used with binary files (some systems make no distinction between binary and text files):

```
size_t  fread(void *p_data, size_t size, size_t number, FILE *stream);
size_t  fwrite(const void *p_data, size_t size, size_t number, FILE *stream);
```

where:

     p_data   is a pointer to the data to be read or written
     size   specifies the size of the object(s) to be transferred
     number   specifies the number of objects to be transferred
     stream   is a pointer to a structure of type FILE

fread attempts to read number objects of size size from stream returning the data in the array pointed to by p_data. It returns as an int function result the number of objects read (which may be less than the number requested). After calling fread the functions feof and ferror should be called to see if end of file was encountered or an error occurred.

fwrite attempts to write number objects of size size from the array pointed to by p_data to stream. It returns as an int function result the number of objects written (which will be less than number if an error occurred).

See Chapter 27.7 for examples of use.

C.13   Utility functions <stdlib.h>

C.13.1   Dynamic memory allocation

```
void *malloc(size_t size);                  /* allocate one object of size bytes */
void *calloc(size_t number, size_t size);
         /* allocate an array of number objects of size bytes, initialised to 0 */
void *realloc(void *pointer, size_t size);
                   /* reallocate storage pointed to by pointer, make it size bytes */
void free(void *pointer);            /* deallocate storage pointed to by pointer */
```

if successful malloc, calloc and realloc return a pointer to the storage area allocated (which must be *cast* to the required type), otherwise NULL is returned.

C.13.2   Pseudo random number generation

```
int     rand(void);                 /* returns the next pseudo random number */
void    srand(unsigned seed);         /* seeds the random number generator */
```

The default seed is 1 and the number range returned by rand is [0, RAND_MAX] (RAND_MAX is defined as a symbolic constant in <stdlib.h>).

C.13.3 Searching and sorting

```
void qsort(void *array, size_t number, size_t size,
                int (*compare)(const void *, const void *));
```

Using the *quick sort* algorithm (see Chapter 29 Exercise 29.1) sorts array of number elements (each of size bytes) into ascending order using the comparison function compare(). The function compare() has two parameters both of which are pointers to elements of array. The function returns an int less than, equal to or greater than zero depending upon whether the element pointed to by the first parameter is considered less than, equal to or greater than the element pointed to by the second.

```
void *bsearch(const void *key, const void *array, size_t number, size_t size,
                int (*compare)(const void *, const void *));
```

Using a binary search searches array of number elements (each of size bytes) for an element which matches the object pointed to by key. The elements in array must be ascending order with respect to the comparison function compare() (specification as for qsort above).

C.13.4 Integer arithmetic

```
int   abs (int x);                              /* returns absolute value |x| */
long labs(long x);                              /* returns absolute value |x| */
div_t div(int numerator, int denom);            /* divide numerator by denom */
ldiv_t ldiv(long numerator, long denom);        /* divide numerator by denom */
```

div and ldiv return the quotient and remainder in a structure:

```
typedef struct {
                int quot;                       /* quotient */
                int rem;                        /* remainder */
                }
                div_t;
```

C.13.5 String conversion

The following functions convert the contents of string to a numeric value (skipping leading white space). The address of the character which stopped the conversion process is placed in endptr (if endptr is NULL the address is not returned). In the case of strtol and strtoul the base of the number may be specified:

```
double  strtod(const char *string, char **endptr);
long    strtol(const char *string, char **endptr, int radix);
unsigned long strtoul(const char *string, char **endptr, int radix);
```

The following are simplified versions of the above:

```
double  atof(const char *string);
int     atoi(const char *string);
long    atol(const char *string);
```

C.13.6 Communicating with the environment

```
void    abort(void);                        /* abnormal termination of program */
int     atexit(atexit_t function);      /* on abnormal termination execute function */
void    exit(int status);                   /* normal termination of program */
char    *getenv (const char *name);         /* get environment string for name */
int     system(const char *command);        /* pass command to operating system */
```

Function atexit may be used to specify up to 32 functions which will be called on program termination, e.g. to disable interrupts, close down I/O devices, etc.

C.14 String processing functions <string.h>

```
char *strcpy(char *destination, const char *source);
```
copy string source to string destination; return a pointer to destination
```
char *strncpy(char *destination, const char *source, size_t maxlen);
```
copy at most maxlen characters from string source to string destination, return a pointer to destination. If the length of source ≥ maxlen the string in destination will not be null terminated (the programmer must watch out for this !).
```
char *strcat(char *destination, const char *source);
```
concatenate string source onto the end of string destination; return a pointer to destination
```
char *strncat(char *destination, const char *source, size_t maxlen);
```
concatenate at most maxlen characters of string source onto the end of string destination; return a pointer to destination
```
int strcmp(const char *string1, const char *string2);
```
compare string1 with string2; return:
  <0 if string1 < string2, 0 if string1 == string2 and >0 if string1 > string2
```
int strncmp(const char *string1, const char *string2, size_t maxlen);
```
compare at most maxlen characters of string1 with string2; return:
  <0 if string1 < string2, 0 if string1 == string2 and >0 if string1 > string2
```
char *strchr(const char *string, int character);
```
search string for character; if found return pointer to first occurrence else NULL
```
char *strrchr(const char *string, int character);
```
reverse search string for character; return pointer to last occurrence else NULL
```
size_t strspn(const char *string1, const char *string2);
```
returns the length of the initial substring in string1 which consists entirely of the characters in string2
```
size_t strcspn(const char *string1, const char *string2);
```
returns the length of the initial substring in string1 which consists entirely of the characters *not* in string2
```
char *strpbrk(const char *string1, const char *string2);
```
search string1 for *any* character in string2; if *any* found return pointer to first occurrence else NULL
```
char *strstr(const char *string1, const char *string2);
```
search string1 for string2; if found return pointer to first occurrence else NULL
```
size_t strlen(const char *string);
```
returns the length of string (excluding terminating '\0')
```
char *strerror(int errnum);
```
Many library functions set up an integer error number in errno (declared in <errno.h>) if an error occurs. strerror returns a pointer to an implementation defined string corresponding to errno (function perror can be used to print the error to stderr)
```
char *strtok(char *string1, const char *string2);
```
searches for tokens in string1 using the characters in string2 as delimiters or token separators. If not found NULL is returned. If a token is found:
  (a) the character immediately following the token is overwritten with '\0',
  (b) the remainder of string1 stored within the system,
  (c) the address of the first character of the token is returned.
Subsequent calls with string1 equal to NULL search the saved part of the original string1 for the next token. If found the address of string (within the system) that contains the next token is returned. If a token is not found NULL is returned.

There are also functions strcoll and strxfrm which process characters using the current *locale* as set up by functions defined in <locale.h> (see compiler manuals for details).
  The above functions (starting with str) are for processing strings terminated with a

null, `'\0'`. The following functions are used to manipulate blocks of memory, of a specified size, as arrays of characters which are not null terminated, e.g. records read from a database which contain character arrays which are not null terminated.

```
void *memchr(const void *string, int character, size_t number);
```
    search at most number characters of string for character; if found return pointer to first occurrence else NULL
```
int memcmp(const void *string1, const void *string2, size_t number);
```
    compare at most number characters of string1 with string2; return:
        <0 if string1 < string2, 0 if string1 == string2 and >0 if string1 > string2
```
void *memcpy(void *destination, const void *source, size_t number);
```
    copy at most number characters from string source to string destination;
        return a pointer to destination
```
void *memmove(void *destination, const void *source, size_t number);
```
    copy at most number characters from string source to string destination;
        return a pointer to destination. This will work even if the objects overlap
```
void *memset(void *string, int character, size_t number);
```
    fill the first number characters of string with character

C.15 Date and time functions `<time.h>`

The `<time.h>` header file defines the following:

```
/* two arithmetic types for representing times */
typedef long clock_t;                                   /* typical definition */
typedef long time_t;                                    /* typical definition */

/* a symbolic constant which defines the number of clock ticks per second */
#define CLOCKS_PER_SEC 18.2              /* typical value for an IBM PC compatible */

/* structure which holds the components of a calendar time */
struct tm
{
   int    tm_sec;                    /* seconds after the minute, range [0, 61] */
   int    tm_min;                      /* minutes after the hour, range [0, 59] */
   int    tm_hour;                      /* hours after midnight, range [0. 23] */
   int    tm_mday;                        /* day of the month, range [0, 31] */
   int    tm_mon;                       /* months since January, range [0, 11] */
   int    tm_year;                                    /* years since 1900 */
   int    tm_wday;                         /* days since Sunday, range 0, 6] */
   int    tm_yday;                    /* days since January 1st, range [0, 365] */
   int    tm_isdst;                          /* daylight savings time flag */
};

clock_t  clock(void);              /* returns clock ticks since start of execution */
double   difftime(time_t time2, time_t time1);  /* returns time2 - time1 in seconds */
time_t   time(time_t *timer);                   /* returns calendar time in *timer */
char *   asctime(const struct tm *tpointer);      /* converts *tpointer to string; */
                                                  /* Fri Nov 20 05:25:17 1992\n\0 */
struct tm *localtime(const time_t *timer);         /* converts *timer to structure */
char *ctime(const time_t *time);                   /* converts *timer to string, is */
                                      /* equivalent to asctime(localtime(timer)) */
struct tm *gmtime(const time_t *timer);            /* converts *timer to structured */
                                                    /* Greenwich Mean Time */
time_t mktime(struct tm *tpointer);                /* converts *tpointer to time */
size_t strftime(char *s, size_t maxsize, const char *fmt, const struct tm *tpointer);
                          /* converts *tpointer into a string, see compiler manual */
```

Appendix D Summary of C syntax

D.1 Outline structure of a C program see Chapters 3, 4, 15, 17 and 21

The program below is a version of Program 5.3 altered to use a modified version of function power from Program 15.1. The page numbers alongside indicate where more details of the statement may be found.

	page
`/* Program Appendix.D - to calculate circle area and check radius */`	33
`#include <stdio.h>` `/* preprocessor directives to include */`	228
`#include <math.h>` `/* standard library header files */`	28
`int main(void)` `/* function header of main */`	16
`{`	16
`    float power(const float number, int exponent);    /* function prototype */`	100
`    /* define internal constants and automatic variables */`	126
`    const float pi = 3.1415926f;         /* non-alterable internal variable */`	30
`    float radius;                                /* a real variable */`	47
`    int converted_ok;                         /* an integer variable */`	40
`    printf("Enter radius of circle (real number) ? ");    /* print message */`	26
`    converted_ok = scanf("%f", &radius);              /* read radius */`	30
`    if (converted_ok != 1)                            /* read radius */`	67
`        printf("invalid input value \a\n");                 /* error ! */`	69
`    else`	67
`        {                                      /* compound statement */`	69
`        float area, radius_check;        /* internal automatic variables */`	126
`        area = pi * power(radius, 2);                 /* calculate area */`	101
`        printf("radius = %f, area = %f", radius, area);`	26
`        radius_check = sqrt(area / pi);            /* calculate radius */`	28
`        printf(", radius check = %f \n", radius_check);`	26
`        }`	
`    return 0;                        /* return success/failure indicator */`	25
`}                                         /* end of function main */`	16
`/*-------------------------------------------------------------*`	
` * Function to raise a float to an integer exponent            */`	101
`float power(const float number, int exponent)        /* function header */`	98
`{`	
`    float result;                /* automatic variable, holds result */`	126
`    for (result = 1; exponent > 0; exponent--)      /* loop exponent times */`	81
`        result = result * number;                    /* calculation */`	
`    return result;                        /* return function result */`	99
`}                                         /* end of function power */`	

D.2 Defining and declaring variables see Chapter 21.2 (page 165)

A *declaration* of a variable specifies its name and type, a *definition* also reserves storage. Thus the majority of 'declarations', as in the above program, are also definitions. Format:

```
variable_type variable_name1, variable_name2, variable_name3, ....;
```

For example:

```
int a, b, c = 6;              /* define integer variables, initialise c to 6 */
float x, y = 100.0f;          /* define real variables, initialise y to 100.0 */
int array[100];                     /* define an array of 100 elements */
static char z;                  /* define static variable z, see below */
```

The const type qualifier is used to define a non-alterable variable (page 171):

```
const float pi = 3.14159f;              /* define a non_alterable 'variable' */
```

D..3 The scope of identifiers see Chapter 17.2 (page 119) and Chapter 21

The scope of a variable (see page 119) determines where it may be used:

External variable: declared outside a function is from the point of declaration to the end of the file.

Internal variable: (called *automatics*) declared within a compound statement is from the point of declaration up to the end of the compound statement.

Functions and external variables may be accessed from other files, i.e. the names are global to the whole program. The storage class specifier static can be used to restrict access to the file concerned (page 166). The storage class specifier extern is used to declare an external variable in one file which is defined in another (see page 166):

```
extern int x, y;         /* declare x and y which are defined in another file */
```

D.4 Allocation of storage see Chapter 21.8 page 169

External variables (page 165) are allocated storage before the program starts and maintained until the program terminates.

Internal automatic variables are allocated storage on entry to a compound statement (page 69) and deallocated on exit from the compound statement (any contents are then lost). The storage class specifier static can be used to allocate permanent storage for an internal variable (page 124); their scope is as for automatic variables.

D.5 Pointer types see Chapter 23 (page 195)

In C a pointer is defined and used (page 196) as follows:

```
int *p_int;                              /* define a pointer to an int */
int number;                            /* define an int variable */

p_int = &number;                      /* point p_int to variable number */
*p_int = 10;                  /* assign the int pointed at by p_int the value 10 */
```

D.6 Defining a new type see Chapter 17.8 (page 126)

The keyword *typedef* enables the creation of new data type names, e.g.:

```
typedef float object_area_t;                     /* define new real type */
typedef int loop_counter_t;                   /* define new integral type */

object_area_t circle_area, sphere_area, cylinder_area;     /* define variables */
loop_counter_t counter_1, counter_2;
```

Note that *typedef* does not create a new type, just an alternative name.

D.7 Arrays see Chapters 18, 19 and 20.

An array is a fixed sized group in which the elements are of the same type:

```
array_type   array_name[array_size];
```

The elements of an array are accessed using an integer subscript or index which ranges from 0 to array_size - 1. For example:

```
int temperatures[100], pressures[100];          /* define two arrays of int */
float matrix[5][5];                             /* define 5 by 5 float array */

temperatures[0] = 0;                   /* zero first element of the array */
temperatures[4] = 20;                  /* assign 20 to the fifth element */
temperatures[99] = 100;                 /* assign 100 to last element */
matrix[0][0] = 5.0f;             /* assign 5 to first element of matrix */
matrix[4][4] = 0.0f;                /* zero last element of matrix */
```

D.8 Structures see Chapter 22.

A structure is a fixed sized group in which the elements are of dissimilar types. For example:

```
typedef struct {                                /* define a new type, student_t */
            char name[20];                          /* student name */
            int age;                                /* student age */
            long int student_identifier;        /* library card identifier */
          }
            student_t;                          /* structure type name */
student_t   student_1, student_2, students[100];        /* declare variables */
```

To access a particular member of a structure the . (dot) structure member operator is used, e.g.:

```
strcpy(student_1.name, "Smith, Bert");                   /* set up name */
student_1.age = 17;                             /* set up age */
printf("student name %s, age %d ",
            student_1.name, student_1.age);             /* print student data */
student_2 = student_1;                   /* copy one structure to another */
```

D.9 The if statement see Chapter 11 (page 67)

```
if (expression)
    statement
```

expression is evaluated and if *true* (non-zero) statement is executed otherwise it is skipped.

```
if (expression)
    statement1
else
    statement2
```

expression is evaluated and if *true* (non-zero) statement1 is executed otherwise statement2 is executed (the statements can be a single program statement or a compound statement). For example, to read a character ch (defined as an int) and test it:

```
ch = getchar();
if (ch == EOF) printf("\n end of file found \a\n");
else            printf("\n Character %c, character code %d \n", ch, ch);
```

D.10 The switch statement see Chapter 14.4 (page 94)

The switch statement is an alternative to using a sequence of if statements when selecting from a number of alternatives:

```
switch (expression)
    {
    case constant1: statement1
    case constant2: statement2
    ......
    default: default_statement
    }
```

For example:

```
ch = getchar();                                    /* read character */
switch (ch)
    {
    case ':':            printf("\n  character was :"); break;
    case 'x': case 'X': printf("\n  character was x or X"); break;
    }
```

the break statement is used to prematurely terminate a do, while, for or switch statement.

D.11 The while loop see Chapter 12.1 (page 76)

```
while (expression)
    statement
```

while expression is *true* execute statement (if expression is *false* on entry statement is never executed).

D.12 The do loop see Chapter 12.2 (page 79)

```
do
    statement
while (expression);
```

execute statement while expression is *true* (statement is executed at least once).

D.13 Example comparison of while and do loops (page 79)

For example, characters are read and processed by a function process_character until terminated by the $ character:

```
while ((ch = getchar()) != '$')        do
    process_character(ch);                 {
                                           ch = getchar();
                                           process_character(ch);
                                           }
                                       while (ch != '$');
```

In the while loop the terminating $ is not processed by the loop, in the do it is.

D.14 The for statement see Chapter 13 (page 81)

The for statement is a shorthand way of writing a while:

```
for (expression1; expression2; expression3)
    statement
```

1   expression1 is evaluated
2   expression2 is evaluated
3   if the result of expression2 is
        true statement is executed followed by expression3 then control returns to step 2
    or *false* the for terminates and execution continues with next statement

Example to evaluate the factorial of an integer number n:

```
factorial_n = 1;                            /* initialise factorial */
for (i = n ; i > 1 ; i--)                   /* loop i = n downto 1 */
    factorial_n = factorial_n * i;          /* N! = N * !(N-1) * .. */
```

D.15 Functions see Chapter 15 (page 98)

The function *definition*, where the body of the function is defined, takes the following general form (see page 98):

```
result_type function_name(parameter_list)
{
    declarations
    statements
}
```

Example function to raise a float to an int exponent, i.e. number^{exponent}:

```
/*--------------------------------------------------------------------------*
 * Function to raise a float to an integer exponent                         *
 * Parameters in: number (float) value to be raise to exponent             *
 *                exponent (int) the value of the exponent                  *
 * Function result: number raised to exponent                             */
float power(const float number, int exponent)          /* function header */
{
    float result;                        /* automatic variable, holds result */
    for (result = 1; exponent > 0; exponent--)           /* loop exponent times */
        result = result * number;                          /* calculation */
    return result;                                /* return function result */
}                                                 /* end of function power */
```

Example function call to evaluate 5.0^7:

```
int main(void)
{
    float power(float number, int exponent);           /* function prototype */
    float answer;                                      /* internal variables */
    answer = power(5.0, 7);                              /* call function */
}
```

When a function is called the compiler uses the *function prototype* to check that the number of parameters is correct and, if necessary, convert the types of the *actual parameters* to those required by the *formal parameters* (see page 100).

Appendix E

Table of operator precedence and associativity

precedence	operators	associativity
highest		
unary	`.  ( )  [ ]  ->`	left to right
	`!  ~  +  -  ++  --  *  &  (cast)  sizeof`	right to left
multiplicative	`*  /  %`	left to right
additive	`+  -`	left to right
bitwise shifts	`<< (left)  >> (right)`	left to right
relational	`<  <=  >  >=`	left to right
equality	`==  !=`	left to right
bitwise AND	`&`	left to right
bitwise OR	`^`	left to right
bitwise XOR	`|`	left to right
logical AND	`&&`	left to right
logical OR	`||`	left to right
conditional	`?:`	right to left
assignment	`=  +=  -=  *=  /=  %=  &=  ^=  |=  <<=  >>=`	right to left
sequence	`,`	left to right
lowest		

References

Bramer, B, 1990, 'Using a common host system to develop software products for a variety of target computer environments', IEE Computer-Aided Engineering Journal, Vol. 7 No. 5, October, pp. 129-134.

Bramer, B & Bramer, S M S, 1991, 'MC68000 Assembly Language Programming', second edition, Edward Arnold.

Bramer, B & Sutcliffe, D C, 1981, ' The use of display file techniques with raster scan displays', Proceedings of Eurographics '81, North Holland.

Bytronic 1989, 'The Bytronic multi-applications board', Bytronic Associates, 27b Cloeshill Road, Sutton Coldfield, B75 7AX, UK.

Bytronic 1991, 'The Bytronic MC68000 Trainer', Bytronic Associates, 27b Cloeshill Road, Sutton Coldfield, B75 7AX, UK.

Chikofsky, E J and Rubenstein, B L, 1988, 'CASE: reliability engineering for information systems', IEEE Software, Vol. 5 No. 2, March, pp. 11-16.

Child, J, 1992, 'C/C++ compilers bring faster code crunching to PC platforms', Computer Design, April, pp 129-133.

Dorn, W S and McCracken, D D, 1972, 'Numerical methods with Fortran IV case studies', Wiley.

Hintz, K J, 1992, 'Merging C and assembly language in microcontroller applications', Journal of Microcomputer Applications, Vol. 15, July, pp 267-278.

HP 1991, 'HP PHIGS FORTRAN Binding References', Vols. 1 and 2, Hewlett Packard, January 1991.

James, K R and Riba, W D, 1992, 'Pascal programming and numerical methods for scientists and engineers', Chartwell-Bratt.

Kernighan, B. & Pike, R., 1984, 'The UNIX programming environment', Prentice-Hall.

Kernighan, B. & Ritchie, D., 1978, 'The C programming language', Prentice-Hall.

Microsoft C, 1990a, "Microsoft C Reference for MS, OS/2 and MS-DOS Operating Systems", Microsoft Corporation.

Microsoft C, 1990b, "Microsoft C Advanced Programming Technqiues", Microsoft Corporation.

Motorola 1983, 'MC68230 Parallel Interface/Timer (PI/T)', MC68230/D, Motorola Inc.

Steward, D, 1987, 'Software Engineering with systems analysis and design', Brooks/Cole.

Tubro C, 1991, 'Turbo C++ user's guide', and 'Turbo C++ programmer's guide' Borland International Inc., PO Box 660001, Scotts Valley, CA 95067-0001.

Oman, P W, 1990, 'CASE analysis and design tools', IEEE Software, Vol. 7 No. 3, May, pp. 37-43.

Wallace, D R and Fujii, R U, 1989, ' Software verification and validation: an overview', IEEE Software, Vol. 6 No. 3, May, pp. 10-17.

Whitesmiths 1986, 'Interface manual for the MC68000', Ver. 3.1, Whitesmiths Ltd., October.

Whitesmiths 1987a, 'C Language Manual', Ver. 3.2, August, Whitesmiths Ltd.

Whitesmiths 1987b, 'Compiler manual for DOS/86', Ver. 3.2, April, Whitesmiths Ltd.

Index